Sustainable Living and Business

Hans-Werner Franz • Gerald Beck
Diego Compagna • Peter Dürr
Wolfgang Gehra • Martina Wegner
Editors

Sustainable Living and Business

Management of Social Innovations as a Shaping of Social Transformation

Springer

Editors
Hans-Werner Franz
ESSI European School of Social Innovation
Dortmund, Germany

Gerald Beck
Hochschule München
München, Germany

Diego Compagna
Hochschule München
München, Germany

Peter Dürr
Hochschule München
München, Germany

Wolfgang Gehra
Hochschule München
München, Germany

Martina Wegner
Hochschule München
München, Germany

ISBN 978-3-658-41834-2 ISBN 978-3-658-41835-9 (eBook)
https://doi.org/10.1007/978-3-658-41835-9

This book is a translation of the original German edition „Nachhaltig Leben und Wirtschaften“ by Franz, Hans-Werner, published by Springer Fachmedien Wiesbaden GmbH in 2020. The translation was done with the help of artificial intelligence (machine translation by the service DeepL.com). A subsequent human revision was done primarily in terms of content, so that the book will read stylistically differently from a conventional translation. Springer Nature works continuously to further the development of tools for the production of books and on the related technologies to support the authors.

This Springer imprint is published by the registered company Springer Fachmedien Wiesbaden GmbH, part of Springer Nature.
The registered company address is: Abraham-Lincoln-Str. 46, 65189 Wiesbaden, Germany

Paper in this product is recyclable.

Contents

Contributors

Theresa Arnold Goethe University Frankfurt, Frankfurt am Main, Germany

Sevda Can Arslan Ludwig Maximilian University, Munich, Germany

Thomas Barth Institute of Sociology, Ludwig-Maximilians-Universität Munich, Frankfurt am Main, Germany

Gerald Beck University of Applied Sciences Munich, Munich, Germany

Tamar Beruchashvili Gender Studies in Engineering at the TU Munich, Munich, Germany

Christine Best Social Research Center Dortmund, TU Dortmund, Dortmund, Germany

Peter Biniok Guild SHK Berlin, Berlin, Germany

Diego Compagna Faculty of Applied Social Sciences, Munich University of Applied Sciences, Munich, Germany

Peter Dürr Munich University of Applied Sciences, Munich, Germany

Florian Engel University of Applied Sciences, Fulda, Germany

Oranna Erb Schäuble Institute for Social Research Munich, Munich, Germany

Hans-Werner Franz ESSI European School of Social Innovation, Dortmund, Germany

Wolfgang Gehra Munich University of Applied Sciences, Munich, Germany

Christian Gelleri Julius-Maximilians-University of Würzburg, Würzburg, Germany

Kerstin Guhlemann Social Research Center Dortmund, TU Dortmund, Dortmund, Germany

Yves Jeanrenaud Institute of Sociology, Ludwig-Maximilians-Universität Munich, Munich, Germany

Robert Jende University of Applied Sciences Munich, Munich, Germany

Georg Jochum Technical University of Munich, Munich, Germany

Janine Kuhnt Institute of Educational Science, Friedrich Schiller University Jena, Jena, Germany

Claudia Obermeier Institute of Social Sciences – Sociology, Christian-Albrechts-Universität zu Kiel, Kiel, Germany

Bastian Pelka Social Research Center Dortmund, TU Dortmund, Dortmund, Germany

Ingegerd Schäuble Schäuble Institute for Social Research, Munich, Germany

Julia Schmidt Munich University of Applied Sciences, Munich, Germany

Study Group Get Online Week

Julia Heidegger, Hannah Klamroth, Friederike Kober, Hannah Leibig, Henrike Naß, Larissa Oliverio, Adina Pauksch, Nathalie Schmitte, Floriane Thies, Cynthia Victoria Seemann, Pia Wolff, Ina Zawadka Faculty of Rehabilitation Sciences, TU Dortmund, Dortmund, Germany

Martina Wegner Faculty of Applied Social Sciencesl, Munich University of Applied Sciences, Munich, Germany

Elisabeth Wiesnet Gender Studies in Engineering at the TU Munich, Munich, Germany

Introduction

Hans-Werner Franz

Abstract

This was the third BDS meeting in a row to focus on social innovation. With each conference, we have tackled the topic more concretely, but at the same time expanded it. Whereas in Frankfurt 2015 the aim was to "understand the phenomenon of social innovation" (cf. BDS 2015), the conference in Dortmund in 2017 focused on "shaping social innovation locally" (Franz and Kaletka 2018).

1 The Book on the Conference

This was the third BDS meeting in a row to focus on social innovation. With each conference, we have tackled the topic more concretely, but at the same time expanded it. Whereas in Frankfurt in 2015 the focus was still on wanting to "understand the phenomenon of social innovation" (cf. BDS 2015), the conference in Dortmund in 2017 already emphasised wanting to "shape social innovation locally" (Franz and Kaletka 2018). In Munich, we placed the topic in the context that is the actual reason for the upswing in the preoccupation with the topic of "social innovation": the necessity of transforming our society(ies) if we want to make the climate change we ourselves have caused livable for all of us. This includes both the efforts associated with our lifestyles to limit it, and all the changes and innovations that

H.-W. Franz (✉)
ESSI European School of Social Innovation, Dortmund, Germany

H.-W. Franz et al. (eds.), *Sustainable Living and Business*,
https://doi.org/10.1007/978-3-658-41835-9_1

help to adapt our lifestyles to the changed conditions and shape them ourselves. For if our society is to move in the direction of sustainable living and economic activity, then “many must do something differently”. This was our initial generic definition of social innovation (in Frankfurt). In Dortmund, we have readjusted it. Because this generic definition, which targets social practices, “could also apply to social change, which is the sum of many innovations, including social ones.” (Franz and Kaletka 2018, p. 1) It is the same with transformation, the theme of Munich 2019, with the crucial difference that social change has no direction, whereas transformation is “directed and shaped social change,” as we wrote in the call for papers for the conference and conference proceedings. The transformation we speak of in this volume, which is considered necessary, means a social development directed towards the goal of sustainability, which is dependent on both technical and social innovations. The way people manage and consume, live in one place and move from place to place, must change in such a way that humane living in the human-designed world on planet Earth is in harmony with the natural conditions required for it. To live, we must be able to breathe the air, drink the water, eat the food, without harm to ourselves and the whole of all life on earth, either now or in the long run. For, as Charles Darwin said, “anything that is against nature (…) has no permanence in the long run.” Innovations by sciences of all kinds are needed as well as the interested innovative action of many people in all areas of society with the aim of changing individual as well as societal habits and behaviours, social practices and praxis. Transformation means living and doing business differently. For many. Actually for everyone.

2 The Book

As already mentioned: Unlike social change, which takes place gradually and quasi surreptitiously, transformation requires shaping: on the one hand, the shaping of social innovation, which can only be considered as such – it should be remembered – “if it is an undeniable fact, a practice practiced by many” (Franz 2015, p. 155), and on the other hand, a shared understanding of sustainability as the goal and direction of this transformation. Both are by no means self-evident, but require constant communication so that as many as possible follow the path and do not lose direction in the process, true to the phrase attributed to Mark Twain: “Having lost sight of our goals, we redouble our efforts.”

3 The More Theoretical Part

Claudia Obermeier pursues reassurance of the required kind when she wants to "understand the effect of social innovations through sociological classics" and assures herself of "Dahrendorf's guidance" in "Weber's shoes". Her thesis: "Social innovations lead to more life chances." "The idea is to conceptually work through, for both the micro and macro levels, the influence of social innovations, which not infrequently lead to social change, on the life chances of individuals and society as a whole." In general, she illustrates this with the changes that come along with digitalization, concretely and on an individual level she proves this by using Dahrendorf's life chances concept based on empirical findings from the lives of senior citizens. "The use of the Internet multiplies not only the potential choices, but above all the *opportunities used* by senior citizens." Drawing on the findings of her dissertation, she comes to impressive conclusions: "By being able to obtain advance information via the Internet, senior citizens feel more self-confident, more responsible, more informed and less dependent on others. They expand their repertoire of actions because they can use the Internet to work out solutions to problems in a targeted manner; they feel more independent and are also more relaxed about times when they are restricted by decreasing mobility. The Internet opens up new creative possibilities, more extensive choices and a broad portfolio of opportunities for participation. Even more far-reaching and significant than the gain in options is the new way of shaping social ties. (…) Through the use of Internet-based communication channels, senior citizens feel much more integrated into the family network. They feel more intensively involved in the lives of their children and their children's children. In addition, they feel that contact with their grandchildren is easier. Overall, senior citizens feel that they are a much more tangible part of society through Internet use" (Obermeier 2020, p. 412 ff.).

Diego Compagna undertakes a par force ride through the theoretical offerings of sociology in order to prove that sustainability is a thoroughly contested concept. "An orientation towards sustainability as well as sustainable innovations seem to be the essence and the result of a reflexive modernity that has completely come into its own and (…) has brought the problem consciousness of late-modern societies 'from the ivory tower' to the streets. In the process, contested and thus contested interpretations of complex referential contexts undergo a not inconsiderable path of trivialization and de-paradoxification in the course of translation from an academic to a lifeworld frame of reference." Underway, he says, is "the construction of sustainability," in which precisely a central requirement of such processes of understanding itself becomes a major problem: "the participation of as many 'citizens' as possible in identifying, shaping, and solving one or more (common) problems." He paints a rather bleak picture, describing modern man as a (tragic, I interpret) "Atlas subject" who has to carry the globe on his shoulders, although he cannot really influence the capitalist structures of this world, which are at the same time responsible for its condition, but rather reproduces them by pursuing his individual interests. Connected with the concept of sustainability, new forms of subjectivation emerge, which, to remain in the image of the "Atlas subject", are difficult to bear for the individual and can hardly be dissolved. How can we not be misled in the face of the best-predicted catastrophe in living memory, in which the analyses of the relevant *scientific community* describe the degree of threat ever more precisely, but the advice of the scientists on how to change course is hardly taken note of by politicians? – As a rule, this is due to fear of the reaction of the citizens to measures that are recognized as correct, but which massively impair their way of life. At the end of his contribution, *Compagna* therefore rightly raises the question of the society in which we want to live. If sustainability is sought, can that be capitalism, which thrives on plundering the earth's resources beyond measure and which exploits and robs primarily, but not exclusively, the people and regions of the less developed parts of the world? Capitalism is in a "pincer" (Dörre 2019) and we with it: dependent on growth, it is in danger of collapsing if it is to function without it, with all the consequences that this entails for the structures and processes of our economies and societies.

"Seen in this light, the sustainability discourse would have to deal centrally with questions of social inequality and the unfair distribution of resources and value creation. The sustainability discourse should focus on power relations and question them, pose the social question anew. Instead, it accepts the (unequal) social order and does not even try to shake it by repeatedly focusing on the practices and orientations of action of each individual."

One could also have *Compagna's* Atlas subject ask the question (in the spirit of Mark Twain's sentence quoted above): How is the individual who is put in charge and feels responsible not to go astray? In the face of a system reproduced by himself through his normal way of life, calibrated for growth, which endangers the survivability of the human species by having led nature to its limits and has thus reached its limits itself.

Georg Jochum and *Thomas Barth* also take up this contradictory nature of the demand for sustainability. They examine "the role of work in the development of sustainable social innovation processes". In a changing world shaped by sustainability, they urge the redefinition of work as one of the most important social innovations with reference to the guiding principle of "sustainable work" formulated by the United Nations Development Programme (UNDP 2015). "In contrast to the previous focus of the sustainability debate on individual consumption patterns on the one hand and companies on the other, this guiding principle, which has also been more widely received in Germany in recent years (…), places workers at the centre of consideration. It goes beyond a perspective limited to gainful employment to include work in the non-wage sector (UNDP 2015, p. 3). The point of reference is a comprehensive concept of development inspired by the 'capability approach' (Sen 1979). The overarching goal is to expand people's choices. In this context, special importance is attributed to work, as human potentials would be developed through work." The UNDP report on "Work and Human Development" (UNDP 2015) also recurs to the "Sustainable Development Goals" adopted in the UN agenda "Transforming Our World" (UN 2015) and their manifold significance for the world of work and the "pathway to sustainable work" (UNDP 2015: p. 153).

4 Innovation and Sustainability in Organisations and Work Organisation

How does sustainability enter companies and other organizations? Authors from the University of Applied Sciences Munich are dealing with this question. One of them, *Peter Dürr,* considers how participation-based processes can lead or be used to lead to the development of guiding principles. The others, *Wolfgang Gehra* and *Julia Schmidt,* have thought very carefully about how a model of the common good balance sheet can be incorporated into corporate performance indicator management with balanced score card models.

Dürr expects reflection processes in companies – be it under the heading of vision, mission, brand, corporate identity or, more generally, the development of guiding principles – to "take into account the long-term consequences of organisational actions through future orientation", whereas "non-sustainable behaviour by organisations is essentially defined by the socialisation of social and ecological costs". Companies would definitely deal with sustainability in their own interest, on the one hand because "unsolved social problems […] eventually [cause] costs in the companies", on the other hand because "ecological and social investments […] contribute in the long run to the motivation of the workforce, to the image gain with customers and to the acceptance in the public." (Lombriser and Abplanalp 2015, p. 248). *Dürr's* contribution focuses on the "development of a novel process logic that bundles recognized pedagogical, engineering and design-oriented design schemes in a so-called 'Interactive Learning Course' and is used as a planning aid. Special attention is paid to the importance of principles such as participation, change of perspective and constructiveness in order to design these processes successfully. In the context of a concrete application example, it will then be examined how the implementation of this planning tool can be designed in practice and what effects this can have on sustainable action in the organization".

Gehra and *Schmidt* want to examine whether the rather elaborate concept of the common good balance sheet, which is now used as an instrument of sustainability certification by more than 400 organizations, mainly in German-speaking countries, can be linked to the widely used international concept of the balanced scorecard (BSC). While the common good balance sheet is practically an evaluation of the results of two (or more) years of business activity, the BSC, as part of the day-to-day management of an organisation by means of key figures, continuously provides key figures in the day-to-day running of the company. In most cases, the data required for this is collected permanently in the company's accounting system and in parallel to the operational performance. This raises the question of the extent to which a convergence of the two concepts can reduce the workload for the common good balance sheet by incorporating its questions into the parallel accounting system of the BSC approach. The actual aim is to "promote the spread of the common good orientation with the help of the common good balance sheet" and to implant it in everyday company policy with the help of the BSC. After a very thorough examination of all the question complexes, they come to a cautiously positive conclusion, but make it clear that a lot of work would still have to be put in here to develop this innovation of a BSC-supported common good orientation in companies into a manageable tool.

Theresa Arnold's contribution has only very indirectly to do with sustainability, but all the more to do with innovative work organisation. She presents the results of an empirical study on open space concepts, in which companies are making the office world more spatially, temporally and socially flexible in response to the challenges of Work 4.0. Indirectly, this has to do with sustainability, because here employees are given the decision as to whether they work at home or in an open office, where, however, they only have one workplace, but no longer their own. This reduces the need for office space and makes much more economical use of the available office space. *Arnold* examines these open and flexible work landscapes from the perspective of the sociology of work.

"This is about the practice of Open Space: What motives and reasons do companies see for introducing these offices? How do employees shape their work under the work-organizational changes? What challenges arise here for employees and how are these solved? These questions will be answered on the basis of empirical data (interviews with employees and change facilitators). In dealing with the changed work environment, areas of tension can be worked out, which are discussed in conclusion, taking into account sociological theories of work and concepts of the subjectification of work."

5 Innovation and Sustainability in Regions, Cities and Municipalities

Three very different perspectives on change processes in regions, cities and municipalities are presented in this section.

Christian Gelleri deals with regional complementary currencies that pursue specific goals. In his most important reference project, the Chiemgauer, for example, the aim is to achieve "the saving of 5000 tonnes of CO_2 over three years in the Chiemgau region" in a first stage. "The rules and regulations of the complementary currency 'climate bonus' serve to motivate people and organisations to reduce CO_2 and to compensate for the remaining footprint." What sounds exotic turns out to be a fairly widespread phenomenon; there are estimated to be over 10,000 complementary currencies (including the 2000 or so cryptocurrencies such as Bitcoin), which are usually linked to specific goals and quite often prove to be a stable support mechanism for regional economies. *Gelleri* analyses complementary currencies as a social innovation that can very well be used for regional governance of sustainability strategies.

Cities and municipalities are important political players when it comes to sustainability. They are the policy level closest to citizens and their living conditions. In many municipalities, strategies for sustainable living and economic activity are being developed with great seriousness and usually with the involvement of the citizens, and these strategies always have to do with the restructuring of the city and its structures. The reason for and background to this is often demographic change.

In the process, as *Bettina Wegner* notes on the basis of many change processes in German municipalities, they sooner or later reach the point "where they have to come to terms with their identity. They cannot plan their future without thinking about their identity. … Therefore, the question arises as to the nature of this identity and whether municipalities as places have an identity of their own or whether this identity is ascribed to them exclusively by people." Based on philosophical approaches, *Wegner* posits that places have an identity of their own independent of the perceptions of the people living in them at any given time. She then tests this thesis of the "inherent logic of cities" on the basis of spatial and urban planning as well as sociological theories and derives criteria for shaping the future of cities and communities in the sustainability discourse.

Ingegerd Schäuble and *Oranna Erb* are actively involved in such discourses and shape them on behalf of municipalities. They note that such "serious, consistently implemented participatory processes in the community hold considerable potential for shaping social transformation." "They are transformation processes at the grassroots level of the population – and *with* the population." They not only deal with the participation of individual citizens, but more precisely also with the mobilization of expertise and multiple perspectives. "Sustainable effective participation networks span different social groups, interests, expertise and hierarchical levels." For the success of such processes, they present a comprehensive set of methods and tools in their contribution, which are, however, always highly prerequisite-rich, which is why they unfortunately often remain vague.

6 Social Science Interventions

Most of the contributions in this volume look at the role of social science actors in the process of change, in addition to the social change they report on. This was just as intentional. The subtitle of the conference and volume: "Management of Social Innovations as Shaping Social Transformation" suggests this. And we had asked for this in our call for papers:

- "What conditions, what processes lead to certain social innovations being taken up? Which actor constellations are most suitable? Which cooperations are entered into in order to launch innovative projects and lead them to success? Which factors prove to be rather favourable or demonstrably obstructive?
- How can we as social scientists facilitate the understanding and development of sustainable social innovation and transformation processes? What roles do we ourselves play in the respective context? Which theoretical and methodological tools do we use for this?
- What social science-reflected examples of social transformation processes in cities, communities and regions can we present on this?"

Up to this point, we have already had to deal with a series of contributions in which the authors were involved not only as academics, but also as social science consultants in the broadest sense, or at least also formulated from this perspective. This is certainly true for all the authors of the last section: for *Christian Gelleri,* who helped to launch the Chiemgauer, for Bettina *Wegner,* who accompanies communal identity-finding processes, and especially for *Ingegerd Schäuble* and *Oranna Erb, who* are active in moderation and mediation projects. This also applies to two of the three contributions in the previous section, "Sustainability in Organizations and Work Organization". *Peter Dürr* also introduces himself as a consultant for strategy/communication in companies; *Wolfgang Gehra* and *Julia Schmidt* come from the common good economy and want to contribute to its better functioning with their expert contribution.

The following contributions are almost universally characterized by a high degree of reflection on their own interventions, not a few of them quite self-evaluative and self-critical.

Peter Biniok got involved most intensively. In his model project with the Berlin Guild of Sanitary, Heating and Air Conditioning Technology, he not only visited and got involved with the industry in phases, as is usual in research projects, but also went through the companies as an employee of the guild in order to "work as a sociologist on the conception of measures against training dropouts [and to support] the processing of empirical-analytical questions." "In the process, social scientists themselves become creative actors in the transformation process." In his specific case, he describes his role as "infiltration" on the one hand and "arrangement" on the other. As "infiltration" because he chose an ethnographic approach that, depending on the situation, can be examined as both observing participation and participant observation, and because he was allowed to influence "the self-direction of the actors". As an "arrangement" "by initiating dynamics", in other words, because in his role he was virtually commissioned to initiate changes against all obstructive and insistent forces, which were to be carried by the practitioners.

In her contribution, *Sevda Can Arslan* deals with the concept of transdisciplinarity. Against the background of Vilsmaier and Lang's analysis of "Transdisciplinary Research" (2014), she brushes her own project "Media Future Lab" against the grain. Her project "is about the future of media. Media, as public channels of communication, are essential for democracy. But they are currently in a crisis: the reach, acceptance and interpretive authority of traditional offerings are declining. Against this background, the project asks what we, the society, expect from media offerings, what we understand by good journalism and what we want to pay for it." In order to do justice to such a complex question with an adequate set of theories and methods, it is important not only to work across the boundaries between academic disciplines, but also to seek cooperation between academia and civil society, for example, and to set up the project as a learning one. *Arslan* examines three central moments of transdisciplinarity: the *contextuality of* research, the *orientation towards society,* and the focus on the *learning process,* and applies them analytically and evaluatively to her own project.

Tamar Beruchashvili, Elisabeth Wiesnet and Yves Jeanrenaud present in their contribution "Interactive formats for the social participation of seniors using the example of socially responsible technology design". The task of the sub-project within the Bavarian research network ForGenderCare was to develop "suitable communication and participation models to allow seniors with different requirements and life realities to participate in the development of social change." Specifically, a participation model for older people in the technological development that directly and indirectly affects them was developed. At the same time, an approach was developed on how companies can be more strongly oriented towards a gender and diversity-oriented culture and customer orientation.

Christine Best and Kerstin Guhlemann dedicate their contribution to the "art of social transformation" or, as it is called in the subtitle, "empowerment through social art". The long-term unemployed are empowered through social art, especially through the JobAct method, to a more self-confident perception of labour market opportunities. Relevant projects, which work with forms of combining theatre work and social work, achieve high integration and placement rates, which in the result are strongly superior to traditional methods of integrating disadvantaged people into the labour market and society. The authors analyse the method itself, which was developed in Germany, as well as the different circumstances and problems of applying the method with two partners in other European countries, namely Italy, France and Hungary.

In many areas, digital media and applications have become such a matter of course that groups of people who cannot or do not want to use them are in danger of being left behind. The Get Online Week, initiated by the EU Commission and held for years, aims to counteract this danger. *Bastian Pelka* and the *Get Online Week study group,* students of rehabilitation education at TU Dortmund University, participated in Get Online Week 2019 in Dortmund with their own offers and evaluated their own "intervention to improve digital participation" with the aim of "preparing the intervention itself, but also its conditions of success for possible transfer to other local campaigns as well as for following student cohorts in Dortmund for imitation." Basically, this is a study to determine how sustainable the learning success has been for the participating groups of young people and senior citizens, specifically: whether the course has been of lasting help to them in coping with digital processes in everyday life. The group itself has since disbanded after passing the exam.

Janine Kuhnt deals with innovation potentials in a now widespread group of civil society organizations: Citizens' Foundations and Volunteer Agencies, whose task is to mobilize and coordinate engagement. They summarize their findings in the succinct headline: "A story about storytellers." In other words: those who tell good, i.e. success stories about themselves and present themselves well are more successful. With her contribution, *Kuhnt* wants to answer the question: "How do community foundations and volunteer agencies, taking into account their organizational constitution, fulfill the innovation function attributed to them by promoting engagement?" She subjects these organizations to a "secondary analysis" and takes into account "both quantitative data, such as the number of organizations, their financial resources and personnel structure, as well as qualitative data generated from scientific findings on the self-assessment of the professionals working in the organizations and their organizational environment".

In their contribution on "RePair Democracy – Social Innovations as Workshops for Democratic Design", *Gerald Beck* and *Robert Jende* pursue the guiding thesis that "citizens need to experience themselves as politically effective in order to build an inclusive and satisfying political community. Conversely, this means that a corresponding disconnect between citizen will and political decision-makers leads to an erosion of democracy." They see this erosion as well advanced and therefore look for repair practices of democratization and understand them as "open workshops, repair cafés, solidarity farms and other social innovations as a contribution to the establishment of *local democracies." (Authors' emphasis)* In them, "the concerns and needs of a city, a neighborhood, or a neighborhood gather, and, as it were, the skills and abilities to address the concerns practically come together here." Their intervention goal is to "anchor democracy cafés in the urban society in order to connect the wishes and needs of citizens with new possibilities for shaping them".

Finally, *Florian Engel* sees "social innovations and sustainability in the phenomenon of bottle collecting" and examines the phenomenon with a detailed sociological approach. Among other things, he comes to a conclusion that is also relevant for many other processes of change: "The sustainable change of urban living space does not only depend on the intentional creativity of its inhabitants. An analytical approach that attempts to understand the visible and invisible contexts of action in their interconnectedness appears to be fruitful".

Engel formulates here one of the requirements of social science research as beneficial in observing and even more so in promoting social change processes beyond the traditional methods and tools of counting, measuring and testing: Empathy, social sensitiveness and social responsibility. Certainly, well-intentioned is far from well-done. But what is well done may also be well meant.

References

BDS. 2015. Soziale Innovation verstehen. Sozialwissenschaften und Berufspraxis (SuB) 38, Nr. 2/2015
Dörre, Klaus. 2019. Risiko Kapitalismus. Landnahme, Zangenkrise, Nachhaltigkeitsrevolution. In Große Transformation? Zur Zukunft moderner Gesellschaften. Sonderband des Berliner Journals für Soziologie, Hrsg. Klaus Dörre, H. Rosa, K. Becker, Sophie Bose und B. Seyd, 3–33. Wiesbaden: Springer VS.
Franz, Hans-Werner, und C. Kaletka, Hrsg. 2018. *Soziale Innovationen lokal gestalten.* Wiesbaden: Springer VS
Franz, Hans-Werner. 2015, Editorial. In: *BDS. 2015.* Soziale Innovation verstehen. Sozialwissenschaften und Berufspraxis (SuB) 38, Nr. 2/2015
Lombriser, R. und P. Abplanalp. 2015. *Strategisches Management: Visionen entwickeln – Erfolgspotenziale aufbauen – Strategien umsetzen.* 6., vollst. überarb. und aktual. Aufl. Zürich: Versus.
Obermeier, Claudia. 2020. *Seniorinnen und Senioren im Kontext der digitalen Revolution.* Eine qualitative Untersuchung der Internetnutzung von Seniorinnen und Senioren. Weinheim: Beltz Juventa.
Sen, Amartya. 1979. Utilitarianism and Welfarism, The Journal of Philosophy, LXXVI, 463–489.
UN (United Nations). 2015. Transforming Our World. The 2030 Agenda for Sustainable Development. New York: United Nations.
UNDP (United Nations Development Programme). 2015. Bericht über die menschliche Entwicklung 2015: Arbeit und menschliche Entwicklung. Berlin: Deutsche Gesellschaft für die Vereinten Nationen.
Vilsmaier, Ulli, J. D. Lang. 2014. Transdisziplinäre Forschung. In: Harald Heinrichs und Gerd Michelsen (Hrsg.): Nachhaltigkeitswissenschaften, Bd. 104. Heidelberg: Springer, S. 87–113.

Hans-Werner Franz, Dr. phil., Dipl.-Üb., studied Applied Languages in Germersheim (Uni Mainz), studied Sociology, Journalism, Political Science and Linguistics at the FU Berlin. Long-term employee and member of the management of the Sozialforschungsstelle Dortmund (TU Dortmund), EFQM assessor, Permanent Advisor to ESSI (European School of Social Innovation, Vienna). Freelance consultant for the quality of organisations.

Latest Publications:

Franz, H.W.; C. Kaletka; B. Pelka; R. Sarcina. 2018. Building Leadership in Project and Network Management – A Facilitator's Tool Set, 2nd ed. Berlin/Heidelberg: Springer.

Franz, H.W.; C. Kaletka. Eds. 2018. designing social innovations locally, Wiesbaden: Springer VS.

Dalluege, A.; H.W. Franz. 2015. IQM – Integrated quality management in education and training. Self-assessment for EFQM, CAF, Q2E, DIN EN ISO 9001 and other QM systems, Bielefeld: wbv (4th revised and expanded edition).

Franz, H.W.; J. Hochgerner; J. Howaldt. eds. 2012. Challenge Social Innovation, Berlin/Heidelberg: Springer.

In Weber's Shoes and with Dahrendorf's Escort: Understanding the Impact of Social Innovation Through Sociological Classics

Claudia Obermeier

Abstract

The knowledge of sustainably changed practices of action and their influence on social structural mechanisms is a genuine sociological one. The social sciences, by virtue of their methods and theories, have the possibility to systematically process and depict structurally effective social transformations and to derive insights from them. Without sociological theorizing, it would be unthinkable to recognize and map the influence of changed repertoires of action on the shaping of individuals' lives (micro level) and on society as a whole (macro level) (in the tradition of Max Weber). The consideration of social innovations is relevant for both the micro and the macro level. This article aims to address the explanatory content of sociological theories for the consideration of socially relevant mechanisms in the form of social innovations. The influence of social innovations, which often lead to social change, on the life chances of individuals and society as a whole will be conceptually explored at both the micro and macro levels. The basic thesis of this analysis is: *Social innovations lead to more life chances.* Ralf Dahrendorf's concept of life chances will serve as a theoretical foundation, which will be used to develop a discussion of social innovations in addition to

C. Obermeier (✉)
Institute of Social Sciences – Sociology, Christian-Albrechts-Universität zu Kiel, Kiel, Germany
e-mail: claudia.obermeier@fau.de

H.-W. Franz et al. (eds.), *Sustainable Living and Business*,
https://doi.org/10.1007/978-3-658-41835-9_2

the basic presentation of the term life chances. The attempt to capture the effect of social innovations on the basis of Dahrendorf's life chances concept will be explicated by means of the empirical findings from my doctoral thesis on the topic of Internet use by senior citizens. The results obtained allow, on the one hand, to show the motivations behind innovative action on the basis of this example, and, on the other hand, to visualize how the effects of a social innovation are realized for the protagonists in the light of the life chances concept. The article aims to provide a perspective on the explanatory power of social science theory concepts with regard to the effects of social innovations, using empirical data from its own survey as support.

1 Social Innovation: Basic Understanding and Frame of Reference

In an increasingly differentiated environment, traditional routines and practices are confronted with questions that seem impossible to deal with in the traditional way. New questions provoke different answers, changing circumstances put previous ways of life of individuals and whole groups of society to the test. Coping mechanisms for the smaller and larger tasks of everyday life that were previously perceived as comfortable or satisfactory now seem rather inadequate. In the confrontation with these very tasks, it becomes clear that the previous practice of action can no longer be considered satisfactory. The challenge that presents itself provokes the orientation towards new options for action or a new coping strategy that (should) reduce or eliminate this dissatisfaction. Zapf formulates this as follows:

> Social innovations are new ways of achieving goals, especially new forms of organization, new regulations, new lifestyles, that change the direction of social change, solve problems better than previous practices, and are therefore worth imitating and institutionalizing (Zapf 1989, p. 177).

The objectives of action adaptation are dispersed. What counts is the social benefit that can be identified in the medium and long term. It should be noted that processes of social change lead to an inducement to modify practices of action in accordance with a perceived pressure to change: "Routine and innovation do not belong to two different worlds, but slide into each other" (Waldenfels 1990, p. 96). Such modifications may arise, among other things, from a more individual motive. A modified design thus reacts to an occurrence that is perceived as inadequate.

With processes of social change[1], which can be driven by very different impulses, there is also an increase in the broad-based need to respond to the changes on offer at the level of action – in other words, comprehensive processes of social change mean that modified practices of action are relevant in many different contexts (Howaldt and Schwarz 2010, p. 25). The *digital revolution* is considered to be one of the most concise influencing factors in postmodernity (Hofstetter 2018, p. 91 ff.; Reutner 2012, p. 9; Stengel 2017, p. 63 ff.). All social sub-sectors are taken by adapting digital principles of organization, administration and design. But this does not just mean the mere intrusion of new kinds of apparatuses and machines.

> Twenty years from now, we will look back on this time at the beginning of the 21st century and recognize in it a crucial turning point in the history of our economy and society. We will understand that we have entered a new age, based on new principles, views and business models, how the rules of the game have changed. (Tapscott and Williams 2007: p. 19)

The current upheavals are taking place through new information and communication technologies. Postmodern man is confronted with a new way of generating knowledge, realizing education and organizing communication and interpersonal relationships. Digitally provided and medially ventilated information, digitally encoded messages conveyed via technical media, location- and time-independent networking via the infrastructure of the Internet – the quasi-permanently available potentials create a new necessity of dealing with these availabilities and offers (Becker 2013, p. 29 f.; Floridi 2015, p. 45 ff.). However, recognising digitality as an organisational principle also means having to adapt one's actions to the new technical circumstances and the manifold digital possibilities – this applies equally to the individual, to certain groups of actors and to social sub- or functional areas. Digitisation also provokes new questions about how social interaction should be shaped at the micro level, which circumstances now have the potential to change or which routines need to be rethought. The change encompassing society, which is given its title by the *digital revolution*, gives rise to the need to question ways of acting or to adapt them in the light of new options. Social change processes thus

[1] At this point, the term societal or social change should only serve as a cornerstone for the argumentation. The abbreviated view and the self-evident operation with this multifaceted term does not happen without the awareness of the necessity of the differentiated use. With reference to Zapf (1994), who in turn takes into account fundamental thoughts of Comte, Marx, Pareto, Durkheim and other greats of the social sciences (Zapf 1994, p. 11 f.), social change is to be understood as such a term, which is differentiated into a structural understanding together with the question of a social order and a further differentiation into the dimensions that attempt to characterise social change (Zapf 1994, p. 14).

form the bracket for social innovations, but can also be the result of socially innovative changes, whereby the change processes themselves only become visible (Braun-Thürmann and John 2010, p. 53). Digitisation is understood as that which creates broadly new potentials for the shaping of social references, connections and relationships, but also of social organisation and administration. The resulting novel practices can themselves be technically and/or socially innovative and, in addition, trigger or entail further innovations because reference points shift and established routines are no longer considered practicable. In this context, the aspect of novelty with regard to social innovations eludes clear contouring[2]. The question arises as to how the novelty of a practice is to be identified. The thesis that a social innovation is rather a modification of an already known practice of action and that the attempt to identify it falls back on the different rather than clearly referring to a novel element seems to be much more accurate. In all attempts to capture this fact in definitional terms, one nevertheless comes back to the characterization explicated by Schumpeter, which so aptly depicts the idea of novelty in social innovations: "the doing of new things or the doing of things that are already being done in a new way" (Schumpeter 1947, p. 151). The novelty of the practices realized in social innovations lies, so to speak, in their otherness. Social innovations do not exist without the element of novelty, but it requires a different connotation of the new that is expressed in a social innovation (Gillwald 2000; Bechmann and Grunwald 1998). Here the problem of the elusiveness of the distinction, which is difficult to grasp and measure, becomes clear (Gillwald 2000, p. 41; Braun-Thürmann and John 2010, p. 54 f.). For, if every difference in behaviour could be an innovation, this would reduce the term and the concept to absurdity. New frameworks provoke new practices of action, and changed practices can subject the frameworks to a need for modification. What seems easily comprehensible at this point in the abstract formulation appears far more complex with regard to a theoretical foundation and in the examination of very concrete moments. Researchers from various disciplines (e.g. Ogburn 1923; Kroeber 1924; Rammert 1993; Mensch 1972) have already discussed the question of what a social innovation is by definition and when a changed practice of action can be identified as socially innovative. In this context, the following aspect seems particularly relevant: "Not everything that we find innovative becomes innovation" (Franz and Kaletka 2018, p. 2). Thus, when the adjective innovative is used in the further course of these remarks, it is used to describe a practice of action that is visualized as actual innovation and has

[2] The assumption that in relation to technical innovations an extremely clear designation of the new can take place must also be critically examined with reference to the explanations of Bechmann and Grundwald (1998: 5) and the view of Luhmann (1990).

consequently found its way into people's repertoire of actions. The claim is therefore not used here to describe something new, but to refer to innovations that actually mean changed action practice. Bearing in mind that this paper pursues a different agenda, we shall stick to this concise and condensed exposition of the subject of *social innovation.* Consequently, the assumption will apply that social innovations can be characterised by the fact that modes of action are designed in a supra-individual and *different way* than before – precisely in the form that many act *differently than before.*

2 Working Thesis and Intention

The thesis that social innovations can lead to *an increase* in satisfaction or a new sense of well-being is by no means new. In the course of this reading, the perspective is shifted, which essentially means that the question of *what* a social innovation is is no longer prominent. Rather, the focus is on the ways of acting that are conceived as changed and that are the result or outcome of social innovation. Drawing out the social occurrences arising from the innovative action appears to be just as great a challenge as finding the dam-breaking argument as to when a social innovation can be designated as such. Inherent in this circumstance is the tentative question of how social innovations can be mapped, how they can be understood in terms of their design, expansion and impact. Social innovations can be understood as social phenomena that need to be described, understood and explained (Braun-Thürmann and John 2010, p. 54 ff.).

If one wants to find out how big the change has to be for it to be considered innovative, it can be useful to look at what has changed in order to be able to uncover the innovative character of a newly implemented practice (Howaldt et al. 2008). The following remarks will attempt to demonstrate the explanatory potential of a social science theory approach for understanding how social innovations work. With the upstream thesis that a social innovation changes a practice of action, a social innovation will be considered quasi a posteriori with the help of Dahrendorf's (1979) life chances approach. The guiding working thesis therefore reads as follows: *Social innovations lead to an increase in life chances.*

The life chances approach is intended to systematise and operationalise this rather abstract result of social innovations in a theory-based manner. The field of tension of digitalisation serves as a frame of reference, and the group of senior citizens – i.e. people who are already retired – is considered.[3] Digitisation is a

[3] The group under consideration is contoured by the theoretical preliminary considerations

phenomenon that takes on different forms depending on the functional system of society. At this point, the focus is not on the various forms and advances in individual fields of application. Rather, the perspective forces what is considered a prerequisite for the individual to be able to participate in digitally designed processes, be it information procurement, everyday organisation or communication. The prerequisite for a digital life is the use of the Internet. With regard to the group under investigation, Internet use is therefore the most relevant factor for participation in an increasingly digitalised society. The group of senior citizens is the only one in current society that can be clearly quantified and differentiated into a group of Internet users and a group of Internet non-users (Initiative D21 e. V. 2018, p. 40 f.). Online users have already completed the *digital turn* brought about by digitalisation (Schramm 1988, p. 341). Those senior citizens who organise their everyday life without the Internet and thus practice an analogue lifestyle have not yet had this experience. With regard to the group of senior citizens, the *digital turn is* considered a divisive element that leads to heterogeneity, especially with regard to the factors of information procurement and communication. The use of the Internet is interpreted as a social innovation for the group of senior citizens for various reasons. This makes it clear that social innovations are not carried out in the same time frame for all population groups and that, in addition, a practice of action does not have to be considered innovative for all population groups, i.e. new and changed compared to existing routines. For younger people, for example, Internet use is not a novel practice – it is rather an internalized cultural practice. Based on this example of Internet use by senior citizens, a proposal is to be made, with the addition of the life chances concept, as to how the effect of a social innovation can be represented by a social science theoretical approach. In order to pursue the thesis, it will first be briefly explained why the Internet use of senior citizens should be understood as a social innovation. Subsequently, the basic features of Weber's concept of life chances and the cornerstones of Dahrendorf's concept of life chances will be outlined, followed by a consolidation of the findings.

---

that were made for the doctoral project (finalised in 2018). The term senior citizens does not refer to a numerical equivalent in the form of an age, but results from the legally regulated terms that apply when a person has reached retirement age and leaves employment or is (early) retired for health reasons. Due to the aforementioned aspects, this article will refer exclusively to senior citizens and not to older people, in order to highlight the distinctiveness with regard to retirement from employment (Obermeier 2020, p. 63 ff.).

3 Internet Use as a Social Innovation

The working thesis can be preceded by the question: How do social innovations work and how are they initiated? The intention is to bring about such a change through social innovation that is ultimately evaluated more positively and results in better designed living conditions (John 2013, p. 71). However, this assumption should be sharpened to the effect that a socially innovative practice of action does not per se have to mean that it is in consequence genuinely positive and better conditions per se. Changed practices can, however, also produce results for others who are only indirectly involved that are not positively evaluated (Gillwald 2000, p. 19 f.). This is to be transferred into the context of the Internet use of senior citizens. From an overall social perspective, against the background of the immense spread and implementation in almost all areas of society, it is no longer possible to speak of Internet use as a partially effective social innovation. Although the argument in itself can apply to certain intentions of use or specific application profiles, changed principles of administration and organisation, the use of the Internet itself should be the focus here, and this aspect can be understood as a broad, comprehensive diffusion and transfer into repertoires of action. For many, the Internet-based and digitally designed environment is now an integral part of their own lifeworld (Krotz 2008; p. 44 ff.). Building on the digital design principles, innovative strategies can be identified in a new way. For all those who use the Internet, further repertoires of action and fields of application arise, the preconditions for which have been created by Internet use. From a macro perspective, this refers, for example, to the organisation and design of interpersonal communication, new types of learning strategies, the nature of information genesis and, per se, to the integration of technical media into everyday life. It can be said that various social innovations have become interwoven and ultimately represent the transformation process of the *digital turn*. However, the digitalised communication, information, organisation and administration principles are to a certain extent opposed by those who do *not use* the Internet and thus *cannot participate in digitalisation*. The majority of this group of people living offline are senior citizens. Alongside education and type of occupation, age is currently the most influential determinant with regard to internet use. In the course of the doctoral project completed in 2018, a study was conducted on the internet use and non-use of senior citizens (Obermeier 2020), which provides all kinds of interesting insights into this context of social innovations and the explanatory potential of Dahrendorf's social science concept of life chances.

The results of the quantitative studies conducted by Initiative D21 show that people are more likely to use the Internet when their professional activities make it necessary to do so. The sooner people are confronted with the topics of digitalisation in their professional environment, the more likely they are to be open-minded and innovative towards the Internet in their private lives. This aspect can be transferred to the group of senior citizens if one understands retirement and thus the end of employment as a kind of caesura in Internet use. It can be seen that people who have used the Internet in a mature and confident manner during their working lives continue to do so in retirement. For those who only became acquainted with the Internet in a rudimentary way during their working life or did not have to use it at all, the studies for the current senior generation show that Internet use is marginalised or completely discontinued in retirement (Obermeier 2020, p. 280 ff.). If the senior citizens have not established any contact with the Internet in the phase of employment, they only find access to it to a limited extent. The decisive factor for the group of offliners with regard to potential Internet use is the existence of family networks. Here, finally, lies the decisive moment: senior citizens living offline who have no children (and thus no grandchildren)[4] *do not* feel disadvantaged in the increasingly digitalised environment and do *not* perceive themselves as excluded – as shown by the results of the qualitative study of the doctoral project (Obermeier 2020, p. 339 ff.). They see no reason from their current life situation to engage with the Internet. The reasons for remaining distanced from the Internet are manifold: a) learning computer technology and handling it seems too time-consuming and costly, b) they reject the Internet as a whole, c) they fear excessive demands, d) they do not see any added value in Internet use, or e) they do not consider it necessary for organising their everyday life. Senior citizens who have children or multi-generational networks have a different view of the necessity of the Internet for their own way of life: they are among those who have dealt intensively with computer and Internet skills and have made their way into the World Wide Web even in retirement, without previously established knowledge. It is not the case that these senior citizens do not share the obstacles and hurdles of the offliners. They are also afraid of risks and excessive demands, they also shy away from the expenditure of time and see in the Internet use a multifaceted challenge, which above all manifests itself in an increased respect for computer technology. The decisive reason why they have acquired the use of the Internet lies in the strong need to be able to use the Internet-based communication channels and thus participate in the exchange within the family. The awareness that Internet-based communication technologies are the primary means of communication and that grandchildren in particular, and the

[4] Own children are not exclusively understood to be biological children. It is essentially about connections and relationships created by mutual care in a supra-generational relationship, which correspond to or resemble a (bodily) parent-child relationship.

younger generations in general, appear to be more accessible through them, is common to all senior citizens. For those senior citizens who do not have family networks, the new communication and information technologies appear to be less significant, as they are less regularly active in intergenerational networks within which digitalised communication is established. The majority of them share their living situation with people who are primarily socialised via analogue communication strategies and who also have stable social relationships in their environment. In this context, it is less relevant for senior citizens to exchange information via digital channels. The situation is different with regard to senior citizens who are, as it were, parents and possibly grandparents/great-grandparents. For them, it is above all the connection to the family that is important – they recognise the advantages offered by Internet-based communication media such as e-mail or messenger services. Turning to the Internet thus follows a clearly identifiable intention: contact with children and grandchildren. This intention is intensified even further when families are fragmented due to geographical circumstances, i.e. (grand)children and (grand)parents tend to live further away from each other, so that personal, direct togetherness is only possible to a very limited extent. For this group of people it is true that, due to a clearly perceived problem and a pressure to suffer, they decide to expand their repertoire of actions so that the goal, contact with the family, can be achieved. This then means for this group of people not only that they find their way to the Internet, but that a new way of communication is practiced. The senior citizens conquer a new way of communication, which is to a large extent characterized by written language and also functions through the use of photos as a carrier medium. In this way, the senior citizens are conquering a multimedia usage behaviour that is based on common moments such as the use of WhatsApp, video telephony, etc. The type of platform or media format is not determined by the user. The type of platform or the media format are not the decisive moments in this context: The fact of the completely new communication is the outstanding element for the senior citizens. In this way, they resolve an event experienced as unsatisfactory by actively striving for a new repertoire of action. Thus, the new way of communication diffuses into their everyday life. Per se, they are thus following a transformation that has already taken place for a large number of groups of people in society. Nevertheless, for seniors living offline, turning to the use of the Internet is a social innovation. Senior citizens who have spent most of their lives using analogue strategies and who have only begun to deal with the Internet at a late stage open up far-reaching insights into their dealings with the newly learned and thus also newly experienced digitalisation in the course of the qualitative analysis. They can provide reconstructive information about how individual lifestyles are shaped and changed by Internet use. The mapping of this change will be done with the help of Ralf Dahrendorf's life chances concept.

4 The Concept of Life Chances

The term *life chances* can be located in the context of questions and analyses of social inequality. Per se, the understanding of this concept can be approached at the micro level and shaped in such a way that it refers to the opportunities for shaping an individual's life, which can unfold in the light of the determinants and dimensions of social inequalities. This immediately implies that not every individual in a society is confronted with the same opportunities. Depending on the manifestations, i.e. the constellation of characteristics, of the determinant (askriptive and acquired) factors of social origin, age, education, income, occupation and gender, different potentials arise with regard to access to (further) socially relevant resources. What is considered a relevant resource (e.g. income, professional status and prestige, etc.) is shaped by societal values and norms and is structurally consolidated.

> For just as life chances are based on the one hand on the objective conditions of life, they are on the other hand influenced by the subjective perception and processing of these conditions by acting individuals. Social structures function as conditions for life chances that are produced and reproduced by human actors. (Meyer and Pöttker 2004, p. 11).

The determinants named limit or open up the opportunities that present themselves, depending on their characteristics. In view of the processes of social change, further factors are added to the systematised influencing variables and shift or expand the canon of socially relevant resources. Internet use and participation in digitisation can be included in this canon and regarded as a significant dimension that can be understood as the result of determinant factors, but which also has an impact on life chances.

Life chances address how individuals shape their lives on the basis of these constellations of characteristics. It is thus inherent in this term that it is aimed at the exploitation of the opportunities that present themselves and considers how individuals evaluate their potential. Thus, life chances are something highly individual: although potentials could be depicted qua the objectively ascertainable constellations of characteristics, the assessment of individuals with regard to the freedom to exploit the potentials and to realise the chances is the decisive evaluation of how life chances present themselves (Sen 2002, p. 94 ff.; Leßmann 2006, p. 35). Thus, the concept of life chances eludes a selective scaling and quantification.

The concept of life chances has its origins in Max Weber, who takes the divergent potentials outlined above (due to the constellations of characteristics and the associated chances of access to socially relevant resources) to extremes by speaking of "survival chances" (Weber 1999 [1922], p. 38). The contextualization is thus different: It is not the individual conduct of life that strives for a happy and successful life that is meant here, but rather a competitive situation that prevails between individuals and that has nothing less than survival as its goal.

> The (latent) struggle for existence of human individuals or types for chances of life and survival, which takes place against each other without any meaningful intention of struggle, is to be called "selection" ("Auslese") [sic!]: "social selcetion" insofar as it is a matter of chances of living, "biological selection" insofar as it is a matter of chances of survival of hereditary property. (Weber 1999 [1922], p. 38)

Weber is concerned with the contestation of positions in the social structure – in doing so, he makes the point that there are limited resources that not every individual can attain.

While *life chances* in Weber's foundation functions more as a term to outline market power and resource distributions in his class conception, Ralf Dahrendorf elevates it to a theoretical concept. Critics accuse Dahrendorf of the fragmentary character of this approach, which is considered to be incomplete, large-framed and little differentiated and concretized (Reichwein and Brandt 1980, p. 376). However, these supposed weaknesses can also be reinterpreted as strengths: The openness and sometimes abstract interpretation of life chances offers room for the personal configurations of the individuals who undertake the evaluation of their life chances for themselves.

The concept of life chances according to Dahrendorf oscillates, as it were, on the micro and macro levels. Relevant for the context of consideration are the explications on the micro level. It has already been outlined that life chances can be understood as the individual conduct of life. Dahrendorf visualizes this in the catchy formulation: "Life chances are the baking forms of human life in society; they determine how far people can develop" (Dahrendorf 1979, p. 24). From a macro perspective, this also means that the life chances of an entire society change as a result of a changed framework, such as a changed legal situation with regard to women's suffrage, and in the course of this, *new* life chances are added because entirely new choices open up. In the case of women's right to vote, it is easy to see that this leads to lasting developments in society as a whole and that new opportunities arise directly for the group of women. These possibilities are conceptually reflected in Dahrendorf's approach to life chances. Life chances are constituted in two elements: options and ligatures.

> Ligatures are affiliations; one could also call them ties. [...] From the point of view of the individual, ligatures present themselves as references. They give meaning to the place he occupies. In general, ligatures mark the element of meaning and anchoring, while options emphasize the goal and horizon of action. Ligatures endow references and thus the foundations of action; options demand choices and are thus open to the [sic!] future. (Dahrendorf 1979, p. 51).

The potentials mentioned several times in advance coincide with the element of options: These are the choices that an individual can make on the basis of his or her available resources. These are very different and relate to aspects such as the educational path, the choice of career, the organisation of leisure activities, etc. Ligatures are moments of meaning that give the individual an anchorage and signify a connection to social networks. Ligatures are the social ties of an individual. Life chances only exist when both options and ligatures are pronounced: "Ligatures without options mean oppression, while options without ties are meaningless" (Dahrendorf 1979, p. 51 f.). Both elements condition individual life chances, whereby the manifestations defy quantification and do not offset each other – the quality of the shaping of the two elements is up to the individual's evaluation. This complex is not further decisively differentiated by Dahrendorf even in this grounding, so that the abstraction does not receive a resolution (Geißler 1987, p. 3). However, this concept can be used in an open, qualitative design to explore how the life chances of senior citizens are shaped when they discover Internet use for themselves.

5 More Life Opportunities Through Internet Use

It became apparent that Internet use for seniors is an innovative practice that goes beyond the mere use of Internet-enabled devices. It is about an immersion in a new way of communicating by using messenger services, sending e-mails and making video calls. In the context of the doctoral project, qualitative in-depth interviews were conducted, which were analysed interpretatively and meaningfully with the help of the life chances concept. The question of which aspects the senior citizens regard as options and ligatures in the Dahrendorfian sense was worked out inductively from the material (Obermeier 2020, p. 280 ff.). The results are clear: the use of the Internet not only multiplies the potential choices, but above all the *options used by senior citizens.* This becomes apparent especially with regard to the procurement of information and the generation of knowledge. Through the possibility of being able to obtain advance information via the Internet, the senior citizens feel more self-confident, more responsible, more informed and less dependent on others. They expand their repertoire of actions because they can use the Internet to work out solutions to problems in a targeted manner; they feel more independent and are also more relaxed about the times in which they are restricted by decreasing mobility. The Internet opens up new creative possibilities, more extensive choices and a broad portfolio of opportunities for participation. Even more far-reaching and significant than the gain in options is the new form of social ties. For the senior citizens, for example, an increase in ligatures can be recorded. Through the use of Internet-based communication channels, senior citizens feel much more integrated into the family network. They feel more intensively involved in the lives of their children and their children's children. They also feel that contact with their grandchildren is easier. Overall, senior citizens feel that they are a much more tangible part of society through Internet use (Obermeier 2020, p. 412 ff.).

This makes it clear that a social innovation, in this case the use of the Internet – together with the new communication and information technologies – *can contribute to an increase in life chances.* The gains can be worked out both for the options and for the ligatures. Through socially innovative action, the senior citizens have succeeded in improving a situation that is perceived as inadequate and in establishing a new practice of action. Using Dahrendorf's life chances concept, it was possible to show one way in which the results of social innovations can be determined.

References

Bechmann, G., und A. Grunwald. 1998. Was ist das Neue am Neuen, oder: wie innovativ ist Innovation? *TA-Datenbank-Nachrichten*, 7. Jg., H. 1: 4–11.

Becker, Jörg. 2013. *Die Digitalisierung von Medien und Kultur*. Wiesbaden: Springer Fachmedien.

Braun-Thürmann, H. und R. John. 2010. Innovation: Realisierung und Indikator des sozialen Wandels. In *Soziale Innovation*, Hrsg. J. Howaldt und H. Jacobsen, 53–69. Wiesbaden: VS Verlag für Sozialwissenschaften.

Dahrendorf, Ralf. 1979. *Lebenschancen. Anläufe zur sozialen und politischen Theorie*. Frankfurt/M.: Suhrkamp.

Floridi, Luciano. 2015. *Die 4. Revolution*. Berlin: Suhrkamp.

Franz, H.-W. und C. Kaletka. 2018. Einleitung. In *Soziale Innovationen lokal gestalten*, Hrsg. H.-W. Franz und C. Kaletka, 1–19. Wiesbaden: Springer VS.

Geißler, Rainer. 1987. *Soziale Schichtung und Lebenschancen in der Bundesrepublik Deutschland*. Stuttgart: Enke.

Gillwald, Katrin. 2000. Konzepte sozialer Innovation, WZB Discussion Paper, No. P 00-519, Wissenschaftszentrum Berlin für Sozialforschung (WZB), Berlin. https://www.econstor.eu/bitstream/10419/50299/1/319103064.pdf. Zugegriffen: 01. Oktober 2019.

Hofstetter, Yvonne. 2018. Digitale Revolution, gesellschaftlicher Umbruch: Eine Technikfolgenbewertung. In *Wissen – Macht – Meinung. Demokratie und Digitalisierung*, Hrsg. Franziska Martinsen, 91–98. Baden-Baden: Nomos.

Howaldt, Jürgen und M. Schwarz. 2010. *Soziale Innovation im Fokus. Skizze eines gesellschaftstheoretisch inspirierten Forschungskonzepts*. Bielefeld: transcript.

Howaldt, J., R. Kopp, und M. Schwarz. 2008. Innovationen (forschend) gestalten – Zur neuen Rolle der Sozialwissenschaften. *WSI-Mitteilungen*, 61 Jg., H. 2: 63–69.

Initiative D21 e. V. 2018. D21 Digital Index 2018/2019. Jährliches Lagebild zur Digitalen Gesellschaft. https://initiatived21.de/app/uploads/2019/01/d21_index2018_2019.pdf. Zugegriffen: 11. Oktober 2019.

John, René. 2013. Innovation als soziales Phänomen. In *Innovationen im Bildungswesen*. Buchreihe Educational Governance, Vol. 21, Hrsg. Rürup, M. und I. Bormann, 71–86. Wiesbaden: Springer VS.

Kroeber, Alfred L. 1924. *Anthropology*. London etc.: Harrap.

Krotz, Friedrich. 2008. Kultureller und gesellschaftlicher Wandel im Kontext des Wandels von Medien und Kommunikation. In *Medienkultur und soziales Handeln*, Hrsg. Tanja Thomas, 44–62. Wiesbaden: Springer VS.

Leßmann, O. 2006. Lebenslagen und Verwirklichungschancen (capability) – Verschiedene Wurzeln, ähnliche Konzepte. Vierteljahrshefte zur Wirtschaftsforschung 75, H. 1: 30–42.

Luhmann, Niklas. 1990. *Die Wissenschaft der Gesellschaft*. Frankfurt/M.: Suhrkamp.

Mensch, Gerhard. 1972. *Das technologische Patt. Innovationen überwinden die Depression*. Frankfurt/M.: Umschau.

Meyer, T., und H. Pöttker. 2004. Rainer Geißler und das soziologische Konzept der Lebenschancen. In *Kritische Empirie. Lebenschancen in den Sozialwissenschaften*, Hrsg. H. Pöttker und T. Meyer, 9–13. Wiesbaden: VS Verlag für Sozialwissenschaften.

Obermeier, Claudia. 2020. *Seniorinnen und Senioren im Kontext der digitalen Revolution. Eine qualitative Untersuchung der Internetnutzung von Seniorinnen und Senioren*. Weinheim: Beltz Juventa.

Ogburn, Wiliam F. 1923. *Social Change. With Respect to Culture and Original Nature*. London: Allen & Unwin.

Rammert, Werner. 1993. *Technik aus soziologischer Perspektive. Forschungsstand, Theorieansätze, Fallbeispiele. Ein Überblick*. Opladen: Westdeutscher Verlag.

Reichwein, R., und G. Brandt. 1980. Ralf Dahrendorf. Lebenschancen. Anläufe zur sozialen und politischen Theorie. *Soziologische Revue*, Jg. 3: 375–388.

Reutner, Ursula. 2012. Von der digitalen zur interkulturellen Revolution? In *Von der digitalen zur interkulturellen Revolution*, Hrsg. Ursula Reutner, 9–32, Baden-Baden: Nomos.

Schramm, Wilbur. 1988. *The Story of Human Communications: Cave Painting to Microchip*. New York: Harper & Row.

Schumpeter, J. A. 1947. The Creative Response in Economic History. *The Journal of Economic* Hostory, 7 Jg., H. 2: 149–159.

Sen, Amartya. 2002. *Ökonomie für den Menschen. Wege zur Gerechtigkeit und Solidarität in der Marktwirtschaft*. München: Deutscher Taschenbuch Verlag.

Stengel, Oliver. 2017. Zeitalter und Revolutionen. In *Digitalzeitalter – Digitalgesellschaft. Das Ende des Industriezeitalters und der Beginn einer neuen Epoche*, Hrsg. O. Stengel, A. Looy und S. Wallaschkowski, 17–50.
Tapscott, Don und A. D. Williams. 2007. *Wikinomics: Die Revolution im Netz*. München: Carl Hanser.
Waldenfels, Bernhard. 1990. *Der Stachel des Fremden*. Frankfurt/M.: Suhrkamp.
Weber, Max. 1999[1922]. *Wirtschaft und Gesellschaft*. Paderborn: Voltmedia.
Zapf, Wolfgang. 1994. *Modernisierung, Wohlfahrtsentwicklung und Transformation: soziologische Aufsätze 1987 bis 1994*. Berlin: Edition Sigma.
Zapf, Wolfgang. 1989. Über soziale Innovationen. *Soziale Welt*, 40. Jg., H. 1–2: 170–183.

Claudia Obermeier, Dr. phil., doctorate in sociology at the Christian-Albrechts-Universität zu Kiel, double master's degree in international comparative sociology and philosophy, research assistant at the Institute for Social Sciences at the Christian-Albrechts-Universität zu Kiel, member of the board of the BDS.

Latest Publications:

Obermeier, Claudia. 2020. *Seniorinnen und Senioren im Kontext der digitalen Revolution. Eine qualitative Untersuchung der Internetnutzung von Seniorinnen und Senioren.* Weinheim: Beltz Juventa.

Obermeier, Claudia. 2018. Wege aus der Einsamkeit, soziale Interaktion neu denken. (Pflege) Roboter als Interaktionspartner älterer Menschen. In *Soziale Innovationen lokal gestalten* eds H.-W. Franz and C. Kaletka, 149-164 Wiesbaden: Springer VS.

The "Atlas Subject" and New Forms of Subjectivation in the Age of Sustainability

Diego Compagna

Abstract

As is well known, in the stories of Greek mythology, the Titan Atlas (Prometheus' brother, by the way) has to carry the vault of heaven (i.e. the globe) on his shoulders as punishment, since he has sided with Kronos and thus against the 'new gods' of Olympus. In my contribution I would like to address a particular (new) form of individualization of late modernity and the negative consequences for social renewal associated with it. Thus, I would also like to address – against the background of a distinction between the dynamics of innovation versus revolution – the orientation towards sustainability as a regime-stabilizing phenomenon that considerably limits the scope for genuine social transformations. Based on alternative models of knowledge production and world interpretation (rhizome, cyborg, Cthulhu), I will formulate a social present-day diagnosis of "total immanence" that can hardly be surpassed in terms of claustrophobic powerlessness effects. Not only does the world seem to us to be "without exit" (Adorno and Horkheimer's almost prophetic heralding of the second modernity), it must now also be saved by each individual – and at any price.

D. Compagna (✉)
Faculty of Applied Social Sciences, Munich University of Applied Sciences, Munich, Germany
e-mail: diego.compagna@hm.edu

H.-W. Franz et al. (eds.), *Sustainable Living and Business*,
https://doi.org/10.1007/978-3-658-41835-9_3

1 The Construction of Sustainability

The orientation towards sustainability fundamentally promises good things and has recently become a (or even the) guiding concept of social change (Neckel et al. 2018; but cf. also, for example, Daschkeit and Dombrowsky as early as 2010), which is now already being used at least as ubiquitously as the once progressive, future-oriented concept of "innovation" (Braun-Thürmann 2005). An orientation towards sustainability as well as sustainable innovations seem to be the essence and the result of a reflexive modernity that has come completely into its own and – in the sense of a double hermeneutics (Giddens 1997) – has brought the problem consciousness of late-modern societies "from the ivory tower" to the streets. In the process, contested *and thus* contested interpretations of complex referential contexts undergo a not inconsiderable path of trivialization and de-paradoxification in the course of translation from an academic to a lifeworld frame of reference, which is not uncommon in the context of double hermeneutics. Moreover, so-called participatory-transformative research legitimizes the leveling of fuzziness and side-effects worthy of criticism (foreseeable and unforeseeable) by barely addressing them. What seems to me particularly problematic, however, is the invisibilization through the non-thematization of (partly) well-known problems and a central imbalance (the highly selective participation) of transdisciplinary-transformative research, which ultimately fall victim to practicability and an imperative of "wanting to implement". It is precisely the (rightly) demanded urgency stemming from the impending "climate collapse" that provides the legitimation for the activists' renunciation and capitulation with regard to this central demand of transdisciplinary-transformative projects: the participation of as many "citizens" as possible in the identification, design, and solution of one or more (common) problems.

The social sciences, on the other hand, have rediscovered the social phenomenon of "sustainability" in recent years and are increasingly interpreting it in terms of the undesirable side-effects it produces – including the effects of power, hierarchy and inequality at the national, supranational and global levels. My contribution is a genuinely sociological one that responds to the desideratum formulated a good year ago by Sighard Neckel and his Hamburg-based team of researchers:

> Sustainability should – in other words – not be studied sociologically from the societal participant perspective, but should serve as an observational category that can shed light on what socio-economic change is taking place, what novel lines of conflict are emerging, and what inequalities and hierarchies are emerging as contemporary societies increasingly integrate criteria of sustainability into their institutions, functional domains, and cultural value patterns. Social science research should pay particular attention to how sustainability is linked to social power relations. For how

> sustainability is defined and who determines sustainability is as much a question of social rankings as the consequences of sustainability can raise problems of social inequalities. (Neckel 2018a, p. 13 f.)

Thus, my contribution will on the one hand deal with the – still urgently needed – social science educational work regarding the unintended and partly undesirable side effects of a (ubiquitous) orientation towards sustainability, and on the other hand with the hubris of affluent societies, *whose* world is to be saved (global), and educated middle-classes, *whose* nature is to be saved (local). Both dynamics result in a reinforcement of social inequality, globally in the sense of a post-colonial world order, locally through the dictates of those who have something to lose compared to everyone else. It can neither be in the sense of a free democratic basic order nor of a "climate change" to further deepen this schism. An orientation towards sustainability, e.g. through the realisation of a decidedly "sustainable lifestyle", is pursued in Germany by a very specific, quite manageable segment. This makes up about 7 percent of the population, is very homogeneous within itself, and can be characterized as an "aspiring middle class" (Neckel 2018b). So let us first soberly note: The pioneers of a lived sustainability can be described as (1) academics who (2) emerged from an educated middle-class milieu and (3) successfully oriented themselves "upwards" (aspiring). This small, very specific group of people, whose lifeworld differs markedly from the vast majority of society, is the nucleus for perhaps the most significant social innovation of the present.

The urgency of a comprehensive orientation towards sustainability is undisputed. However clear the insight into the need for far-reaching change at all levels may be, it is all the more important to deal with undesirable side-effects and impacts that are either imminent or already in full swing. It therefore seems to me to be indispensable, especially in the sense of an overall societal (at best global) orientation towards sustainability that leads to concrete forms of successful implementation of climate-friendly action and economic activity, to deal with the undesirable side-effects, which admittedly also include effects that affect the dimension of the social (cohesion, integration, etc.) in a narrower sense. Here I understand sustainability or an orientation towards sustainability to mean the evaluation of options for action which then lead to corresponding decisions – from these two points of view:

1. "[T]o ensure the *regenerativity of* ecological, economic, social, and subjective resources that social institutions and functional areas need for their existence and must use for their further development. Increasingly urgent are forms of using resources that, when used, do not consume themselves without residue

but are renewable, which is why "Vernutzung" – i.e. consumptive use – is the antithesis of the regenerative principle of sustainability." (Neckel 2018a, p. 16)
2. "Here, the second social reproduction problem of sustainability is the safeguarding of the *potentiality of* future development opportunities, which are not to be destroyed or considerably restricted by the resource problems of the present. Sustainability here serves to secure a stock of possibilities for action that should no longer be made scarce in the present. Its counter-concept is determination, which transforms open futures into closed ones." (Neckel 2018a, p. 16)

A clarification of terms is necessary, since the concept of sustainability is highly "contested" precisely because of its dominant general-societal, trend-setting effect (in an analogous way, Jutta Weber (2003) presented the sociologically also highly presuppositional concept of "nature" as contested years ago). Gaining – or retaining – the power to define promises improbably great advantages, because depending on how it is defined, certain interests can be met more readily than others. This paper will focus primarily on the effects of the current sustainability discourse at the individual level, although some social effects can be derived directly from it to some extent. The global, postcolonial level requires a discussion dedicated to it, which will have to be further elaborated elsewhere.

Despite the not exactly small risk of being misunderstood, I would like to point out an important aspect. Herbert Blumer's (2013) description of the production of facts that are socially identified as a problem can be excellently transferred to the sustainability discourse and the demand for an orientation towards sustainability. A state of affairs has to overcome a whole series of communicative hurdles until it is considered a socially more or less generally accepted problem. Quite in the sense of a "career" of socially produced and thus on the one hand contingent, on the other hand materially no less imposing interpretations of reality, the demand for sustainability orientation must be deconstructed. By stating that no one directly perceives CO_2 as a problem in everyday life, it is by no means intended to claim that the problem has been invented. Nevertheless, as much as scientific (objective) observations, evaluations and assessments of experts unmistakably and unambiguously entail an orientation towards sustainability, they say little about the fact that the "problem" of a "climate crisis", which can be traced back to a too CO_2 -intensive lifestyle, must be constructed, because no one directly perceives it that way and can consequently comprehend it. This leads, on the one hand, to a relative openness to interpretation and, on the other hand, to the eminent difficulty of a very broad, intrinsic willingness to participate.

For, despite all the media's visualisation of the consequences of climate change, from the directly accessible local experience of the vast majority of the population there is both a lack of direct access and the possibility of insight into the complex interrelationships (Luhmann 1996, p. 10 f.). The connection between the consumption of a curry sausage in the snack bar and crop failures or even the increase in the flow of refugees (which is partly due to climate change) may seem obvious to the readers of this article – but when viewed soberly, this connection involves many mediating steps that run through several corners and are simply *not* accessible to direct life experience. The sustainability discourse, the climate crisis (as much as it is scientifically obvious) are – like almost everything else we orient ourselves to in everyday life – the result of a narrative (Hall 2004). In a lifeworld characterized by mediocrity (typical for functionally differentiated, modern societies and even more so for those that are situated within the framework of a globalized structure), not only the "stories" of capitalists or transport ministers are fictitious, but also those of climate activists. To deceive oneself in this is grist to the mill of those who fear that they would have to give up a piece or a large part of their privileges if the demands of the activists were followed by deeds.

So focusing on "storytelling" is entirely in the spirit of sustainability. What can a new narrative for society as a whole look like that does not give rise to resentment? How to put those in the foreground of the story *as protagonists* who do not belong to the "usual suspects" (urban gardening investors, eco-house owners, regional currency advocates, common good economy entrepreneurs, etc.)? But it is equally important to critically accompany the narrative of the current sustainability discourse and to be aware that the voices of those who are in the process of telling this "new" story are different. Some voices are framed by dominant interpretive patterns in such a 'sideways' way that they may not be heard at all (cf. Spivak 2008).

2 The Time Dimension of Sustainability

In his structuration theory, Giddens (1997) distinguishes (rightly and momentously) between the irreversible time of the individual and the reversible time of the social or society. Irreversible is the time of the actors in a society because their life span is finite. Reversible, on the other hand, is social time insofar as it extends into infinity (measured against the human horizon of experience); a society, can – in principle – set its own clock to zero again and again. In Giddens' theory of structuration, this distinction is important insofar as it marks an important feature of the duality of action and structure: The (usually) unintended reproduction of social structures takes place on the basis of an orientation towards personal needs and motives. These are, of course, not only culturally shaped, but can be directly traced back to a socially given frame of reference into which every human being is born. In recourse to the mode of action of unintended consequences of action, Giddens succeeds in describing and explaining structural reproduction as not directly motivated, thus circumventing the "functionalist dilemma" of a "puppetishness" of people who function as vicarious agents of social order through functional contributions. In contrast, Giddens repeatedly points out that only people can have needs, whereas social systems have neither needs nor motives, and in this respect must always be traced back to the satisfaction of needs by the people who place themselves in social contexts. As socialized people (social actors), however, they are always already embedded in social structures and frameworks that favor certain dispositions of needs and make others unlikely, sometimes even impossible. Social actors do not reproduce the structures (i.e. rules and allocative as well as authoritative resources) intentionally insofar as in the vast majority of cases they do not seek out certain social contexts with the intention of reproducing the structures, but rather act in a motivationally oriented manner in order to achieve a certain goal, satisfy a need, etc. Who studies in order to reproduce the structures of the educational system? Who attends a concert, a party with the intention of reproducing the structures of corresponding institutionalized practices? No, students want to obtain a degree, further their education, take up a particular profession, etc. And the same is true for concert and party-goers, consumers, company employees, etc.

One of the reasons why the time dimension is so important for Giddens' (1997) theory is that the motivation of individuals to enter a certain context without critically reflecting on the structures also stems from the fact that their time is precisely finite (irreversible). In this way, Giddens succeeds, at least in part, in explaining the inertia of social structures. In casual terms, this circumstance can be described in terms of the so-called opportunity costs: A student who, in the fourth semester of her bachelor's degree, realises that a different course of study would probably have been more in line with what she actually wanted to study, will think twice about changing her course of study.

For a concern with sustainability, this means two things above all: first, it is another facet that can be held responsible for the inertia of a structural change; second – and this is the aspect I am primarily concerned with here – social time has changed with hardly foreseeable consequences for the construction or confirmation of social reality on the basis of an unintended structural reproduction: What does it mean when social time also becomes (has become) irreversible? What performance must be rendered by individuals in order to find their way motivationally in the timeline of a society that has become finite "all at once"? If each individual integrates the climate emergency into his/her life, can structures still be reproduced at all on the basis of unintended consequences? Can a highly differentiated and specialized society afford such a comprehensive irritation? Can I pursue my job if I have to commute? Can I keep studying if job prospects don't play into the hands of sustainability? Can I buy pickled cucumbers if they are not local? Better in a jar, in a can, or only if they're not packaged at all?

In Giddens' (1997, p. 65) "stratification model of action", the reflexive control of action is distinguished from action rationalization and motivation. (Highly) individualized actors of late modern societies are already practiced in having to constantly reposition and reorient themselves by having to constantly question and reassess their lifeworld on the level of action rationalization and motivation. However, the burden of the late-modern (second) push towards individualization (cf. Beck and Beck-Gernsheim 2008) to be borne by each individual pales in the face of the tasks facing the atlas subject. The time of society, which has become irreversible, synchronizes personal with social needs in such a way that structural reproduction would be massively endangered. A highly specialized, highly differentiated society is dependent on generic (e.g. with the help of generalized interaction media) patterns of action and orientation. A structure that has to be negotiated over and over again means a structure that is threatened by collapse. If sustainability were to provide the frame of reference for the logic of all situations and the individual had to choose the logic of action selection accordingly, the actors would be overwhelmed and the structures would be in danger.

The time dimension in Giddens' theory gives us an indication of how little modern societies can afford to locate and play out sustainability at the individual level. Structural reproduction becomes a deliberate enterprise of each individual. This may be possible in a tribal society – which Durkheim (Durkheim 1999; cf. Luhmann 1999, p. 24) saw, not without reason, as being sustained by a collective consciousness – but hardly in a differentiated modern society. From Max Weber's Lebensführung (Weber 1994, p. 20 f.) to the domestication of the inner nature of the Frankfurt School (Horkheimer and Adorno 1997, p. 61 ff.) to Foucault's (2004, p. 39 f.) diagnosis of a present characterized by subjectivation and further to Ulrich Bröckling's (2007) "entrepreneurial self", the fate of modern actors continues in a straight line and culminates in a further (highest?) level of self-thematization and self-disciplining, for which there can be no more apt expression than the mythological template of Atlas, who is condemned to carry the earth on his shoulders and, thus fixed, loses any chance of freedom, development, and shaping. Atlas had to carry the earth for all eternity; we must continually repair it.

3 The Subjectification of Sustainability

In the stories of Greek mythology, the Titan Atlas (incidentally: Prometheus' brother) must carry the firmament (i.e. the globe) on his shoulders as punishment, since he has sided with Kronos and thus against the 'new gods' of Olympus. The Atlas subject primarily means a further intensification of self-disciplining brought about by the sustainability discourse, insofar as sustainable action or an orientation towards sustainability in action is negotiated at the individual level and in many cases (medially) attributed to each individual. The attribution of co-responsibility and thus implicitly also co-blame for the impending climate-related catastrophe is unmistakably made as an appeal, which has already been plausibly described as the subjectification of sustainability by Pritz (2018). That humans as social actors of modern societies have become masters of 'sub-jection' (sub-iactare) is commonly known and a commonplace in the social sciences. Therefore, I will only cursorily take up the topic in order to then resume the thread that will lead us to the atlas-subject and the death of utopias.

Durkheim (1999) already pointed out the interdependent relationship between individualisation and modernity against the background of functional differentiation. Following in Durkheim's footsteps, functionalist approaches have spelled out the facts with further theoretical acuity (cf. Parsons 1994, p. 185 ff.; Luhmann 2008b). On the part of the individuals, identity is constituted here on the one hand as a necessary condition of the management of the most diverse role expectations and the most diverse subsystems, in which they participate in the mode of partial inclusion (cf. Schneider 2002, p. 158 ff.; Parsons 1975). On the other hand, the difference between self-reference and other-reference imposes a continuous reflection on the individuals, which simply results from the circumstance of embarrassment regarding the manifold possibilities of choice:

> Society no longer indicates the direction of the solution, but only the problem; it no longer confronts man as a demand for moral conduct of life, but only as complexity, to which one has to relate contingently and selectively in each individual way. (Luhmann 2008a, p. 194)

If the description of the individualization process has been presented as ambivalent from the very beginning – Durkheim's concept of morality is due to the lack of correspondence between socially demanded organic solidarity and individual insight (Müller 1992) – the concept of subjectivation is skeptical of the program of modernity as a whole. Thus, subjectivation can, on the one hand, be perceived as an effect of individualization qua functional differentiation with more or less negative connotations (cf. Hahn 1986) or, on the other hand, as its necessary condition and reverse side: The perspective circumscribed by subjectification and subjectivation consequently conceives of the subject rather as the substantivization of a characteristic of certain practices, which only lead to the formation of an individual producing himself as a subject (cf. e.g. Butler 2010, p. 35 ff.; Habermas 2008). Here, subjectification is understood on the one hand as "becoming a subject, whereby subject status can be claimed in certain social roles", and on the other hand as the "process of submission to the normative discursive rules that constitute this status" (Villa 2010, p. 203; cf. Butler 2010, p. 8; Wetzel 2004, p. 252). From this latter perspective, individual and subject are not identical:

> In her writings, Butler makes a clear distinction between subjects and individuals, the former being a kind of neat and properly intelligible discursive position, the latter being, as it were, messy complexities. Subject positions are expressed in socially recognized and valid social titles such as woman, manager*, father, gay/lesbian, sociologist*, etc., which are highly constituted by norms. If we follow Butler [...], persons do not embody norms directly. Rather, norms regulate the conditions under which concrete actions of concrete persons are intelligible, i.e. recognizable [...]. (Villa 2010, p. 204; cf. Butler 2010, p. 15 f.)

In this context, Foucault analytically separates two dynamics: on the one hand, the genesis of the subject as an 'individualized actor', and on the other hand, the social disciplinary techniques that follow on from this and reinforce this process and/or vice versa (Foucault 2002, p. 258 ff.; Foucault 1997, p. 34 f., 88 f.; cf. Lemke 2001, p. 85 ff.). The two moments are to be understood as brackets that refer to each other, without it being possible to specify a 'one-sided' conditional relationship:

> Only the knowledge of one's own self that emerges through the subjectification of the individual allows the individual to recognize what the disciplining gaze grasps when it is directed at the individual. Moreover, the Foucauldian genealogy of sexuality shows that even the most intimate areas of human life are placed in the service of disciplinary society [...]. The constructive effects of the modern crystallization points of power relations alone, that is, of the disciplinary techniques that first produce the modern individual as a product of subjection, make possible the irreversible constitution of disciplinary society. (Hillebrandt 1999, p. 207)

From the effects of panoptic procedures presented in his early writings to the confessional practices of the late series on "Sexuality and Truth", some of which were only published posthumously, the genesis of the subject runs as a leitmotif through Foucault's works. This is presented not only as a "double movement of liberation and enslavement" (Foucault 2003, p. 480), but at the same time as a 'double bind of individualization and totalization' (Hillebrandt 1999, p. 207):

> In the example of the reform efforts from which the psychiatric asylum and clinical psychology emerge, Foucault finally develops that inner kinship of humanism and terror which gives his critique of modernity its sharpness and ruthlessness. In the birth of the mental institution from the humanitarian ideas of the Enlightenment, Foucault demonstrates for the first time that 'double movement of liberation and enslavement' which he later recognizes across the board in the reforms of the penal system, the educational system, health care, social welfare, and so on. The humanitarian-based liberation of the insane from the squalor of internment camps. The creation of hygienic clinics with medical objectives. The psychiatric treatment of the insane, the right they acquire to psychological understanding and therapeutic care. All this is made possible by an institutional order that makes the patient the object of continuous surveillance, manipulation, isolation and regimentation, above all the object of medical research. The practices that are institutionally solidified in the inner organization of institutional life are the basis for a knowledge of madness that only gives it the objectivity of a pathology reduced to a concept and thus places it within the universe of reason. (Habermas 1996, p. 289 f.)

For the thematization of sustainability and subjectivity that I propose, Foucault's account of a double bind of the relationship between subject and social reality is particularly important. Max Weber had developed this train of thought quite similarly with the concept of 'Lebensführung'. Lebensführung is characterized by him as a 'hinge' of the mediation of the actor and the social, which is generated as an emergence of precisely this mediation and at the same time constitutes the characteristic feature of the modern actor. The modern subject thus owes its individuality to a specific relation to what it is not; Weber's retreat into the 'pianissimo of the closest relations' (Weber 1994, p. 22 f.) corresponds in the context of such a confrontation to Foucault's call for the proactive living out of subversive 'self-practices', which is cautiously described in the second volume of Sexuality and Truth as the actor's space of movement vis-à-vis the order represented and produced by the 'code' (cf. Foucault 2004, p. 39 f.).

In an interview, Foucault unequivocally expresses that in this 'space', which is also initially very private, the techniques of the self can be transversal to the 'code' and thus the relationship "between ethics and social, economic or political structures [...] are mutable" (Foucault 1984a, p. 80). The practices or technologies of the self are at once means of subjugation as well as liberation, the mode of change thus remains subject to the same conditions that produced the modern subject and to which its 'individuality' remains attached (cf. Butler 2010, p. 89).

Unlike Weber, Foucault thus arrives at the question, "[W]hat can one play with and how can one invent a game?" (Foucault 1984b, p. 93) The actor, however, can only establish distance from himself on the basis of 'new' performances of subjectivation and thus experiences himself as a 'subject' who can inscribe a distinction in 'his' life, but actor and subject do not come apart: The subject coincides with the actor, as it is only in the mode of subjectivation that it can inscribe a distinction into its life; for Foucault there is no 'pianissimo' of intimate relations, which for Weber marks the threshold to the outside, the subject is the result of a 'self-technification' and as such, as an actor, he remains entrenched in the mechanisms of action of social space and subject to the same reality-constituting techniques. Against this background stands the notion that the episteme 'man' is temporally limited (Foucault 1995, p. 462).

Against the backdrop of the necessary orientation towards sustainability, however, it would appear that the episteme of man is facing a glorious future, for the stronger the need to mediate between self- and other-reference, the more urgent the balancing of individual needs with socially approved means of achieving goals. The Atlas subject presents a historically unique situation. In the myth of Odysseus, Adorno and Horkheimer (1997) show how the modern actor was laid out in the cradle of occidental culture, as a cunning, forward-planning individual who is able to rise above external nature (the sirens) by taming his inner nature (allowing himself to be tied to the mast). The domineering relationship between man and nature is traced in the myth in an almost caricatured manner, whereby clearly the interdependent relationship of domestication of outer and inner nature can hardly be brought out more succinctly than in this episode from Homer's Odyssey. Odysseus conquers nature and pays the price of losing his freedom. Until some time ago, we could indulge in the (still improbable) hope that this domination-like relationship could somehow still be overturned, dissolved.

The Dialectic of Enlightenment begins by stating, "Enlightenment, in the comprehensive sense of progressive thought, has always had as its aim the removal of fear from men and the installation of them as masters. But the fully enlightened earth shines with the sign of triumphant calamity." (Horkheimer and Adorno 1997, p. 19) By disaster is meant first and foremost the catastrophe of civilization, the inconceivable crime of National Socialism. An essential feature of precisely this "dialectic" of the Enlightenment lies in the transfer of hierarchy to the social, among other things due to the self-disciplining that is just as effective in the social, which is the basis for (willing) submission to social structures that are perceived as imperatives. What is remarkable about the sustainability discourse is that it turns one side of this equation 180 degrees and potentiates the other. The domineering relationship towards nature must be abandoned; on the contrary, we must put ourselves at the service of nature. Within the current format of social reality, however, this can (apparently) only be achieved by making self-binding, subjugation and disciplining all the more absolute. These two sides of modern Enlightenment hybridity can be resolved with the concepts of Baconism (knowledge is power, or domestication of external nature) and subjectification (submission to social imperatives leads to a self capable of action, or domestication of internal nature), and in this way considered separately (cf. Jochum 2017). Baconism refers to Francis Bacon (cf. Horkheimer and Adorno 1997, p. 19) and the foundation of the modern modern worldview attributed to him, especially with regard to the relation of (modern) scientific methods respectively generated knowledge in the service of a mastery of nature *and* the world. The distinction between (modern scientific mastery of nature and subjectivation), which until recently was a purely analytical one relevant to the history of science, is undergoing a precarious empirical "realization" in the sustainability discourse.

In saving the self-inflicted destruction of nature, we finally submit to self-inflicted immaturity in such a way that we (must) give up hope for a free society shaped by free individuals in order to save the world. The unconditional, survival-necessary requirement of a sustainable way of life makes this prospect impossible, insofar as the decision, voluntary for Odysseus, to choose to outwit the sirens (nature) and against his desire to surrender to them, now presents itself as a non-negotiable and insofar imperative one: The subjectification narrated in the Odysseus myth is (in principle) reversible, whereas that of the Atlas subject is not. Or, can a different narrative be found for how to deal with environmental destruction? And, who benefits from this version just outlined, who is left out in the cold in a social reality characterized by Atlas subjectification? Do we perhaps still have a choice? Should we, then, still (for all the compelling and insofar obligatory arguments) remain restless (Haraway 2018)?

4 The Death of the Utopia of Sustainability

Jason W. Moore (2019) has recently reiterated that talk of the Anthropocene obscures an essential aspect of responsibility, since characterizing the current era as the Anthropocene suggests that all humans are equally responsible for influencing, for example, the climate of planet Earth. Rather, we should be talking about the Capitalocene, because this immediately takes into account the inherent unequal distribution of resources, wealth and the associated environmental destruction (both locally and globally). In this way, it is at least more difficult, and thus less likely, to fall prey to the diffusion of responsibility that accompanies the term

"Anthropocene." To some, this description and the associated proposal may seem old-fashioned Marxist. However, this addresses an important aspect, namely the obvious influence of the connotations of the designation of a fact that is plausible in itself, on the other hand, the logic of a distribution of responsibility that does not do justice to the simple causal nexus "polluters for environmental destruction". I am surprised at how little effort is made to bring this relationship into sharp focus and to make demands accordingly, as well as to pronounce clear apportionments of blame. Nothing would be more surprising if the existing power relations (both local, nation-state, continental and global) were not reflected in the distribution of the burden of "repairing" the damaged Earth ecosystem that now obviously has to be borne. I am surprised that there is so little debate about who has to pay what price (what sacrifice) when it comes to distributing the burden of repair fairly (according to the polluters). Seen in this light, the sustainability discourse should be centrally concerned with issues of social inequality and unfair distribution of resources and value creation. The sustainability discourse would have to focus on power relations and question them, posing the social question anew. Instead, it accepts the (unequal) social order and does not even try to shake it by repeatedly focusing on the practices and orientations of each individual.

The authors' collective Tiqqun described this stocktaking in 2007 with the words: Already in 2007, in an exaggeration that has rightly been criticized for being simplistic, the authors' collective Tiqqun described this stocktaking in a similar way:

> Our fathers were hired to destroy this world, now they want us to work on its reconstruction, and that it will be profitable. […] Voluntary asceticism is on their banner, and they [the "avant-garde of disaster"] work for free to adapt us to the 'coming ecological state of emergency'. […] 'Each individual has the task of changing his or her behaviour', they say, if we want to save our beautiful civilisational model. You have to consume less in order to still be able to consume. Produce organically in order to still be able to produce. One must force oneself in order to still be able to use coercion. This is how the logic of a world intends to go on living, by giving itself the appearance of a historical turn. […] The new bio-asceticism is the self-control required of everyone to negotiate the bailout into which the system has driven itself. People will now have to tighten their belts in the name of ecology – as they did yesterday in the name of economics. […] The present paradox of ecology is that, under the pretext of saving the earth, it is only saving the foundations of what has made it this dismal star. (Tiqqun 2007, p. 56 f.)

Although the choice of words and the description are sometimes powerful and exaggerated, this appeal nevertheless contains an important hint, namely the distinction that is decisive for the sustainability discourse, which was mentioned above in connection with the discrepancy between the mastery of nature and subjectivation.

It can also be paraphrased as the distinction between the economic system and epistemology, or between capitalism and Baconism, or between social reality and a constitution of actors that is essentially characterized by subjectivation. No matter how the distinction is framed, they are all relevant to the sustainability discourse in very similar ways: They span the horizon in which sustainability is discussed and possibly decided upon in ways that will result in the reproduction of inequality. Questions about the stability of modern societies (see above the point about the "time of sustainability") as well as about global justice and the advancement of human culture and civilization (see above all "The subjectification of sustainability") benefit from an awareness of the effects that a solution to the "climate question" would have on the individual level. Precisely because there is a social dynamic that plays into the hands of this tendency, which can commonly be depicted as the coupling of a neoliberal orientation with subjectification and, casually put, potentiates Max Weber's concept of Lebensführung (cf. Hennis 1987; Schluchter 1994) (Scharff 2016).

As frightened and panicked as some may feel (and probably rightly so), it would now be dangerous to put up with anything that benefits saving the world. The sustainability discourse invites the sell-out of utopias. Who can still afford to cling to a utopia, the utopia of a world society of free individuals, while the *world itself* is at stake? When the future closes in on itself, when the horizon of possible (better) futures narrows to just one point, namely to escape the impending "climate collapse", there is no time, no resources, no legitimacy left for alternatives. This prospect is dangerous insofar as it provides an ideal breeding ground for the perpetuation of social and global structures that are not significantly different from the current ones, and may even worsen in terms of the unequal distribution of privileges. Insofar as the willingness to discipline oneself grows and subjectification becomes more inevitable, the structures that promote inequality can only profit from this.

At the same time, however, the demand for sustainability in the face of the "climate crisis" also holds a historic opportunity for fundamental clarification and renegotiation. It could open up the space of the radically new and placeless (utopian) instead of closing it. A particularly noteworthy proposal has recently been put forward by Donna Haraway (2018). She proposes to undo the domination-like relationship between humans and nature in a way that equally undoes the fixation of humans on the other side of the equation (Baconism or subjectification or domestication of inner nature to save Outer Nature). Unlike the apprehension advocated here, which would lead to a forcing of the subject, thus further enriching the breeding ground for a hierarchical relationship between humans, Haraway proposes that humans should mix with nature. In this way, the fixation on a particular format of "personhood" is deprived of any material and ideal basis. Alongside the Anthropocene and the Capitalocene, it adds a third alternative (prospectively), that of the "Chtulucene" (cf. Flatschart 2017). No question, if we became a being that is both plant and animal (including Homo Sapiens parts), endowed with both a consciousness and a biographical memory, we would live as climate-friendly as we avoid cutting our fingers off with a knife while eating. With the implosion of the human-nature difference, a new form of sociality would emerge at the same time, which the self-absorbed Homo Sapiens might not like to imagine, but which would (finally) free him from himself.

5 Addendum from the Off...

Recently, in a course in a social science master's program, I was surprised to discover (once again) that Max Weber's (1988) Protestantism thesis is hardly part of the canon of a basic social science education. In the discussion that followed my brief description of Max Weber's "The Ethics of Protestantism and the Spirit of Capitalism" (1988) – which was partly characterized by the students' amazement at Weber's attempt at a sociological explanation of how personal, intrinsically comprehensibly motivated actions of many people give rise to a social order that no one really wanted – I lost myself in thoughts... about a future in which our descendants will similarly wonder how it can be that the many practiced renunciation at that time, further optimizing their subjectivizing actions and taking advantage of the historically favorable opportunity of a renegotiation of social reality, the power- and domination-shaped relations on both sides of the equation (Baconism – man vs. nature – and subjectivism – man vs. social order).

References

Beck, Ulrich, und E. Beck-Gernsheim. 2008. *Individualisierung in modernen Gesellschaften – Perspektiven und Kontroversen einer subjektorientierten Soziologie*. In *Riskante Freiheiten. Individualisierung in Modernen Gesellschaften*, Hrsg. Dies., 10–39. Frankfurt a. M.: Suhrkamp.

Blumer, Herbert. 2013 [1971]. *Soziale Probleme als kollektives Verhalten*. In *Symbolischer Interaktionismus. Aufsätze zu einer Wissenschaft der Interpretation*, Hrsg. Ders., 141–154. Frankfurt a. M.: Suhrkamp.

Braun-Thürmann, Holger. 2005. *Innovation. Einsichten*. Bielefeld: Transcript.

Bröckling, Ulrich. 2007. *Das unternehmerische Selbst. Soziologie einer Subjektivierungsform*. Frankfurt a. M.: Suhrkamp.

Butler, Judith. 2010 [1997]. *Psyche der Macht. Das Subjekt der Unterwerfung*. Frankfurt a. M.: Suhrkamp.

Daschkeit, Achim und W.R. Dombrowsky. 2010. *Die Realität einer Katastrophe. Gesellschaftliche Diskurse zum Klimawandel.* In *Ökologische Aufklärung*, Hrsg. C. Büscher und K.P. Japp. Wiesbaden: Springer VS Verlag.

Durkheim, Emile. 1999 [1893]. *Über soziale Arbeitsteilung. Studie über die Organisation höherer Gesellschaften*. Frankfurt a. M.: Suhrkamp.

Flatschart, Elmar. 2017. *Anthropozän oder Kapitalozän? Der emanzipatorische Gehalt ökologischer Krisenbearbeitung zwischen Gesellschaft und Technik.* In *Kybernetik, Kapitalismus, Revolutionen. Emanzipatorische Perspektiven im technologischen Wandel*, Hrsg. P. Buckermann, A. Koppenburger, S. Schaupp, 127–161. Münster: Unrast Verlag.

Foucault, Michel. 1984a. *Sex als Moral. Gespräch mit Hubert Dreyfus und Paul Rabinow*. In *Von der Freundschaft als Lebensweise*. Im Gespräch. Hrsg. Ders., 69–83. Berlin: Merve.

Foucault, Michel. 1984b. *Von der Freundschaft als Lebensweise. Gespräch mit René de Ceccatty, Jean Danet und Jean le Bitoux.* In *Von der Freundschaft als Lebensweise. Im Gespräch*, Hrsg. Ders., 85–93. Berlin: Merve.

Foucault, Michel. 1995 [1966]. *Die Ordnung der Dinge. Eine Archäologie der Humanwissenschaften*. Frankfurt a. M.: Suhrkamp.

Foucault, Michel. 1997 [1976]. *Der Wille zum Wissen. Sexualität und Wahrheit 1.* Frankfurt a. M.: Suhrkamp.

Foucault, Michel. 2002 [1975]. *Überwachen und Strafen. Die Geburt des Gefängnisses.* Frankfurt a. M.: Suhrkamp.

Foucault, M., 2003. *Wahnsinn und Gesellschaft – Eine Geschichte des Wahns im Zeitalter der Vernunft*, 15. Aufl., Frankfurt a. M.: Suhrkamp

Foucault, Michel. 2004 [1984]. *Der Gebrauch der Lüste. Sexualität und Wahrheit 2.* Frankfurt a. M.: Suhrkamp.

Giddens, Anthony. 1997 [1984]. *Die Konstitution der Gesellschaft. Grundzüge einer Theorie der Strukturierung*. Frankfurt a. M., New York: Campus-Verlag.

Habermas, Jürgen. 1996 [1988]. *Der philosophische Diskurs der Moderne. 12 Vorlesungen.* Frankfurt a. M.: Suhrkamp.

Habermas, Jürgen. 2008 [1988]. *Individuierung durch Vergesellschaftung. In Riskante Freiheiten. Individualisierung in modernen Gesellschaften*, In *Riskante Freiheiten. Individualisierung in modernen Gesellschaften*, Hrsg. U. Beck und E. Beck-Gernsheim, 437–446. Frankfurt a. M.: Suhrkamp.

Hahn, Alois. 1986. *Differenzierung, Zivilisationsprozeß, Religion. Aspekte einer Theorie der Moderne*. In *Kultur und Gesellschaft. René König, dem Begründer der Sonderhefte, zum 80. Geburtstag gewidmet*, Hrsg. F. Neidhardt, M.R. Lepsius, J. Weiß, 214–231. Opladen: Westdt. Verl.

Hall, Stuart. 2004. *Identität, Ideologie und Repräsentation. Ausgewählte Schriften 4.* Hamburg: Argument Verlag.

Haraway, Donna J. 2018. *Unruhig bleiben. Die Verwandtschaft der Arten im Chthuluzän.* Frankfurt a. M. und New York: Campus Verlag.

Hennis, Wilhelm (1987): *Max Webers Thema. ‚Die Persönlichkeit und die Lebensordnungen'.* In *Max Webers Fragestellung. Studien zur Biographie des Werks*, Hrsg. Ders., 59–114. Tübingen: Mohr.

Hillebrandt, Frank. 1999. *Exklusionsindividualität. Moderne Gesellschaftsstruktur und die soziale Konstruktion des Menschen*. Opladen: Leske+Budrich.

Horkheimer, Max und T.W. Adorno. 1997 [1944]. *Dialektik der Aufklärung. Philosophische Fragmente*. Frankfurt a. M.: Suhrkamp.

Jochum, Georg. 2017. *"Plus Ultra" oder die Erfindung der Moderne. Zur neuzeitlichen Entgrenzung der okzidentalen Welt*. Bielefeld: Transcript.

Lemke, Thomas. 2001. Max Weber, Norbert Elias und Michel Foucault über Macht und Subjektivierung. *Berliner Journal für Soziologie* 11: 77–95.

Luhmann, Niklas. 1996. *Die Realität der Massenmedien*. Opladen: Westdeutscher Verlag.

Luhmann, Niklas. 1999 [1977]. *Arbeitsteilung und Moral. Durkheims Theorie*. In *Über soziale Arbeitsteilung. Studie über die Organisation höherer Gesellschaften*, E. Durkheim, 19–38. Frankfurt a. M.: Suhrkamp.

Luhmann, Niklas. 2008a [1989]. *Copierte Existenz und Karriere. Zur Herstellung von Individualität*. In *Riskante Freiheiten. Individualisierung in modernen Gesellschaften*, Hrsg. U. Beck und E. Beck-Gernsheim, 191–200. Frankfurt a. M.: Suhrkamp.

Luhmann, Niklas. 2008b [1987]. *Die gesellschaftliche Differenzierung und das Individuum*. In *Die Soziologie und der Mensch. Soziologische Aufklärung 6*, Hrsg. Ders., 121–136. Wiesbaden: VS Verl. für Sozialwiss.

Moore, Jason W. 2019. The Capitalocene and Planetary Justice. *Maize* 6: 49–54. Online: https://jasonwmoore.com/wp-content/uploads/2019/07/Moore-The-Capitalocene-and-Planetary-Justice-2019-Maize.pdf. (Zugriff: 08.12.2019).

Müller, Hans-Peter. 1992. Gesellschaftliche Moral und individuelle Lebensführung. Ein Vergleich von Emile Durkheim und Max Weber. *Zeitschrift für Soziologie* 21: 49–60.

Neckel, Sighard. 2018a. *Die Gesellschaft der Nachhaltigkeit. Soziologische Perspektiven*. In *Die Gesellschaft der Nachhaltigkeit: Umrisse eines Forschungsprogramms*, Hrsg. S. Neckel, N. Besedovsky, M. Boddenberg, M. Hasenfratz, S.M. Pritz, T. Wiegand. Bielefeld: Transcript.

Neckel, Sighard. 2018b. *Ökologische Distinktion. Soziale Grenzziehung im Zeichen von Nachhaltigkeit*. In *Die Gesellschaft der Nachhaltigkeit: Umrisse eines Forschungsprogramms*, Hrsg. S. Neckel, N. Besedovsky, M. Boddenberg, M. Hasenfratz, S.M. Pritz, T. Wiegand. Bielefeld: Transcript.

Neckel, Sighard, N. Besedovsky, M. Boddenberg, M. Hasenfratz, S.M. Pritz, T. Wiegand (Hrsg.). 2018. *Die Gesellschaft der Nachhaltigkeit: Umrisse eines Forschungsprogramms*. Transcript: Bielefeld.

Parsons, Talcott. 1975 [1966]. *Gesellschaften. Evolutionäre und komparative Perspektiven*. Frankfurt a. M.: Suhrkamp.

Parsons, Talcott. 1994. *Aktor, Situation und normative Muster. Ein Essay zur Theorie sozialen Handelns*. Frankfurt a. M.: Suhrkamp.

Pritz, Sarah Miriam. 2018. *Subjektivierung von Nachhaltigkeit*. In *Die Gesellschaft der Nachhaltigkeit: Umrisse eines Forschungsprogramms*, Hrsg. S. Neckel, N. Besedovsky, M. Boddenberg, M. Hasenfratz, S.M. Pritz, T. Wiegand. Bielefeld: Transcript.

Scharff, Christina. 2016. The Psychic Life of Neoliberalism: Mapping the Contours of Entrepreneurial Subjectivity. *Theory, Culture and Society* 33: 107–122.

Schluchter, Wolfgang. 1994. *Die Entstehung der bürgerlichen Lebensführung*. In *Max Webers Wissenschaftslehre. Interpretation und Kritik*, Hrsg. G. Wagner, H. Zipprian, 700–712. Frankfurt a. M.: Suhrkamp.

Schneider, Wolfgang L. 2002. *Grundlagen der soziologischen Theorie (Band 1). Weber – Parsons – Mead – Schütz.* Wiesbaden: Westdt. Verl.
Spivak, Gayatri Chakravorty. 2008. *Can the Subaltern Speak? Postkolonialität und subalterne Artikulation.* Wien: Verlag Turia + Kant.
Tiqqun. 2007. *Kybernetik und Revolte.* Zürich: Diaphanes Verlag.
Villa, Paula-Irene. 2010. *Verkörperung ist immer mehr. Intersektionalität, Subjektivierung und der Körper.* In *Fokus Intersektionalität. Bewegungen und Verortungen eines vielschichtigen Konzeptes*, Hrsg. H. Lutz, M.T.H. Vivar, L. Supik, 203–221. Wiesbaden: Springer VS Verlag für Sozialwissenschaften.
Weber, Jutta. 2003. *Umkämpfte Bedeutungen. Naturkonzepte im Zeitalter der Technoscience.* Frankfurt a. M. und New York: Campus-Verl.
Weber, Max. 1988 [1904–1905, 1920]. *Die protestantische Ethik und der Geist des Kapitalismus.* In *Gesammelte Aufsätze zur Religionssoziologie I*, Hrsg. Ders., 17–206. Tübingen: Mohr.
Weber, Max. 1994 [1919]. *Wissenschaft als Beruf.* In *Wissenschaft als Beruf. Politik als Beruf*, Hrsg. Ders., 1–23. Tübingen: Mohr.
Wetzel, Dietmar. 2004. *Macht und Subjektivierung im flexibilisierten Kapitalismus. Nach Foucault und Butler.* In *Vernunft – Entwicklung – Leben. Schlüsselbegriffe der Moderne. Festschrift für Wolfgang Eßbach*, Hrsg. U. Bröckling, A.T. Paul, S. Kaufmann, 245–262. München: Fink.

Diego Compagna, (Dr. phil.) is Professor of Theories of Social Transformation at the Faculty of Applied Social Sciences at the University of Applied Sciences Munich and focuses on the anthropological foundations of sociological theories as well as the formulation of alternative actor models and their spaces of action (e.g. cyborgs, robots, avatars, simulacra, hyper- and virtual reality).

On the Way to Sustainable Work? The Role of Work in the Development of Sustainable Social Innovation Processes

Georg Jochum and Thomas Barth

Abstract

The article discusses the role of work for the development of sustainable social innovation processes. Up to now, transformation policies towards sustainability have often been aimed at sustainable consumption on the one hand, and at production that is as sustainable as possible through the assumption of corporate social responsibility on the other. However, employees and their concrete forms of appropriation of nature are often lost from view. Their work activities, however, are significant in their productive as well as destructive aspects from a socio-ecological point of view and therefore form a crucial site for the development of social innovations for sustainable living and working. With reference to the guiding principle of "sustainable work" formulated by the UNDP (Human Development Report 2015: Work and Human Development, German Association for the United Nations, Berlin, 2015), this article presents these innovation potentials for the transition towards sustainability. Innovations in the sphere of gainful employment are discussed first. Employees will be considered here both as protagonists and as those affected by conversion processes. A socially ac-

G. Jochum (✉)
Technical University of Munich, Munich, Germany
e-mail: thomas.barth@lmu.de

T. Barth
Institute of Sociology, Ludwig-Maximilians-Universität Munich, Frankfurt am Main, Germany

H.-W. Franz et al. (eds.), *Sustainable Living and Business*,
https://doi.org/10.1007/978-3-658-41835-9_4

ceptable and participatory design of the transformation processes is seen as an indispensable prerequisite for their success. Based on the expanded concept of work, which takes into account not only gainful employment but also non-paid work (e.g. care work, personal work and community work), the potentials of a redefinition of the relationship of these different spheres to each other for the sustainability transformation are then shown. Finally, a plea is made for a political design of the structural framework that supports the innovations in the ecology of work.

1 Introduction

In the context of global sustainability policy, the assumption is shared that the currently dominant structural patterns of production and consumption are arranged in an unsustainable way. In order to fundamentally change them, "social innovations" are crucial. According to Howaldt (2019, p. 17), these are to be understood "in terms of creative and purposeful changes in social practices [and] relate to the way we live (together), work and consume". On the whole, however, sustainability policies have so far, when they specifically address responsibility, been aimed on the *one hand at* those who consume as sustainably as possible, whose primarily consumption-related everyday practices are focused on areas such as energy use or mobility. *On the other hand,* the focus is on companies that produce as sustainably as possible, and here often rather on technological innovations. Work is still at best a marginal topic.

Interestingly, this means that the very sphere and actors that, to a certain extent, connect the two sides are lost from view: the activities of workers as a concrete form of appropriation of nature. However, according to our thesis, it is precisely work that is decisive for more sustainable ways of living and doing business, and this in several respects. Work is the basic "process between man and nature […] wherein man mediates his metabolism with nature by his own act" (Marx 1962, p. 193) – both in its productive and destructive aspects. The acceptance of ecological policy measures also depends on the specific involvement of workers, as the current disputes over the coal phase-out in Germany illustrate. The way in which one is integrated into the employment system determines the income earned and thus to a large extent the material and energy consumption of households as well as the time available to live ecological everyday practices. In general, the historically specific form in which work is socially organised is decisive for the social and ecological (non-)sustainability of societies. The world of work can thus be seen as a central sphere of possible social innovations for the transition towards sustainability.

In the following, we will describe these innovation potentials in more detail with reference to the guiding principle of "sustainable work" formulated by the *United Nations Development Programme* (UNDP 2015). Following an outline of this model (Sect. 2), innovations in the sphere of gainful employment will first be discussed. Here, employees appear both as protagonists and as those affected by conversion processes (Sect. 3). Based on an expanded concept of work that takes into account not only gainful employment but also non-paid work (e.g. care, personal and community work), the potentials of a redefinition of the relationship of these different spheres to each other for the transformation towards sustainability are then shown (Sect. 4). Finally, in the concluding outlook, ways of a socio-ecologically positive mediation of the two spheres of gainful employment and non-gainful employment are outlined (Sect. 5).

2 The Guiding Principle of Sustainable Work

By referring to "sustainable work", we are, on the one hand, following on from a debate on the connection between ecology and work that has been going on for some time, but has only started to expand again in recent years (see, among others, Brandl and Hildebrandt 2002; Diefenbacher et al. 2016; Barth et al. 2019). Second, we refer to the UNDP report "Work and Human Development" (UNDP 2015). In this report, with reference to the "Sustainable Development Goals" adopted in the UN agenda "Transforming Our World" (UN 2015) and their manifold relevance for the world of work,[1] the pursuit of the "path(s) to sustainable work" (UNDP 2015, p. 153) is called for. This is "defined as work that is conducive to human development while reducing or eliminating negative externalities that may be experienced in different geographical and temporal contexts. It is crucial not only for the preservation of our planet, but also to ensure that future generations continue to have work." (ibid., p. 45).

In contrast to the previous focus of the sustainability debate on individual consumption patterns on the one hand and companies on the other, this guiding principle, which has also been more widely received in Germany in recent years (cf. Barth et al. 2016; AG Nachhaltige Arbeit 2019; Becke 2019), places workers at the

[1] Reference is made in particular to Goal 8 "sustainable economic growth, full and productive employment and decent work for all"; but Goals 2, 3, 5 and 9 also have relevance for work (cf. UN 2015; UNDP 2015: 20).

centre of consideration. It goes beyond a perspective limited to gainful employment and also includes work in the non-wage sector (UNDP 2015, p. 3). The point of reference is a comprehensive concept of development inspired by the "capability approach" (Sen 1979). The overarching goal is to expand people's choices. In this context, special importance is attributed to work, as human potential would be developed through work.

Unsustainable work is characterized by both contradicting the goal of good, developmental work in the present and undermining future work opportunities. Sustainable work, on the other hand, enables the current realization of work potentials while minimizing the environmental side-effects of these activities to ensure the future realization of human potentials. In a matrix structured along the axes of sustainability and development (cf. Fig. 1), the dual objective is presented.

The guiding principle of sustainable work thus combines development and environmental goals. It aims at innovations for a socio-ecological transformation of the global labour society, which should preserve the natural foundations of present and future work and promote human development through work.

In the following, we want to identify central fields of social innovation for sustainable work. In doing so, we link up with the preliminary work of the DKN

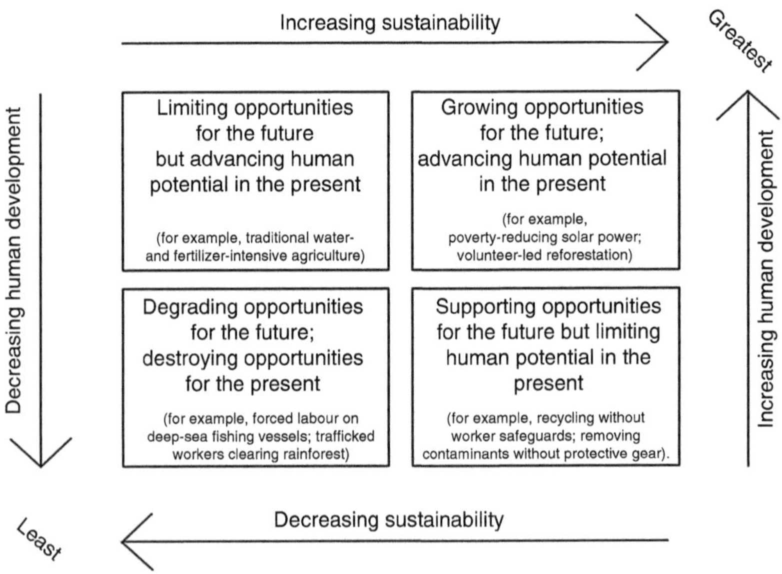

Fig. 1 The matrix of sustainable work. (Source: UNDP 2015, p. 130)

Future Earth working group on "Sustainable Work – The Socio-Ecological Transformation of the Labour Society".[2] This WG, of which the authors of this paper were also members, set itself the task of exploring key research questions on sustainable work. In its final report, which was completed in 2019, the following central guiding themes of a research agenda on sustainable work were identified:

1. "changes in the ratio of paid and unpaid work.
2. innovations and transformations in the sphere of gainful employment
3. global contexts of the labour society(ies)
4. digitalisation of work and sustainable work
5. governance of the social-ecological transformation." (WG Sustainable Work 2019, p. 4)

Due to the focus on a research agenda, the question of social innovations is not explicitly addressed in the report. However, the implicit basic assumption is that the identified fields have a particular relevance for social innovations for sustainable work and should therefore receive special attention in the accompanying and supporting scientific research. The WG assumes that

> The transition to sustainable work must be conceived as a comprehensive socio-ecological transformation of the working society that goes far beyond technological and economic innovations. The aim of research must be, on the one hand, to undertake analyses of current socio-ecological transformation and, on the other hand, to investigate the conditions and possibilities of potential development paths towards sustainable work. (ibid., p. 8).

In the following remarks, these potentials implicitly assumed in the Working Paper for – to adopt a successful neologism by Becke – "work-ecological innovations" (Becke 2019, p. 37)[3] towards sustainable work will be made explicit. Since not all areas can be elaborated in this paper, we will focus exemplarily on innovations in the sphere of gainful employment as well as changes in the relationship between paid and unpaid work.

---

[2] For the Sustainable Work Group, see: https://www.dkn-future-earth.org/activities/working_groups/084759/index.php.de. Acc. 17 November 2022.

[3] In the discourse on social innovations, ecological innovations and innovations in the world of work have so far hardly been related to each other. An exception is the recent publication by Becke, in which the "concept of work-ecological innovations [...] is developed as a bridging concept" that focuses on "the relationship between the work-related and the ecological dimension of sustainable work" (Becke 2019, p. 37).

3 Innovations and Transformations in the Sphere of Gainful Employment

The sphere of gainful employment shapes the modern working society and is thus an essential field of transformation in the transition to sustainable work. Innovations have already been initiated in this area, although they are largely of a technical nature. Entrepreneurs and management are primarily addressed as the carrier group of sustainability innovations. We consider this level and the demand for corporate social responsibility to be quite important against the background of the power relations in the companies. However, as will be shown in the following, the contribution that wage-earners and their organisations can make to a social and ecological transformation of paid work is lost from view. Their involvement is also necessary in order to take into account at an early stage the interests of those directly affected by ecological conversion processes.

3.1 Extended Subject Claims and Sustainable Work

Becke and Warsewa (2017) argue that in the course of a general norm-building process, i.e. the diffusion of ecological sustainability concerns into almost all social spheres and milieus, employees bring their also ecological attitudes and evaluation criteria into company processes in the sense of an "expanded subjective perspective", thus "opening up opportunities for a more sustainable and socially acceptable design of work" (ibid. 20). This by no means presupposes that the majority of employees hold ecological positions, but the opportunities to do so tend to be greater insofar as companies are increasingly called upon to respond to social demands and those of employees.

While Becke and Warsewa assume that sustainability-oriented attitudes on the part of employees could be carried over into the workplace, i.e. transferred from the sphere of everyday life into the sphere of "gainful employment", it is also possible to start directly with the concrete work activity itself. In this case, the question is whether the empirically verifiable "work content demands" of employees, i.e. to perform an activity that is experienced as meaningful and, for example, to produce socially meaningful products, also has an ecologically sustainable dimension (Nies 2019).

However, it must be taken into account that the power potentials are still very asymmetrically distributed both inside and outside companies (cf. Barth et al. 2019): Sustainability innovations in the field of labour see themselves caught in a complex power web within companies, and outside of companies, the mere discursive questioning of corporate sovereignty over what is produced and how provides strong resistance. Subjectification of work can only contribute to sustainable work in the sense of a socio-ecological transformation if employees' scope for decision-making is unequally increased. Thus, the question of a more extensive participation of working people and their organizations also becomes relevant for the implementation of work-ecological innovations.

3.2 The Guiding Principle of Sustainable Work in Conflictual Conversion Processes

This participation is particularly necessary when employees are affected by ecologically based transformation processes. This is illustrated by the current debates on the conversion of fossil fuels to renewable energies through a phase-out of coal, or in the automotive industry as a result of the transition from the internal combustion engine to other forms of propulsion (especially electric mobility) and to more sustainable mobility systems. It is precisely in these areas that the integrative guiding function of "sustainable work" could become significant. This is because the transformation processes are likely to be accompanied by a loss of jobs or at least a devaluation of previous qualifications – for example, between 125,000 and up to 360,000 of the 800,000 jobs in the automotive industry are considered to be at risk (cf. Die Welt 2019).

In this field of conflict, the guiding principle of sustainable work does not provide a clear direction due to its dual objective of both advancing ecological transformation and maintaining or creating decent, good work that promotes development. As the UNDP report makes explicitly clear, conflicting interests may arise and therefore "measures to manage conflicting objectives" (UNDP 2015, p. 209) become necessary. This implies that the interests of those previously employed in these areas should be seen as perfectly legitimate. Work-ecological innovations must therefore not take place over the heads of the employees. Rather, the transition towards ecologically sustainable work must take place with due regard for the goal of social compatibility and the preservation of human development opportunities. The various forms of trade union organisation of interests and participation of employees in the world of work would therefore rather have to be strengthened, and – according to Becker et al. (2019) referring to the change supplier industry in the automotive industry in view of the transition to electromobility – a "participation-oriented industrial policy for dealing with socio-ecological transformation conflicts" (ibid. 254) is necessary. This is the only way to avoid social upheavals.

Instead of driving forward a more ecological technical innovation that is blind to social impacts, the guiding principle of sustainable work could contribute to a conflict-mediating, integrative socio-ecological innovation process.

3.3 Education for a New Sustainability-Oriented Professional Ethos

However, debates on labour-ecological innovations towards sustainable work should not be conducted solely with regard to the sectors currently at the centre of public controversy. Nor is it a question of promoting special green jobs with particular positive effects on the environment. From our perspective, it should rather be noted that every activity is associated with specific material-energy prerequisites and effects. Technological as well as social innovations in all fields of activity and occupations can thus contribute to a transition towards sustainable work. In this sense, the UNDP report also stresses that it is not just a matter of ending certain types of work and creating new forms of work, but above all of transforming jobs (UNDP 2015, p. 18). New skills and an ecological modernisation of occupations and a new sustainability-oriented work and professional ethos are therefore needed for the transition towards sustainability.

A major contribution to this can be made by giving greater consideration to sustainability issues in vocational education and training. Although innovation processes in this direction have already been taking place for several years (cf. BMBF 2018), if one looks at the concrete design of curricula and teaching in vocational education and training, the conclusion is rather sobering. Relevant teaching content is taught additively, if at all; a systematic integration of sustainability concerns into all areas of activity, on the other hand, is still a desideratum. The dual system of vocational education and training that is characteristic of Germany would be particularly well suited to contribute to such a change in training and thus also in the professional ethos imparted.

On the one hand, specialist training can create an awareness of the specific ecological relevance of one's own activity, both in the companies and in the vocational school. On the other hand, the importance of vocational education for a "civic education" (Kerschensteiner 1901), which was particularly relevant for the 'father of the vocational school' Georg Kerschensteiner and which goes beyond pure technicality, could undergo a fundamental reorientation. This concern, which is still reflected today in the inclusion of the subject "social studies" in the curriculum, resulted around 1900 from the goal of integrating male youth into the nation-state. Today, in our view, it would primarily be a matter of a cosmopolitan education, which has as its content the integration of the modern working society (and thus also the work of the individual) into the ecosystem and a consideration of the consequences of one's own work for the work and life of people in other regions of the world. This could impart a new integrative sustainability ethos which, together with subject-specific sustainability-relevant knowledge, would contribute to a fundamental innovation of the profession. It should be added that similar innovations would also have to be introduced for the area of academic education, since the demand for a systematic integration of education for sustainability is still largely unfulfilled there as well.

4 Redefining the Relationship Between Paid and Unpaid Work

In contrast to a narrowing of work to gainful employment, as can sometimes be observed in the debate on ecological jobs and green jobs, the guiding principle of sustainable work aims at the sustainability of all (re-)productive activities. In this sense, the aforementioned UNDP report points out that "from a human development perspective [...] the concept of work encompasses more than jobs or employment relationships" and also includes "work in the home and in the area of care and nursing, voluntary work and engagement, as well as creative activities" (UNDP 2015, p. 3).

Following on from this, the Sustainable Work WG explicitly uses a broader concept of work, which includes not only market-oriented gainful employment, but also, in addition to the above-mentioned activities, care work, welfare work and 'own work'. Such an extended concept of work implies that these activities cannot be considered additively, but that their interactions in their dynamics of change must be taken into account. In this context, it is also necessary to problematize the hierarchies frequently associated with the division between formal and informal or marketable and non-market work. The redefinition of the relationship between paid and unpaid work represents, as will be shown in the following, a central field of social innovation for a transformation towards sustainability.

Building on debates in women's and gender studies, the industrial society's focus on gainful employment was problematized early on in connection with sustainability: Around the turn of the millennium, the project "Work and Ecology" (HBS 2000) systematically addressed this issue by examining the combination of different activities with different design principles and requirements, and by including work beyond gainful employment in the analysis of work with the concept of 'mixed work' (Brandl and Hildebrandt 2002) (see Fig. 2).

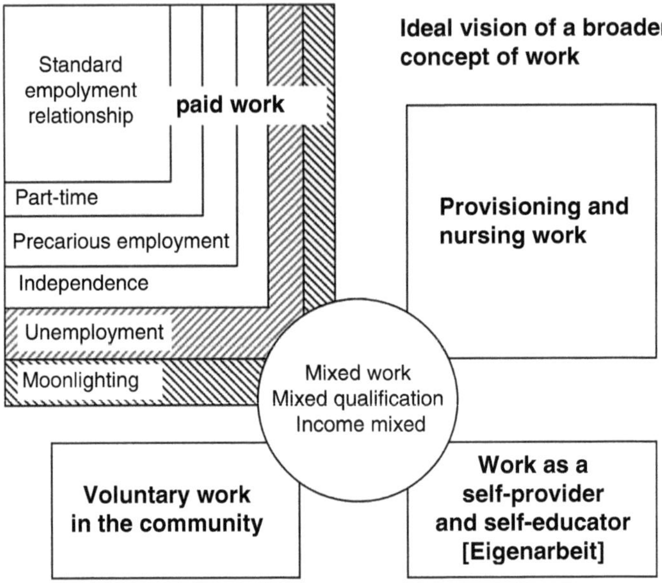

Fig. 2 Mixed work as an ideal type of an expanded concept of work (Brandl and Hildebrandt 2002, p. 105; source: Spangenberg and Lorek 2022)

The concept, which is regarded as a reference when it comes to spelling out an alternative, expanded concept of work, combines various activities from which mixed qualifications, burdens and incomes result. In addition to gainful employment, community work, in which useful things are produced for society and services are rendered free of charge, self-sufficient work, and care work, i.e. care work, especially in the family, are also taken into account. Mixed work is to be seen as an analytical and at the same time as a sustainability-oriented normative concept. In the project "Work and Ecology", guidelines for ecological, economic and social sustainability were defined and the transition to a "sustainable work […] that enables a sustainable lifestyle" was called for (HBS 2000, p. 33).

In order to implement sustainable work and mixed work as its guiding concept, specific political measures such as a socio-ecological tax reform and, in particular, a general (working) time reduction (to 25–30 hours per week) were considered necessary, through which a redistribution of work should be achieved. The reception of the concept of mixed work, however, remained predominantly limited to academic circles, and overall the connections between sustainability and work were addressed only sporadically around the turn of the millennium.

In recent years, however, interest in concepts for a redistribution of labour has increased, especially in the so-called post-growth discourse. This is justified above all by the fact that a decoupling of economic growth and resource and energy consumption has not yet succeeded and that technical solutions to remedy the ecological crisis phenomena are insufficient. The goal is the transition from a working society currently based on economic growth and gainful employment to a socio-ecological activity society. Models of far-reaching social innovations are discussed, which are usually based on a reduction of working hours, often flanked by a guaranteed basic income and an upgrading of the informal, unpaid activity sector (cf. in overview Littig 2016, Schmelzer and Vetter 2019). These demands are based on findings that long working hours are usually accompanied by a high ecological footprint due to the environmental consumption associated with production. With reference to OECD countries, it was calculated that the limit for sustainable working hours was already reached at six hours (Frey 2019). In addition to this so-called scale effect, so-called composition effects are also cited. For example, people with long working hours tend to use more time-saving devices and technologies in their own households, which are generally more environmentally intensive (cf. Liebig 2019, p. 214 f.). Various alternative concepts to full-time (gainful) employment are discussed. Niko Paech proposes a division of working time, as a result of which only 20 hours (per week) are devoted to monetarily remunerated activities. The other 20 hours are worked in the decommercialised sector and are determined by subsistence-oriented activities (self-production, non-profit work, etc.) as well as a sufficiency-oriented lifestyle (Paech 2014, p. 151). Diefenbacher et al. also consider it necessary to minimize the current dominance of gainful employment and to upgrade informal work (2016, p. 314). The latter include activities in three areas, namely in the household economy, which has a more feminine connotation, in the self-sufficiency economy (craft activities and gardening), and in the self-help economy (e.g. helping neighbours) (ibid., p. 299).

Thus, there are already some concepts that provide an orientation for social innovation in the direction of sustainability through a redefinition of work. However, with regard to some concepts in the post-growth discourse[4] it must be critically noted that in some cases a romanticising glorification of activities in the informal, unpaid sector can be observed and an underestimation of the importance of formal, paid work for identity formation, the development of individual potentials and social integration that goes beyond income security.

---

[4]This does not apply to all approaches in the very heterogeneous post-growth discourse (see Schmelzer and Vetter 2019 for an overview), but mainly to the value-conservative oriented concepts.

This critique does not imply that we do not consider a redefinition of the relationship between paid and unpaid work to be a central field of social innovation towards sustainability. However, social science-informed work-ecological innovation must include barriers and possible problematic side-effects of the shift. Research for social innovation to promote sustainable work should therefore also question and test some of the underlying assumptions. To this end, (a) the thesis of an ecologically positive effect of a reduction in working hours is discussed below, and then (b) work in the informal sector is examined in more detail.

(a) The thesis of ecologically positive effects of a reduction in gainful employment can at least be put into perspective. A study carried out within the framework of the joint project "Work and Ecology" on the effects of a reduction in working hours and flexibilisation at Volkswagen AG with the aim of securing jobs on time well-being, lifestyle and socio-ecological commitment comes to a sobering conclusion:

> The assumption that a process of reflection would be set in motion 'by itself', as it were, by the time potential gained through the reduction in working time, at the end of which a change in lifestyle could take place according to socio-ecological aspects, is […] not substantiated. […] The hypotheses about positive interactions between new working time patterns and sustainable lifestyles have not been confirmed (Hildebrandt 1999, p. 35).

Hildebrandt sees a major reason for this in the fact that the subjects were hardly able to bring in their own interests and that the flexibilisation and reduction of working time tended to take place according to the specifications of the interests of the company (ibid., p. 36). Also, the expectations that the availability of more time could lead to an ecological commitment were not fulfilled. This was also due to the specific infrastructure of the car city of Wolfsburg and the consumerist model of affluence and lifestyle that dominates there (ibid., p. 37). Although these findings from 1999 do not refute the possibility of a change in lifestyle towards sustainability brought about by reductions in working time, they do relativise the assumption of an automatic connection.

In the years that followed, the issue of reducing working time in Germany was no longer important, at least on the trade union side, so that corresponding studies were not carried out in other contexts. In recent years, however, in addition to demands for higher pay, the possibility of more flexible working time arrangements has been increasingly demanded and stipulated in some collective agreements of IG Metall and in ver.di choice models, which give employees the individual option between a pay increase or additional days off. In this context, a surprisingly large number of employees chose the option of more time off (cf. Liebig 2019, p. 225).

However, the ecological effects of this gain in free time depend on its individual use. If it is used to reduce weekly working time, these tend to be positive, whereas in blocked form it can also serve to extend holiday time, leading to additional travel, for example, so that the ecological balance is negative (ibid., p. 225). Despite this limitation, Liebig comes to the overall conclusion "that a reduction in working time is admittedly not a socio-ecological panacea. But it should equally not be underestimated, for it may well serve positive social and ecological ends." (ibid.) He adds, however, that these positive effects also depend on extra-firm contextual conditions, such as an ecological tax reform that promotes ecological behavioural options, as well as a more egalitarian distribution of domestic work.

For the currently persisting unequal distribution of this work between the sexes due to traditional role attributions can be seen as a further possible shortcoming of a reduction and flexibilisation of working time. Already today, due to the higher part-time quota, many women are characterised by a working reality that to a certain extent corresponds to the models outlined above – however, this is associated with a reduction in income and pensions and a permanent double burden, whereas men still tend to follow the classic full-time model with regard to working time. A reduction in working hours could result in men gaining more real free time, whereas for women the burdens are still increasing. Even though the demand for a revaluation of informal, non-market work was originally raised by women's and gender studies, these gender policy considerations are not present in all growth-critical approaches. However, their inclusion is indispensable in order to avoid a deepening of the gender-specific unequal division of labour as a result of a redefinition of the relationship between paid and unpaid work (cf. Littig 2016).

Finally, the argumentation put forward by many advocates of a reduction in working time, according to which the increase in productivity made possible by technical progress makes a reduction in working time not only practicable, but also ecologically as well as socially necessary in order to avoid increased environmental consumption and unemployment (cf. e.g. Schor 2016, p. 136 f.), must also be questioned. For it must be taken into account that the productivity increases in industrial society were also made possible by the use of so-called "technical slaves" (Staudinger 1947), which not only simplified work in the private household, but also revolutionized gainful employment. Living human labor and biotic energy were supplemented and replaced by fossil fuels and the machines they powered. The result was a significant increase in resource consumption. Automation processes and productivity gains enabled by digitalization are also likely to result in a renewed increase in global material flows and increased energy consumption. Protagonists of Industry 4.0 hope that the current digital revolution will lead to smarter, sustainable production. Critics, however, warn of a "resource curse 4.0"

(Pilgrim et al. 2017), as "dematerialization (is) to be seen as an unredeemable promise of Industry 4.0" (ibid., p. 38) (see also Jochum and Matuschek 2019). For a transition to a post-fossil society, it could thus become necessary to use more human labour again – at least if the bioeconomic hopes for an easy substitutability of the high consumption of fossil energy and non-renewable resources by renewable energies and renewable raw materials also prove to be an illusion.

Moreover, it must be asked whether new work will not even be created as a result of the increasing ecological crises in order to prevent the disasters (e.g. building dams) or to cope with the consequences of the disasters (e.g. reconstruction and relocation of cities destroyed by flooding). Whether this work will then take place in the context of formal acquisition work or in the informal sphere is, of course, an open question. Overall, however, it can be assumed that the volume of work will increase in certain areas – which does not, of course, imply that reductions in work are not possible in those areas where the social utility of the goods is highly questionable (e.g. armaments).

The simplifying glorification of informal work and the problematisation of formal work, as seen for example in the concept outlined by Diefenbacher et al. (2016), must also be regarded as truncated. In particular, a look at the global South, but also the consideration of the reality of work in the North, makes a differentiated view seem necessary. Already for the last decades a "transformation of work into informality" (Mahnkopf 2003, p. 65) is stated – with mostly negative consequences for the working people and with at least open ecological effects. In the so-called developing countries, more people are employed informally than formally, and a high proportion of them live in extreme poverty (cf. UNDP 2015, p. 75).

In the sociological discussion of work, the term informal work is used to describe not only private work that is more concerned with self-sufficiency, but also the heterogeneous totality of 'atypical' work that deviates from the 'ideal type' of formal work associated with the normal employment relationship in industrialised countries. Formal work is wage work in permanent employment with private companies or in the public sector, and it can be captured by statistics. It is also associated with inclusion in social security programmes, occupational health and safety laws apply, and it is usually based on formal qualifications and relatively good pay. Informal work tends to be unregulated, underpaid, unprotected and unorganised in the negative sense of the term, and has similarities to precarious work (Mayer-Ahuja 2013, p. 56 f.). Many forms of informal work are indeed part of the capitalist market economy and serve to earn money, but those who work there are only involved in a subordinate form. Accordingly, the ILO and the UNDP see the establishment of "labour standards to curb the informal economy" as a "new milestone" that could lead to "decent jobs" (UNDP 2015, p. 183).

However, feminist critics in particular have rightly pointed out that normal employment relationships and formal wage labour have always been primarily specific to the male population (Mahnkopf 2003, p. 60 f.). It has also been argued that the tension between formal wage labour and informal forms of labour and the frequently associated opposition between productive and merely reproductive labour is also a reflection of a relationship of exploitation: Through the devaluation of the latter, this socially necessary labour, which is also necessary for capitalism, can be appropriated cheaply (Patel and Moore 2018); this labour is made available for capitalist exploitation by being removed from informal, but subsistence-securing autonomous and self-sufficient traditional contexts.

The demand raised in the post-growth discourse for a revaluation of informal work can certainly also be seen as an attempt to counteract this devaluation. However, the focus on the household economy, the self-sufficiency economy and the self-help economy does not adequately capture the problematic reality of informal work, especially from a global perspective. This must be taken into account, however, if a redefinition of the relationship between formal and informal work is to promote sustainable work that also meets the requirement of good employment conducive to development.

5 Summary and Outlook

For social innovations concerning the redefinition of the relationship between paid and unpaid work, the following conclusions can be drawn from these considerations:

- The tendency in the post-growth discourse and other concepts based on an expanded concept of work to focus one-sidedly on the non-employment sector and a simplistic demand for a reduction in the importance of gainful employment (secured by a guaranteed basic income) must be critically questioned. It is just as one-sided as the focus on gainful employment in the hegemonic discourse on the transition to a Green Economy. The potentials of work-ecological innovations within gainful employment outlined above are therefore to be regarded as a central component of a transformation under the given conditions. In particular, the subjective potentials and interests of employees in developing their own potentials within gainful employment must be taken seriously. Social innovations in both gainful and non-gainful employment are important for a socio-ecological transformation of the labour society, and their interactions, possible synergies as well as areas of conflict and side-effects of changes must be systematically taken into account.

- Current efforts by trade unions to change working time patterns as part of collective agreements should be brought together with the socio-ecological debates on a reduction of working time (cf. Liebig 2019). In this context, the organisation of time should neither be adapted solely to the needs of companies nor should it be carried out solely according to the rigid specifications of an ecological time regime. Rather, the goal must be a flexibilization and reduction of working time in which subjects can bring in their own interests and needs. And, in view of the problems outlined above, it must also be gender-sensitive.
- With regard to the relationship between gainful and non-gainful, formal and informal work, paid and voluntary work, marketised and non-market work, and production and reproduction work, integrative innovation concepts are necessary. We share the call for a revaluation of work located at the latter pole. These 'social re-novations' in the sense of rediscovering and strengthening forms of work that have been devalued and marginalised in the course of industrial social modernisation can make an important contribution to the transition to more sustainable working.

This does not imply, however, that only a new one-sidedness of perspective should take the place of the old one. Potentials of work-ecological innovations through shifts and new connections would also have to be tapped. We too have simplistically used the polar pairs of opposites in the paper and assumed their extensive congruence. On closer examination, however, it becomes clear that there are combinations that deviate from this. For example, formal, paid work does not necessarily have to take place in a market society – at least not in a growth-oriented, capitalist economy. The regulations associated with formal work, which also imply security for employees and recognition of their qualifications, could be maintained without this entailing adherence to the ecologically problematic growth economy. The concept of formal work and the demands associated with it could also undergo an ecological renewal if the standardisation associated with it also included consideration of environmental standards.

- Particularly high innovation potentials could thus be expected in the development of new mixed forms of work between the formal and informal economy. Many hope for such a change through the expansion of the "sharing economy". Although this "sharing economy" is not dependent on digitalisation, digital platforms have contributed significantly to the boom of the sharing economy. This has already promoted a change in the world of work in recent years,

> eroding the boundaries between consumption and production and giving rise to new prosumer networks and forms of collaborative consumption. Despite the implied resource problems of digitalisation, the overall balance here could also enable more ecologically sustainable ways of working, In this sense, Rifkin proclaimed in "The Zero Marginal Cost Society" (2014) a genesis of "collaborative commons" and a "sustainable cornucopia" made possible by the intelligent use of new technologies. In light of the experiences of recent years, however, these hopes had to be put into perspective. The adoption of the idea of an economy of sharing by profit-oriented companies of platform capitalism has rather resulted in an erosion of labour standards and ecologically negative rebound effects, as consumption opportunities have multiplied for consumers. As Loske argues, there is therefore a need for political design and regulation if the positive effects of the sharing economy are to be promoted: "Sharing can [...] make a contribution to sustainable development if it succeeds in keeping the tendency towards the collective use of goods and services predominantly in the socio-ecological mode. However, this does not happen by itself, but needs political will." (Loske 2019, p. 70)

This plea for accompanying political governance is, as will be argued here in conclusion, to be held for all work-ecological social innovations. It is true that innovations can be initiated and driven by actors within the world of work, especially by the workers themselves. However, the conditions in gainful employment as well as in the sphere of informal work are always dependent on the overall economic structures and the regulating political frameworks. Innovation policy to date has been aimed primarily at technical innovations. For a socio-ecological transformation of the labour society, however, far-reaching structural innovations are necessary, which also support the social, labour-ecological innovations outlined above.

References

AG Nachhaltige Arbeit. 2019. *Nachhaltige Arbeit – Die sozial-ökologische Transformation der Arbeitsgesellschaft.* Positionspapier der Arbeitsgruppe "Nachhaltige Arbeit" im Deutschen Komitee für Nachhaltigkeitsforschung in Future Earth. Hamburg: DKN. http://www.dkn-future-earth.org/data/mediapool/190820_dkn_working_paper_19_1_ag_nh_arbeit.pdf. Zugegriffen: 2. November 2019.

Barth, Thomas, G. Jochum, Georg und B. Littig (Hrsg.). 2016. *Nachhaltige Arbeit. Soziologische Beiträge zur Neubestimmung der gesellschaftlichen Naturverhältnisse.* Frankfurt/New York: Campus.

Barth, Thomas, G. Jochum, Georg und B. Littig. 2019. Machtanalytische Perspektiven auf (nicht-) nachhaltige Arbeit. *WSI-Mitteilungen* 1/2019: 3–12.

Becke, Guido (Hrsg.). 2019. Arbeitsökologische Innovationen – Konzept und zentrale Erkenntnisse. In: *Gute Arbeit und ökologische Innovationen Perspektiven nachhaltiger Arbeit in Unternehmen und Wertschöpfungsketten*, Hrsg. G. Becke. 35–63. München: oecom.

Becke, Guido und G. Warsewa. 2017. Erweiterte Subjektperspektive – Neue Ansprüche an Arbeit und Nachhaltigkeit. In: *Arbeits- und Industriesoziologische Studien.* Jahrgang 10, Heft 2, November 2017: 20–36.

Becker, Karina, M. Ehrlich und M. Holuschuh. 2019. Das Wertschöpfungssystem "Automobil" im Umbruch. In: *Große Transformation? Zur Zukunft moderner Gesellschaften.* Hrsg. Dörre, K., Rosa, H., Becker, K., Bose, S., Seyd, B. 245–258. Berlin: Springer.

BMBF. 2018. *Nachhaltigkeit im Berufsalltag. Berufsbildung für nachhaltige Entwicklung.* BMBF: Bonn.

Brandl, Sebastian, und E. Hildebrandt. 2002. *Zukunft der Arbeit und soziale Nachhaltigkeit. Zur Transformation der Arbeitsgesellschaft vor dem Hintergrund der Nachhaltigkeitsdebatte.* Opladen: Leske + Budrich.

Die Welt. 2019. 360.000 *Jobs in der deutschen Autoindustrie gefährdet.* https://www.welt.de/wirtschaft/article202844490/BUND-360-000-Jobs-in-deutscher-Autoindustrie-gefaehrdet.html. Zugegriffen: 2. November 2019.

Diefenbacher, Hans, O. Foltin, B. Held, D. Rodenhäuser, R. Schweizer und V. Teichert. 2016. *Zwischen den Arbeitswelten. Der Übergang in die Postwachstumsgesellschaft.* Frankfurt a. M: Fischer.

Frey, Philipp. 2019. *The Ecological Limits of Work: on carbon emissions, carbon budgets and working time.* Hampshier: Autonomy. http://autonomy.work/wp-content/uploads/2019/05/The-Ecological-Limits-of-Work-final.pdf. Zugegriffen: 2. November 2019.

HBS (Hans-Böckler-Stiftung) (Hg.). 2000. *Wege in eine nachhaltige Zukunft. Ergebnisse aus dem Verbundprojekt Arbeit und Ökologie.* Düsseldorf.

Hildebrandt, Eckart. 1999. Flexible Arbeit und nachhaltige Lebensführung, *WZB Discussion Paper,* No. P 99–507.

Howaldt, Jürgen. 2019. Soziale Innovation im Fokus nachhaltiger Entwicklung. In: *Netzwerke und soziale Innovationen*, Hrsg. Christian Neugebauer, Sebastian Pawel und Helena Biritz, 13–30. Wiesbaden: Springer VS.

Jochum, Georg und I. Matuschek. 2019. Arbeit im Spannungsfeld von digitaler und sozial-ökologischer Transformation – Interferenzen, Synergien und Gegensätze. In: *Gute Arbeit und ökologische Innovationen Perspektiven nachhaltiger Arbeit in Unternehmen und Wertschöpfungsketten*, Hrsg. Guido Becke. 81–100. München: oecom.

Kerschensteiner, Georg. 1901. *Staatsbürgerliche Erziehung der deutschen Jugend.* Erfurt: Villaret.

Liebig, Steffen. 2019. Arbeitszeitverkürzung für eine nachhaltigere Wirtschaft? In: *Große Transformation? Zur Zukunft moderner Gesellschaften.* Hrsg. Dörre, K., Rosa, H., Becker, K., Bose, S., Seyd, B. 211–228. Berlin: Springer.

Littig, Beate. 2016. Nachhaltige Zukünfte von Arbeit? Geschlechterpolitische Betrachtungen. In: T. Barth, G. Jochum, Georg und B. Littig. (Hrsg.). 2016. *Nachhaltige Arbeit. Soziologische Beiträge zur Neubestimmung der gesellschaftlichen Naturverhältnisse.* 77–100. Frankfurt/New York: Campus.

Loske, Reinhard. 2019. Die Doppelgesichtigkeit der Sharing Economy. Vorschläge zu ihrer gemeinwohlorientierten Regulierung. *WSI-Mitteilungen* 1/2019: 64–70
Mahnkopf, Birgit. 2003. Zukunft der Arbeit: Globalisierung der Unsicherheit. *Kurswechsel* 3/2003: 63–74.
Marx, Karl, 1962 [1867]. *Das Kapital: Kritik der politischen Ökonomie*, Band 1, Marx-Engels-Werke, Bd. 23, Berlin: Dietz Verlag.
Mayer-Ajuda, Nicole. 2013. Prekär, informell – weiblich? Zur Bedeutung von ‚Gender' für die Aushöhlung arbeitspolitischer Standards. In: *Arbeit in globaler Perspektive*, Hrsg. N. Weinmann, S. Peters, H. J. Burchardt. 123–148. Frankfurt a. M/New York: Campus.
Nies, Sarah. 2019. Verwertungszwang und Eigensinn. Inhaltliche Ansprüche an Arbeit als Perspektive für Nachhaltigkeit? In: *WSI-Mitteilungen* 1/2019: 13–21.
Paech, Niko. 2014. *Befreiung vom Überfluss. Auf dem Weg in die Postwachstumsökonomie.* München: oekom.
Patel, Raj, und J.W. Moore. 2018. *Entwertung. Eine Geschichte der Welt in sieben billigen Dingen.* Berlin: rowohlt.
Pilgrim, Hannah, Groneweg, Merle, Reckordt, Michael. 2017. *Ressourcenfluch 4.0. Die sozialen und ökologischen Auswirkungen von Industrie 4.0 auf den Rohstoffsektor*, Berlin. Verein für eine ökologisch-solidarische Energie-und Weltwirtschaft e.V. [https://power--shift.de/ressourcenfluch-4-0/ Letzter Zugriff: 29.09.2019]
Rifkin, Jeremy. 2014. *Die Null-Grenzkosten-Gesellschaft. Das Internet der Dinge, kollaboratives Gemeingut und der Rückzug des Kapitalismus.* Frankfurt M. u.a: Campus-Verl.
Schmelzer, Matthias, und A. Vetter. 2019. Degrowth/Postwachstum. Zur Einführung. Hamburg: Junius
Schor, Juliet. 2016. *Wahrer Wohlstand. Mit weniger Arbeit besser leben.* München: oekom.
Sen, Amartya. 1979. Utilitarianism and Welfarism, *The Journal of Philosophy*, LXXVI, 463–489.
Spangenberg, Joachim H.; S. Lorek. 2022. Who Cares (For Whom)? In: *Frontiers in Sustainability* 3: 835295. https://doi.org/10.3389/frsus.2022.835295.
Staudinger, Hermann. 1947. *Vom Aufstand der technischen Sklaven.* Essen: Chamier.
UN (United Nations). 2015. *Transforming Our World. The 2030 Agenda for Sustainable Development.* New York: United Nations.
UNDP (United Nations Development Programme). 2015. *Work for Human Development.* Human Development Report. United Nations Development Programme, New York : United Nations.

Jochum, Georg (†), Dr. phil.; Dipl. Soz., studied sociology (LMU Munich). Research assistant at the TU Munich; TUM School of Governance, Chair of Sociology of Science.

Latest Publications:

Jochum, G. 2022. Jenseits der Expansionsgesellschaft. Nachhaltiges Dasein und Arbeiten im Netz des Lebens. Munich: oekom.

Jochum, G. 2021. Dialectics of Technical Emancipation—Considerations on a Reflexive, Sustainable Technology Development. In: NanoEthics 15 (1), pp. 29–41. doi.org/10.1007/s11569-021-00387-7.

Barth, Thomas, Dr. phil., Master's degree in sociology and political science (University of Jena). Institute for Social Research at Goethe-University Frankfurt.

Latest Publications:

Barth, T.; S. Lessenich. 2022. Nachhaltige Arbeits- und Sozialpolitik. De-Formation des Wohlfahrtsstaats in der sozial-ökologischen Transformation? In: Betzelt, S.; T. Fehmel (Ed.): Deformation oder Transformation? Analysen zum wohlfahrtsstaatlichen Wandel im 21. Jahrhundert. Wiesbaden: Springer, pp. 297.316.

Barth, T.; B. Littig. 2021. Labour and Societal Relationships with Nature. Conceptual Implications for Trade Unions. In: Räthzel, N.; D. Stevis; D. Uzzell (Ed.): The Palgrave Handbook of Environmental Labour Studies. Cham: Springer, pp. 769–792.

Leitbild Development in Organizations

An Interactive Learning Process for Sustainable Transformation

Peter Dürr

Abstract

Even if current dynamics of change in business and society seem to suggest that the paradigm of the agile is gaining the upper hand over the strategic, the search for a compass for the future remains unchanged in organizations or is even gaining in importance. Whether under the heading of vision, mission, brand, corporate identity or, more generally, *Leitbild* – a German term combining the concept of mission statement and guiding principles – , organisations in practice attempt in a variety of ways to distill the holy grail of universal principles and guidelines for further development from the multiplicity of all possibilities and translate it into a communicable format. This article examines the extent to which *Leitbild* processes, with their focus on questions of values and the future, are suitable for initiating sustainable change in organizations. The focus is on the development of a novel process logic that bundles recognized pedagogical, engineering and design-oriented design schemes into a so-called "Interactive Learning Path" and is used as a planning aid. Special attention is paid to the importance of principles such as participation, change of perspective and constructiveness in order to design these processes successfully. In the context of a concrete application example, it will then be examined how the implementation

P. Dürr (✉)
Munich University of Applied Sciences, Munich, Germany
e-mail: peter.duerr@hm.edu

H.-W. Franz et al. (eds.), *Sustainable Living and Business*,
https://doi.org/10.1007/978-3-658-41835-9_5

of this planning tool can be designed in practice and what effects this has on sustainable action in the organization.

1 *Leitbilder* as Impetus for Sustainability

Even if the current change dynamics in businesses and society seem to suggest that the paradigm of agilitymay be gaining the upper hand over strategy, the search for an organizational compass for the future remains unchanged or is even becoming more important (Farjoun 2007; Mancesti 2015; Teece et al. 2016). Be it under the heading of *vision, mission, brand, corporate identity* or, more generally, *Leitbild,* organisations in practice try in a wide variety of ways to distill the holy grail of universal principles and guidelines for further development from the multitude of all possibilities and translate them into a communicable format. For all their diversity, these *Leitbilder* usually contain statements about the long-term orientation and value foundation of the organization. Following an analysis of the different objectives of *Leitbild* processes, the first step is to examine the extent to which grappling with values and the future leads to organisational action being more strongly oriented towards socio-ecological objectives.

Leitbilder emerge as the result of a structured process in which different managers, employees or even external stakeholders can be involved. In a second step,the significance of process design on the result is examined. Since the process is described in very different detail in the literature reviewed, each using its own systematics, a generic model for learning-solution processes is first presented for better comparability. In this model, the close ties between solving and learning is revealed and activities are differentiated both according to the type of engagement with the problem and according to the form of communicative exchange between the participants. The sequential linking of these activities describes a kind of exercise course, here referred to as a *parcours.* The model serves as a basis for examining the extent to which the process design supports a sustainable orientation of the organization.

In a subsequent application example, the principles are illustrated busing a development process carried out in practice.

2 The Function and Content of *Leitbilder*

2.1 Conceptual Framework

A *Leitbild* is generally understood as a "guiding idea", an "ideal" or "role model" (Duden 2019). While in the management literature the development of *Leitbilder* is predominantly understood as a task of strategic management (Bleicher 2004; Graf and Spengler 2016; Greiner 2018; Grünig and Kühn 2011; Hinterhuber 2011; Klaußner 2016; Lombriser and Abplanalp 2015; Müller-Stewens and Lechner 2016; Paul and Wollny 2014), the understanding of the components contained therein and their meaning differs, sometimes considerably. Among other aspects, this is attributable to different professional approaches and an associated heterogeneous application practice with fluid boundaries between management consulting and scientific theory building.

For example, Klaußner (2016, p. 3) writes that a "*Leitbild* of an organization [...] briefly and concisely [formulates] the mission, the strategic goals (vision), and the essential orientations for the way they are to be implemented (values)." It includes descriptions of tasks and goals, ways of achieving goals, and the "basic ideas" of an organization. Greiner (2018, p. 125) also assigns the components vision and mission to a *Leitbild*, supplemented by "principles" and "values" of the company. In contrast, according to Paul and Wollny (2014, p. 51), *Leitbild* and mission statements only refer to the present and the vision statement is complementary to this. Similarly, Grünig and Kühn (2011, p. 129 f.) do not see the vision as a component of the *Leitbild*. In contrast, it includes the mission as a description of the company's purpose, self-image, supreme goals and value attitudes. According to Lombriser and Abplanalp (2015, p. 252), on the one hand, the vision should be included in a *Leitbild*, but on the other hand, the authors no longer list it alongside strategic mission, core values, strategic intent, basic thrusts, core competencies and framework conditions (ibid., p. 252). Hinterhuber (2011, p. 99) also does not see the vision as part of the *Leitbild*, which he sometimes puts on a par with the corporate policy (mission), sometimes next to it, in order to depict a "corporate philosophy" in sum (ibid., p. 100). According to Graf and Spengler (2016, p. 62), in turn, *Leitbilder* "deal with the long-term, global goals and the long-term valid principles, norms and rules of the game of an organization, which should ensure its viability and ability to develop". Among other components, they contain statements on self-image, goals, tasks and structures as well as the (desired) behaviour of their members and serve as a "common orientation framework" (ibid., p. 62).

If we move down to the level of the individual *Leitbild* components, the range of conceptual heterogeneity decreases significantly.

As Lombriser and Abplanalp (2015, p. 244) conclude from a comparison of different definitions for an organisation's *vision,* what they have in common is the "idea of directional thoughts for the future development of the company" and it thus has an "orienting", "motivating" and "meaning-giving" function (ibid., p. 244).

The *mission* or *mission statement* legitimizes why the organization exists, what its purpose is, and what tasks are derived from it in relation to different stakeholders. Greiner (2018, p. 132), for example, attributes this statement to answers to three core questions: "Why do we exist? What mission do we fulfill? What added value do we offer our customers and society?".

In the case of *core values* and *principles,* a general distinction is made between the way in which the company acts and wishes to be seen from the outside, and the expectations placed on employees and managers. In this context, Lombriser and Abplanalp (2015, p. 252) formulate the question "How do we do it?", which needs to be answered, and Greiner (2018, p. 146 f.) uses the English terms *company values* and *people values* to differentiate the different perspectives. Hinterhuber (2011, p. 103) and Lombriser and Abplanalp (2015, p. 252) also assign *core competencies* to these corporate principles.

Some authors also see the *self-image* or *identity* as part of the mission statement, which expresses how the company (currently) sees itself (Grünig and Kühn 2011, p. 129, Lombriser and Abplanalp 2015, p. 252). Hinterhuber (2011, p. 101) refers to "traditional values" of the company as well as to a form of "self-confidence" (ibid., p. 102) that generates pride among employees. "Zukunft braucht Herkunft" (a future requires a past) was already written by philosopher Odo Marquard (Marquard 2015), from which emerges the link between the development of a vision for the future and identity, which according to Wagner (2010, p. 499) is defined by "value orientations that guide joint action".

2.2 Differentiation of Statement Characteristics

According to Greiner (2018, p. 124), *Leitbilder* are to be understood as an "emotional and factual superstructure of strategy work", the orientation and motivation function of which is essentially shared by the authors cited here. However, an analysis shows that information on the components contained and their respective statement intentions often diverge with regard to the following characteristics:

- *Function:* Does the statement serve to describe a target state *(normative),* a methodologically more or less well-founded result of an investigation (*analytical)* or an instruction for action *(action-oriented)?*
- *Orientation:* Are the statements directed more towards customers, suppliers, partners and the public *(outside)* or more towards your own organisation with its employees and managers *(inside)?*
- *Time reference:* Do the statements refer rather to conditions or developments in the future *(tomorrow)* or to descriptions of the present *(today)?*
- *Degree of abstraction:* Are the statements formulated more generally for holistic orientation or are they specific and implementation-oriented *(high – medium – low)?*
- *Development context:* Are the statements rather developed in connection with the superordinate *Leitbild development* or the subordinate *strategy development*?

According to this logic of differentiation, a distinction can be made between the instruments frequently attributed to *Leitbilder* and the statements generated with their help, as shown in Table 1, and a boundary can be drawn between *Leitbild* development and strategy development.

Table 1 Differentiation of elements in *Leitbild* and strategies. (Own representation)

		Function			Orientation		Time frame		Abstraction level		
	Instrument/Element	normative	analytical	action-oriented	outside	inside	tomorrow	today	high	medium	low
***Leitbild* development**	Vision	■				■	■		■		
	Mission	■			■		■		■		
	Corporate values	■			■			■	■		
	Corporate culture	■				■		■	■		
	Identity/self-image	■	■			■		■	■		
	Corporate identity	■	■		■	■		■	■		
	Market position/USP		■		■			■	■		
Strategy development	Opportunities/threats analysis		■		■		■			■	
	Market/competition analysis		■		■			■		■	
	Strengths/weaknesses analysis		■			■		■		■	
	Strategic fields of action			■		■	■			■	
	Strategic directions	■		■		■	■			■	
	Strategic goals	■				■	■				■
	Impact models		■			■	■	■			■
	Strategic measures			■		■		■			■

Roughly speaking, a distinction can be made between *Leitbild* and strategy development in that *Leitbilder* are predominantly normative in character, while strategies are formulated in a more action-oriented manner. In this context, the focus is increasingly directed inwards towards the organisation itself and the creation of the preconditions for goal-oriented management.

With this differentiation, we will now examine the extent to which the statements developed in *Leitbild* processes have a positive effect on the sustainability of an organisation.

2.3 A Holistic View of the Future

A *vision* is a narrative of the future that describes in a highly compressed way a target state of the organization in the future. The addressees of the contained statements are usually employees and managers of the organization. They have a sense-making effect (Müller-Stewens and Lechner 2016, p. 235, Paul and Wollny 2014, p. 51; Greiner 2018, p. 124), are oriented towards value attitudes of the stakeholders involved (Hinterhuber 2011, p. 84; Lombriser and Abplanalp 2015, p. 248) and are accordingly holistically oriented (Lombriser and Abplanalp 2015, p. 248). In the view of Porter and Kramer (2011), this in conjunction with the long-term orientation leads to the concept of *shared value* and thus to a shift from shareholder to stakeholder focus.

A long-term and holistic orientation that takes into account the values of a wide range of stakeholders has an impact on the sustainable actions of an organization. Thus, non-sustainable behaviours of organisations are essentially defined by the collectivization of social and ecological costs, while long-term consequences of organisational actions are taken into account through future orientation. Lombriser and Abplanalp (2015, p. 249 ff.) emphasize that, on the one hand, "unsolved social problems […] eventually [cause] costs in companies", while on the other hand "[making] ecological and social investments [...] contributes to motivating the workforce in the long term, enhancing the image with customers and gaining public acceptance" (ibid., p. 248).

A "vision generates confidence, freedom from fear, pride and joy of being there" (zur Bonsen 2012, p. 35), which are important ingredients for creating meaning for the employees of an organization, creating loyalty and enthusiasm (Greiner 2018, p. 124) and thus leading to more sustainable behavior. A holistic understanding of values that go beyond business economics leads to negotiation processes in which social and ecological aspects in particular are given greater consideration.

A *mission* tends to be outward-looking and focuses on the organisation's reason for being. It is a promise to customers and/or society as a whole, and therefore a universe of values also comes into focus here, which tends to be oriented towards sustainable principles, as it is hardly possible to exclude social and ecological side effects in the long term.

An examination of *basic values* (Lombriser and Abplanalp 2015, p. 248) usually leads to a stronger orientation towards "social standards", "spiritual quality of life" and humanistic thinking, with short-term and material references taking a back seat (Warwitz 2016, p. 260 ff.). In this context, the humanistic image of man encompasses elementary needs such as freedom, justice, self-development and participation (Schlösser 2007).

Impulses for sustainability that arise from the work on mission statements can therefore be summarized by the characteristics of *long-term, holistic* and *meaningfulness*. What role does the design of the development process play here?

3 *Leitbild* Development as a Process

"The decisive factor is less the content than the way in which a *Leitbild* is developed and introduced" Lombriser and Abplanalp (2015, p. 252) observe in their book on strategic management. Overall, in the literature the process for developing a *Leitbild* is described in very different detail, both in terms of the selection of process steps (core process only vs. including upstream and downstream processes) and in terms of the specific implementation of individual activities. This diversity is rooted in the business models of the respective providers of process support. To illustrate this, a selection of formative characteristics is presented below.

3.1 Process Models

The importance of a heterogeneous *team composition* is emphasized by many authors (cf. Hilb 2017, p. 43, Grolmann 2015, p. 198 f., Graf and Spengler 2016, p. 84, Lombriser and Abplanalp 2015, p. 255, Paul and Wollny 2014, p. 53, Hinterhuber 2011, p. 88 ff.). Klaußner (2016, p. 15) points out that heterogeneity also increases the complexity of the project, resulting in a more open-ended process.

These decisions are linked to the question of whether the *control* of the process should be more top-down or bottom-up (Klaußner 2016, p. 13 ff.). In the former case, the main decisions are made by top management; in the latter, a strong power to shape the process is guaranteed by employees on a wide variety of hierarchical levels. Lombriser and Abplanalp (2015, p. 255) emphasize the importance of combining these approaches, which is referred to as the countercurrent approach.

Furthermore, Hilb (2017, p. 42) points to the importance of *analyses* of environment, stakeholders and the organization in order to create a robust foundation for developing a *Leitbild*. In Graf and Spengler (2016, p. 86 ff.), these also have an important preparatory function before the actual creative work can begin.

Grolmann (2015, p. 203) divides the overall process into different *phases:* preparation, the actual *Leitbild* development – organization and implementation of workshops, reflection loop, lessons learned and evaluation – , editorial follow-up, decision with adoption and rollout. In particular, preparation is given an important role for ensuring that a "functionally and culturally compatible process architecture" is created (ibid., p. 211). For better structure, Graf and Spengler (2016, p. 85) recommend the creation of a process plan, where all relevant planning steps are summarized.

Several authors also develop concrete ideas on how *communication* and interaction between the participants can be organized in the respective process phases. Detailed suggestions in this regard can be found in Klaußner (2016, p. 97 ff.), Grolmann (2015, p. 203 ff.) and Eisenschmidt (2015, p. 73 ff.), while Graf and Spengler (2016, p. 85) explicitly refer to the "didactic structure".

Hinterhuber (2011, p. 87 ff.) chooses a different form of presentation by not describing process phases or interaction formats, but *attitudes of mind* that serve as guiding principles for visioning. Among other things, he recommends that participants in these processes observe with open senses, think in terms of alternatives, gain experience and put themselves in the shoes of others.

In order to be able to classify and evaluate these different solution processes, which are always linked to learning processes, a newly developed description format is presented below.

3.2 A Generic *Parcours* Model for Learn-Solve Processes

3.2.1 Interweaving Solving and Learning

Leitbild development, like all organisational processes, is connected to a learning and a solving task. On the one hand, as described in the previous section, it is important to achieve a work result that points the way to a successful future and has a meaningful effect on employees. On the other hand, achieving this goal requires that robust foundations for the desired positioning are created through reflective discourse in the first place. In order to express the dual nature of these requirements, we will speak of *learn-solve processes* furtheron.

Learn-solve processes are essentially characterised by providing for a sequence of activities to achieve a given goal. These are described very inconsistently in the literature due to the different disciplinary perspectives and contexts. In the educational context, we often speak of "learning steps" (Leisen 2015; Wahl 2013), "learning elements" (Wannemacher et al. 2016), "learning opportunities" (Seidel et al. 2008) or "learning activities" (Pfäffli 2015; Kosslyn 2017), a term that is also taken up in the more technically oriented field of collaboration engineering (Leimeister 2014, Briggs et al. 2003, de Vrede et al. 2009). In the corporate context, especially in project management, the terms "work steps", "tasks" or "work packages" are used analogously (Kraus and Westermann 2019; Kuster et al. 2019).

3.2.2 Cognitive Engagement

Since learning is a process of appropriation (Seidel et al. 2008, p. 260), knowledge must not only be transmitted, but also examined, reflected upon, contextualized, applied, and linked to existing knowledge (Fost et al. 2017, p. 168). By using the term "inquiry-based learning," Mayer (2004, p. 94) refers to the various activities that are engaged in during a research process. These include the formation of hypotheses, experimental testing and the repeated application of solutions, as can also be found in problem-based learning (Barrows 1994; Walker et al. 2015).

In his research on principles of successful learning, Kosslyn (2017, p. 154 f.) emphasizes the variety of cognitive operations as a prerequisite for deep processing of information, repetition to create multiple mental representations of information (generation effect), and the importance of feedback to correct faulty mental models. In order to deepen what has been learned, forms of explanation such as presentations are also suitable (Chi et al. 1994).

From an analysis of different studies on active learning and their own experiences, Kosslyn (2017, p. 169) and his colleagues derived different bundles of activities that can be assigned to either the creation of outputs, the investigation of viewpoints, the targeted activation of students, or the synthesis or evaluation of work results (see also Table 2).

A completely different view of differentiating characteristics of learning processes is offered by approaches from the field of design. In this context, the question is which spatial requirements result from different activities of learning and solving. For this purpose, stringent concepts have been developed by Jenull and Jacobson (2013), Doorley and Witthoft (2012), Kohlert and Cooper (2017), Mokosch-Wabnitz (2014), and Gensler (2015), among others (see also Table 2).

Table 2 Comparison of different classification schemes for learning activities

Cognitive engagements	Learning typologies (Jenull and Jacobsen 2013)	Learning actions (Doorley and Witthoft 2012)	Ways we learn (Gensler 2015)	ThinkLets (Colt pods et al. 2004)	Activity tags (Kosslyn 2017)
Frame				Understand problem	(Focus question)
Source	Discover	Saturate	Acquire		Transfer information
Explore	Analyze	Reflect	Reflect, collaborate	Evaluate alternate	Discuss, debate
Consolidate		Synthesize			Synthesize, evaluate write, diagram, math, code, brainstorm
Construct	Create	Flare		Develop alternate	Write, diagram, math, code, storm
Deliver	Share	Saturate	Convey		Speak, present
Feedback			Master	Monitor outcome	Respond
Select		Focus		Choose an alternative	
Implement		Realize	Experience	Take action	

Since these are closely related to the form of interaction, they will be discussed in more detail in the next section.

From these heterogeneous findings and perspectives, a classification of learning activities can be developed. Following Kosslyn's (2017) terminology, these are described as *cognitive engagements* indicating which form of learner engagement with the knowledge object dominates:

- *Frame:* Activities that clarify the context, problem and learning task. In this process, objectives are formulated and normative and project-specific boundaries are set. This is a necessary prerequisite for guiding research and creation.
- *Source:* Activities that serve to gather information in any form, for example by listening, reading or observing in the field. These are prerequisites for subsequent analysis or creation.
- *Explore:* Activities whose aim is to investigate phenomena and statements, for example by means of reflective discourse, data analysis or simulation. The un-

derstanding thus gained is a prerequisite for deriving meaning and patterns for subsequent synthesis steps.
- *Consolidate:* Activities that contribute to structuring and evaluation through heuristic pattern generation or mathematical optimization. These consolidated results are a prerequisite for subsequent creation or a selection decision.
- *Construct:* Activities directed at developing one's own ideas and producing new outputs – conceptually or physically. Brainstorming, writing, and prototyping are prerequisites for subsequent revision based on testing or analysis.
- *Deliver:* Activities that serve to make results of learning and work visible to a selected group of addressees. These include, for example, conducting experiments or examinations as well as presentations. These are the basis for obtaining external feedback and possible further iterations in the learn-solve process.
- *Feedback:* Activities that focus on critical evaluation and constructive reflection of the content presented. Feedback points the way to iterative improvement of learning and work results.
- *Select:* Activities that aim to select one option from several based on a previously developed evaluation scheme. This can be done using appropriate choice methods or mathematical selection procedures.
- *Implement:* Activities aimed at applying developed solutions to real-world contexts. Implementations are to be understood as practical outputs of learning processes and provide important inputs for subsequent learn-solve processes.
- *Manage:* Activities dedicated to project management, in particular team communication, coordination and controlling. These activities typically run parallel to all other activities and are particularly important in longer-term processes. They will not be discussed further below.

This classification of learning activities can be contrasted with other classification schemes aligned with learning functions from the fields of design, collaboration engineering and pedagogy, as shown in Table 2. It can be seen that there are many similarities in terms of information gathering *(source)* and creating *(construct)*. *Framing* as preparation for learn-solve processes, on the other hand, is often not explicitly identified. The boundaries between analysis and synthesis *(explore, consolidate)* are not always clear and thus often identified as a single learning process. Deciding *(select)* and implementing *(implement)* is rare in teaching contexts, where the focus is usually on the learning experience rather than the solution.

Learning and problem-solving processes, as they are carried out in courses, workshops, research or practice projects, can thus be described comprehensively as sequences of these engagements. Here, these sequences of activities are referred to as a *parcours* in reference to athletic runs to overcome obstacles, a term already used by Jenull and Jacobsen (2013, pp. 27-28) with the *innovation parcours* as a spatial implementation of learning stations on learning paths.

3.2.3 Communicative Interaction

Another important characteristic of learn-solve processes is the way in which the people involved interact with each other. In educational contexts, a distinction is usually made between the roles of teachers and learners due to knowledge asymmetry, whereas in practical contexts this distribution of roles is less pronounced and, depending on the phase, different people can take on leader or facilitator functions.

Jonassen and Hung (2015, p. 15) refer to the importance of self-activity, exchange between learners as well as the change of interaction formats in order to take on different roles, to approach questions from different sides and thus to develop one's own positioning (Reinmann-Rothmeier and Mandl 2001). In a meta-study of 225 individual studies, Freeman et al. (2014, pp. 8413–8414) showed the advantages of active learning over frontal teaching formats. In comparison with other teaching methods such as service learning and learning communities, Kilgo et al. (2015) also show that the combination of active and collaborative learning is most effective.

Simplified, five typical *interaction patterns* can be distinguished in learning settings (cf. Dürr et al. 2016, p. 6), which dominate in today's practice:

- Plenary input (e.g. lecture, film screening, pitch/slam)
- Plenary interaction (e.g. fishbowl, business game, panel discussion)
- Group coaching (team coaching, peer instruction, feedback)
- Group work (e.g. World Café, online chat, brainstorming)
- Individual work (e.g. online research, writing, flash)

By combining these two aspects, *cognitive engagement* and *interaction patterns,* learn-solve processes can now be described and evaluated comprehensively.

3.3 The Added Value of Interactive Learning Processes

According to Paul and Wollny (2014, p. 51), a development process leads to the emergence of a common understanding about the organizations's future direction. Joint elaboration creates a certain consensus and thus acceptance, which leads to better coordination for subsequent strategic decisions (ibid., p. 53). Lombriser and Abplanalp (2015, p. 258) add that the process serves team development and integration and also activates an emotional core of values that includes "fairness, justice, harmony, trust, respect, openness, joy, fun, courage and community spirit". The attitude of those involved in the process is also important, for which openness, understanding other opinions, putting oneself in their shoes and active listening are necessary prerequisites (Hinterhuber 2011, p. 86).

Effects on sustainability can essentially be determined by the process characteristics presented below.

Participation

Leitbilder contain fundamental statements about long-term orientation and the cultural self-image of an organization. If these commitments are not simply generated top-down, but are developed jointly with employees at different hierarchical levels, this strengthens identification with the results. Those involved in the process can recognise the consequences of their interventions even if the perspective they brought in could not prevail in the negotiation process, sine any result is always associated with the offered competing designs and related exchange of arguments.

The workbook *Gemeinwohlökonomie* (Blachfellner et al. 2017, p. 68 f.) sees employee co-decision-making as a central aspect of an organisation's orientation towards the common good. This is strengthened by their influence on "long-term relevant fundamental decisions" (ibid., p. 69). These are flanked by other aspects such as the legitimacy of managers and internal transparency (ibid., pp. 66-68). The standards of the Global Reporting Initiative, an international organization that has been developing sustainability reporting for more than 20 years, provide information on the process of how value positions are developed (Disclosure 102-16: Values, principles, standards, and norms of behavior), how employees (Disclosure 102-19: Delegating authority) and other stakeholders (Disclosure 102-21: Consulting stakeholders on economic, environmental, and social topics) are involved for this purpose (GRI 2018, pp. 16-19).

The international research and consulting institute Great Place to Work® has developed an auditing model that is intended to help organizations determine the status of their corporate culture (GPTW Germany 2019). The great places to work are derived from surveys in which employees provide information about different cultural characteristics and their satisfaction with their employer. Using this model, Schubert and Kast (2015, p. 216 f.) point out how a value-based culture can activate employees' respect, pride and team spirit and promote them through participative processes. Hollmann (2013, p. 7 f.) also confirms a connection between employee participation in decision-making processes and sustainable (HR) leadership.

Change of Perspective

Processes in which the participants are recruited from different fields of work are characterised by a natural diversity of perspectives, provided that the respective rights of co-determination are not too severely restricted. In stringent participation concepts, this heterogeneity relates not only to the respective knowledge bases and working environments, but also to individual value attitudes. The longer-term perspective in the *Leitbild* is thus also supplemented by a wider range of effects of organisational action that need to be taken into account. As described in Sect. 2.3, this leads to a more stakeholder-oriented orientation of the organisation and thus positive effects on sustainability (Lombriser and Abplanalp 2015, p. 248, Porter and Kramer 2011).

As explained in Sect. 2.2, the development of different perspectives has not only to do with the provenance of participants, but also with the variety of roles they take on in the course of processing as well as the form in which interaction between them is organised. Alternating between a facilitator, researcher, leader and listener role in different group contexts leads to an enhancement of exchange that inspires, integrates and generates new approaches (Reinmann-Rothmeier and Mandl 2001, Jonassen and Hung 2015, p. 15, Schubert and Kast 2015, p. 217). This in turn promotes aspects of a sustainable corporate culture such as team spirit, credibility and respect (Schubert and Kast 2015, p. 216).

Last but not least, changes in perspective are also forced by the iterative process activating different cognitive operations, as explained in the context of the parcoursconcept, since changes in the processing mode lead to new insights (Kosslyn 2017, p. 154 f.; Chi et al. 1994).

Constructivity

Just as learning is an individual construction process (cf. Becker 2006; Mayer 2004; Seidel et al. 2008), carving out the essence – often referred to in practice as the *core* (The Living Core 2019), *DNA* (Neilson and Pasternack 2006) or *operating system* (Resourceful Humans 2019) of an organization – can be understood as a joint construction process. This is characterized by having multiple iterations of divergent and convergent phases, being creative, nonlinear, and thus open-ended.

This is also one of the major challenges for corporate management: To what extent must it provide guidelines or be prepared to accept results that do not meet its expectations? Basically, the combination of top-down and bottom-up is the chosen compromise in order to preserve the emergent character without completely giving up management authority.

The connection to sustainability can be justified analogously to participation: Only if involved employees have the impression that their voice has an influence does this awaken a sense of recognition, self-efficacy and pride in the jointly achieved result (Schubert and Kast 2015, p. 216, GRI 2018, p. 16, Hollmann 2013, p. 7 f.).

4 Practical Example: Applying the Parcours Model to *Leitbild* Development

Context

In 2018, the parcours model was applied to a medium-sized transport company under the project name "Development of the organization's brand core". The results were to serve as basis for strategy development and contain image/text combinations for the brand values *identity, differentiation, vision* and *promise* shown in Fig. 1. In contrast to the *Leitbild* concepts mentioned in Sect. 2, corporate values

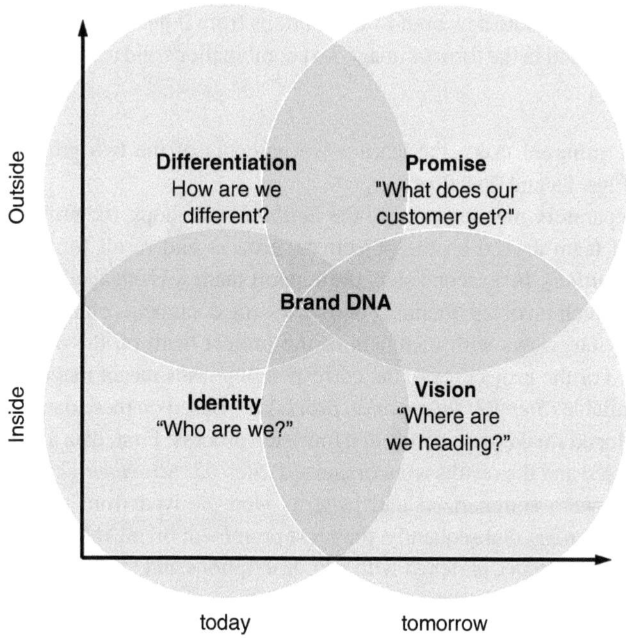

Fig. 1 Differentiation of the value dimensions of the developed brand core. (Own representation)

are not shown here as a separate element, but are integrated as formative components of all other brand values, especially *identity, differentiation* and *promise. Instead* of a *mission,* the *promise* takes the perspective of the customer, i.e. a description of what added value is to be perceived when using the service.

Process Design

The methodology of the learn-solve parcours with changing interaction formats introduced in Sect. 2.2 was used here for the first time outside the university. Two groups were formed:

- The *project team* was made up of members from different hierarchical levels. In addition to the upper management, employees from all departments were involved, who were to act as multipliers. The task of the project team was to develop the four brand values in an iterative process involving the support team.
- The *support team* essentially had the task of structuring the process and carrying out syntheses of the various discussion results. For this purpose, the parcours model was first developed with the management. In the process, the main task was to generate new brand value options from inputs and feedbacks. These were presented in the form of image/text combinations and referred to as (brand) worlds.

Due to the different tasks, the learn-solve parcours of the two groups differ, as shown in Figs. 2a and 2b below.

In a preparatory meeting prior to the *Leitbild* workshops, the project team and the support team agreed on the objectives, process and result formats *(step 01: Project definition).* In a second step, the support team was engaged in information gathering, which involved obtaining and reviewing documents on the one hand and conducting interviews with members of the project team on the other *(Step 02: Research).* For the project team, the corresponding tasks meant making this information available *(Step 02: Information provision).* Based on these data, the support team developed image-text worlds in a four-step process: First, data and interviews were analyzed and the results were organized *(Step 03: Structuring)*, then the analysis results were summarized and patterns were derived from them *(Step 04: Pattern production).* Subsequently, the most prominent brand values were focused on *(step 05: Selection),* enriched with text descriptions and visualization examples in a creative association process and brought into a comprehensible, but also emotionalizing form *(step 06: Universe production).*

The results of this work formed the basis for the subsequent *Leitbild* workshops with the project team, which proceeded in the following steps:

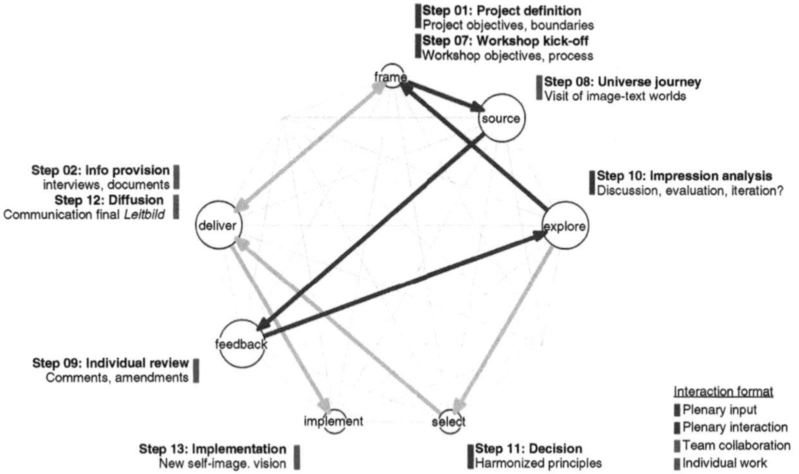

Fig. 2a Learn-solve parcours for the **project team**. (Own representation)

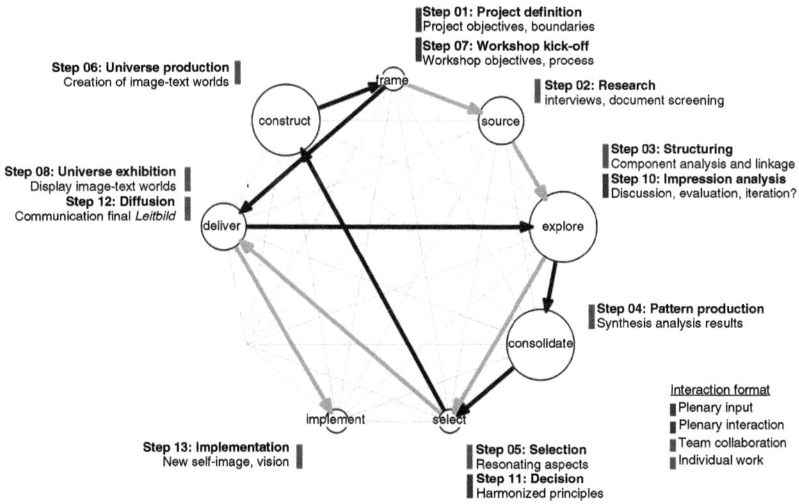

Fig. 2b Learn-solve parcours for the **support team**. (Own representation)

After clarifying the objectives and procedures in the respective workshop *(Step 07: Workshop kick-off)*, the participants were given the task of first making a silent tour of each of the initially ten different worlds individually, as in an exhibition *(Step 08: Universe journey)*. They were asked to first only look, not to evaluate, and only in a second round to make notes on a pad. The aim of this procedure was to suppress stereotypical reaction patterns of evaluation and to take in the worlds with an open mind. In a next round, the exhibits were allowed to be commented on – still silently – and supplemented by the image and text materials provided (Step 09: Individual review). Only during the next joint tour were perceptions and arguments regarding each world exhibit exchanged verbally and documented by the support team (Step 10: Impression analysis). At the end of the workshop, a decision was made as to whether a further iteration was required or whether to proceed to the final agreed brand values *(Step 11: Decision)*. In the former case, the process was repeated from step 04. After the conclusion of the workshops and the decision, the final *Leitbild* was communicated *(Step 12: Diffusion)* and rolled out in the company *(Step 13: Implementation)*.

Results and Conclusion

A total of three iterations were carried out, in the course of which, through selection, recombination and synthesis, four of the ten initial image-text worlds remained. Fig. 3 shows an intermediate result to illustrate the concept of the image-text worlds, and Fig. 4 shows the headings of the final brand values, which together form the brand core of the company and were subsequently formulated as a holistic *Leitbild*.

Some specific features of the process will be highlighted here in order to establish links between work result, process and sustainability:

- The *vision* contains a clear reference to sustainability through the idea of offering intelligent, i.e. environmentally and user-friendly mobility. The *promise* is to offer users and employees the greatest possible scope for development. In describing their *identity*, the project team came to the conclusion that it is not the service developed but the way in which they work together in an appreciative manner that is the defining characteristic of the company. No clear reference to sustainability is discernible in the *differentiation* characteristic alone.
- One challenge in the process was the composition of the project team, which was comparatively management-heavy and did not reflect the entire diversity of the company. As a result, hypotheses made in some phases of the process were not challenged and clarified enough. Some participants also had difficulties

Fig. 3 Example of an image-text world to describe a brand value. (Own representation)

with the degree of abstraction of the image worlds and searched in vain for iconic references that were closer to their everyday work.

- As a result of these two factors, there was a tendency for some to look concretely at the core of their being and their future in terms of the obvious and the familiar rather than in terms of higher, related ideas.

5 Reflection and Outlook

The constituent features of *Leitbilder* are defined very differently in the literature, but despite this diversity there is a high degree of agreement as to their effects. As a foundation for strategies to be developed , they have a strong reference to the future and a clear value orientation, which should have an effect both internally and externally. *Long-term orientation, holism* and a *sense of purpose* were identified as key drivers in the direction of sustainability. The question of whether a *Leitbild* leads to more sustainability in an organization can therefore be confirmed.

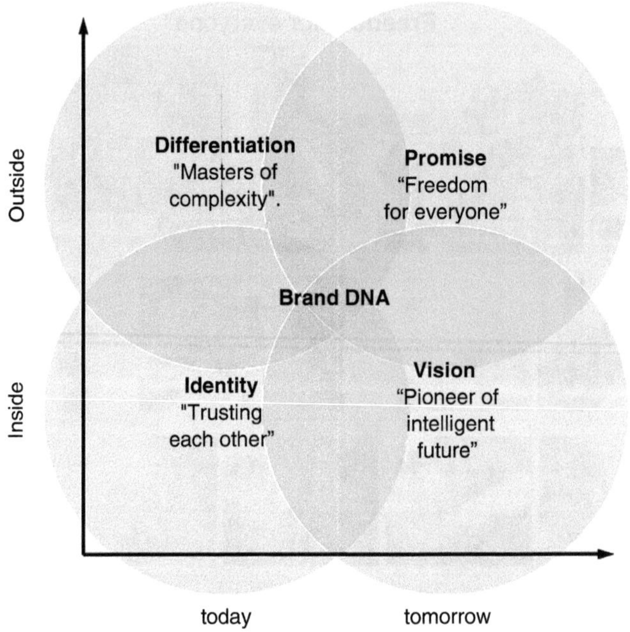

Fig. 4 Final definition of the brand core via four brand values. (Own representation)

The second hypothesis related to the effects that the design of the development process has on a sustainable orientation of the organisation. Here, too, it should first be noted that the approaches described differ, in some cases significantly, in terms of team composition, decision-making logic, work content, phasing and forms of communicative exchange. This often only reflects the competing literature universes, on the one hand the business-oriented management literature with its focus on instruments and results, and on the other hand social-psychologically oriented publications with their focus on processes and communication.

In order to be able to compare and evaluate the recommended approaches, the concept of the *learn-solve parcours* was presented, in which solution steps and forms of communicative interaction are combined into an integrated model. With the help of this model and the descriptions from the literature, principles for successful processes can be derived, which were summarised with the terms *participation, change of perspective* and *constructiveness* and which have a positive effect on the sustainability of the organisation.

To illustrate the importance of the content and process of *Leitbild* development, a real-world application example was presented. While a clear sustainable profile is visible in the developed *Leitbild* content, referred to in the example as *brand values,* the limited heterogeneity of the process participants led to rather limited participation and subsequently to a lower degree of openness towards potentially emergent options. The sustainability objectives were therefore only partially achieved in this respect. The lithmus test for successful implementation can only be carried out years later anyway, when the strategy based on the *Leitbild* leads to changes in the organisation and the environment it influences.

The main task of *Leitbilder* is to lead an organization to long-term success. This paper concludes that with this goal also positive effects on society in general take place in terms of more sustainable behavior patterns. However, sustainability has very many dimensions, which could only be described here on a comparatively abstract level. In fact, there are numerous examples of how success in one sustainability dimension can be counteracted by losses in another. This highlights the need for further research into a differentiated representation and evaluation of the multilayered effects of organisational action.

References

Barrows, Howard. 1994. *The Tutorial Process*. Carbondale: Southern Illinois University Press.

Becker, Nicole. 2006. Von der Hirnforschung lernen? Ansichten über die pädagogische Relevanz neurowissenschaftlicher Erkenntnisse. In *Biowissenschaft und Erziehungswissenschaft. Zeitschrift für Erziehungswissenschaft*, 9. Jg., Beiheft 5/06, Hrsg. A. Scheunpflug und C. Wulf, 177–200. Wiesbaden: Springer.

Blachfellner, Manfred et al. 2017. *Arbeitsbuch zur Gemeinwohlbilanz 5.0 – Vollbilanz.*

Bleicher, Knut. 2004. *Das Konzept Integriertes Management. Visionen – Missionen – Programme*. 7. Aufl. Frankfurt: Campus.

Bonsen, Matthias zur. 2012. *Führen mit Visionen: Der Weg zum ganzheitlichen Management.* Wiesbaden: Gabler.

Briggs, R., de Vreede, G.-J. und J.F. Nunamaker Jr. 2003. Collaboration Engineering with ThinkLets to Pursue Sustained Success with Group Support Systems. *Journal of Management Information Systems*, Vol. 19(4): 31–64.

Chi, M., de Leeuw, N., Chiu, M.-H. und C. Lavancher. 1994. Eliciting self-explanations improves understanding. *Cognitive Science* 18: 439–477.

de Vreede, G.-J., Massey, A.P. und R.O. Briggs. 2009. Collaboration Engineering: Foundations and Opportunities. *Journal of the Association for Information Systems* 10(3): 121–137.

Doorley, S. und S. Witthoft. 2012. *Make Space: How to Set the Stage for Creative Collaboration*. Hoboken: John Wiley & Sons.

Duden. 2019. *Deutsches Universalwörterbuch: Das umfassende Bedeutungswörterbuch der deutschen Gegenwartssprache*. 9., überarb. und erw. Aufl. Berlin: Duden.

Dürr, P., Spier, P., Lödermann, A.-M. und A. Nissler. 2016. Lehrraum der Zukunft. *Schriftenreihe Innovation und Qualität der Lehre*, Hochschule München.

Eisenschmidt, Kerstin. 2015. Visions- und Strategieprozess für ein internationales Architektur- und Designunternehmen. In *Vision – Mission – Werte: Die Basis der Leitbild- und Strategieentwicklung*, Hrsg. Dagmar Werther, 68–86. Weinheim: Beltz.

Farjoun, M. 2007. The end of strategy? *Strategic Organization* (3): 197–210.

Fost, J., Levitt, R. und S. Kosslyn. 2017. Fully Active Learning. In *Building the Intentional University: Minerva and the Future of Higher Education*. Hrsg. Kosslyn, S. und B. Nelson, 165–178. Cambridge: MIT Press.

Freeman, S. et al. 2014. Active learning increases student performance in science, engineering, and mathematics. *Proceedings of the National Academy of Sciences of the United States of America* 111(23): 8410–8415.

Gensler (2015) Reimagining Learning: Strategies for Engagement. https://www.gensler.com/uploads/document/406/file/Reimagining-Learning-US.pdf. Zugegriffen am 12.10.2019.

GPTW Deutschland. 2019. Great Place to Work® – Was wir machen. https://www.greatplacetowork.de/ueber-uns/was-wir-machen. Zugegriffen am 29.11.2019.

Graf, P. und M. Spengler. 2016. *Leitbild- und Konzeptentwicklung*. 6. Aufl. Regensburg: Walhalla.

Greiner, Oliver. 2018. *Touchdown! Wie Unternehmen unschlagbar werden. Das Strategiebuch*. Hamburg: Murmann.

GRI. 2018. *Consolidated Set of GRI Sustainability Reporting Standards*. Amsterdam: Global Reporting Initiative.

Grolmann, Florian. 2015. Leitbildentwicklung in größeren Unternehmen und Konzernen. In *Vision – Mission – Werte: Die Basis der Leitbild- und Strategieentwicklung*, Hrsg. Dagmar Werther, 197–211. Weinheim: Beltz.

Grünig, R. und R. Kühn. 2011. *Methodik der strategischen Planung: Ein prozessorientierter Ansatz für Strategieplanungsprojekte*. 6. Aufl. Bern: Haupt.

Hilb, Martin. 2017. *Integriertes Personalmanagement: Ziele, Strategien, Instrumente*. 21., aktual. Aufl. Berlin: Luchterhand.

Hinterhuber, Hans. 2011. *Strategische Unternehmensführung: I. Strategisches Denken Vision – Ziele – Strategie*. 8., neu bearb. Aufl. Berlin: Erich Schmidt.

Hollmann, Sebastian. 2013. *Sustainable Leadership: Modellentwicklung, empirische Überprüfung und Gestaltungshinweise*. Wiesbaden: Springer.

Jenull, S. und J. Jacobsen 2013. *Kreative Zusammenarbeit im Innovation Space*. Bene Research + Design.

Jonassen, D. und W. Hung. 2015. All Problems are not equal: Implications for Problem-based Learning. In *Essential Readings in Problem-Based Learning: Exploring and Extending the Legacy of Howard S. Barrows*, Hrsg. A. Walker, P. Ertmer, C. Hmelo-Silver, H. Leary. West Lafayette: Purdue University Press.

Kilgo, C., Ezell Sheets, J. und E. Pascarella. 2015. The link between high-impact practices and student learning: some longitudinal evidence. *Higher Education* 69(4): 509–525.

Klaußner, Stefan. 2016. *Partizipative Leitbildentwicklung: Grundlagen, Prozesse und Methoden*. Wiesbaden: Springer.

Kohlert, C. und S. Cooper. 2017. *Space for Creative Thinking: Design Principles for Work and Learning Environments*. Munich: Callwey.

Kosslyn, Stephen. 2017. The Science of Learning: Mechanisms and Principles. In *Building the Intentional University: Minerva and the Future of Higher Education*. Hrsg. Kosslyn, S. und B. Nelson, 149–164. Cambridge: MIT Press.

Kraus, G. und R. Westermann. 2019. *Projektmanagement mit System: Organisation, Methoden, Steuerung*. 6., aktual. und erw. Aufl. Wiesbaden: Springer.

Kuster, Jürg et al. 2019. *Handbuch Projektmanagement: Agil – Klassisch – Hybrid*. 4., vollständig überarb. und erw. Aufl. Wiesbaden: Springer.

Leimeister, Jan Marco. 2014. *Collaboration Engineering: IT-gestützte Zusammenarbeitsprozesse systematisch entwickeln und durchführen*. Heidelberg: Springer Gabler.

Leisen, Josef. 2015. Lernumgebung und Lernschritte durch Moderation steuern: Wie man "anders" im Unterricht kommunizieren kann. *Pädagogik* 11: 14–17.

Lombriser, R. und P. Abplanalp. 2015. *Strategisches Management: Visionen entwickeln – Erfolgspotenziale aufbauen – Strategien umsetzen*. 6., vollst. überarb. und aktual. Aufl. Zürich: Versus.

Mancesti, Marco. 2015. Is VUCA the end of strategy and leadership? International Institute of Management Development. https://www.imd.org/research-knowledge/articles/is-vuca-the-end-of-strategy-and-leadership. Zugegriffen am 27.11.2019.

Marquard, Odo. 2015. *Zukunft braucht Herkunft. Philosophische Essays*. Ditzingen: Reclam.

Mayer, Richard. 2004. Should There Be a Three Strikes Rule Against Pure Discovery Learning? The Case for Guided Methods of Instruction. *American Psychologist* 59 (1): 14–19.

Mokosch-Wabnitz, Robert. 2014. Work in Flow: Impulse zur Struktur innovationsfördernder Arbeitswelten. *Open Innovation Sommerzirkel*, Bad Wörishofen, 25.–27. September.

Müller-Stewens, G. und C. Lechner. 2016. *Strategisches Management: Wie strategische Initiativen zum Wandel führen*. 5. überarb. Aufl. Stuttgart: Schäffer-Poeschel.

Neilson, G. und B. Pasternack. 2006. *Erfolgsfaktor Unternehmens-DNA: Die vier Bausteine für effektive Organisationen*. Frankfurt a. M.: Campus.

Paul, H. und V. Wollny. 2014. *Instrumente des strategischen Managements. Grundlagen und Anwendungen*. 2. aktual. und erw. Aufl. München: Oldenbourg.

Pfäffli, Brigitta. 2015. *Lehren an Hochschulen: Eine Hochschuldidaktik für den Aufbau von Wissen und Kompetenzen*. 2. Aufl. Stuttgart: UTB.

Porter, M. und M. Kramer. 2011. Creating Shared Value: How to reinvent capitalism – and unleash a wave of innovation and growth. *Harvard Business Review* 1: 1–17.

Resourceful Humans. 2019. The operating model to turn your organisation into an entrepreneurial network. https://resourceful-humans.com. Zugegriffen am 29.11.2019.

Schlösser, Hans-Jürgen. 2007. Wirtschaftspolitik und gesellschaftliche Grundwerte. Bundeszentrale für Politische Bildung. Informationen zur politischen Bildung 294/2007. https://www.bpb.de/izpb/8449/wirtschaftspolitik-und-gesellschaftliche-grundwerte. Zugegriffen am 30.11.2019.

Schubert, A. und R. Kast. 2015. Partizipative und wertebasierte Entwicklung von Unternehmensleitbildern. In *Vision – Mission – Werte: Die Basis der Leitbild- und Strategieentwicklung*, Hrsg. Dagmar Werther, 212–222. Weinheim: Beltz.

Seidel, T., M. Prenzel, und R. Rimmele. 2008. Konstruktivistische Überzeugungen von Lehrpersonen. In Perspektiven der Didaktik. Zeitschrift für Erziehungswissenschaft, Sonderheft 9/08, Hrsg. M. Meyer, M. Prenzel, S. Hellekamps, 259–276.

Teece, D., M. Peteraf, und S. Leih. 2016. Dynamic Capabilities and Organizational Agility: Risk, Uncertainty, and Strategy in the Innovation Economy. *California Management Review* 58(4): 13–35.

The Living Core. 2019. Arbeitsweise und Haltung: Konzepte, die in unserer Arbeit eine zentrale Rolle spielen. http://www.thelivingcore.com/arbeitsweise-haltung. Zugegriffen am 29.11.2019.

Wagner, Peter. 2010. Hat Europa eine kulturelle Identität? In *Die kulturellen Werte Europas*, Hrsg. H. Joas und K. Wiegandt, 494–511. Frankfurt a. M.: Fischer.

Wahl, Diethelm. 2013. *Lernumgebungen erfolgreich gestalten. Vom trägen Wissen zum kompetenten Handeln*. 3. Aufl. Bad Heilbrunn: Julius Klinkhardt.

Wannemacher, Klaus. 2016. Digitale Lernszenarien im Hochschulbereich. *Hochschulforum Digitalisierung. Arbeitspapier* 15.

Warwitz, Siegbert. 2016. *Sinnsuche im Wagnis: Leben in wachsenden Ringen. Erklärungsmodelle für grenzüberschreitendes Verhalten*, 2., erw. Aufl. Baltmannsweiler: Schneider.

Walker, Andrew Elbert, H. Leary, C. E. Hmelo-Silver, P. A. Ertmer. Hrsg. 2015. *Essential Readings in Problem-based Learning*. West Lafayette Indiana: Purdue University Press

Peter Dürr, Prof. Dr.-Ing., MSc., studied Economics (UC Irvine), Transportation (MIT), PhD Urban and Transportation Planning (TU Munich). Director Research Think Tools AG, Senior Manager Horváth & Partners, Chair of Knowledge and Communication Management and co-head of the Management of Social Innovations program at Munich University of Applied Sciences, Visiting Scholar UC Berkeley CITRIS-DDI, independent consultant Strategy & Communication.

Latest Publications:

Dürr, P., P. Spier, A.M. Lödermann, A. Nissler. 2016. teaching space of the future. *Schriftenreihe Innovation und Qualität der Lehre*, Munich University of Applied Sciences.

Dürr, P., N. Tschauner, G. Zollner. 2015. insurance companies as communities of solidarity. In *Making sustainability measurable*, ed. Sprinkart KP, 245-270. Regensburg: Walhalla.

Hipp, M., P. Dürr, K. Sailer, K.P. Sprinkart. Eds. 2015. *practice of social innovation*. Regensburg: Valhalla. Sprinkart, K.P., Dürr, P., Hipp, M., Sailer, K., eds. 2015. *networks of societal innovation*. Regensburg: Walhalla.

Common Good Balance Sheet and Balanced Scorecard – Considerations for an Approach

Wolfgang Gehra and Julia Schmidt

Abstract

Since 2010, the initiative of the Common Good Economy in Europe and South America has inspired a large number of people, companies and communities to align their actions with the common good. The background to the vision of the Common Good Economy is to establish a market economy that brings economic activity into harmony with ethical values. A values-reference-group matrix serves as an orientation system for reporting and development as well as a target system for the external evaluation of entrepreneurial action. This paper presents the link between the common good matrix and the balanced scorecard. By linking the two systems, the common good matrix functions beyond its functions as a sustainability report and organizational development tool, also as part of business management control, thus benefiting from the strategic relevance of the established management tool. The data basis available in many organisations for the determination of key figures in the context of the balanced scorecard facilitates the entry into a common good-oriented management and fertilises the strategy implementation through simple adjustment processes. It is assumed that the deeper the goal orientation towards the common good is implanted in the DNA of the economic thinking and acting of organisations, the more effective a sustainable influence will be.

W. Gehra (✉) · J. Schmidt
Munich University of Applied Sciences, Munich, Germany
e-mail: wolfgang.gehra@hm.edu

H.-W. Franz et al. (eds.), *Sustainable Living and Business*,
https://doi.org/10.1007/978-3-658-41835-9_6

1 Introduction

The concept of the Common Good Balance Sheet as an instrument of sustainability certification is a catalogue of criteria now used by over 400 organisations, mainly in German-speaking countries. Among them are well-known companies such as Sparda Bank Munich, the health insurance company BKK ProVita or the sports goods manufacturer Vaude. With the aid of a matrix comprising 20 fields, a maximum of 1000 plus points or a maximum of 3600 minus points are awarded. The certificate of the common good balance sheet is valid for 2 years. Due to the minimum two-year rhythm, some companies prepare their subsequent balance sheet later, the public welfare balance sheet has more of a certification character with a not inconsiderable additional effort of preparation. This contrasts with the widespread concept of the Balanced Scorecard, which is implemented as part of the day-to-day management of an organisation by means of key figures. In most cases, the data required for this is collected permanently in the company's accounting system and in parallel with the operational performance creation.

This raises the question for the following considerations as to what extent a convergence of the two concepts of the common good balance sheet and the balanced scorecard would allow the labour-intensive certification character of the former concept to be transferred to the parallel accounting system of the latter approach, in order ultimately to promote the spread of common good orientation with the help of the common good balance sheet.

2 The Common Good Balance Sheet

The common good economy sees itself as an intrinsically motivated, global open source movement with the goal of implementing an ethical market economy that does not strive for the increase of monetary capital, but for a good life for all. The highest value here is human dignity, but ecological responsibility also plays a major role (Internationale Delegiertenversammlung 2018). With the help of the Common Good Balance Sheet and the Common Good Matrix (Matrix-Entwicklungsteam 2017), companies should be able to obtain governmental and corporate advantages, e.g. in taxes, loans and contracts. The common good economy movement sets new values in business and society. All ideas for a changed sustainable economic order are developed in democratic processes. These values are to be lived in everyday business life. Another goal is to limit capitalist economic activity and unequal distribution of profits. Accordingly, economic growth should only take place within the framework of social and economic compatibility, so that even in the overall political context no excessive power can arise through financial means (Internationaler Verein zur Förderung der Gemeinwohl-Ökonomie e. V. 2019).

The balance sheet appears in the form of a matrix (see Fig. 1). The vertical line, i.e. the Y axis, maps the various stakeholder groups, in this case touch groups, with letters from 'A' to 'E'.

(A) "Suppliers
(B) Owners and financial partners
(C) Employees
(D) Customers & Co-entrepreneurs
(E) social environment" (Matrix-Entwicklungsteam 2017, p. 8).

On the X axis, the values essential to the common good economy are shown in the opposite direction. These are:

1. "Human Dignity,
2. Solidarity and justice,

VALUE / STAKEHOLDER	HUMAN DIGNITY	SOLIDARITY AND JUSTICE	ECOLOGICAL SUSTAINABILITY	TRANSPARENCY AND CODECISION
A: SUPPLIERS	**A1** Human dignity in the supply chain	**A2** Solidarity and justice in the supply chain	**A3** Environmental sustainability in the supply chain	**A4** Transparency and co-decision in the supply chain
B: OWNERS & FINANCE PARTNERS	**B1** Ethical attitude in dealing with financial resources	**B2** Social attitude in dealing with funds	**B3** Social-ecological investments and use of funds	**B4** Ownership and co-decision
C: CO-WORKERS	**C1** Human dignity in the workplace	**C2** Drafting of employment contracts	**C3** Promoting the ecological behavior of employees	**C4** Internal co-decision and transparency
D: CUSTOMERS & CO-ENTERPRISES	**D1** Ethical customer relations	**D2** Cooperation and solidarity with fellow companies	**D3** Ecological impact of use and disposal of products and services	**D4** Customer participation and product transparency
E: SOCIAL/SOCIETAL ENVIRONMENT	**E1** Meaning and social impact of products and services	**E2** Contribution to the community	**E3** Reduction of ecological impacts	**E4** Transparency and social co-decision

Fig. 1 Common good matrix 5. 0 (Matrix-Entwicklungsteam 2017)

3. environmental sustainability,
4. Transparency and co-decision" (Matrix-Entwicklungsteam 2017, p. 8).

For example, A1 corresponds to human dignity in the supply chain, B2 corresponds to social attitude towards handling funds, etc. (Matrix-Entwicklungsteam *2017)*.

3 Balanced Scorecard

The Balanced Scorecard is a strategic measurement tool developed by Kaplan and Norton in 1992 (Kaplan and Norton 2018, Preface VIII). Over time, with the help of various international consulting firms, an improved system of key performance indicators has become a recognized management system. Due to practical experience and growing interest, further developments are constantly being published (Kaplan and Norton 2018, Preface VIII f.).

"[The BSC] (It) promotes dialogue between business units, division managers, and board members, not only in terms of short-term financial goals, but also in terms of formulating and executing a breakthrough strategy for the future" (ibid. p. 13). The aim of introducing a BSC in the company is to implement a continuous process that integrates the "long-term goals and strategies" of the business units into the company (ibid. p. 13).

The Balanced Scorecard is a system of indicators that combines data from different sources into a statement system (Kühnapfel 2019, p. 1). "These input data are of a very different nature, sometimes quantitative and objectively ascertainable (e.g. they come from cost accounting or personnel accounting), sometimes they are subjective expected values" (ibid. 2019, p. 1). In addition to monetary targets, non-monetary targets such as customer satisfaction are also taken into account, as they contribute to the fulfilment of the targets and should not be disregarded. In contrast to the mere financial ratios, these are early indicators, which means that a negative change can be detected and prevented at an early stage (Barthélemy 2011, p. 59).

The four individual perspectives of a BSC (see Fig. 2) deal with different issues. The 'financial perspective' discusses the question of which target values can be derived from the financial expectations of the investors as stakeholders. The 'customer perspective' examines which objectives can be derived from the requirements of customers. The 'process perspective' analyses internal processes, e.g. in production, services or marketing. In the 'potential, learning or employee perspective', the potentials of human resources management must be analysed (Gerberich et al. 2006, p. 41).

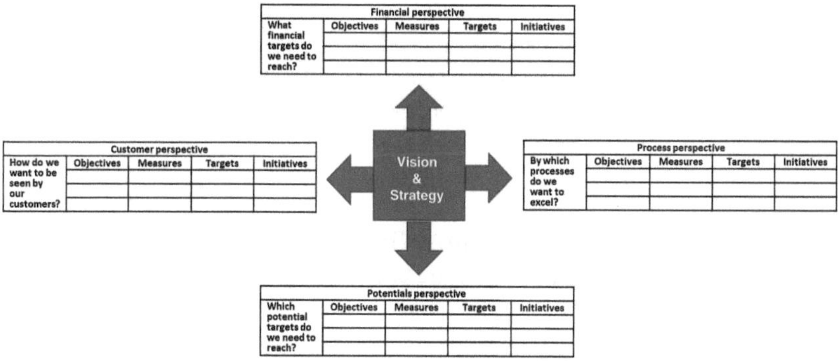

Fig. 2 Categorisation of the BSC according to perspectives – representation based on Kaplan and Norton (1997), p. 9 after. (Gerberich et al. 2006)

Year	Author	Country	Application of the BSC
2002	Horváth & Partners	D	Study with 97 companies following the introduction of a BSC: 78% of the participants rated the benefits of the BSC as positive, and for 89% of the study participants the concept will still be of great importance in the next three years.
2002	Tomschi et al.	D	38% of the companies surveyed have implemented a BSC
2002	Töpfer/Lin dstädt/Förster	D	Study with 194 companies, 17.2% have implemented a BSC
2003	Speckbacher/Bischof/Pfeiffer	D	Study with 174 companies, 26% have implemented a BSC
2006	Schachner/Speckbacher/Wentges	D	Study with 205 companies, 35% have implemented a BSC
2014	Hans-Jörg Vohl	D	Study with 138 medium-sized companies, 14% of the companies with up to 100 employees and 27% of the companies with more than 100 employees have implemented a BSC.

Fig. 3 Table of studies on the application of the BSC in organizations, (Vohl 2014, p. 2)

According to Horváth and Partners, the great interest in the Balanced Scorecard is due to a number of management problems. The dynamic working environment requires an efficient implementation of the necessary strategies. Here in particular, there are considerable shortcomings, as the implementation of poorly measurable statements in clearly defined target formulations and the associated measures cause enormous difficulties. The 2014 study by Vohl, "Balanced Scorecard im Mittelstand – Studie zum Einsatz der BSC in mittelständischen Unternehmen" (Balanced Scorecard in medium-sized companies – study on the use of the BSC in medium-sized companies), shows that the BSC is definitely also anchored in medium-sized companies. A comparison (in the form of a table, see Fig. 3) with other previous studies illustrates how high the interest is in implementing the BSC in companies. Horváth and Partners obtained the result that 78 percent of all companies surveyed considered the benefits of a BSC to be positive. The other studies, on the other hand, directly examined the degree of implementation in the companies and showed implementation in 17.2 percent to 38 percent of the companies surveyed (Vohl 2014, p. 2).

4 Analysis of the Common Good Balance Sheet and the Balanced Scorecard

The detailed analysis for commonalities follows the systematic of a qualitative content analysis according to Kuckartz 2018), to which the *"deductive-inductive category formation"* corresponds (ibid, 2018, p. 95). Here, "[…]a priori categories are started and in the second step the formation of categories or subcategories on the material […]" follows.

Using a kind of grid, the Common Good Balance Sheet and the various Balanced Scorecard questions are scanned, i.e. the existing material is searched for the corresponding content and categorised in the process, also referred to as "tag" in the following. In the second step, the formation of subcategories then takes place inductively, whereby only the material assigned to the respective main category is used (ibid. 2018, p. 96).

The investigation, analysis and categorization is done with Microsoft Excel, a standard tool in many companies. This allows free access to the created data for possible further use and adaptation to the organization.

5 Analytical Comparison of Key Figures and Mandatory Indicators of the Common Good Balance Sheet

The difficulty of a comparative analysis of both systems lies in their openness. The specifications in both the Balanced Scorecard and the Common Good Matrix are rather vaguely formulated.

However, the balanced scorecard as an extension for traditional accounting includes the valuation of intangible and intellectual assets of a company that has become necessary. Moreover, traditional financial measures only represent past events (cf. Kaplan & Norton, 1997 from Boersch and Elschen 2007, p. 139). Organisations are not required to adhere to a certain set of metrics for successful implementation of the BSC. These are [seen] as a "manifestation of a strategy" "because all metrics are linked in a cause-effect relationship" (ibid. 2007, p. 144). It can be concluded that depending on the strategy for the particular type of company, other key figures have the greatest significance and are therefore valid.

The common good economy is aimed at all types of organisations and companies. However, smaller companies are allowed to prepare an abbreviated compact balance sheet in order to clear the first hurdles. Micro-enterprises with less than ten employees can also execute it permanently. For the preparation of this paper, the so-called 'mandatory indicators' of the full balance sheet were used as a data basis. All questions of the report form were nevertheless screened. The almost 450 different questions of the report form that exist here are very long in terms of content, partly too public interest specific or contain questions that cannot be recorded in the regular operating procedure, without public interest accounting.

An example of such a question is: "Which of the products and services are luxury products that mostly 'just' serve one's status and can be replaced by cheaper, less resource-consuming products and services of the simple or good life?".

In this respect, the mandatory indicator of the ARC report "Share of benefit type in % of total sales: status symbols or luxury (... %)" was taken into account to ensure the completeness of the work. (Matrix Development Team 2017, p. 92).

The often shorter and more directly written 'mandatory indicators' of public good accounting are easier and quicker to answer, therefore the 'first-time user' can find his way around better. The selection of questions dealt with in the analysis is therefore not to be seen in a judgmental way, but rather serves to reduce complexity for newcomers to the field of public good accounting.

For the sake of readability, there is no separate source reference for the individual key figures. However, the Excel file prepared (in particular the tab of the table of the entire audited key figures with the name 'Key figures tag hits') shows the origin of the questions in individual columns in each case in order to ensure constant traceability.

The complete questions of the common good balance sheet originated from the "Workbook on the Common Good Balance Sheet 5.0" of the Matrix Development Team (Matrix-Entwicklungsteam 2017), they are the mandatory indicators for the preparation of the full balance sheet.

The indicators and questions of the Balanced Scorecard originate from different sources in order to represent a range of different types of scorecards. Due to this, the mass of BSC metrics analysed is to be considered relevant in this case. It ensures that as many different organisations as possible are addressed and that generalisation takes place through different approaches.[1]

[1] 'Classic metrics' of the BSC can be found from Hennig et al. (2008), from the title "100

The table (see Fig. 4) comprises 400 different key figures, each of which can be found in the rows under the heading Question/KPI[2] in 'Column A'. The next four columns sort the measures into the perspectives 'Process B', 'Customers C', 'Employees D' and 'Finances E', as defined by Kaplan and Norton's Balanced Scorecard.

The following columns F-J sort the key figures according to their origin. The order here is freely chosen. To ensure traceability and objectivity in all steps, all data of origin can be found in the table. The key figures from the book by Hennig et al, "100 Key Figures of the Balanced Scorecard", are marked with 'BSC 100′ and are located in 'Column F'. This is followed by 'G' with the metrics titled 'BSC Wissen' (Knowledge); these are the metrics from the book or the website of Dr. Fleig (2019). 'Column G' shows the data of the common good economy (GWM); this was marked by the column heading 'GWM Pflicht' (Compulsory). Labelled in 'Column I' is the data with the heading 'CSR-BSC' and is from the book by Neßler and Fischer (2013). The last column with data on origin is 'Column J', which shows data from the pocket guide to the BSC by Friedag and Schmidt (2011).

Subsequently, the sorting was done according to attributes, which can be found in the column with the heading 'Tag'. A 'tag' is a "marking element of description languages (e.g. HTML) for structuring documents" (Duden 2019) and marks the respective data with attributes or also codes. In the first step, these sort only generally and a-priori, which serves the overview and sorting. This means that a 'tag' does not necessarily have to be correct in the scientific sense. For example, the tag 'customer preferences' here is merely an attribute indicating that the metric is related to customers and the potential expectations of customers. Thus, data such as "number of product and service innovations with socio-ecological improvement that resulted from customer input" or "proportion of products with designated ingredients (as % of sales)" can be found under the aforementioned 'tag'. Another example for clarification can be found under the 'tag' 'employee satisfaction'. Here, both the metric 'costs due to workplace accidents' and 'implementation of suggestions for improvement' have been coded. Both key figures link 'the

metrics of the Balanced Scorecard"and Jürgen Fleig (2019) from the chapter on the Balanced Scorecard of the Management Handbook. To expand the portfolio, two specialized sources were additionally chosen: Friedag and Schmidt (2011) with the paperback book "Balanced Scorecard"and Neßler and Fischer (2013) with the book "Social-Responsive Balanced Scorecard". Both sources also deal with social aspects of the BSC and provide corresponding key figures in the analysis.

[2] KPI stands for Key Performance Indicator. However, this abbreviation has only been used in the table to improve readability.

Question/KPI	Process	Customers	Employees	Finances	BSC 100	BSCWisser	GWMPflict	CSRBSC	BSC Fried	Tag
Average sickness rate			Employees			BSC				Absence
Average sickness rate			Employees				GWM			Absence
Health/sickness ratio (depending on demographic distribution), number of days on which employees come to work despite sickness			Employees							Absence
Sickness rate			Employees		BSC 100				Friedag	Absence
Sickness ration (only Mondays and Fridays, in %)			Employees							Plants/ equipment
Yearly absence structure					BSC 100					Plants/ equipment
Plants/equipment yield (quality efficiency)	Process				BSC 100					Plants/ equipment
Plants/equipment performance (performance efficiency)	Process				BSC 100					Plants/ equipment
Plants/equipment availability (availability efficiency)	Process				BSC 100					Plants/ equipment
Additions to assets (in 1000 EUR)				Finance			GWM			Plants/ equipment
Up to three main financial partners; for each partner name, financial product and sales volume per year				Finance			GWM			Investment strategy
Country-specific reporting from 10 % of turnover: investment volume				Finance			GWM			Investment strategy
Country-specific reporting from 10 % of turnover: renting and leasing				Finance			GWM			Investment strategy
Age structure			Employees		BSC 100					Employment contracts
Share of part-time jobs; distribution of flexible working time models			Employees					CSR BSC		Employment contracts
Share of fixed-term contracts			Employees				GWM			Employment contracts
Number of employees (incl. temporary staff)			Employees				GWM			Employment contracts
Number of dismissals			Employees					CSR BSC		Employment contracts
Number of executives/employees with individual working models (e.g. part-time, job sharing			Employees				GWM			Employment contracts
Number of hierarchical levels per 100 employees			Employees			BSC				Employment contracts
Number of men/women in management positions			Employees					CSR BSC		Employment contracts
Number of zero-hours contracts			Employees				GWM			Employment contracts
Number of lump-sum contracts			Employees				GWM			Employment contracts
Number of temporary employees			Employees				GWM			Employment contracts
Number of paternal/maternal leaves in months			Employees				GWM			Employment contracts

Fig. 4 Extract of the table in Excel, analysis of the key figures sorted. (Own representation 2019)

well-being of employees', even if occupational accidents cannot be linked to general satisfaction in this way.

The filter function of the 'tags' is important to find the greatest possible overlaps and replaces the coding in the qualitative analysis. The process was checked in several loops so that individual key figures were partially tagged with the best possible tag in order to create as little data as possible with individual tags without duplication. This was checked and evaluated in a pivot table. Thus, the rows of 400 metrics in the table have been tagged with a total of 50 tags. These are:

Absence	Social/societal responsibility	Environmental sustainability
Attachments	Profit Taxes	Pricing
Investment strategy	Production costs	Product age
Employment contracts	Information	Production
Workload Employees	Innovations	Productivity
Committee	Capital	Process
Reporting	Corruption	Range
Length of service	Customer turnover	Software
Application	Customer requests	Donations Turnover
Cash Flow	Customer satisfaction	Sales
Contribution margin	Stock	Further education
Lead time	Deliveries	Advertising
Success rate	Lobby	Reseller
Trade press	Market share	Drawings
Fluctuation rate	Employee engagement	Investments in the future
contractors	Employee satisfaction	Products
Borrowed capital	Co-determination	

The indicators with the tags 'investment strategy', 'future investments' and 'lobby' are omitted from the further analysis, as they only occur in the common good economy and thus have no application in the Balanced Scorecard.

The same was done with the data with the tag 'donation turnover'. Here, there was a match between the GWÖ and the BSC according to Friedag. However, the individual examination showed that the common connection is missing. In Friedag, donations are to be seen as turnover, since the key figures are applied in the area of a non-profit association. In the GWM question, the 'disclosure of party donations on the basis of turnover' was asked; there is no counterpart to this in the other key figures.

The opposite test in a pivot table resulted in a further reduction of the key figures to be compared. All 'tags' that contain data from questions of the BSC but no further questions from the common good economy were not included in the further analysis. Commonality or overlap is excluded due to the lack of a basis for comparison.

Omitted for this reason are:

Utilization	Stock
Employees	Deliveries
Committee	Lobby
Contribution margin	Product age
Lead time	Production
Success rate	Productivity
Trade press	Process
Production costs	Range
Information	Software
Innovations	Reseller
Customer turnover	Drawings
Customer satisfaction	

The selection processes do not arise from the importance or necessity for the respective source, but result purely from the analytical and qualitative consideration regarding commonalities.

The only verbatim match can be found in the key figures of the tag 'fluctuation rate' (cf. Fig. 5).

This key figure can be found in the 'BSC 100', in 'BSC Knowledge' as well as in the 'Gemeinwohlökonomie'. A detailed examination of the complete tag "Fluctuation rate" takes place in the separate analysis item 'Fluctuation rate'.

In alphabetical order follows the content analysis of the 'tags' and key figures based on existing literature.

Question/KPI	Process	Customers	Employees	Finances	BSC 100	BSCWissen	GWMPflicht	CSRBSC	BSC Fried	Tag
Fluctuation rate			Employees			BSC				Fluctuation rate
Fluctuation rate			Employees		BSC 100					Fluctuation rate
Fluctuation rate			Employees				GWM			Fluctuation rate

Fig. 5 Extract from the Excel spreadsheet for analysis – Questions on the tag – 'Fluctuation rate'. (Own representation 2019)

5.1 Absence

The ratios under the ‘tag’ ‘absence’ (cf. Fig. 6) differ only minimally in their wording and can be regarded as straightforward ratios.

In the question, the common good economy additionally considers the “days on which employees come to work despite illness”. Here, the value would have to be estimated. An exact recording of this data appears difficult within the framework of the creation of a balanced scorecard. All key figures can be found in the perspective area of the employees. Due to the repeated occurrence in the various Balanced Scorecard areas, the probability of use as a BSC key figure is high.

5.2 Reporting

The analysis of the ‘tag’ ‘reporting’ (cf. Fig. 7) shows that there are no similarities. The reporting question of the Economy of the Common Good is specific and only refers to the recording of publications of a social or ecological nature. The two BSC indicators in the reporting area do not provide any information on this.

5.3 Seniority

The “seniority structure” (cf. Fig. 8) and the “average length of service” correspond to the same key figures and would therefore be straightforward for the user of an existing balanced scorecard in GWÖ accounting.

Question/KPI	Process	Customers	Employees	Finances	BSC 100	BSCWissen	GWMPflicht	CSRBSC	BSC Fried	Tag
Average sickness rate			Employees			BSC				Absence
Health/sickness ratio (depending on demographic distribution), number of days on which employees come to work despite sickness			Employees				GWM			Absence
Sickness rate			Employees		BSC 100					Absence
Sickness ration (only Mondays and Fridays, in %)			Employees						Friedag	Absence
Yearly absence structure			Employees		BSC 100					Absence

Fig. 6 Extract from the Excel spreadsheet for analysis – Questions on the tag – ‘Absence’. (Own representation 2019)

Question/KPI	Process	Customers	Employees	Finances	BSC 100	BSCWissen	GWMPflicht	CSRBSC	BSC Fried	Tag
Number of key figures included in reporting	Process					BSC				Reporting
Speed of final reports			Employees			BSC				Reporting
Publication of a public interest report or equivalent reporting of a social nature	Process						GWM			Reporting

Fig. 7 Extract from Excel spreadsheet for analysis – Questions on the tag – ‘Reporting’. (Own representation 2019)

Question/KPI	Process	Customers	Employees	Finances	BSC 100	BSCWissen	GWMPflicht	CSRBSC	BSC Fried	Tag
Length of service			Employees		BSC 100					Length of service
Average length of service			Employees				GWM			Company affiliation

Fig. 8 Extract from the Excel spreadsheet for analysis – Questions on the tag – 'Length of service'. (Own representation 2019)

Question/KPI	Process	Customers	Employees	Finances	BSC 100	BSCWissen	GWMPflicht	CSRBSC	BSC Fried	Tag
Fluctuation rate			Employees			BSC				Fluctuation rate
Fluctuation rate			Employees		BSC 100					Fluctuation rate
Fluctuation rate			Employees				GWM			Fluctuation rate

Fig. 9 Table in Excel. Analysis of the ratio – Applications.PNG. (Own presentation 2019)

Question/KPI	Process	Customers	Employees	Finances	BSC 100	BSCWissen	GWMPflicht	CSRBSC	BSC Fried	Tag
Fluctuation rate			Employees			BSC				Fluctuation rate
Fluctuation rate			Employees		BSC 100					Fluctuation rate
Fluctuation rate			Employees				GWM			Fluctuation rate
Early turnover rate			Employees		BSC 100					Fluctuation rate
Cancellation rate			Employees		BSC 100					Fluctuation rate
Quit rate for employees hired in the last five years			Employees			BSC				Fluctuation rate
Cancellation rate in the last five years			Employees		BSC 100					Fluctuation rate
Number of new hires/fluctuations disaggregated by dimensions (e.g. age, gender, ethnicity, physical/mental disabilities, sexual orientation, religion - if collectible and relevant) and separately by management levels										

Fig. 10 Extract from the Excel table for analysis – Questions on the tag – 'Fluctuation rate' total. (Own representation 2019)

5.4 Application

The same applies to the key figures from the area of applications (cf. Fig. 9). Although the questions differ minimally, the general number of applications must be determined in order to record an "increase in applications". The data basis for the question on public interest accounting is therefore even easier to obtain.

5.5 Fluctuation Rate

The key figure "fluctuation rate" (cf. Fig. 10) from the same 'tag' has already been mentioned; this is where the only word-for-word correspondence between the two systems arises. The 'turnover rate' does not exist as a key figure in the common good economy and must therefore be neglected for further analyses. An additional required mandatory question in the common good accounting requires a breakdown by management levels, ethnic groups or religions.

5.6 External Companies

The ‘tagging’ for the key figure ‘external companies’ comprises a lot of data (cf. Fig. 11). Here, coding into a second level is necessary in order to be able to carry out an analysis for similarities. Under the ‘tag’ ‘contractor share’, similar questions can be found, both for the common good balance sheet and for the ‘BSC Friedag’ and ‘BSC 100’. However, it should be distinguished that the ‘contractor share’ is not the same as the ‘contractor employee share’, whereas contractor employees are part of the ‘contractor share’.

The question about “purchased services” is similar to Friedag’s question about the “share of (third-party) services in total sales”, and a recording of the data must be available for this question in the Friedag BSC. Thus, it is usable for public good reporting.

In the second question in the picture, the common good economy aims at the “equitably distributed share in the value creation process of all suppliers” (Matrix Development Team 2017, p. 21). It is not possible to use the BSC data because the questions of the BSC are too different compared to the GWÖ.

The four questions under the term ‘outside companies – ethics’ have no correspondence in the area of BSC and GWÖ (cf. Fig. 12).

Question/KPI	Process	Customers	Employees	Finances	BSC 100	BSCWissen	GWMPflicht	CSRBSC	BSC Fried	Tag	Tag
Share of (third-party) services in total sales (in %)	Process								Friedag	Contractors	Share
Proportion of external employees			Employees		BSC100					Contractors	Share
Share of purchased products/services in total purchasing volume in tabular form	Process						GWM			Contractors	Share
Estimated ratio of share of value added between enterprise and supplier	Process						GWM			Contractors	Share

Fig. 11 Extract from the Excel spreadsheet for the analysis – Questions on the tag – ‘contractor share’. (Own representation 2019)

Question/KPI	Process	Customers	Employees	Finance	BSC 100	BSCWissen	GWM Pflicht	CSR BSC	BSC Fried	Tag	Tag
Proportion of suppliers with whom fair and solidarity-based dealings with stakeholders were discussed or who were selected on this basis.	Process						GWM			Contractors	Ethics
Proportion of suppliers with whom a transparent and participatory approach to stakeholders was discussed or who were selected on this basis.	Process						GWM			Contractors	Ethics
Number of lawsuits for anticompetitive behavior Principles of conduct in dealing with business partners regarding fair business practices	Process							CSR BSC		Contractors	Ethics
Principles of conduct in dealing with competitors	Process							CSR BSC		Contractors	Ethics

Fig. 12 Extract from the Excel spreadsheet for analysis – Questions on the tag – ‘Contractors – ethics’. (Own representation 2019)

Two questions for the preparation of the CSR BSC include “dealing with competitors” and “possible complaints in competition”; the common good economy deals with “dealing with suppliers” in each case.

In the entire area of the key figures for the ‘tag’ ‘external companies’, no further agreement can be found; the Gemeinwohlökonomie has a unique selling point here. For ‘cooperation’, ‘the valuation of comparisons with competitors in communication’ and the ‘duration of business relationships’ cannot be found in the audited BSC key figures.

5.7 Debt Capital

The book with the key figures ‘BSC 100’ contains the question about the “debt coefficient”, here it is about the “share of debt capital in equity capital “(Hennig et al. 2008, p. 134).In the GWÖ this question is also present and can be easily adopted (cf. Fig. 13). A commonality in the question “financing, broken down by type of financing “of GWÖ cannot be clarified exactly. The ratios cannot be recorded as a commonality. Although it is likely that for a listing of the borrowed capital, the origin of the funds must be clarified and recorded.

5.8 Profit Taxes

The reporting questions of the common good balance (cf. Fig. 14) are asked in great detail in this ‘tag’. The question about the “difference between gross and net payroll “is related to the “net tax ratio“, therefore it is not a value which falls under the tag ‘labour contracts’ and thus justifies tagging (Matrix Development Team 2017, p. 98).

Furthermore, the common good balance sheet asks for “country-specific reporting “on “taxes ““profit “etc., these points can most likely be answered if the controlling key figure is available in the company. Each company is free to decide

Question/KPI	Process	Customers	Employees	Finance	BSC 100	BSC Wissen	GWM Pflicht	CSR BSC	BSC Fried	Tag
Financing by type (EUR thousand)				Finance			GWM			Borrowed capital
Debt ratio (% share of debt)				Finance			GWM			Borrowed capital
Debt coefficient				Finance	BSC 100					Borrowed capital

Fig. 13 Extract from the Excel spreadsheet for analysis – Questions on the tag – ‘Debt capital’. (Own representation 2019)

Question/KPI	Process	Customers	Employees	Finances	BSC 100	BSCWisse	GWMPflict	CSRBSC	BSC Fried	Tag
EBIT				Finance	BSC 100					Profit Taxes
Capital income to be distributed (in EUR thousand, as a % of the share capital)				Finance			GWM			Profit Taxes
Difference between gross and net payroll (sum of wage tax and SI contributions of salaried employees), less all company-related subsidies and grants. "These net levies are related to the reported value added (profit before tax plus interest on borrowed capital plus income from rents and leases) and thus result in the net levy ratio.			Employees	Finance			GWM			Profit Taxes
EBITDA				Finance	BSC 100					Profit Taxes
profit or revenue				Finance		BSC				Profit Taxes
profit before tax				Finance	BSC 100					Profit Taxes
Profit due to employees				Finance			GWM			Profit Taxes
Net income (profit)				Finance	BSC 100					Profit Taxes
Country-specific reporting from 10% of sales: tax performance and social security contributions (broken down by tax type: income tax, payroll tax, etc.)				Finance			GWM			Profit Taxes
Country-specific reporting from 10% of sales: Value added: profit before taxes plus interest on borrowings plus income from				Finance			GWM			Profit Taxes
Net cash provided by operating activities (in EUR thousand)				Finance			GWM			Profit Taxes
Net tax ratio: income taxes actually paid (income tax, corporate income tax) payroll taxes and employers' social security contributions				Finance			GWM			Profit Taxes
Gross profit margin				Finance	BSC 100					Profit Taxes

Fig. 14 Extract from the Excel spreadsheet for analysis – Questions on the tag – 'Profit Taxes'. (Own representation 2019)

which data is included in the BSC; however, since strategy development should be communicated and implemented across all levels in the company, country-specific reporting is likely. “A proliferation of scorecards must be prevented, so this is another reason why the process should be started at the highest possible level.” (Horváth and Kaufmann 1998, p. 49).

To facilitate the analysis, a second column is also used in the second ‘tag’ ‘profit taxes’ (cf. Fig. 15). Profit’ is present as a key figure in both classic BSC variants and in the common good economy. The key figures are identical and can clearly be used for both types of reporting.

“EBIT” and “EBITDA” are “cash flow” approximations. For both ratios (cf. Fig. 16), the tax-adjusted income is determined including any rental and leasing income, but also before interest (Hennig et al. 2008, 115 f.).

In addition to the data already mentioned, the common good economy asks for social security contributions. Provided that these and the associated wages are known, the result of the ratios can be used for common good accounting. The same database allows for simplification and can be considered as a figure that is already known. A transfer to the “country-specific reporting” is also possible if the “EBIT” or “EBITDA” have already been calculated for this country (see point 3.3.11 Profit Taxes). The question about the “investment income to be distributed” refers primarily to the social or ethical use of funds, e.g. no distribution of income as long as there is still debt capital in the company (Matrix Development Team 2017, 39f.).

No comparable key figure can be found here in the BSC.

5.9 Capital

The ‘tag’ ‘capital’ also consists of many key figures and questions. Here, the analysis by a second set of attributes becomes necessary in order to be able to analyze in the exclusion procedure (cf. Fig. 17).

Under the tag ‘capital – equity’, two different questions of the common good economy can be found. The “average equity ratio compared to other industries” is

Question/KPI	Process	Customers	Employees	Finances	BSC 100	BSCWissen	GWMPflicht	CSRBSC	BSC Fried	Tag	Column I
Profit or revenue				Finance		BSC				Profit taxes	Profit
Profit before tax				Finance	BSC 100					Profit taxes	Profit
Profit due to employees				Finance			GWM			Profit taxes	Profit
Net income (profit)				Finance	BSC 100					Profit taxes	Profit
Gross profit margin				Finance	BSC 100					Profit taxes	Profit

Fig. 15 Extract from the Excel spreadsheet for analysis – Questions on the tag – ‘Profit Tax – Profit’. (Own representation 2019)

Question/KPI	Process	Customers	Employees	Finances	BSC 100	BSCWissen	GWMPflicht	CSRBSC	BSC Fried	Tag	Column I
EBIT				Finance						Profit taxes	other
Capital income to be distributed (in EUR thousand, as % of share capital)				Finance			GWM			Profit taxes	other
Difference between gross and net wage bill (sum of wage tax and SI contributions of salaried employees), less all company-related subsidies and grants " These net levies are applied to the reported value added (profit before tax plus interest on borrowings plus income from rents and leases) and thus result in the net tax ratio."			Employees	Finance			GWM			Profit taxes	other
EBITDA				Finance	BSC 100					Profit taxes	other
Country-specific reporting from 10 % of turnover: tax performance and social security contributions (broken down by tax type: income tax, payroll tax, etc.)				Finance			GWM			Profit taxes	other
Country-specific reporting from 10% of sales: Value added: profit before taxes plus interest on borrowings plus income from				Finance			GWM			Profit taxes	other
Net cash provided by operating activities (in EUR thousand)				Finance	BSC 100		GWM			Profit taxes	other
Net tax ratio: income taxes actually paid (income tax, corporate income tax) payroll-related taxes and employers' social security contributions				Finance			GWM			Profit taxes	other

Fig. 16 Extract from the Excel spreadsheet for analysis – Questions on the tag – 'Profit – other'. (Own representation 2019)

Question/KPI	Process	Customers	Employees	Finances	BSC 100	BSCWissen	GWMPflicht	CSRBSC	BSC Fried	Tag	Tag 2
Average equity ratio of the industry				Finance			GWM			Capital	Equity
Equity share				Finance			GWM			Capital	Equity
Equity ratio				Finance	BSC 100					Capital	Equity
Return on equity				Finance	BSC 100					Capital	Equity
Return on equity				Finance		BSC				Capital	Equity

Fig. 17 Extract from the Excel spreadsheet for analysis – Questions on the tag – 'Capital – equity'. (Own representation 2019)

Question/KPI	Process	Customers	Employees	Finance	BSC 100	BSCWissen	GWM Pflicht	CSR BSC	BSC Fried	Tag	Tag
Distribution of equity (equity structure in %, each from 0 to 100 %): Managers				Finance						Capital	Share
Distribution of equity (equity structure in %, each from 0 to 100 %): Customers				Finance			GWM			Capital	Share
Distribution of equity (equity structure in %, each from 0 to 100 %): Suppliers				Finance			GWM	CSR BSC		Capital	Share
Distribution of equity (equity structure in %, each from 0 to 100 %): Employees				Finance			GWM	CSR BSC		Capital	Share
Distribution of equity capital (equity capital structure in %, from 0 to 100 % in each case): non-participating				Finance			GWM			Capital	Share
Distribution of equity (equity structure in %, each from 0 to 100 %): Female entrepreneurs				Finance			GWM			Capital	Share
Distribution of equity (equity structure in %, each from 0 to 100 %): Other environment				Finance			GWM			Capital	Share

Fig. 18 Extract from the Excel spreadsheet for analysis – Questions on the tag – 'Capital – Share in'. (Own representation 2019)

not found in any of the BSC key figures. However, the required "equity ratio" is the same as the key figure from BSC 100 of the "equity ratio" and is therefore identical. It can be used both in the BSC and in public good accounting.

The "distribution of equity to stakeholders, e.g. customers" is a question specific to the common good economy (cf. Fig. 18) and is not reflected in any of the BSC indicators. All other indicators under this point are not found in the common good economy and can therefore be neglected in the analysis.

5.10 Customer Requirements

There are four key figures in the 'tag' of 'customer desires' (cf. Fig. 19) that originate from the GWÖ. Data from the 'CSR – BSC' are similar to these.

The question about "lack of declaration of hazardous substances" can be equated with the question from the CSR BSC: "Proportion of products with declared ingredients". This correspondence leads to the facilitation of the public good balance sheet preparation.

Furthermore, the 'CSR – BSC' question on "voluntary information" can address two GWÖ questions at the same time, namely the "share of published price components" and the question on the "number and type of incidents in which voluntary and statutory information obligations" are compared.

Question/KPI	Process	Customers	Employees	Finances	BSC 100	BSCWissen	GWMPflict	CSRBSC	BSC Fried	Tag
Number and type of incidents of non-compliance with voluntary and statutory information requirements		Customers						CSRBSC		Customer requests
Voluntary information		Customers						CSRBSC		Customer requests
Number of newly identified customer requests	Process					BSC				Customer requests
Share of products with declared ingredients (in % of sales)	Process						GWM			Customer requests
Percentage of products containing hazardous substances or posing a risk in use that are not transparently declared to the public (in % of sales)	Process						GWM			Customer requests
Share of products and services with published price components (in % of sales)	Process						GWM			Customer requests
Number of product and service innovations with socio-ecological improvement, which were created through the participation of female customers.	Process	Customers					GWM			Customer requests

Fig. 19 Extract from the Excel spreadsheet for analysis – Questions on the tag – 'Customer wishes'. (Own representation 2019)

Question/KPI	Process	Customers	Employees	Finances	BSC 100	BSCWissen	GWMPflicht	CSRBSC	BSC Fried	Tag	Column 1
Share of recognised trade unions in total existing trade unions			Employees					CSR BSC		Employee engagement	Union
Proportion of employees involved in committees			Employees			BSC				Employee engagement	Union
Number/content of complaints from the works council, the AK or the trade union in the reporting period and reaction to these complaints			Employees				GWM			Employee engagement	Union
Works council: present/absent; since when?)			Employees				GWM			Employee engagement	Union
Statement by works council and/or personnel department on these issues (inhumane working conditions)sales)			Employees				GWM			Employee engagement	Union

Fig. 20 Extract from Excel spreadsheet for analysis – Questions on the tag – 'Employee Engagement – Trade Union'. (Own representation 2019)

However, due to the extremely vaguely formulated CSR BSC question, an answer can be given in such a differentiated way that an aid for the preparation of the ARC is questionable and thus not recognizable.

5.11 Employee Engagement

The topic 'Employee Engagement' contains key figures from both systems (see Fig. 20). For structuring purposes, the table was provided with a second 'tag' in order to be able to analyse similarities.

The table in Fig. 20 shows the question with the 'tag' 'employee engagement' and 'union'. Even if membership of a trade union is not necessary in the works council, this is often common and thus justifies the tagging.

The 'BSC Knowledge' question about "employees involved in committees" can be equated with the question about the "existence of a works council" in GWÖ. Here, in any case, an involvement in the works council would have to be mentioned.

Question/KPI	Process	Customers	Employees	Finances	BSC 100	BSCWissen	GWMPflicht	CSRBSC	BSC Fried	Tag	Column I
Number and extent of occupational accidents			Employees				GWM			Employee satisfaction	Industrial accidents
Costs due to occupational accidents	Process					BSC		CSR BSC		Employee satisfaction	Industrial accidents
Accident rate			Employees		BSC 100					Employee satisfaction	Industrial accidents
Injuries, occupational diseases, days lost (as a percentage of employees)	Process							CSR BSC		Employee satisfaction	Industrial accidents

Fig. 21 Extract from the Excel spreadsheet for analysis – Questions on the tag – 'Employee satisfaction – occupational accidents'. (Own representation 2019)

However, the statement from the works council cannot be answered with questions from the BSC. The "complaints and related claims" are also not to be found in a BSC.

All other tags have no content of the common good economy and therefore do not require analysis.

5.12 Employee Satisfaction

The tag "Employee satisfaction" (cf. Fig. 21) contains a lot of data, so that the analysis was supported here with an additional column.

The question of the common good economy regarding 'occupational accidents' includes the "number and extent". Both the CSR BSC and the BSC 100 record occupational accidents. The data from the BSC 100 records the 'accident rate'. This captures all hours lost due to accidents (including non-occupational). This is therefore irrelevant to the GWÖ question.

In order to record the "costs due to industrial accidents", one needs the "number of these accidents". Here, a match can be recorded, which leads to the facilitation of the public good balance sheet preparation.

The remaining metrics of the Employee Satisfaction tag are not consistent with the Common Good Economy or are not included in it.

5.13 Environmental Sustainability

Ecological sustainability consists of many key figures, here again a division into further 'tags' is necessary (cf. Fig. 22).

The question of the common good economy about the "use of other consumables in kilograms" finds a match.

Question/KPI	Process	Customers	Employees	Finances	BSC 100	BSCWissen	GWMPflicht	CSRBSC	BSC Fried	Tag	Tag 2
Number of recyclable materials/total materials Biodiversity:	Process							CSR BSC		Environmental sustainability	Material
Average product life		Customers						CSR BSC		Environmental sustainability	Material
Use of regenerable substances/total substances	Process							CSR BSC		Environmental sustainability	Material
Use of hazardous substances/total substances	Process							CSR BSC		Environmental sustainability	Material
Use of other consumables (kg)	Process						GWM			Environmental sustainability	Material
Optimization of resource and energy use along the value chain	Process							CSR BSC		Environmental sustainability	Material

Fig. 22 Extract from the Excel spreadsheet for analysis – Questions on the tag – 'Environmental sustainability – Material'. (Own representation 2019)

Question/KPI	Process	Customers	Employees	Finances	BSC 100	BSCWissen	GWMPflicht	CSRBSC	BSC Fried	Tag	Tag 2
Degree of acceptance of the ecological company offer among employees in %.	Process		Employees							Environmental sustainability	Employees
Proportion of travel by car, public transport, bicycle or on foot			Employees				GWM			Environmental sustainability	Employees
Proportion of catering from organic sources	Process		Employees				GWM			Environmental sustainability	Employees
Behavioural principles relating to the environmentally conscious use of resources in the workplace			Employees					CSR BSC		Environmental sustainability	Employees
Provision of the necessary expertise to anchor environmental problems in the consciousness of employees			Employees					CSR BSC		Environmental sustainability	Employees

Fig. 23 Extract from the Excel spreadsheet for analysis – Questions on the tag – 'Environmental sustainability – Employees'. (Own representation 2019)

Question/KPI	Process	Customers	Employees	Finances	BSC 100	BSCWissen	GWMPflicht	CSRBSC	BSC Fried	Tag	Tag 2
Projects financed (in EUR thousand; % of investment) Social-ecological				Finance			GWM			Environmental sustainability	Projects
Fund investments (in EUR thousand; % of investment) Social-ecological				Finance			GWM			Environmental sustainability	Projects
Capital expenditure related to uni-environmental protection measures	Process						GWM	CSR BSC		Environmental sustainability	Projects
Investment plan incl. ecological refurbishment requirements (in thou.)				Finance						Environmental sustainability	Projects
Realisation of ecological refurbishment (in EUR thousand and %)				Finance			GWM			Environmental sustainability	Projects
Relevant comparative values regarding environmental accounts or (see E3.1) in the sector or region Impact indicators	Process						GWM			Environmental sustainability	Projects

Fig. 24 Extract from the Excel spreadsheet for analysis – Questions on the tag – 'Environmental sustainability – Projects'. (Own representation 2019)

The value chain also includes, for example, the administrative area. In order to be able to optimise "resources and energy use", the current use must be recorded.

This makes it easier to answer the question in the public good accounting, provided that this indicator is available in the CSR BSC.

There is no agreement on the point of 'environmental sustainability' in relation to 'employees' (cf. Fig. 23); the questions differ in principle.

The 'CSR BSC' asks about "principles and transfer of expertise", the common good economy uses questions about "acceptance and share level of environmental sustainability" in the various sectors.

Under the tag 'Environmental Sustainability – Projects' (cf. Fig. 24), there is no further correspondence; the Social Responsibility Scorecard asks the question about "capital expenditure in relation to environmental protection measures", while the Gemeinwohlökonomie asks about the "amount of financed projects of social-ecological origin".

It should be noted here that the GWÖ questions under the item "financed projects" examine the investment strategies of financial resources, for example in funds or the granting of mini-loans. (Matrix Development Team 2017, 42f.)

The necessary reporting on the consumption of resources (cf. Fig. 25) is available in great detail in the common good economy.

The 'CSR BSC' offers two metrics on this topic. The 'energy efficiency' does not find a match in the GWÖ, but the 'direct and indirect energy consumption' can be equated with the indicators for 'electricity consumption' and 'heating energy'. Here, the CSR BSC offers support for public good accounting.

No further hits could be determined.

5.14 Turnover

Despite a wealth of data from key figures and questions, this 'tag' does not require any further sorting (cf. Fig. 26).

The questions about the "subsidy amount and interest payments for intangible services" are not found in any of the BSC indicators.

The "allocation to reserves" is also not included in any of the key figures.

An "ethical approach to products and services" is also not present in the BSC.

'Sales' as a metric is used in many ways in the Balanced Scorecard; as discussed in the 'Profit' tag, this also applies to foreign based subsidiaries/branches/production facilities.

None of the BSC metrics address the issue of "sales targets" separately; however, if "sales" is present as a metric in the company, there will be a target for this.

This ratio can therefore be used to answer the first question in the table and is a facilitator in the preparation of the public good balance sheet.

5.15 Continuing Training and Education

The key figures on the subject of continuing training (cf. Fig. 27) require a more differentiated view and have been subdivided into 'tags' once again.

The key figures with the attributes on the topic 'number' (related to hours/days or employees) are similar. The common good economy poses the question of "development opportunities per employee".

Question/KPI	Process	Customers	Employees	Finances	BSC 100	BSCWissen	GWMPflicht	CSRBSC	BSC Fried	Tag	Tag 2
Emissions of climate-impacting gases [kg	Process						GWM			Environmental sustainability	Consumption
Petrol consumption (and its CO2 equivalent) | litres or kg	Process						GWM			Environmental sustainability	Consumption
Chemical consumption (toxic, non-toxic) [kg]	Process						GWM			Environmental sustainability	Consumption
Direct and indirect energy consumption	Process						GWM	CSR BSC		Environmental sustainability	Consumption
Energy efficiency along the use phase		Customers					GWM	CSR BSC		Environmental sustainability	Consumption
Gas consumption (and its CO2 equivalent) | kWh or kg	Process						GWM			Environmental sustainability	Consumption
Heating energy (in relation to the respective average temperature) | kWh/°C							GWM			Environmental sustainability	Consumption
Artificial lighting | Lumen, kwh	Process						GWM			Environmental sustainability	Consumption
Paper consumption [kg]	Process						GWM			Environmental sustainability	Consumption
Pollutant emissions and other environmental impacts | according to the respective standard impact category	Process						GWM			Environmental sustainability	Consumption
Electricity consumption (and its CO2 equivalent) | kWh or kg	Process						GWM			Environmental sustainability	Consumption
Transport (and its CO2 equivalent) | km or kg	Process						GWM			Environmental sustainability	Consumption
Consumption of drinking water and rainwater m3	Process						GWM			Environmental sustainability	Consumption

Fig. 25 Extract from the Excel spreadsheet for analysis – Questions on the tag – ‘Environmental sustainability – Consumption’. (Own representation 2019)

Question/KPI	Process	Customers	Employees	Finances	BSC 100	BSCWisser	GWMPflict	CSRBSC	BSC Fried	Tag
Internal sales targets from the company: yes/no?				Finance			GWM	CSRBSC		Sales
Country-specific reporting from 10 % of turnover: subsidy amount				Finance			GWM	CSRBSC		Sales
Country-specific reporting from 10% of turnover: Turnover				Finance			GWM			Sales
Country-specific reporting from 10 % of sales: interest payments and payments for intangible services (especially license fees) to foreign branches or partners				Finance			GWM			Sales
Sales				Finance			GWM			Sales
Share of sales of the unethical products and services listed here	Process						GWM			Sales
Allocation to the reserve (in EUR thousand)				Finance			GWM			Sales
Duration of the invoicing and collection period	Process					BSC				Sales
Scope of solvency				Finance		BSC				Sales
Paragraph change		Customers			BSC100					Sales
Markdown rate	Process				BSC100					Sales
Offer success rate (response rate)		Customers			BSC100					Sales
Days Sales Outstanding (DSO)				Finance	BSC100					Sales
Human capital return on investment (HCROI)			Employees		BSC100					Sales
Second degree liquidity				Finance	BSC100					Sales
Turnover per joint engineering day	Process					BSC				Sales
Turnover per employee				Finance	BSC100					Sales
Return on sales				Finance						Sales
Return on sales				Finance		BSC				Sales
Sales growth						BSC				Sales
Value added per hour					BSC100	BSC				Sales
Payment target deviation		Customers		Finance	BSC100					Sales
Purchasing Power Index		Customers		Finance	BSC100					Sales
Return on capital employed (ROCE)				Finance	BSC100					Sales

Fig. 26 Extract from the Excel spreadsheet for analysis – Questions on the tag – 'Turnover'. (Own representation 2019)

Question/KPI	Process	Customers	Employees	Finances	BSC 100	BSCWissen	GWMPflicht	CSRBSC	BSC Fried	Tag	Column I
Development opportunities offered and taken advantage of (professional and personal) in hours per employee or according to management level			Employees				GWM			Continuing education	Number
Number of training and further education courses			Employees					CSR BSC		Continuing education	Number
Number of training days per full-time equivalent and year			Employees		BSC 100					Continuing education	Number
Average number of hours for training/employee			Employees					CSR BSC		Continuing education	Number
Use of training courses (in days)			Employees						Friedag	Continuing education	Number
Percentage of employees trained/total number of employees	Process							CSR BSC		Continuing education	Number
Qualification structure			Employees		BSC 100					Continuing education	Number
Number of employees trained in health and safety/total number of employees	Process							CSR BSC		Continuing education	Number

Fig. 27 Extract from the Excel table for analysis – Questions on the tag – 'Continuing education number'. (Own representation 2019)

Question/KPI	Process	Customers	Employees	Finances	BSC 100	BSCWissen	GWMPflicht	CSRBSC	BSC Fried	Tag	Column I
Offers taken up by employees: Content and number of hours per employee - Occupational health and safety			Employees				GWM			Continuing education	Safety
Training of employees with regard to health and safety standards		Customers	Employees					CSR BSC		Continuing education	Safety

Fig. 28 Extract from the Excel spreadsheet for analysis – Questions on the tag – 'Continuing education safety'. (Own representation 2019)

The CSR BSC, the BSC 100 and Friedag record the "number of training and development days per employee". The key figure can be used to answer the GWÖ without any further action.

No further agreement is found on the topic of "safety" (cf. Fig. 28). Although both systems ask about "training on the topic of safety", the GWÖ question refers to "occupational health and safety" (Matrix Development Team 2017, p. 51), while the CSR question refers to "training in the area of product standards". (Neßler and Fischer 2013, p. 74).

All other tags under the topic "safety" respectively "security" do not contain questions of the common good economy.

5.16 Advertising

The 'tag' 'advertising' contains three questions from the GWÖ balancing (cf. Fig. 29).

The question about the "number of people reached" is designed to disseminate social and ecological principles and therefore does not receive any further attention (Matrix Entwicklungsteam 2017, 93f.)

Question/KPI	Process	Customers	Employees	Finances	BSC 100	BSCWissen	GWMPflicht	CSRBSC	BSC Fried	Tag
Proportion of advertising spend allocated to ethical and unethical campaigns	Process	Customers					GWM			Advertising
Number of people reached, e.g. readers, visitors	Process	Customers					GWM			Advertising
Overview of budgets for marketing, sales, advertising: Expenditure on measures or campaigns	Process						GWM			Advertising
Analysis of media reports	Process							CSR BSC		Advertising
Proportion of employees Vehicles with company sticker			Employees			BSC				Advertising
Reach of a campaign	Process				BSC 100					Advertising
Growth of the advertising budget		Customers				BSC				Advertising
Recommendation rate		Customers			BSC 100					Advertising

Fig. 29 Extract from the Excel spreadsheet for analysis – Questions on the tag – ‘Advertising’. (Own representation 2019)

A differentiation of “advertising campaigns to ethical and unethical campaigns” is omitted, it is not provided for in the key figures of the BSC, although these also consider the “advertising budget”.

In this ‘tag’ there is a match with the question from the GWÖ catalogue shown in the third line: The overview of the ‘budget for advertising and marketing’. The BSC Knowledge provides the question about the “growth of the advertising budget”.

In order to be able to calculate a delta with regard to growth, one needs the basis, i.e. the sum of the expenditures for advertising and marketing.

It can be noted a facilitation in the preparation of the common good balance sheet.

6 Presentation of Results

A total of 298 questions were examined more closely for correspondence between the common good economy and the various BSC sources. In the process, 58 questions were identified with a positive result, i.e. with a match between the data. For a total of 240 more closely examined data sets, the result was negative; these are not usable for the creation of a common good balance sheet based on the Balanced Scorecard data (see Fig. 30). The results are presented below as a table and graphically processed.

The highest number of matches are found in area with the tag ‘Turnover’, a total of nine, in second place the tag ‘Profit Tax’, followed by the ‘Tag’ ‘Absence’ (see Fig. 30).

The largest number of questions in the ‘tags’ with *no* correspondence between the common good economy and the balanced scorecard are found in ‘employment

Question/KPI	Match analysis		
	Positive	Negative	Overall result
Advertising	3	5	8
Further education	4	10	14
Sales	9	15	24
Products		36	36
Pricing		4	4
Ecological Sustainability	5	32	37
Co-determination		2	2
Employee satisfaction	2	16	18
Employee engagement	2	9	11
Market share		3	3
Customer requests	2	6	8
Corruption		2	2
Capital	2	17	19
Profit Taxes	8	2	10
Social/societal responsibility		5	5
Borrowed capital	2	1	3
Contractors	2	15	17
Fluctuation rate	4	6	10
Cash Flow	4	5	9
Application	2		2
Length of service	2		2
Reporting		3	3
Employment contracts		42	42
Attachments		4	4
Absence	5		5
Overall result	**58**	**240**	**298**

Fig. 30 Table Number of matches sorted by tags from GWÖ and BSC (Schmidt 2019)

contracts' with 42 metrics, followed by 'products' with 36 metrics, and in third place here are the questions from 'environmental sustainability' with 32 values.

The list in the table (Fig. 30) does not indicate whether the questions are always the same or whether they differ, but only whether there is agreement in these fields.

The graph "Number with match by source" (Fig. 31) and the corresponding table (Fig. 32) show a high density for the metrics from the source 'BSC 100′, followed by 'BSC Knowledge'.

Likewise, the data reveals the number of questions from the common good economy. Out of a number of 302 questions checked for content, 35 come with matches from the four Balanced Scorecard data; there are no matches in 129 data sets from the Balanced Scorecard; leaving 136 metrics from the common good economy. Here there are 113 with no matches. This leaves 23 questions from the

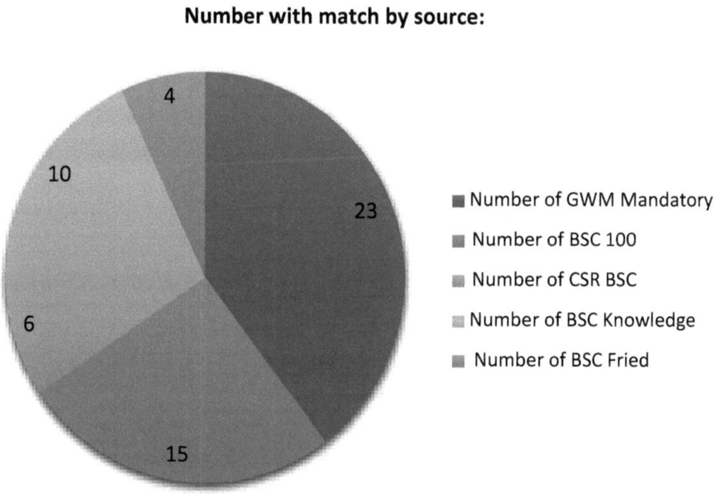

Fig. 31 Graph from the number of matches in questions sorted by source. (Own representation 2019)

Values	Yes	No	Overall result
Number of GWM Mandatory	23	113	136
Number of BSC 100	15	53	68
Number of CSR BSC	6	41	47
Number of BSC Wissen (knowledge)	10	33	43
Number of BSC Fried	4	3	7

Fig. 32 Table of the number of matches in questions sorted by source. (Own representation 2019)

mandatory indicators of the common good economy that can be answered using the Balanced Scorecard. (Fig. 32).

The graph of 'agreement by perspectives' (Fig. 33) shows that the number is particularly high in the areas of "Finance", but also among employees. This can be explained by the fact that the Balanced Scorecard is located in the financial area, but also by a high number of used key figures after sorting to tags from the sources BSC 100 (68 pieces) and BSC Knowledge (43 pieces). Both sources are located in the classical business management area.

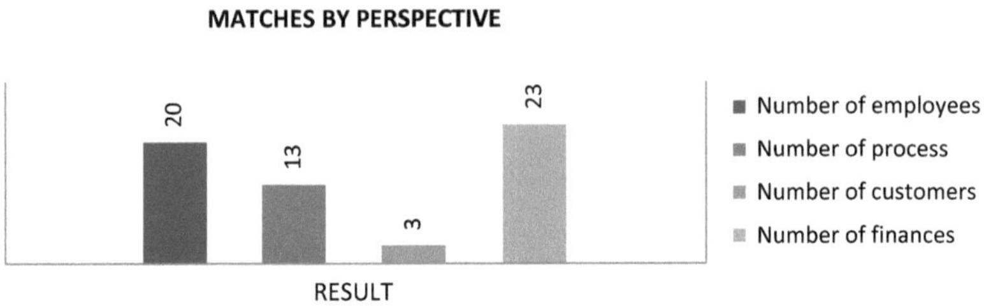

Fig. 33 Table of the number of matches in questions sorted by perspectives. (Own representation 2019)

7 Discussion of the Results

The results show that a total of 23 questions of public good accounting can be taken from the indicators of the Balanced Scorecard. After sorting them, it is striking that seven indicators come from the process perspective, eight from the employee or development perspective and nine indicators from the financial perspective; in contrast, there is no hit (in the common good questions) from the customer perspective. This result is surprising because in both systems, i.e. in the Balanced Scorecard as well as in the Economy of the Common Good, the stakeholder group of customers plays an important role.

The questions of the Economy of the Common Good mainly contain "measurable", i.e. easily recorded data, such as: hours, shares of turnover, input in kg. The key figures in the area of finances correspond to a cross-section of the existing questions, such as: "surplus funds from ongoing business activities (in EUR thousand)" or "equity ratio". In the process key figures, one finds for example the question "Overview of budgets for marketing, sales, advertising: expenditure on measures or campaigns", in the development perspective: "Number and extent of operational accidents".

Critically, the set of 23 indicators out of 144 mandatory indicators for the common good balance sheet preparation corresponds to just under 16 percent of the total set. If the comparative quantity is applied to all possible questions of the common good economy, namely 448, the existing 23 questions correspond to only about 5% of the balancing process. In addition, the question arises whether the use of the Balanced Scorecard leads to the desired strategy fulfilment through exactly these questions. The absence of the customer perspective in the questionnaire makes the use of other 'non-conforming' metrics likely. Only in this way, in the balance of the process levels, is the scorecard balanced.

8 Entrepreneurial Advantages and Practical Relevance in Companies

A company that is actively engaged with the common good economy and the associated common good accounting could quickly be deterred by the flood of information requested and to be provided. The Common Good Accounting Workbook 5.0 contains a total of 114 pages and is only part of a whole process.

A well-known and established instrument such as the Balanced Scorecard can help companies in this point. The fact that already 23 key figures with the creation of the (existing) Balanced Scorecard do not require any further considerations benefits companies in practice. Synergy effects in the creation of a balanced scorecard and the simultaneous use of the collected data for the common good balance sheet could thus convince companies of the use of sustainable and common good-oriented goal orientation.

9 Summary and Outlook

The Balanced Scorecard metrics analysed in these considerations are already generally accepted in business management and are used in a large number of companies to control and audit processes. (cf. Vohl 2014). An expansion of the already known system is easily possible.

Both Porter and Kramer (2011) and Kaplan and Norton (2008) insist that the processes for strategy development and goal achievement in companies are changeable and need to be adjusted in regular loops. "Companies [...], in order to do this, must first identify all social needs, benefits and problems related to their products." (Porter and Kramer 2011, p. 67) "They quickly identify how these decisions affect operations and strategy and can make strategic course corrections if necessary." (Kaplan and Norton 2008, p. 19).

When implementing the common good economy in companies, the first step is to provide the strategy implementation in everyday life with an appropriate orientation towards the common good. The identification of existing data from the Balanced Scorecard can help in this regard.

Due to the analysis in the context of qualitative social research, a "rigid system" for identifying commonalities results, justified by the method of attributing individual key figures. The desired objectivity and reliability lead to a quick exclusion of individual key figures without an examination of adaptation or application possibilities on both sides. It is precisely at the process level of the customers that key figures are found in the common good economy that are suitable for a balanced scorecard.

At first glance, the direct points of contact based on the analysis carried out here between the Common Good Balance Sheet and the Balanced Scorecard seem small in comparison to the several hundred criteria that both approaches have as their content. This was to be expected due to the different approaches and originally different goal orientations.

Nevertheless, at second glance, a certain confidence arises that, with a little "translation help", a balanced scorecard can be developed that comprehensively integrates the criteria of the common good balance sheet.

This could create an offer for companies that, firstly, reduces the workload for the preparation of the common good balance sheet, since it switches from a certification paradigm with long audit cycles to a paradigm of everyday accounting and data generation, and the collected data is used multiple times. Secondly, the criteria of a common good balance sheet in combination with the balanced scorecard become even more of an operational tool that supports the implementation of strategies and thus the day-to-day management of an organization and its actions in society.

References

Barthélemy, Frank. 2011. *Balanced Scorecard: Erfolgreiche IT-Auswahl, Einführung und Anwendung: Unternehmen berichten.* Wiesbaden: Vieweg+Teubner Verlag/Springer Fachmedien Wiesbaden GmbH Wiesbaden.

Boersch, Cornelius, und R. Elschen, Hrsg. 2007. *Das Summa Summarum des Management.* Wiesbaden: Gabler.

Duden. 2019. Wörterbuch online, Tag,. https://www.duden.de/rechtschreibung/Tag_Strukturelement_Markierung. Zugegriffen: 10.06.19.

Fleig, Jürgen. 2019. Balanced Scorecard (BSC). Management Handbuch. Kapitel 035 (b-wise GmbH, Hrsg.), Karlsruhe. Verfügbar unter https://www.business-wissen.de/kapitel/balanced-scorecard-bsc/. Zugegriffen: 30.04.2020.

Friedag, Herwig R., und W. Schmidt. 2011. *Balanced Scorecard*, 4. Aufl. Freiburg: Haufe-Lexware GmbH & Co. KG.

Gerberich, Claus W., T. Schäfer, und J. Teuber. 2006. *Integrierte Lean Balanced Scorecard: Methoden, Instrumente, Fallbeispiele.* Wiesbaden: Gabler.

Hennig, Alexander, W. Schneider, U. Wiehle, M. Diegelmann, und D. Henryk. 2008. *100 Kennzahlen der Balanced Scorecard.* Wiesbaden: Cometis.

Horváth, Péter, und L. Kaufmann. 1998. Balanced Scorecard-ein Werkzeug zur Umsetzung von Strategien. *Harvard-Business-Manager: das Wissen der Besten* 20:39–50.

Internationale Delegiertenversammlung. 2018. Die Vision der GWÖ. https://www.ecogood.org/de/vision/die-vision-der-gwo/. Zugegriffen: 18.05.19.

Internationaler Verein zur Förderung der Gemeinwohl-Ökonomie e. V. 2019. Theoretische Basis. https://www.ecogood.org/de/vision/theoretische-basis/. Zugegriffen: 18.05.19.
Kaplan, Robert S., und D. P. Norton. 1997. *Balanced scorecard: Strategien erfolgreich umsetzen*. Stuttgart: Schäffer-Poeschel Verlag
Kaplan, Robert S., und D. P. Norton. 2008. Management mit System. *Harvard Business manager* (Mai 2008): 2–19.
Kaplan, Robert S., und D. P. Norton. 2018. *Balanced scorecard: Strategien erfolgreich umsetzen*. Stuttgart: Schäffer-Poeschel Verlag.
Kuckartz, Udo. 2018. *Qualitative Inhaltsanalyse. Methoden, Praxis, Computerunterstützung*, 4. Aufl. Weinheim, Basel: Beltz Juventa.
Kühnapfel, Jörg B. (Hrsg.). 2019. *Balanced Scorecards im Vertrieb*. Wiesbaden: Springer Fachmedien Wiesbaden.
Matrix-Entwicklungsteam. (Hrsg.). 2017. Arbeitsbuch zur Gemeinwohl-Bilanz 5.0 Vollbilanz, o.O. Verfügbar unter: https://www.ecogood.org/de/unsere-arbeit/gemeinwohl-bilanz/gemeinwohl-matrix/arbeitsmaterialien/. Zugegriffen: 30.04.2020.
Neßler, Christian, und M.-T. Fischer. 2013. *Social-Responsive Balanced Scorecard: Wie Unternehmen gesellschaftliche Verantwortung in Kennzahlen umsetzen*. Wiesbaden: Springer.
Porter, Michael E., und M. R. Kramer. 2011. Die Neuerfindung des Kapitalismus. *Harvard-Business-Manager: das Wissen der Besten* 33 (2): 58–75.
Schmidt, Julia. 2019. *Excel-Datei zur Bachelorarbeit "Die Gemeinwohlökonomie im Unternehmenskontext"*.
Vohl, Hans-Jörg. 2014. Balanced Scorecard im Mittelstand, Studie zum Einsatz der BSC in mittelständischen Unternehmen. http://www.bsc-im-mittelstand.de/0105_buch-download.html. Zugegriffen: 17.05.19.

Gehra, Wolfgang, Prof. Dr., Diplom-Kaufmann (Univ.), Chair of Social Management and Public Relations, Faculty of Applied Social Sciences, Munich University of Applied Sciences, Germany.

As a graduate in business administration and as co-director of the study programme, he represents the economic sciences in the interdisciplinary study programme Management of Social Innovations. 20 years of management experience as a medium-sized entrepreneur, managing director of organic certified monastery operations and commercial director of the German Franciscan Province with many social institutions, as well as many years on the board of foundations, mean diverse expertise for innovative change processes in society and organizations in the area of tension between business constraints and idealistic goals, especially sustainability. Member of various advisory and supervisory boards. The focus on entrepreneurial action in a social and ecological context forms both background experience and research interest.

Last published:

Freiburg, M.; W. Gehra, 2020 (in press). Hybrid business models of social enterprises in the field of tension between teaching and practice. In: WiSt – Wirtschaftswissenschaftliches Studium, Zeitschrift für Studium und Forschung.

Schmidt, Julia, B.A. Management of Social Innovations. Bachelor's degree in Management of Social Innovations (HM Munich), tax clerk, many years of experience in business organisation and controlling. Specialization in the common good economy, advanced training in common good accounting through the Association for the Common Good Economy.

Open Space: Spatial, Temporal and Social Flexibilization of the Office World as an Answer to the Challenges of *Work 4.0* – Empirical Findings

Theresa Arnold

Abstract

Learning from each other, mutual inspiration, interactive exchange and innovative solutions: Companies have recently been leaning more towards new spatial concepts to design agile and flexible workspaces (The Berlin Smart City Vision. A discourse-analytical future research, Institut Futur, Berlin, 2017). These can be conceived as open space offices, designed as open and flexible working landscapes (Work of the Future: Digital, Multi-local, Dynamic. Theses and design approaches for the workplace of the future, ISF Munich, Munich, 2018). This paper presents the results of an empirical research study in which the phenomenon of "Open Space" is investigated from a sociology of work perspective. The focus is on the practice of Open Space: what motives and reasons do companies see for introducing these offices? How do employees shape their work under the work-organizational changes? What challenges do employees face here and how are they solved? These questions will be answered on the basis of empirical data (interviews with employees and change facilitators). In dealing with the changed work environment, areas of tension can be worked out, which are then discussed taking into account theories of the sociology of work and concepts of the subjectification of work.

T. Arnold (✉)
Goethe University Frankfurt, Frankfurt am Main, Germany

H.-W. Franz et al. (eds.), *Sustainable Living and Business*,
https://doi.org/10.1007/978-3-658-41835-9_7

1 Introduction

With the change in work processes, a change in the design of office space is also taking place. The increasing flexibilization of life and work demand new forms of coexistence, so that in addition to innovative living space concepts such as "Smart City", new work organizations such as "Open Space" are becoming increasingly relevant as a modern office model (Priebe 2017, p. 8). Across architectural construction, a trend development towards flexible, multi-local workspaces can be seen, which correspond to flexibilisation and individualisation in terms of the organisation of workflows (Kratzer 2018). In addition to the trend of those offices looking confusingly similar to stylish lofts or boutique hotels, open space offices are understood as a continuous office working environment without partition walls. The new work organisation is conceived as a modern, flexible working landscape that offers different rooms or room zones for different work requirements (ibid. 2018). Here, similar to open plan offices, a larger number of workers share an open space. However, unlike open plan offices, a continuous working landscape with both open and closed areas is found here. The different design of the room types is aimed at the respective activity profiles with their specific requirements, such as concentrated, undisturbed work or routine work. While traditional office spaces show an arrangement that functions as a spatialisation of division of labour and systematic control, openness, transparency and the reduction of hierarchy are currently the top priorities (Petendra 2015). Thus, open, flexible office spaces with increasing space for communication, creativity and agility are given special importance. The pursuit of agility can be seen not only in the agile methods such as "Scrum" that companies have been increasingly using recently (Lühr et al. 2018; Haack and Müller-Trabucchi 2017). Well-known companies such as Siemens and Adidas have restructured their work organization according to the open space principle, thus pursuing a flexible working style that is reflected in the layout of the space (Kratzer and Lütke Lanfer 2017). This paper is about the constitution of open space office spaces as space formation processes in the interaction of structural conditions and subjectivized actions of employees. Their practices of action and their perceptions were examined, taking into account changed work organizational conditions.

After outlining the relevance of the topic of Open Space, the second chapter presents the research questions and the research design used for the analysis of the study. This is followed by a section based on the data analysis, which explains the expectations and motives for the transformation to Open Space from the perspective of the companies. The following part deals with the perspective of the employees and with the experiences and actions made with the new working landscape. Finally, these are summarized in the form of areas of tension. This is followed by a presentation of the employees' strategies for dealing with the changed working conditions in Open Space. Finally, the empirical results are discussed and summarized, taking into account sociological theories on the subjectification of work.

2 Research Question and Research Design

On the one hand, the study records the motives and motivations of companies that switch from a traditional office form to Open Space. Furthermore, from the perspective of sociology of work and industry, the orientations of action and subjectification potentials in everyday practices are examined against the background of flexibilized work processes. With regard to the activities examined in the changing world of work, there are some empirical contributions in the sociology of work and industry that increasingly identify freedom of action and autonomy for project-based work, which lead to subjectivised performance regulation and increasing self-organisation as well as self-rationalisation (Kratzer 2003). Work in open space also tends to become more interactive, reflexive and individual, and thus raises the question of the extent to which a (new) active co-creation of the work subject is also present and demanded here, and to what extent companies build on the use of the potentials, resources and competences of the workforce. The question of the thesis is:

1. What motives and expectations lead companies to set up Open Space workplaces?
2. What tensions arise for employees in this context and to what extent are subjectivized action strategies and design options of adaptation and appropriation used in order to perform under the changed spatial and temporal conditions?

The theoretical approaches to the subjectification and dissolution of boundaries in work were used for the qualitative investigation. A mixed-method approach was chosen for the methodological procedure in order to achieve a comprehensive and multi-layered perspective on the research object (Flick 2012). The combination of methods used for data collection lent itself to this: expert interviews, observation, and guided interviews with employees. For the expert interviews, so-called change facilitators were interviewed who accompany the transformation process to Open Space in three different companies (n = 4). The selection of the sample for the guided interviews was based on employees from different companies and organisations in the service sector, especially in the consulting sector (n = 4). For the analysis of the data, the qualitative content analysis according to Mayring (2015) was used and an inductive category development was chosen.

3 Company Motives and Expectations for Open Space

For companies, the office form represents a central cost factor, especially with regard to the high rental prices of office space, which is factored in and reflected in the design of office space. In this context, open space offices are increasingly proving to be efficient and economical where a partial physical absence of employees is assumed. In addition to the economic efficiency of the concept, Open Space is also proving to be suitable for changing business processes, as it allows management to plan staff flexibly and agilely. This applies to staff increases and decreases as well as to the formation of new teams. With the open space unit, there is the possibility to react flexibly and agilely to the constantly changing organisational structures.

Other motives are innovation and communication. It is assumed that the office structure promotes communication within the team, as it is easier to make contact and interact due to the open design. Companies aim to create new encounters in order to boost innovation processes. In this way, they try to generate interactions across departments as well as teams. Spatially, this is usually achieved with the help of shared lounge areas in order to create a "place to meet" and to break down silo thinking in companies. Furthermore, Open Space can be seen as part of a trend development in order to present itself to (potential) employees as a digitized company that is attractive in competition with other employers. In addition, companies intend with this concept to be innovative and to be able to present strength with regard to the topics of digitalisation and globalisation. In summary, Open Space is intended to promote profitability, efficiency, flexibility and the promotion of interdepartmental communication and innovation.

4 The Perspective of the Employees

Restructuring according to the Open Space principle can prove to be a profound change in working life for some employees. First and foremost, it usually means the loss of the "personal" workplace, especially if this is accompanied by desk sharing and the workplace has to be chosen anew every day. With regard to the behaviours in Open Space, the following chapter focuses on the experiences and challenges of employees in the open working landscape.

4.1 Areas of Tension in Open Space

The changes in work organisation in the course of Open Space form the starting point for changes in the way employees work. These are understood in the following as areas of tension.

4.1.1 Tension: Fixed Workplace vs. Flexible Workplace

More flexibility in the choice of work locations

The concept of open space includes working elsewhere, for example at other locations or in a home office. The respondents make use of the large number of flexible spatial workplaces. It was shown that for the employees this is also accompanied by increased spatial flexibility, which is characterised by working at other locations or in a home office. The possibility of working from home is included in the Open Space concept.

Mobility and reorganization through digitalization

This flexibility in terms of work locations was definitely appreciated by the employees, but negative aspects also emerged with regard to the loss of personal workplaces. A distinction was made between this and traditional offices.

> In the past, of course, you had your fixed workplace. You come in in the morning, bring your cup of coffee and you can [...] start right away and that's such a problem with open workplaces that you can have mobility, but it doesn't work that wirelessly either. (No. 6, lines 389–396).

In the Open Space office, a high degree of digitalization is strived for and this is also used by the employees through the flexible choice of the work location in the home office or elsewhere. In this context, one interviewee mentioned the principle of "paperless work" that is strived for in the Open Space. In line with the clean desk policy, employees are encouraged not to leave documents or other work material at the workplace once they finish their working day. The interviewee felt restricted because the work material has to be stowed away again and again.

> There are simply still companies that still work a lot with paper. […] And it is not yet possible to do without it. Paper simply needs space and that is also a shortcoming. Of course, in Open Space you no longer have your 2.40 m wide tables, but only 1.20 m […] You are then somewhat restricted. Exactly, that is now also such a negative case with us, that you can no longer spread out as you want (No. 6, lines 526–536).

Scope for action and self-organisation

Open Space requires an increased self-organisation of work. This goes hand in hand with an increase in autonomy and new freedom of action in the execution of work.

> But then that's structure. Everybody, how they want to do it. Digitally, you make a to-do list and have it there as a hard copy. There everyone is responsible for himself, how he does his tasks (No. 6, lines 555-558).

In terms of the organisation of working time, there are company-established framework conditions and trust-based working time, which are, however, accompanied by flexible handling and allow opportunities for greater autonomy.

> In principle, no one tells me when I come and when I go, unless I have appointments, of course. So the working hours are actually completely flexible, and we live by that (no. 5, lines 55–57).

Although working hours are flexible, they are mainly determined by the deadlines of the projects being worked on. An ambivalent discourse emerged with regard to the potential changes in the way work is structured in the course of the Open Space organization. On the one hand, the majority of employees stated that they did not consciously structure their working day differently. On the other hand, all interviewees implicitly showed characteristics that pointed to a changed spatial, temporal and organisational design of their work. In most cases, these only became noticeable in the survey and in consideration of their environment and social actions.

Depersonalization of the workplace

Since, for employees, work takes place not only in different spatial zones in the Open Space, but also in other locations, such as in the home office, it points to a depersonalisation of the workplace. Thus, although there is an expansion of work location options, at the same time the territorial claim to one's personal, own workplace is dwindling. One interviewee, for example, felt the creeping decline of privacy in open space.

> While positive [...] that it's so open and everything is free [...], at some point you often lose your privacy [...]. I think that's the biggest change. Of course, you used to put up your picture frames, family photos and so on (No. 6, lines 368-373).

Personal features such as the display of pictures and family photos represent both a form of identification and territorialisation that 'mark' and individualise the workplace. While not having a personal workspace was not perceived as negative or disruptive by the majority, having a personal workspace was perceived as a positive factor. However, a promotion and the prospect of a personal workspace is associated with a positive feeling of having earned it.

4.1.2 Tension: Privacy vs. Transparency

The subjective understanding of performance

In the analysis of the data collected, it became apparent on several occasions that employees have a contradictory understanding of their performance in the Open Space. On the one hand, a flexible way of working supported by the company applies, which is characterized by autonomy of action in terms of time and space. On the other hand, ambivalences emerged with regard to the freedom of action that is restrictively influenced by the environment in Open Space. Thus, in the course of indirect control, forms of autonomy restrictions emerged, such as when doing private things. All interviewees commented on the feeling of observability, which is perceived in particular through the strong transparency in the open working environment and has an effect on the subjective understanding of performance. Employees move within the flexible working arrangements allowed by the company according to the principle of trust. On the other hand, employees felt "caught" not having done their work and having done private things.

> I remember, as a beginner, I was somehow a bit inhibited [...] to call my client [...]. I thought they were all listening to me [...] and I don't really know what to ask them anyway (No. 5, lines 337–342).

The majority of employees had difficulties making loud phone calls in Open Space, especially at the beginning of their career in the company. However, according to the respondents, this inhibition disappears with increasing experience. When asked how the Open Space environment affected their own performance, all respondents indicated that they were not significantly affected. Although all interviews showed an impact on the ability to concentrate, this was not significantly perceived as a reduction in performance. The majority of the interviewees emphasised the rapid flow of information as a positive effect of the Open Space organisation, which was perceived as decisive for the performance. However, for activities that required a high degree of concentration, it was rather counterproductive.

Confidentiality

Another issue that emerged in the Open Space was the handling of confidential information. All employees report situations in which their work involves confidentiality, such as the planning of an IPO of clients. In addition to confidential conversations that already require discretion at the beginning and for which the employees seek out places of retreat, confidential conversations often arise unexpectedly.

> Typically (…) a conversation is started in Open Space. One has probably assumed that it is suitable for Open Space and then it is not. Then you have to see how you can get the cow off the ice. Then everyone finds out where and how the conversation is conducted (No. 4, lines 342–347).

For the employees, a delicate situation arises in which they have to decide for themselves how to deal with the situation appropriately. This is usually a fine line, as employees do not want to cause a stir.

Work and private life

Another central factor is the overlapping of work and private life, which is perceived as a potential conflict in Open Space due to the increased transparency. At this point it becomes apparent that in Open Space not only the professionalism of the worker is observed, but also the person as such becomes the focus of attention. This turned out to be a difficulty for the employees when personal problems cannot be sufficiently suppressed emotionally and have an impact on the design of work.

> It can also be that you are sad because something happened at home, or someone was fired. […] Then you notice something like that, and maybe you don't want to […]. And you still have to work when you are sad (no. 6, lines 567–571).

Some employees described this as critical, as they do not necessarily want to allow so much privacy and closeness. Overall, transparency and openness could be identified on the one hand as a difficulty for the treatment of confidential information.

At the same time, the open office unit, characterised by more proximity, was perceived as a positive factor for the feeling of togetherness, as can be seen in the following quote:

> Because it's really nice, because you also notice your colleagues in everyday life [...] you just see what they're up to and you get it and it's such a sense of togetherness (no. 4, lines 212–216).

4.1.3 Tension: Communication Vs. Concentration

Communication

Respondents highlighted an increase in interaction and thus an improvement in the way they communicate with colleagues and superiors. As already noted, there is more room for informal conversations in Open Space. These do not only result from the observability of seeing and being seen more often. Rather, a mutual openness also contributes to an active exchange with each other, as a result of which interactions are increased. The transparency in the Open Space also leads to an easy "orientation" and a quick finding of the employees.

> In fact, in Open Space, [...] you can tell when who is there and then you can look to communicate briefly (no. 4, lines 39–42).

Here the comparison was drawn with the individual office, as in this case one had often walked unnecessary distances, although the colleagues were then in an appointment or out of the office. Overall, the informal conversations that arise, for example, on the way to the coffee machine, were perceived as very important. In addition, it was rated as easier to make arrangements with superiors compared to traditional offices. This was also justified by the actual proximity to the supervisor.

> If the boss is sitting in a room, you don't dare knock at first. And if it's in an open room, [...] then you have a question, then you can ask directly (No. 6, lines 407–411).

This also showed a dismantling of hierarchical structures, as the superior's office is still often connoted with a status symbol.

In addition to communication with superiors, particular emphasis was placed on interaction with colleagues, which helped to provide mutual support in the work process and produced joint approaches to solutions.

> If you overhear something and they're talking about problems and you already know the problem, you can still say "Hey, I know the problem. Then you help out. (no. 6, lines 297–300).

On the one hand, however, it was seen as negative that colleagues were more quickly involved in other areas of responsibility. On the other hand, this aspect was also seen as positive, as it served the interests of the company as a whole.

> Which is good in so far as, for the overall company, because you could probably avert the damage, but you get dragged into it because you can't prevent it from happening at all (no. 4, lines 234–237).

It can be stated that the interactive work in Open Space partially leads to an expansion of one's own tasks or area of responsibility, which is characterized by the co-operation of the colleagues.

Distraction, acoustics and intensity of influences

With regard to the distraction caused by Open Space, various factors were mentioned.

> That the conversations of others or telephone calls distracted me. That I thought, I have to concentrate now, but I can't really because so many people are talking (No. 5, lines 419-422).

Distraction factors include loudness, the perception of which varied depending on whether it was perceived as background noise or consciously as conversations. According to all interviewees, the volume in the Open Space offices has an effect on the employees' ability to concentrate. Thus, fewer disruptions occurred due to "chit-chat" and more due to phone calls or conversations going on next to them. One interviewee pointed out that some colleagues might deliberately put themselves in the spotlight by deliberately talking loudly so that everyone would hear their "problems". It should also be noted that the problems of acoustics and loudness are also related to the number of places of retreat and lead to an increase in stress.

All three identified areas of tension are characterised by a specific ambivalence. They point to a changed spatial arrangement for employees in which they have to develop special ways of dealing and coping strategies for themselves. How this is done is discussed in the following section.

4.2 Dealing with Areas of Tension

The employees reported special adaptations and structuring services with which they shape their work according to their own and the company's performance requirements.

Adaptation services

Employees try to counteract the general noise level and the conversations of their colleagues by listening to music with headphones. Listening to music with headphones serves on the one hand as a help to be able to work concentrated and undisturbed. On the other hand, it puts the worker in an ambivalent situation, as in this way potentially incoming calls cannot be heard.

Furthermore, the employees reported a kind of "tunnel effect" and a fading out, which they would develop over time in the Open Space in order to be less aware of their surroundings.

> They're talking something, I catch it briefly, but I tune it out and I move on. That is also a skill that you actually have to learn in Open Space, that you decouple yourself (No. 4, lines 173–177).

In this context, "emotional endurance" was also mentioned, which refers to the fact that, depending on the situation, prioritisation decisions have to be made again and again with regard to whether to allow oneself to be distracted or to concentrate more on one's own work.

> Then it is a good thing if I manage to bear it emotionally that then also the other things that [...] I [...] actually have to do in peace [...] then just [...] are postponed or have to be interrupted (No. 4, Z. 279–283)

This was perceived as an inner conflict, whereby one always had to weigh things up and prioritise. Subjective demands are made on one's own time management in that priorities are set, whether spontaneous disruptions may be allowed or whether these are regulated in terms of deadlines. This makes it difficult to plan work and work can never be completed undisturbed. Overall, all respondents stated that they had become accustomed to the working conditions in Open Space after a while. Here, the personal adaptability was also emphasized.

Appropriation strategies

Furthermore, employees tended to look for places of retreat in order to avoid disturbances or distractions and to be able to concentrate on their work. These were, for example, project rooms, telephone boxes, corridors or terraces outside the office or the home office. The places of retreat were perceived as extended spaces for action.

> We have spaces where you can work in a concentrated way, quiet areas [...] You always have the opportunity to get up and leave if it doesn't get better with the volume (no. 6, lines 266–272).

The evaluation made it clear that the aspect of retreat, i.e. a place to work undisturbed, is extremely important. Retreat locations are also often sought due to the increased proximity and transparency in Open Space, as the hierarchies become significantly flatter in the course of Free Seating and Clean Desk. For this reason, some employees are uncomfortable working so close to their superiors or colleagues.

> Here it is relatively open and so is the hierarchy, then it can be that your boss squats next to you, but [...] if it makes you uncomfortable, you can escape (no. 6, lines 236–239).

The way of dealing with the disruptive factors in Open Space varied significantly among the respondents. For the individual strategies of action, the practices led by the company or the team were just as important as the personal behaviour. The employees considered being able to deal with this on the one hand as a requirement of the job profile, and on the other hand as part of their own personality.

> People choose their job by their nature. For example, someone who loves regular procedures, who loves his peace and quiet, will tend not to choose a job like the one I have. If the job is designed to have regular working hours and then an open space is imposed on it, then that doesn't work either (No. 5, lines 582–588).

All in all, the subjective expectations and demands also embodied their own standards with regard to the acceptance and regulation of individual needs, whereby the conditions in the Open Space were relativized or even legitimized.

Another strategy was the direct approach. Employees reported that they openly approached colleagues if the conversations in the Open Space became too loud.

> The important strategy is to be direct. That you also allow this directness with each other, in a positive way. If you just say that your colleague is always so gruff. That is of course stupid, you have to agree with each other (no. 4, lines 395–398).

There was also a form of indirect communication in which employees visibly stuck post-its on their screens as warning signals so as not to be disturbed. With regard to the appropriation strategies, it became apparent that respectful interaction with each other was sought by choosing quiet places or a telephone box. Furthermore, mindfulness and respect, which are associated with reflection and emotional intelligence, also showed that employees recognized stressful situations of their colleagues and reacted to them. The granting of a mutually preferred seating structure could also be recognised as a sign of respectful interaction, as the employees' favourite places were known and respected.

5 Summary and Outlook

With regard to the research questions, the following can be stated in consideration of the empirical findings: Even if open space offices differ in their design in terms of size, room zones, work structures and "policies", the flexibility of the use of space as well as workplaces is the constituent feature. These offices have different activity-specific room zones and workplaces that employees can use flexibly to organize their work. This freedom of choice is the difference to traditional offices. Open space offices incorporate flexibility, agility and mobility, whereas traditional offices such as single or smaller offices are less focused on the conditions for communication and interaction required in today's working world and instead tend to offer space for concentrated work. With regard to the goals and expectations of companies, it was found that this concept is associated with increased efficiency and cost reduction, as well as flexibility, communication and innovation. In this context it can be assumed that with the Open Space concept companies find a suitable form to be able to react to the changing demands of the market. In this way, it is possible to react more flexibly to staff increases and reductions, the adjustment of the workforce to the order situation or the formation of new agile teams in the course of competition (Huchler et al. 2007; Böhle 2010). In addition, companies are attempting to respond to the new challenges of the digital world of work by using the philosophy of open space to demonstrate their competitiveness and agility to their environment and to appear as attractive employers to employees and potential employees.

In terms of work organisation, due to the more flexible spatial and temporal organisation of work, Open Space supports an increased orientation towards *indirect control, control of results* and a general loosening of rigid work execution, which takes place in the course of project work and the unregulated or flexible working conditions. Thus forms of temporal, *spatial and content-related delimitation* of work are emerging (Moldaschl and Sauer 2000).

Increasingly, technical and organisational changes form an important component for new forms of business and work organisation (Böhle and Bolte 2002). Open Space becomes possible at all in the course of the progress of technology, as the philosophy is oriented towards the concept of "Paperless Office" and is based on a functioning telecommunication (Sellen and Harper 2002). Information and communication technologies are increasingly used not only to carry out work, but also to communicate within the team and with customers.

In addition, by offering flexible workplace options, companies not only want to create individual incentives, but also expand scope for action (Kleemann et al. 2002). Companies have meanwhile found that incentives are created less by material recognition. Accordingly, the values and goals employees used to aspire to, such as the prospect of a company car and "making a career", are increasingly taking a back seat, with stronger performance incentives being provided instead by issues such as work-life balance, good working conditions or sustainability. A reference to sustainability can be assumed insofar as "sharing" (car sharing, food sharing, etc.), are becoming increasingly relevant and in the open space concept desk sharing can be seen as positive. In terms of society as a whole, a new view of the importance of possessions and territorial claims is emerging. Following on from this, innovation processes are proving to be social processes that are shaped by norms and social values (Blättel-Mink 2019).

The increasingly project-based organization in the Open Space results in new requirements for employees in terms of *self-direction, self-control* and *self-rationalization* (Böhle 2010; Voß and Pongratz 2004). With the possibility of flexible choice of work location, work is multilocated in and out of the office. In this context, the coordination of teamwork represents a central factor, which requires not only the control of one's own capacities, but also that of the project team. In addition, aspects of subjectivised work are becoming apparent in the company's organisation of work, in that the ability to self-direct is expected of the company and the inclusion of personal competences is demanded of the workforce: the increasing use of subjective structuring services in the company's organisation of work and increased access to the subjective potential of workers (ibid.; Kleemann et al. 1999).

In the course of this *reduction of domineering control* and the *increase of indirect control in* the Open Space, the employees themselves are increasingly responsible for the transformation of their own abilities into work performance, even if the given conditions partly impair the work design due to loudness, distraction or interruptions. It was apparent that some workers shared less private information at work, although this sometimes inevitably happened due to transparency. Others, however, perceived this as a positive factor, in that one gets to know the colleagues as a person and "as a whole" with their personality and in this way can also better assess the colleagues in terms of work. In connection with this, the openness in Open Space was perceived as a feeling of togetherness.

For employees, work is in any case accompanied by the use of emotional labour due to their service activity, whereby interaction work is an important component for service provision (Huchler et al. 2007; Böhle 2006). In this context, actors have to coordinate their actions so that joint co-production succeeds (Dunkel and Rieder 2004). For the employees, this situation is associated with the particularity of a double control, on the one hand by the company (enterprise and management), on the other hand by the customers (Böhle 2006). For the employees this represents a daily challenge, which can be partially affected by the interactive work in the Open Space. Thus, employees are increasingly required to perform *"extra-functional functions"* such as creative or social-communicative problem-solving skills (Frey 2009).

In the course of company strategies for *self-organisation,* partial characteristics of a new type are becoming visible here, following on from the *"worker-entrepreneur thesis"*: a worker who becomes an entrepreneur of his or her own labour and knows how to use his or her own potential efficiently and entrepreneurially (Pongratz and Voß 1998). In addition, the flexible organisation of work in terms of time and space can be understood as a sign of a change in self-organisation. This includes a way of working oriented towards *self-organisation,* which at the same time means autonomy and new freedom of action in the execution of work and can be associated with a clear gain in autonomy for employees (Voß 2007). External organisation and control through the specification of regulations and formalised procedures are increasingly being replaced by *self-control, self-economisation* and *self-rationalisation,* while freedom of *action* and *autonomy* are being extended (Lohr and Nickel 2005). Thus, the changes towards Open Space can be understood as a change in company strategies for using and shaping the labour input of the workforce. The changed work organisational conditions associated with flexibilisation and self-organisation represent new circumstances which are equally associated by the interviewees with extended scope for action and incentive structures (Kratzer 2003). For the employees, there are opportunities to individually influence their own work organisation. These opportunities were perceived by the interviewees as a concession on the part of the company. Employees saw this as a self-determined, independent way of working, which they are largely free to shape through the choice of work locations, the use of different work zones and home office options (Moldaschl 2001). These are seen as part of the concept and are rather perceived as *autonomy of action.* Agreements with colleagues and superiors on flexible working time arrangements turn out to be individual *autonomies of negotiation.* The aspect of possible autonomy potentials proves to be central for the high acceptance of the concept, whereby the traceability of the activity-specific (service) work also contributes in the majority.

As stated in the empirical results, the employees have developed certain ways of dealing with the changed conditions in order to carry out their work and to perform well. The main adaptation was the suppression of the environment – volume, acoustics and the high intensity of the influences. On the one hand, this was achieved technically by listening to music with headphones. On the other hand, it was a cognitive (self-)performance in that the environment was mentally blanked out. Here the employees developed special filter mechanisms, a "tunnel vision". In order to react to the conditions in the Open Space, the respondents mostly used places of retreat such as project rooms, telephone boxes or the home office. In order to prevent disruptions and to flexibly adapt their practice-related actions to the complex and structurally prevailing working conditions, the employees intervene in a regulating manner and thus develop a *compensatory subjectivity* (Kleemann et al. 2002). They demonstrate a high *willingness to structure* (Matuschek et al. 2004) through efficient time management taking into account interruptions, activity-specific space management under criteria of acoustics and technical conditions, and a generally structuring prioritization and evaluation of their own capacities to achieve performance demands. In this way, efficient work processes are ensured through subjective-individual adaptations. In this way, a fit of operational demands is achieved (Kleemann et al. 2002).

With regard to a *practical-acting appropriation level*, it can be seen that employees maintain certain options for action despite restrictive working conditions. This occurs, for example, through a preferred choice of seats and through adherence to a general seating structure. Thus, it was shown that employees not only cooperate for professional agreements, but also interact to demand better working conditions from each other. These are perceived as individual *autonomy of action* (Kleemann et al. 2002).

It becomes apparent that strategies are not only developed individually, but also negotiated collectively in the interaction with colleagues by establishing common guidelines for behaviour. In this way, it can be seen that the working methods in Open Space also mean a piece of corporate culture, which is also strived for as a strategic (value) change in the context of operational reorganisation. This can also give rise to shared visions and guiding principles within the workforce, which can contribute to appropriate action within the organisation.

References

Blättel-Mink, B. 2019. Innovationen in Wirtschaft und Gesellschaft. *Organisationsberatung, Supervision, Coaching,* 26 (1): 53–56.

Böhle, F., und A. Bolte. 2002. Die Entdeckung des Informellen. Der schwierige Umgang mit Kooperation im Arbeitsalltag. München: ISF München.

Böhle, F. 2006. Typologie und strukturelle Probleme von Interaktionsarbeit. In *Arbeit in der Interaktion. Interaktion als Arbeit.* Hrsg. Böhle, F., und J. Glaser, 325–347. Wiesbaden: VS Verlag für Sozialwissenschaften.

Böhle, F. 2010. Neue Anforderungen an die Arbeitswelt. Neue Anforderungen an das Subjekt. In *Erschöpfende Arbeit. Gesundheit und Prävention in der flexiblen Arbeitswelt.* Hrsg. Keupp, H., und H. Dill, 77–95. Bielefeld: Transcript Verlag.

Dunkel, W. und K. Rieder. 2004. Interaktionsarbeit zwischen Konflikt und Kooperation. In *Dienstleistung als Interaktion. Beiträge aus einem Forschungsprojekt. Altenpflege – Deutsche Bahn – Call Center,* Hrsg. Dunkel, W., und G. G. Voß, 211–226. München/Mering: Rainer Hampp Verlag.

Flick, U. 2012. Qualitative Sozialforschung. Eine Einführung. Reinbek bei Hamburg: Rowohlt Taschenbuch Verlag.

Frey, M. 2009. Autonomie und Aneignung in der Arbeit. Eine soziologische Untersuchung zur Vermarktlichung und Subjektivierung von Arbeit. Buchreihe *Arbeit und Leben im Umbruch. Schriftenreihe zur subjektorientierten Soziologie der Arbeit und der Arbeitsgesellschaft*, Bd. 18, Hrsg. G. G. Voß, München/Mering: Hampp.

Haack, B., und M. Müller-Trabucchi. 2017. Agile Methoden als Moderatoren zur Steuerung der sozialen Beschleunigung. *Zeitschrift der Technischen Hochschule Wildau* 21: 83–88.

Huchler, N., G. G. Voß, und M. Weihrich. 2007. Soziale Mechanismen im Betrieb. Theoretische und empirische Analysen zur Entgrenzung und Subjektivierung von Arbeit. München/Mering: Rainer Hampp Verlag.

Kleemann, F., I. Matuschek, und G. Voß. 1999. Zur Subjektivierung von Arbeit, Berlin: Wissenschaftszentrum Berlin für Sozialforschung (WZB).

Kleemann, F., I. Matuschek, und G. Voß. 2002. Subjektivierung von Arbeit – Ein Überblick zum Stand der soziologischen Diskussion. In *Zur Subjektivierung von Arbeit,* Hrsg. Moldaschl, M., und G. G. Voß, 53–100. München/Mering: Rainer-Hampp.

Kratzer, N. 2003. Arbeitskraft in Entgrenzung. Grenzenlose Anforderungen, erweiterte Spielräume, begrenzte Ressourcen, Berlin: edition sigma.

Kratzer, N. 2018. Arbeit der Zukunft: Digital, multilokal, dynamisch. Thesen und Gestaltungsansätze für den Arbeitsplatz der Zukunft. München: ISF München.
Kratzer, N., und S. Lütke Lanfer. 2017. Open-Space-Büros und psychische Gesundheit – Eine Trendanalyse. *Zeitschrift für Arbeitswissenschaft.* 71 (4): 279–288.
Lohr, K., und H. M. Nickel. 2005. Subjektivierung von Arbeit – Riskante Chancen. In *Subjektivierung von Arbeit – Riskante Chancen,* Hrsg. Lohr, K., und H. M. Nickel, 207–239. Münster: Verlag Westfälisches Dampfboot.
Lühr, T., T. Kämpf, und B. Langes. 2018. 3 Lean und agile Methoden in der Praxis. Der Umbruch in der Organisation von Arbeit und die Folgen für die Beschäftigten. "Lean" und "agil" im Büro. Neue Organisationskonzepte in der digitalen Transformation und ihre Folgen für die Angestellten. Buchreihe Forschung aus der Hans-Böckler-Stiftung Bd. 193, Hrsg. Lühr, T., T. Kämpf, und B. Langes. Bielefeld: transcript Verlag.
Matuschek, I., Kleemann, F., und C. Brinkhoff. 2004. "Bringing Subjectivity back in". Notwendige Ergänzungen zum Konzept des Arbeitskraftunternehmers. In *Typisch Arbeitskraftunternehmer. Befunde der empirischen Arbeitsforschung,* Hrsg. Pongratz, H. J., und G. G. Voß, 115–138. Berlin: edition sigma.
Mayring, P. 2015. Qualitative Inhaltsanalyse. Grundlagen und Techniken. Weinheim: Beltz Verlag.
Moldaschl, M. 2001. Herrschaft durch Autonomie - – Dezentralisierung und widersprüchliche Arbeitsbeziehungen. In *Entwicklungsperspektiven von Arbeit. Ergebnisse aus dem Sfb 333 der Universität München.* Hrsg. B. Lutz, 132–164. Berlin: Akademie-Verlag.
Moldaschl, M., und D. Sauer. 2000. Internalisierung des Marktes – Zur neuen Dialektik von Kooperation und Herrschaft. In *Begrenzte Entgrenzungen. Wandlungen von Organisation und Arbeit*, Hrsg. M. Heiner, 205–224. Berlin: Ed. Sigma.
Petendra, B. 2015. Räumliche Dimensionen der Büroarbeit. Eine Analyse des flexiblen Büros und seiner Akteure. Wiesbaden: Springer Fachmedien.
Pongratz, H. J., und G. G. Voß. 1998. Der Arbeitskraftunternehmer. Eine neue Grundform der Ware Arbeitskraft? *Kölner Zeitschrift für Soziologie und Sozialpsychologie* 50: 131–158.
Priebe, M. 2017. Die Berliner Smart City Vision. Eine diskursanalytische Zukunftsforschung. Berlin: Institut Futur.
Sellen, A. J., und R. Harper. 2002. The myth of the paperless office. Cambridge: MIT Press.
Voß, G. G. 2007. Subjektivierung von Arbeit und Arbeitskraft. Die Zukunft der Beruflichkeit und die Dimension Gender als Beispiel. *In Arbeit und Geschlecht im Umbruch der modernen Gesellschaft. Forschung im Dialog,* Hrsg. Aulenbacher, B., M. Funder, H. Jacobsen, und S. Völker, 97–113. Wiesbaden: VS Verlag für Sozialwissenschaften.
Voß, G. G., und H. J. Pongratz. 2004. Arbeitskraft und Subjektivität. Einleitung und Stellungnahme. In *Typisch Arbeitskraftunternehmer. Befunde der empirischen Arbeitsforschung*, Hrsg. Pongratz, H. J., und G. G. Voß, 7–31. Berlin: Ed. Sigma.

Arnold, Theresa, M.A., studied sociology at the Goethe University Frankfurt am Main. Theresa Arnold's research areas are sociology of work and organization, social psychology and systemic consulting.

Complementary Currencies and Monetary Tools as Social Innovation

Christian Gelleri

Abstract

Many social and ecological innovations often fail because of the need for a return on investment. Many economists believe that money has a neutral character. This stems from the idea that money is a thing over which man has only limited influence. A look at the historical development of the monetary system casts strong doubt on this theory: Money comes into being already in antiquity, but at the latest in modern times, through collectives that, starting from certain goals and norms, determine an abstract standard of value and calculation and realize it by means of a payment system. With this perspective, money itself opens up as a malleable institution. On the one hand, the scope for action is greatly expanded by the additionality of a currency, but on the other hand it is also limited by rules and norms. Using examples of regional currencies in Wörgl, Chiemgau and Sardinia, different environmental conditions are considered and the objectives and solutions of the respective currency initiatives are presented. The newly created "money" acts as a binding agent that encourages the participants to cooperate dynamically and permanently. What contribution do such alternative currencies make with regard to global challenges such as demographic change, global warming and social inequality? Are they perhaps even paving the way for a fundamental transformation process in the monetary system?

C. Gelleri (✉)
Julius-Maximilians-University of Würzburg, Rosenheim, Germany
e-mail: christian.gelleri@uni-wuerzburg.de

H.-W. Franz et al. (eds.), *Sustainable Living and Business*,
https://doi.org/10.1007/978-3-658-41835-9_8

1 Money as an Object of Social Innovation

At the beginning of 1980, according to Bernard Lietaer, there was one complementary currency in the world: the Swiss WIR (Lietaer 1999, p. 292). In addition, there were isolated other small and relatively unknown systems such as the Bethel money introduced in 1908 (Hardraht and Godschalk 2004, p. 29). After the establishment of the first barter ring in 1983, the number increased rapidly during the 1980s and 1990s to about 1900 in 1998 (Lietaer 1999, p. 281). By 2013, there were nearly 4000 complementary currencies in 23 different countries (Seyfang and Longhurst 2013). The number is now estimated to be around 6000. In addition, there are another 21,000 "cryptocurrencies" (according to coinmarketcap.com, as of 22/11/2022). This dynamic indicates that beyond the 160 existing national and supranational monetary systems, there is an increasing variety of monetary tools that can serve the needs, goals and purposes of citizens. Yet complementary currencies are still perceived as a marginal or niche phenomenon. The design of the rules of money is mostly seen as the subject of political decision-making processes in expert bodies of central banks (Dietsch 2017, p. 232). Thus, changes in the institutional framework are at best "political innovations" (Rammert 2010, p. 42). In turn, the development of means of payment is perceived as economic innovations, but often associated with negative externalities (Paech 2012; Lessenich 2016). The change of money itself seems unusual at first sight, as the objective of high value stability seems unchallenged and independent central banks strive to maintain it (McGinnis and Roche 2017, p. 11). Participants in the monetary system so far move like fish in water and do not care about the medium that surrounds them (Lietaer 1999, p. 18). When individual "fish" talk about money, it seems more like a given "thing" to be maximized:

> I like money. I'm very greedy. I'm a greedy person. I shouldn't tell you that, I'm a greedy – I've always been greedy. I love money, right?... But, you know what? I want to be greedy for our country. I want to be greedy. I want to be so greedy for our country. I want to take back money.(Donald Trump on February 11, 2016).

Donald Trump represents the image of economic people who strive for profit. Trump transfers this image to the state, which as a "Swabian househusband" should also generate as much profit as possible. Theoretically, money as a thing is founded on the modelling of markets with sellers who offer their goods for sale. Since in this fictitious market it is difficult to find someone who needs exactly what I offer and conversely offers what I need, the need for an "innovation" arises (Rammert 2010, p. 39). This simplifies the exchange process by introducing a good as a standard that is accepted by market participants. The problem of double coincidence is solved by introducing a numéraire (Ingham 1996, p. 513). The standard good is easy to measure, easily transferable and enjoys general esteem. Economists usually derive three basic functions from it: Medium of exchange, store of value, and measure of value (Mankiw and Taylor 2008, p. 709). The medium that best and most cheaply covers these functions prevails in the market as money in the sense of the "applicable medium of exchange". Those who make significant progress in fulfilling the functions are considered innovative (Ingham 1996, p. 511).

2 Narrative of Metallism

The focus is on an economic-technical view in which efficiency considerations play the main role. This narrative has a long tradition and is referred to by Goodhart as "M-theory" (Goodhart 1998). The "M" stands for metallism, because it represents a certain equivalent value such as gold or silver. In many economic models this narrative is implicitly adopted and not further reflected (Şener 2014, p. 8). Perfect money has no transaction costs and always has the same value everywhere. With this assumption, money disappears from economic models, and what remains are, for example, exchange situations on Robinson Crusoe's famous island. In such a model world, currency crises and disturbances caused by the monetary sphere do not occur. The idea that new money could bring about something constructive in society is also rejected.

If one remains attached to the narrative of M-theory, money itself will hardly become an object of reflection. Apart from technical developments of the money media, there is little room for manoeuvre. Whoever owns the "thing" should be able to hold it and increase it. Scarcity is good because it guarantees value as a medium of exchange. A problem arises, however, when the distribution becomes highly imbalanced and there is underutilization, unemployment, and poverty. States are strongly challenged in these situations because they have to protect the property of the haves on the one hand, and on the other hand they have to bring about a social balance in case of too much scarcity. The claims of the needy and the protective rights of the owners are opposed to each other and are discharged in political conflicts. Some parallel currencies like the Bitcoin based on M-theory are trying to profit from this conflict. They are characterized by scarcity, by a blindness to social and ecological interests and by the focus on individual interests (Gelleri 2021).

3 Figure of Thought of Chartalism

A relatively new "school" of money narratives was founded by Georg Friedrich Knapp in his book "The State Theory of Money" published in 1905 (Knapp 1905). In it, he argues that money emerged at the latest in modern times through the sovereign acts of collective, mostly state institutions. The starting point was markets, for which secular and ecclesiastical governments provided money that facilitated exchange on the one hand and ensured the collection of taxes on the other. Being able to create money is thus closely linked to the power to levy taxes and contributions. Since taxes may only be redeemed in the unit of money issued, this creates a general compulsion to accept (Wray 2018, p. 60). While agents in the economic circuit are free to use another unit of currency before making the final payment, this increases the transaction cost and requires at least one additional exchange of money before paying taxes (Mundell 1961, p. 662). The value of the unit minted was usually higher than the pure metal value for sound states. This expressed the confidence of the population in the security and efficiency benefits of the collective currency (Desan 2014). Historically, there were quite a few local payment and credit systems that were essentially an accounting of the local community. Graeber suggests that this type of bank-like current account system has even formed the basis for the majority of transactions (Graeber 2011). Here, too, there were often local representatives who collected contributions and taxes, such as religious communities or political institutions like a "community council".

Money creation and the acceptance of taxes, while logically related, are not coupled in a legal sense. This non-reciprocity allows the state or a collective some leeway to issue money into economic spaces without expecting the full amount to be returned in the form of taxes (Wray 2016). Legally, these are uncertain liabilities. The gain realised over time between issuance and reflux is known as 'seignorage'.

4 Creating Money Out of Nothing

The Chartalist view emphasizes the power and ability of the state or another collective to create money out of nothing (Fig. 1). It thus follows a creative understanding of innovation "ex nihilo" (Rammert 2010, p. 31). This money can be used to pay companies and employees to provide public or community goods. With the newly created money, economic activities are set in motion on the goods markets and income is generated. In today's monetary policy we do not find a state-determined

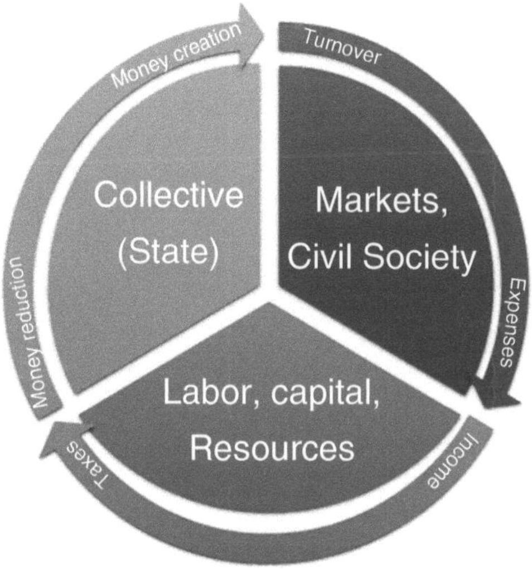

Fig. 1 Chartalistic money creation. (Own graphic)

chartalistic pure form at all, but a very far-reaching delegation of money creation to commercial banks. This has developed successively over centuries (Desan 2014). But why does the state give up this powerful instrument? One of the reasons given is the ability of commercial banks to identify innovative firms that increase potential output through their investment and spending (Weber 2018). The interest rate favours the companies with high growth potential and filters out ventures and projects with low growth potential. Aspects such as sustainability and solidarity play a subordinate role in business calculations. The decisive factor for the bank is repayability, including interest. Political economy findings on the drifting apart of rich and poor (Dietsch 2017, p. 237) and the increasing burden on the environment (Lessenich 2016) play a secondary role here at best. A much higher priority in the legal system is the safeguarding of payment transactions and acquired monetary and material property (Teubner 2012, p. 56). The principle of freedom is cited as a guiding principle: free market economy, free trade and a neoliberal economic concept (Riles 2018, p. 50f.). Often, the highest profits are made where the highest externalities are generated. If one understands money as the original communication medium of the economy, as Luhmann does, then one must look at the way money is created, since this is the source point of economic activity (Luhmann 1994).

In today's dominant form of money creation, banks put money into circulation through credit (Fig. 2). Lending is closely linked to the securing of property and

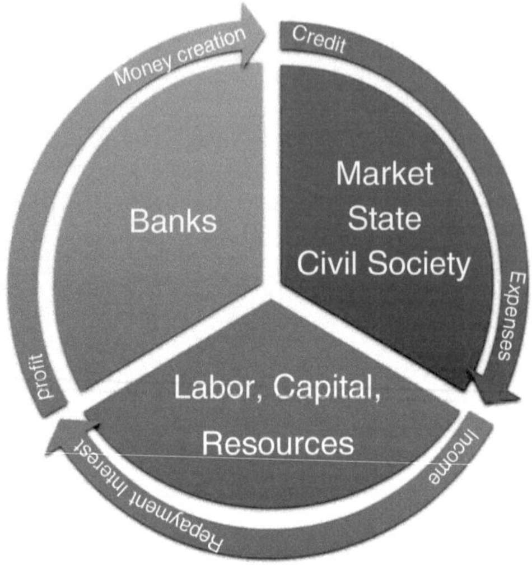

Fig. 2 Money creation by banks. (Own graphic)

other collateral (Heinsohn and Steiger 2006). Only those with collateral can access the medium of the economy directly at the source. In return, banks receive an interest rate for their services, which they use to hedge risks, cover administrative costs and pay a return to capital providers. Currently, governments and large corporations are managing to negotiate a low or even negative real interest rate. Whether this is just a temporary post-traumatic state or the beginning of a "post-growth economy" (Paech 2012), history must teach. For most individuals and firms, however, positive real interest rates are the norm even in an era of low interest rates. In addition, not all regions of the world have functioning banking structures. The pressure among small business owners is relatively high. After all, they represent 99.8 percent of businesses in the European Union (Eurostat 2019). Small and medium-sized enterprises pay on average more than one percentage point higher interest rates than large companies, according to a 2019 OECD survey. In many countries, the interest rate differential is significantly higher, and a high proportion of credit requests are rejected outright (OECD Scoreboard 2019). The proportion of people disconnected and excluded from the monetary system is correspondingly high. If, in addition, recessions occur in the economic cycle, banks hold back on lending for security and return reasons, and economic downturns are procyclically amplified. From a non-bank perspective, there is currently no alternative to commercial bank money. Taxes, rents and many other relevant items of expenditure can only be paid for with giro money. Via laws and jurisdiction we have imposed the "cross" on ourselves in the last decades and currently we can hardly choose freely. All the more important are experimental alternatives that can contribute to a major transformation with the help of the figure of thought of chartalism and collective design (Desan 2017; Feichtner 2018). There are three levels of innovation that can be addressed:

- Public banking to counteract over- and understatements macro-economically
- Monetary innovations through the bottom-up development of mutual self-help instruments
- Public-Commons-Partnerships as a combination of the first two approaches

If one follows Rammert's view, only the last two levels would be defined as "social innovations" because they emerge outside politics and connect with political institutions over time (Rammert 2010, p. 43). However, local networking often starts through civil society initiatives and later connects with local government institutions or vice versa. Therefore, the boundaries at the local level tend to be fluid and mutual networking is a key success factor.

5 Types of Social Innovation in the Monetary Field

In the field of complementary currencies, we use four criteria to distinguish between different forms of money:

1. Issuance of the money by a public body
2. Issue in digital form
3. Use of money via central offices or peer-to-peer
4. Characterization of money as a social innovation

The first criterion follows from the discussion so far: because of the power to levy taxes, a public money can potentially also be issued. Without this property, strictly speaking, one cannot speak of "money" or "currency" in the jurisprudential sense, because the legal normative recognition in the political sphere is missing (Omlor 2014). The second criterion describes a technical property that enables the scaling and programming of goals and properties. This is contrasted with multiple material forms of money. Similarly, the third criterion is decentralized peer-to-peer use without the intervention of a central authority. In the case of cash, the transfer is direct. Similarly, with blockchain-based currencies, the register is distributed and complex operations allow for decentralized pass-through (Bech and Garrat 2017). With a bank's book money, transactions are recorded centrally. The fourth criterion

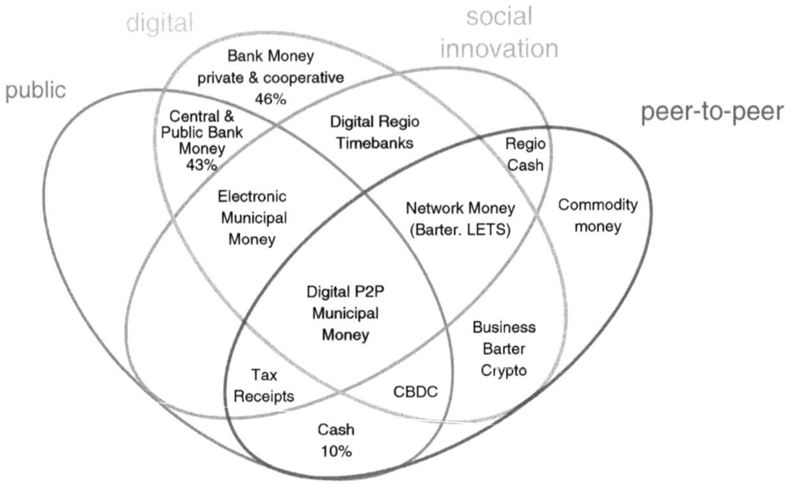

Fig. 3 Money Flower. (Own graphic)

that distinguishes social innovation from other innovations is that it intentionally intervenes in the development of society to bring about and shape social change (Hochgerner et al. 2012, p. 7). Researchers and practitioners from different sectors of society participate in 'real laboratories' through democratic processes and pursue transformative goals (Defila and Di Giulio 2018, pp. 40–41). When money is shaped in this way, it becomes a driver of cultural development beyond purely technological or economic factors (Howaldt and Schwarz 2010, p. 102).

The first three criteria were taken from a model of the "Money Flower" (Bech and Garrat 2017; Bofinger 2018). The fourth criterion was varied for this paper (Fig. 3). The graphical visualization is done using a Venn diagram that integrates the criteria in binary form, i.e. as applicable or not applicable (Micallef 2018).

Because of the great importance of political and economic institutions in the field of money, the two most important forms will be briefly outlined.

5.1 Central Banks and Commercial Banks

In addition to cash, central banks issue digital central bank money. With a share of 10 percent (cash) and 20 percent, the central banks thus issue almost a third of the total money volume (Bundesbank 2019) Central bank money is needed by commercial banks to deposit minimum reserves with the central bank and to settle balances between banks. In Germany, commercial banks represent a good two-thirds of the total money volume and 90 percent of the transaction volume between non-banks. Three types of banks share almost equally the market of the bank money: savings banks as local state banks (in Austria, however, largely privatized), the cooperative banks and the private commercial banks. In their origins, cooperative groupings and savings bank associations as local credit unions were a means of self-help without major regulatory requirements. Through networks and rules, socially relevant and legally recognised institutions have gradually emerged. So what were "social innovations" 150 years ago with cooperative banks and savings banks are today established and traditional forms of the monetary system. They thus lack the aspect of the "new" that belongs to an "innovation" (Rammert 2010, p. 29). Occasionally, there are new forms of banking in this sector, which, as in the case of GLS Bank, see themselves as social innovations in the monetary system (Jorberg and Landwehr 2017, p. 287). Globally, the market shares of private commercial banks are much higher and, accordingly, the focus is much more on returns. Since in many countries, fiat money is the only medium of exchange that can be used to officially pay taxes, commercial bank money has the actual role of official money. Surprisingly, cash often cannot be used to pay taxes, so there are certain question marks about its legal designation as "money".

5.2 First Generation Cryptocurrencies as Economic Innovation

In the case of the cryptocurrency Bitcoin, there is no obligation to redeem it, neither in another currency nor in the form of taxes, benefits or the like. Many cryptocurrencies therefore have the reputation of only being about maximizing the profits of the money creators. It is against this backdrop that the waves of outrage that have arisen in the wake of Facebook's announcement and creation of its Libra project should be understood. One of the sticking points is that while the Libra is to be sold against hard currencies, there is no formal guarantee of redemption. Thus, the issuance of the currency would create a full seignorage for the benefit of the issuer club, which consists only of members who can afford to put in more than US$ten million. Although the Libra Foundation is supposed to form a currency reserve with interest-bearing bonds, there is only an intention to buy Libra for the purpose of exchange rate maintenance, but precisely no guarantee (Bofinger 2018). In terms of legal structure, the Libra concept is limited to a small oligarchic circle. This form of cryptocurrencies can be seen as "economic innovations" with certain technical and utility maximizing aspects. A transformative contribution inherent in social innovations is currently not discernible. Auch die später erfolgte Neukonzeption und Umbenennung des Projekts.

6 Case Studies of Monetary Tools as Social Innovation

More important, therefore, are approaches that are democratically designed and focus on goals such as social justice, solidarity and sustainability (Lietaer et al. 2012). This does not exclude the use of blockchain technology, but a potentially promising technology alone is not sufficient to be considered a transformative "social innovation".

6.1 The Use of Tax Credits at Local Level with Municipal Money (Tax Tokens)

Complementary currencies often emerge in times of major economic crises and high unemployment. A well-known example is the "Miracle of Wörgl" in 1932 and 1933 (Onken 1997). The mayor, Michael Unterguggenberger, had studied the theories of Silvio Gesell (2009) for years and was faced with unemployment of over 20 percent in the small Tyrolean town. With the help of his wife, who ran a business in Wörgl, he developed a local free money concept and convinced the local council of the idea. The mayor hired job seekers to tackle one project after another: A kindergarten was refurbished, a road was repaired, a bridge was built, a hiking trail for tourists was established, and even a ski jump was built. The workers were not paid with the national currency, but with "work certificates" in nominal values of the national currency of 1, 5 and 10 shillings (Fig. 4).

Businesses were motivated to accept the local currency, and in return it was promised that municipal taxes could be paid. A chartalistic cycle was born, which took its starting point from the common collective (Nakayama and Kuwata 2019). To prevent distrust, the full amount was deposited in Austrian shillings at the local Raiffeisen bank. However, this reserve was neither formally nor practically necessary because businesses preferred free redemption for settlement in tax debts to a fee-based exchange into the national currency. The local bank note described the objectives and the idea of the project and also announced that any surpluses would go to local poor relief.

A special feature was a circulation security in the amount of 1 percent per month. With the help of adhesive stamps, the work certificates were regularly revalued. The revaluation was always due on the first of the month. This meant that

Fig. 4 Work confirmation Wörgl from the year 1932. (© Unterguggenberger-Institut Wörgl e. V., Wörgl)

the local currency circulated very quickly. Shortly before expiry, the notes mostly ended up in the community coffers, because businesses used them to pay their taxes (Broer 2013). The community rejoiced in the bubbling revenue, and business occupancy increased significantly. While surrounding communities continued to sink into economic depression, the community thrived and unemployment dropped by a quarter. Surrounding communities adopted the model, and communities from all over Austria showed strong interest.

Shortly after the launch of the local currency, the Austrian central bank saw its monetary monopoly violated and pursued a ban on the local currency. On the administrative level, the central bank was soon able to assert itself. Resistance within the local government and a lawsuit by the municipality were able to delay the stop of the project for a few months, but after the legal defeat in the last instance and a threat of punishment against the local government, the project had to be stopped after only one year in the summer of 1933. The brief glimmer of hope was followed by a fascist dictatorship in Austria, which was later replaced by the National Socialist dictatorship. Nevertheless, the municipality succeeded in bringing a "blueprint" into the world that was the model for the Swiss WIR system (Dubois 2014), the Chiemgauer (Gelleri 2008) and the Sardex (Sartori and Dini 2016).

In the classification as a "social" or "political" innovation, the case of Wörgl is interesting because it was born out of the need of the population and was launched together with local actors. As a democratically legitimated political institution, the municipality ensured the activation of local economic cycles, while the central bank had completely failed in fulfilling its political task. The money creation took place in conjunction with the creation of public goods, some of which are still of use to the residents today and have a sign indicating that they were financed by the free money project at the time.

6.2 Barter Systems for Self-Help Using the Example of Sardex

The term "barter" means "to exchange" and usually refers to the direct exchange between the participants. However, a barter system goes far beyond simple direct exchange. The performance of the network increases with the number of offers and approaches a "universal money" in large systems. Therefore, overcoming a critical mass is crucial and, as in the case described below, the term "network money" is more appropriate.

Even in modern times, there are many regions that are affected by high unemployment and low utilization of regional production potential. For example, the island of Sardinia has been considered a very economically weak region in Italy for decades. The situation worsened with the financial crisis in 2008. Unemployment rose to over 20 percent and youth unemployment even to over 50 percent. The 60,000 small and medium-sized enterprises suffered from low capacity utilization. A startup of five young entrepreneurs came across the topic of complementary currencies and analyzed different types. The most promising appeared to be a barter system, which enables a mutual liquidity framework. By being closed, participants act as providers and as demanders ("prosumers").

Despite underutilization, the scepticism towards another means of payment was very high. Through a lot of persuasion and personal networking, it was possible to motivate a critical mass of 237 companies to participate at the start in 2010 (Sartori and Dini 2016). The companies paid a fixed membership fee for participation, which was based on the number of employees (from EUR 300 per year). Because there are no other fees besides the annual fee, it is attractive for firms to implement as much as possible in the network. The amount of the liquidity limit was also based on the number of employees. The regional cash cycle begins with the interest-free overdraft of the Sardex account. Those who take in Sardex immediately look for further opportunities to spend it again. Over time, employees were also included in the cycle, receiving up to 300 Sardex per month. The network grew rapidly to include 1000 companies three years after launch and counts over 4000 companies in 2019. According to personal information from Giuseppe Littera,

CEO of Sardex, the turnover in 2019 was 48 million Sardex. The average turnover per company was 20,000 Sardex, which is about eight percent of an average company turnover in Sardinia. Media dubbed the project the "Sardex factor" because sales reached a significant share of regional value added of about half a percent. According to the company's own estimate, about 1000 new jobs were created on the island. The focus of value creation is in the south and southwest of the island, where the initiative is also based. Since 2016, the operating company has been a limited company with investors from all over Italy. The founders emphasise that their aim is to maximise the social impact on the region, but do not see the corporate form as a "democratic legal form". Some argue that barter networks are a separate legal entity. The operating organization merely acts as a service provider to ensure technical processing and security. However, the dependency of the network on the operator organisation is very high and the expertise about the network is concentrated with the operator. Therefore, a democratic legal form would in principle be preferable.

Reflecting on the Sardex as a social money innovation, the money creation process is similar to that of a bank. Due to the regional closedness of the system, expenditures in Sardex are more likely to come back as income. There is no compulsion to grow because no additional interest is charged. The cost recovery contributions are manageable at two percent of sales. On the one hand, they should be seen as a financing contribution to liquidity and, on the other, as marketing costs for the visible offer on the Internet. Those who own Sardex actively search for regional offers and reduce advertising costs for service providers. An additional "circulation impulse" exists through the obligation to reduce the liquidity framework to zero within one year. If this is not achieved, participants will have to pay Euros, which they usually do not have enough of. Therefore, on the demand side there is the urge to spend Sardex again soon in order to preserve one's own euro liquidity as much as possible, and on the supply side there is the compulsion to balance minus holdings to zero within twelve months. The logic of reciprocal give and take is comprehensible to all participants, and the more that join in, the more efficiently and cost-effectively the island's economic potential is exploited. For the state and society, the activity is attractive in several ways: rising sales with a high regional value-added content increase employment, raise incomes and taxes, and make it possible to finance public goods. As the activities take place on the island, transport distances are shorter and the external effects on the environment tend to be lower than with import- and export-oriented forms of value creation.

Economists often throw in the argument of "protectionism" here, but only free capacities are used. Value creation in euros is therefore neither impaired nor reduced at the expense of other regions. The alternative to regional exchange in

Sardex would therefore be no value creation at all or black labour. The accusation of an "underground economy" cannot be made against Sardex, as the sales take place completely digitally and can be viewed in recorded form by the tax authorities at any time. With an annual turnover of 48 million Sardex (2019), the tax revenue is likely to be over eight million euros. These taxes must be paid in euros and, due to Sardinian autonomous status, 60 percent of them are at the disposal of the Sardinian regional government. The Sardex cycle would close if the Sardinian government were to accept and spend the additional tax revenues in Sardex. It would even be conceivable to integrate a chartalist perspective, in that the Sardinian government could first spend Sardex and then, after one year, repay the spent Sardex. The liquidity framework would be at least eight million Sardex, but much more would be possible due to the high unemployment and the great need for public goods.

This is where the potential of so-called public-commons partnerships, which rely on close cooperation between state institutions and civil society networks, becomes apparent (Helfrich and Bollier 2019). At the level of one-off investment, such partnerships have long been taking place. For example, the European Union has provided the Sardex initiative with multiple amounts of money as a subsidy for the development of the software platform. There are also initial small-scale projects of cooperation at the local level when it comes to payment in municipal schools in Sardinia and aid services. The example of Wörgl, however, shows a much greater potential with the help of an active local government role in conjunction with democratic sponsorship.

6.3 Chiemgauer Regional Currency Cash and Digital

The fact that complementary currencies do not have to be born out of necessity is shown by the example of the Chiemgauer regional currency (Fig. 5). The Chiemgau region in the districts of Traunstein and Rosenheim is characterised by relative prosperity, unemployment is far below the European average and the corporate structure is a healthy mix of regionally oriented and export-oriented businesses. At the time of its foundation, aspects of underutilisation were not too much in the foreground, although at that time there was a recession with a strongly depressed consumer mood. Instead, aspects such as sustainability, promoting education and experimenting with economic theories were discussed and enshrined in the founding statutes.

The examples of complementary currencies, which were still rare at the time, were analysed in advance, in particular the Wörgl Free Money Project, the WIR

Fig. 5 Chiemgauer regional currency, 2019–2022 series. (© Chiemgauer e. V., Traunstein)

Bank and, with regard to the legal assessment, the Bethel-Euro of the Bodelschwingh'sche Anstalten in Bielefeld. The sponsors of the initiative in this case were the author, who at the time was a teacher at the Chiemgau Waldorf School in Prien at Lake Chiemsee, and six schoolgirls who had voluntarily signed up for the pupil enterprise project. The legal form was initially an unregistered association, which was converted into a registered association a short time later. Due to the rural structure and the increasing dominance of corporations and chain stores, it was evaluated how many enterprises were willing to participate in the project. The results indicated about 35 owner-operated regional businesses in the same locality. 20 companies declared themselves willing to accept, provided that due to the small network a re-exchange into Euro is possible. The Chiemgauer differs from a closed barter system in that it can be exchanged into the national currency on both sides. The currency name was borrowed from the Chiemgau region and the exchange rate was set at one euro to one Chiemgauer. As a bonus for the exchange, a desired project receives three percent of the exchange amount. The payment of the three percent is refinanced from the five percent due for the re-exchange. Two percent is used to cover operating costs. Oriented on the free money idea (Rogoff 2016), the Chiemgauer also has the principle of circulation impulse through semi-annual adhesive tokens that cost three percent of the nominal value.

On the digital Chiemgauer accounts, the negative interest rate is six percent per year.

The network of the Waldorf School, built up over decades, had a favourable effect on the diffusion of the Chiemgauer. At the start date in January 2003 30 parents and teachers exchanged 2000 EUR for 2000 Chiemgauer. At the same time subscriptions were agreed with monthly exchange sums of between 20 and 200 Chiemgauers. A few days after the launch, companies expressed the wish to be able to exchange their Chiemgauers back into euros. After deducting the exchange fee, the amount was transferred to the companies' account. In the beginning, the Chiemgauer was more of a voucher system because the amounts were exchanged into euros relatively quickly. Due to lively reporting in the school news and in local newspapers, the number of acceptance points rose to 100 at the end of 2003. The total turnover was 70,000 Chiemgauers. In the second year, the exchange tripled and the number of acceptance points doubled. The dynamic continued in the following years, and more and more regional circuits were formed with the Chiemgauer. With the onset of the financial crisis, public and media interest increased once again. Concerned members suggested thinking about the further development of the Chiemgauer, and drafts of a value-covered regional currency were created. At the same time, the digital Chiemgauer was developed, which greatly simplified payment transactions. The development took place in close cooperation with cooperative banks and savings banks. Larger companies were thus enabled to participate. In 2013, Stadtwerke Rosenheim was acquired as a municipal company offering a regional green electricity product in Chiemgauer. Today, the total sales are more than six million Chiemgauer per year. More than 700 businesses and non-profit-organizisation and over 4000 people from the region participate. This makes the initiative the largest of its kind in Germany and a model for many more hundreds of regional currencies worldwide.

Inspired by complementary currencies in Brazil (Curitiba) and Belgium (Torekes), the Chiemgauer Initiative began developing a climate bonus concept in 2017 in cooperation with two other regions. The concept was selected from a large number of proposals by the National Climate Protection Initiative of the German Federal Ministry for the Environment, so that in summer 2019, for the first time in Germany, a public commons project could be launched in the field of regional currencies. As a first stage, the saving of 5000 tons of CO_2 over three years in the Chiemgau region was set as a goal. The rules of the climate bonus serve to motivate people and organisations to reduce CO_2 and to compensate the remaining footprint. The revenue for offsetting is used to finance the reduction incentives. The complementary currency serves as the vehicle. After three years, the climate bonus project has nowsaved more than 10,000 tonnes of CO2 (Gelleri 2022).

The idea is not entirely new: in Ghent, there is a local currency called "Torekes", which are paid out to residents of a neighbourhood when they collect litter (Lietaer et al. 2012). Torekes are paid as a reward. The torekes, in turn, can only be used for very specific purposes, such as renting a small garden area. On this, residents can grow and harvest vegetables. The climate bonus is applied in a similar way: For example, if someone brings a broken appliance to a Repair Cafe and the appliance can be repaired, the person who brings the appliance and the person who repairs the appliance receive a climate bonus. This can be used, for example, for a regionally produced climate-friendly product.

In these approaches, money sets a reciprocal dynamic in motion. By changing the institution of money through grassroots or representative-democratic procedures, it unfolds a steering effect which, while not forcing anyone to act, constantly and repeatedly "reminds" the individual of the jointly agreed action. The one-time common imagination of a future becomes a "recycling re-imagining". In itself, this is certainly not sufficient, but money as a regional infrastructure can stimulate further social innovation and form an ecosystem of transformation with further initiatives (Domanski and Kaletka 2018). If this is implemented in accordance with the basic principle of "back to human scale" (Kohr 2002) and oriented towards principles such as subsidiarity and decentralisation, the likelihood of sustainable development paths being entered into in manageable and transparent spaces increases.

Acknowledgments The article presents and discusses results in the context of the research project "Democratization of Money and Credit", which is a subproject of the research association ForDemocracy. The author thanks the project leader, Prof. Isabel Feichtner, for enabling and supporting the research. The paper represents the thoughts and opinions of the author.

References

Bech, Morten, und Rodney Garrat. 2017. Kryptowährungen von Zentralbanken. https://www.bis.org/publ/qtrpdf/r_qt1709f_de.htm. Zugegriffen: 14. Dezember 2018.

Bofinger, Peter. 2018. Digitalisation of money and the future of monetary policy. *Vox*.

Broer, Wolfgang. 2013. *Schwundgeld: Bürgermeister Michael Unterguggenberger und das Wörgler Währungsexperiment 1932/33*, 2. Aufl. Innsbruck u. a: Studien Verlag.

Bundesbank, Deutsche. 2019. Monatsbericht Oktober 2019 71 (10).

Defila, Rico, und Antonietta Di Giulio. 2018. Partizipative Wissenserzeugung und Wissenschaftlichkeit: ein methodologischer Beitrag. In *Transdisziplinär und transformativ forschen: Eine Methodensammlung*, Hrsg. Rico Defila und Antonietta Di Giulio, 39–68. Wiesbaden, Germany: Springer VS.

Desan, Christine. 2014. *Making Money: Coin, Currency, and the Coming of Capitalism.* Oxford: Oxford University Press.

Desan, Christine. 2017. Constitutional Approach to Money. In *Money talks: Explaining how money really works*, Hrsg. Nina Bandelj, Frederick F. Wherry und Viviana A. Rotman Zelizer, 109–130. Princeton, NJ, Oxford: Princeton University Press.

Dietsch, Peter. 2017. Normative dimensions of central banking. In *Just financial markets?: Finance in a just society*, Hrsg. Lisa Herzog, 231–250. Oxford, New York: Oxford University Press.

Domanski, Dmitri, und Christoph Kaletka. 2018. Lokale Ökosysteme sozialer Innovation verstehen und gestalten. In *Soziale Innovationen lokal gestalten*, Hrsg. Hans-Werner Franz und Christoph Kaletka, 291–308. Wiesbaden: Springer Fachmedien Wiesbaden.

Dubois, Hervé. 2014. *Faszination WIR: Resistent gegen Krisen, Spekulationen und Profitgier.* Lenzburg: Faro.

Eurostat. 2019. Number of enterprises in the non-financial business economy by size class of employment. https://ec.europa.eu/eurostat/tgm/table.do?tab=table&init=1&plugin=1&language=en&pcode=tin00145. Zugegriffen: 26. Oktober 2019.

Feichtner, Isabel. 2018. Public Law's Rationalization of the Legal Architecture of Money: What Might Legal Analysis of Money Become? In *Democracy and Financial Order: Legal Perspectives*, Hrsg. Matthias Goldmann und Silvia Steininger, 197–227. Berlin, Heidelberg: Springer Berlin Heidelberg.

Gelleri, Christian. 2008. Theorie und Praxis des Regiogeldes. In *Der Geldkomplex: Kritische Reflexion unseres Geldsystems und mögliche Zukunftsszenarien*, Hrsg. Mathias Weis. Bern, Stuttgart, Wien: Haupt.

Gelleri, Christian. 2021. Reshaping the Future of Europe with Complementary Currencies. *European Papers* (6): 1–12. doi: https://doi.org/10.15166/2499-8249/511.

Gelleri, Christian. 2022. Creating Monetary Collaborative Spaces for Social and Ecological Transformation. Sustainability 14 (23). doi: https://doi.org/10.3390/su142315528.

Gesell, Silvio. 2009. *Die natürliche Wirtschaftsordnung durch Freiland und Freigeld*, 4. Aufl. Kiel: Gaucke Verl. für Sozialökonomie.

Goodhart, Charles A.E. 1998. The two concepts of money: implications for the analysis of optimal currency areas. *European Journal of Political Economy* 14 (3): 407–432. https://doi.org/https://doi.org/10.1016/s0176-2680(98)00015-9.

Graeber, David. 2011. *Debt: The first 5000 years.* New York.

Hardraht, Klaus, und Hugo Godschalk. 2004. Komplementärwährungsgutachten: Erstellt im Auftrag der Sparkasse Delitsch-Eilenburg. https://monneta.org/wp-content/uploads/2015/04/Delitzsch_Rechtsgutachten.pdf. Zugegriffen: 11. Dezember 2018.

Heinsohn, Gunnar, und Otto Steiger. 2006. *Eigentum, Zins und Geld: Ungelöste Rätsel der Wirtschaftswissenschaft*, 4. Aufl. Marburg: Metropolis.

Helfrich, Silke, und David Bollier. 2019. *Frei, fair und lebendig – Die Macht der Commons.*

Hochgerner, Josef, A. Kesselring, K. Handler, P. Moser. 2012. Solidarische Ökonomie als Feld Sozialer Innovation. Endbericht. Ein Forschungsprojekt gefördert vom Jubiläumsfonds der österreichischen Nationalbank. Hg. v. Josef Hochgerner. Wien. Zentrum für Soziale Innovation. Online verfügbar unter https://www.zsi.at/object/project/1005/attach/P13733-Endbericht___Solidarische_%C3%96konomie_als_Feld_sozialer_Innovation.pdf. Zugegriffen: 03. 09. 2018.

Howaldt, Jürgen, und Michael Schwarz. 2010. Soziale Innovation: Konzepte, Forschungsfelder und -perspektiven. In *Soziale Innovation: Auf dem Weg zu einem postindustriellen Innovationsparadigma*, Hrsg. Jürgen Howaldt und Heike Jacobsen, 87–108. Wiesbaden: VS Verlag für Sozialwissenschaften.

Ingham, Geffrey. 1996. Money is a Social Relation. *Review of Social Economy* 54 (4): 507–529. https://doi.org/https://doi.org/10.1080/00346769600000031.

Jorberg, Thomas, und Werner Landwehr. 2017. Die Rolle von Investoren zur Förderung sozialer Innovationen am Beispiel der GLS Bank. In *Soziale Innovationen für nachhaltigen Konsum*, Hrsg. Melanie Jaeger-Erben, Jana Rückert-John und Martina Schäfer, 287–295. Wiesbaden: Springer Fachmedien Wiesbaden.

Knapp, Georg Friedrich. 1905. *Staatliche Theorie des Geldes*. Leipzig.

Kohr, Leopold. 2002. *Das Ende der Großen – Zurück zum menschlichen Maß*, 2. Aufl. Salzburg: Müller.

Lessenich, Stephan. 2016. *Neben uns die Sintflut: Die Externalisierungsgesellschaft und ihr Preis*. München: Hanser Berlin im Carl Hanser Verlag.

Lietaer, Bernard A. 1999. *Das Geld der Zukunft: Über die destruktive Wirkung des existierenden Geldsystems und die Entwicklung von Komplementärwährungen*. [München]: Riemann.

Lietaer, Bernard A., Christian Arnsperger, Sally Goerner, und Stefan Brunnhuber. 2012. *Money and sustainability: The missing link*. Dorset: Triarchy Press.

Luhmann, Niklas. 1994. *Die Wirtschaft der Gesellschaft*.

Mankiw, Nicholas Gregory, und Mark P. Taylor. 2008. *Grundzüge der Volkswirtschaftslehre*, 4. Aufl. Stuttgart: Schäffer-Pöschel.

McGinnis, John O., und Kyle W. Roche. 2017. Bitcoin: Order without Law in the Digital Age. *SSRN Electronic Journal*. https://doi.org/https://doi.org/10.2139/ssrn.2929133.

Micallef, Luana. 2018. Visualizations with Venn and Euler Diagrams.

Mundell, Robert. 1961. A Theory of Optimum Currency Areas. *The American Economic Review* 1961 (51): 657–665.

Nakayama, Chikako, und Manabu Kuwata. 2019. *An Investigation of social and credit theory of money focusing on regional and crypto currencies*, Takayama, 2019. Accessed 19 Oktober 2019.

OECD Scoreboard. 2019. *Financing SMEs and Entrepreneurs 2019*. Paris: OECD.

Omlor, Sebastian. 2014. *Geldprivatrecht: Entmaterialisierung, Europäisierung, Entwertung*. Tübingen: Mohr Siebeck.

Onken, Werner. 1997. *Modellversuche mit sozialpflichtigem Boden und Geld*. Lütjenburg: Fachverl. für Sozialökonomie.

Paech, Niko. 2012. *Nachhaltiges Wirtschaften jenseits von Innovationsorientierung und Wachstum: Eine unternehmensbezogene Transformationstheorie*, 2. Aufl. Marburg: Metropolis-Verlag.

Rammert, Werner. 2010. Die Innovationen der Gesellschaft. In *Soziale Innovation: Auf dem Weg zu einem postindustriellen Innovationsparadigma*, Hrsg. Jürgen Howaldt und Heike Jacobsen, 21–52. Wiesbaden: VS Verlag für Sozialwissenschaften.

Riles, Annelise. 2018. *Financial Citizenship: Experts, Publics, and the Politics of Central Banking*. Ithaca: Cornell University Press.

Rogoff, Kenneth S. 2016. *Der Fluch des Geldes: Warum unser Bargeld verschwinden wird*. München: FinanzBuch Verlag.

Sartori, Laura, und Paolo Dini. 2016. From complementary currency to institution: A micro-macro study of the Sardex mutual credit system. *Societ Editrice Il Mulino* 2016 (2): 273–304.

Şener, Ulaş. 2014. *Die Neutralitätstheorie des Geldes: Ein kritischer Überblick.* Potsdam: Univ.-Verl.

Seyfang, Gill, und Noel Longhurst. 2013. Growing green money? Mapping community currencies for sustainable development. *Ecological Economics* 86:65–77. https://doi.org/https://doi.org/10.1016/j.ecolecon.2012.11.003.

Teubner, Gunther. 2012. *Verfassungsfragmente: Gesellschaftlicher Konstitutionalismus in der Globalisierung.* Berlin: Suhrkamp.

Weber, Beat. 2018. *Democratizing money?: Debating legitimacy in monetary reform proposals.* Cambridge: Cambridge University Press.

Wray, L. Randall. 2016. *Modern Money Theory: A Primer on Macroeconomics for Sovereign Monetary Systems.* London: Palgrave Macmillan UK.

Wray, Larry Randall. 2018. *Modernes Geld verstehen: Der Schlüssel zu Vollbeschäftigung und Preisstabilität.* Berlin: Lola Books.

Gelleri, Christian, Dipl.-Hdl., Dipl.-Betriebswirt (TH), studied business education (Uni Munich), studied economics (Uni Munich), studied business administration (TH Rosenheim). Research assistant at the Institute for International Law, European Law and European Private Law, Professorship Feichtner within the research project “Democratisation of Money and Credit”, Managing Director of Regios eG, founder of the regional currency Chiemgauer.

Latest Publications:

Gelleri, Christian. 2022. Creating Monetary Collaborative Spaces for Social and Ecological Transformation. Sustainability 14 (23). doi: 10.3390/su142315528.

Gelleri, Christian. 2022. Local currencies in the context of climate protection: A circular and decentral economy approach based on real experiments. *Energy Proceedings* (29): 1–6. doi: 10.46855/energy-proceedings-10,286.

Gelleri, Christian. 2021. Reshaping the Future of Europe with Complementary Currencies. *European Papers* (6): 1–12. doi: 10.15166/2499-8249/511.

A Philosophical Approach to the Identity of Places

Martina Wegner

Abstract

The results of the project "Demografiewerkstatt Kommunen" show that municipalities that want to find viable solutions in response to demographic change will sooner or later reach the point where they have to deal with their identity. They cannot plan their future without thinking about their identity. Therefore, the question arises as to the nature of this identity and whether municipalities as places have an identity of their own or whether this identity is exclusively ascribed to them by people. This consideration will be pursued on the basis of philosophical approaches in order to enrich discourses conducted in other disciplines. This philosophical search will look for clues in identity theory, but also in anthropology, metaphor and topography.

1 Introduction

The following search for clues comes from practice: as part of the Demografiewerkstatt Kommunen (DWK) project, which has been funded by the Federal Ministry for Family Affairs, Senior Citizens, Women and Youth (BMFSFJ) since 2015, the cities and districts participating in it are to develop a demographic

M. Wegner (✉)
Faculty of Applied Social Sciences, Munich University of Applied Sciences, Munich, Germany
e-mail: martina.wegner@hm.edu

H.-W. Franz et al. (eds.), *Sustainable Living and Business*,
https://doi.org/10.1007/978-3-658-41835-9_9

strategy[1]. During the strategy development process, the municipalities initially focused their attention strongly on the demographic changes they are facing in each case and on the measures that could be used to cope with them. Some municipalities changed focus during the process; while all population groups are important to them, of particular importance are young people and how they are likely to want to live in the future. The question of the future living conditions of the place also raises the question of how the place should develop and what its identity should be. In Adorf in the Vogtland region of Saxony, for example, it was considered that as a municipality in a structurally weak area it would not be able to compete with the economically stronger towns, but that as a traditional music town in beautiful natural surroundings it could become an attractive residential town for commuters. In the steel town of Riesa, proud in GDR times, there are still numerous commercial enterprises, but the town has to find a new self-image after a strong loss of population after the reunification. In the town, Immendorff's monumental cast steel sculpture "Elbquelle" (Elbe Spring) is a reminder of times gone by, while a game board is used to discuss the city of tomorrow with schoolchildren. In Grabow in the district of Ludwigslust-Parchim, the old town has been redeveloped with housing that also takes into account people with disabilities, and the market square has been provided with new shopping facilities and meeting places. In addition, the tradition of Sunday concerts in the park was revived.

These few examples already show that the idea of the identity of places plays an important role in their further development. In municipal practice, in situations of upheaval or transformation, a mission statement was and is often developed – partly together with the citizens, partly by marketing agencies. The aim is to highlight the unmistakable core of the place, the region, and thus keep people in the city or interest them in it. However, this often involves an identity reference that is very superficial and geared more towards marketability than towards a theory of identity. But how can this identity be grasped? The examples given suggest that identity is about historical imprints, about traditions, about the location of the place in a certain region or nature, and also about a uniqueness reflected by architecture, landmarks or monuments. With the search for identity, communities strive for social sustainability, i.e. they want to shape the living conditions of the people in such a way that there is cohesion, shared values against the background of experienced history, and an interest in participation.

The question of identity arises in different disciplines. With regard to the identity of a city, it is naturally the disciplines that deal with urban planning and urban development that research and work in this field. However, as will be shown below,

[1] The author has been advising the BMFSFJ on the implementation of the project since 2015.

this research is primarily concerned with the patterns of action of people in the respective city and strongly related to the interaction of place and people. In contrast, an attempt will be made here to take up the issue of the identity of place from the discipline of philosophy and to analyse whether cities and towns have an identity of their own beyond the attributions made by people. While the question of identity and identification of people with a place is common and subjectively answerable by them, the question of whether and under what assumptions places can be ascribed an identity of their own is little discussed. Philosophical identity theory aims to establish whether places have an existence and identity of their own, detached from patterns of action and attributions or constructions by people.

The study is made difficult by the fact that the terms place and municipality are not congruent. Municipalities are politically determined territorial authorities that are endowed with rights according to planning, economic or political aspects and are democratically constituted and can group together or meet places with their own history and identity. At the same time, the process of (re)municipalisation (cf. e.g. Dahme and Wohlfahrt 2013, p. 239 ff.) places a great emphasis on the self-organisation of local authorities, which often have to cooperate across newly drawn administrative structures. That this distinction between evolved localities and municipalities defined by planning/policy is significant is evident in the recurring difficulties that arise in intra- and inter-municipal cooperation after territorial reforms, or can be seen in feelings of disruption among the population, who cannot emotionally or identificationally comprehend the divisions or designations of their locality that have arisen out of practical considerations. As Mattenklodt puts it, the territorial reform in Germany in the 1960s and 1970s "was characterized by the transition from historically grown units to planned supply bodies that were as effective as possible. An abstractly conceived network of municipal service units was superimposed on a structure of municipal and district-level bodies that had become historical" (Mattenklodt 2013: 161), which was supposed to better meet citizens' demands for a modern administration.

When we speak of the identity of communities, however, we can only mean places in their growth, in their spaces that have been shaped over decades and centuries and changed by the political and social course of time and dynamics. These are spaces that are culturally and anthropologically significant, since the inhabitants have experienced sociality and participation here, which existentially belong to human existence and life and represent the background foil for their lives.

2 The Inherent Logic of Cities as a Sociological Reference Point

If one looks for the discussion of the identity of places or communities in sociology, one comes across the discussion of the "inherent logic of cities". The research tradition in urban sociology refers to "city" as a particular entity that has characteristics that distinguish it from the countryside. Thus, housing in the city, the living conditions of families in the city, etc. have been researched, but only in so far as they are symptomatic of the entity "city", but not with a view to whether there is also something typical of the city here, i.e. something that characterises cities per se. Little research has been done, on the other hand, on how cities differ (cf. Löw 2018; Frank 2012).

In the past 10–15 years, urban sociology has taken up Henri Lefèbvre's reflections on the city (cf. Frank 2012). and the reception of his ideas will be briefly taken up here. Lefèbvre described "city" as a complex "work of art", as a become object with history (Löw 2018). According to Lefèbvre, the city imposes itself on people in its facticity, it directs action along certain lines, and at the same time, it is only through this action that the city realizes itself. Lefèbvre thus sees here an interaction between the identity of the place and its imprinting by people. On this basis, Lefèbvre called upon sociology to direct its gaze no longer only to social structures, but increasingly to cities and their specifics.

In this context, sociologists are now considering whether the city has a certain habitus (cf. Lindner 2008; Bockrath 2008), whether physical characteristics can be transferred to the city, or whether it is not rather a question of the worlds of meaning that cities offer their inhabitants (Löw 2018). Against this background, a research project entitled "Eigenlogik der Städte"[2] has been launched, focusing on questions of the specificity of individual cities: What is city, what is common to all cities? Do cities function differently, and what characterizes these differences? "The knowledge that Hamburg is quite different from Munich and that Cottbus feels different from Leipzig is deeply anchored in everyday human experience. But why is this so? Why is it that not only 'the city' is commonly imagined as different from 'the country', but also that cities are imagined and experienced as social entities that are distinct from each other, each with its own social characteristics?" (Frank 2012, p. 289) How can the particular reality of *this* city as distinct from *that* city – in the example of Hamburg as distinct from Munich called upon here, or even of Cottbus as distinct from Leipzig – be captured theoretically and empirically?

[2] For this reference I thank my colleague Gerald Beck (cf. his contribution in this book).

The concept of “self-logic” wants to

> describe the amalgamation of something general (logic) – density and heterogeneity as spatial structural principles of the city – with a respective site-specific (own) manifestation – locally specific modes of densification and heterogenization, a respective specific natural attitude towards the world. Eigenlogik’ consequently thematizes the specific density of local practices as well as the locally specific patterns of action, perception and experience in cities as institutionalized, routinized practices of densification. It is these local practices, it is argued, that ultimately make cities distinct from one another. (Frank 2012, p. 299)

With regard to these sociological theses, the following assessment can be made (Frank 2012, p. 303 ff.): Everyone agrees that the Eigenlogik approach provides an innovative research perspective that is suitable for breaking open traditional thought structures and breaking new ground in urban sociology in an interdisciplinary way. However, there is criticism of the “almost complete lack of empirical data” (Sept 2009: 248) with which the theoretical considerations could be substantiated. Empirical research still seems to be in its infancy, as the research design is quite challenging if cities are to be compared synchronously and diachronically – and are “moving targets” due to their change and the very different impact factors. Initial results suggest that cities are developing their own logics of action. Frank quotes Löw with the approach that uncovering cities’ own logics can help them break through routines and bring about change (cf. Frank 2012, p. 305 ff.). Löw describes research approaches that read patterns of action pursued in a city in the stratifications of history and seek to trace them back to them (ibid.) Against this background, Löw explains the need for an urban sociology that understands meaning, since “urban sociology [lacks] a building block of theory building if it primarily makes statements either about the city in and of itself as a social whole or about milieus in cities.” (Löw 2018, p. 135 ff.) With sense-understanding urban sociology, Löw attempts to grasp the actions of people in the city in a multi-layered way and to place them in an overall context. The Eigenlogik der Städte is thus strongly concerned with how a city develops its own logic through its history and social, economic and cultural conditions. As a result, the identity of the municipality is directly related to the patterns of action of the people, i.e. the identity is created by the people and can be read from their actions.

The following reflections on identity are intended to examine the place itself as a bearer of identity. The philosophical considerations deliberately disregard the imprinting and attributions by people and focus on the place and on what it brings along for its emergence from within itself. With recourse to philosophical figures of thought, the existence of a place’s own identity is to be substantiated and analysed in terms of its procurement and significance. The point is not to prove a logic to specific cities, but fundamentally whether a place has an identity of its own that goes beyond the purposeful planning and design by humans.

3 The Concept of Identity in Philosophy

In philosophy, two fundamental questions arise concerning identity. The first is about who or what has an identity and whether this identity is actually unique. Thus, it is discussed whether two things are identical with each other and whether a being is identical with itself (Weissmahr 2010). One can use logic to represent identity as a relation, i.e., a is identical to b. Aristotle assumed that a and b are identical if everything that is predicated of a is also predicated of b. However, Leibniz's principle states that "there cannot be two perfectly identical, indistinguishable things in the world" (Ulfig 1999, keyword identity). The identity principle states that a "being is identical with itself" (Ulfig 1999, keyword identity), which is not a tautology by the statement of Leibniz's principle. For the identity of places this would basically mean that the place as something existing or as a thing indeed has an identity and that it cannot be identical with any other place.

Another aspect in the philosophical consideration of identity is diachronic identity (Weissmahr 2010), i.e. the discussion of the extent to which something retains its identity (with itself) over time. The phenomenon of changeable identity, which nevertheless has a recognizable core, knows a metaphysical and a logical dimension. The Theseus paradox, handed down by Plutarch, makes clear the logical problematic of identity, which already arose in antiquity.

> The ship in which Theseus sailed with the young men and also returned safely, a galley with 30 oars, was kept by the Athenians until the time of Demetrios Phaleros. From time to time they removed from it old planks and replaced them with new intact ones. The ship, therefore, became a constant illustration to the philosophers on the question of dispute as to its further development; for some maintained that the boat still remained the same, while others maintained that it was no longer the same. (Quote from Philoclopedia)

The model of thought is further extended by the question of what influence it would have on the question of the identity of the ship if a new ship had been built from the old planks – and what identity which ship would have had at the respective times of construction. As a solution to this complex question, reference is made to the difference between material and function, with function ultimately being the deciding factor. So if the entity can continue to exist and function, even with exchanged materials, this would secure its identity.

For the identity of places, this would confirm, on the one hand, that despite its change, it maintains its identity, and this as an entity, i.e. out of itself, and not through attribution. Nevertheless, the question of function cannot be neglected here: In one variant of the story, it is reported that every year the victorious and happy return of Theseus was celebrated on this ship. Thus the ship must not only function as a ship, but above all be able to serve as a symbol that has a certain charisma.

While the logical argument strengthens the identity of place independent of man, the metaphysical dimension brings place and man into a relationship. Weissmahr points out that we humans have a consciousness of identity, that we have an a priori knowledge that allows us to experience ourselves as identity in difference. With the knowledge of the spatial and temporal identity in difference of our bodily person, we have "the knowledge of space and time as such or also of the identifiability of persons and things at different times" (Weissmahr 2010). This means that the human being understands transformations of identity and can identify a core that defies change and allows recognition, but also further development.

Since it has now been clarified that, from a philosophical perspective, places can have their own, unattributed identity, some hypotheses of this identity formation will be discussed philosophically below. The first relates to the change of identity in the course of history, in the course of time, and to its significance for man. Here, too, place is to be seen as an existence with its own identity and described in terms of its effect on man. In doing so, the anthropological preconditions of man's perception of change will be illuminated. The second hypothesis relates to identity, which is established through metaphorical elements of place. Even though these elements may be man-made, they are fused with the identity of the place and have an effect on humans. The fact that they can have different effects in this regard is illustrated by the juxtaposition of memory and recollection. A third hypothesis refers to the topography of the place and shows how, on the one hand, the geographical coordinates and, on the other hand, the imprint of a particular landscape or nature contribute to the shaping of the identity of the place.

4 Identity in Change as an Anthropological Challenge

Places change in their identity in the course of history. This history usually takes place gradually, and only the place knows about it in its entirety and in its objectivity. The identity of the place is characterized by the history it presents to the people at a point in time X. In this point in time X, the past and the present resonate. At this time X, the past and the course of time resonate and the future is foreshadowed. For people, this presentation of history is a formative factor that knows an anthropological necessity. The history of the place is a timeline on which people live a certain slice of time and feel connected to what has gone before them and what will happen in the future. This also reflects man's capacity for transcendence and his desire to know about the past and to think in terms of futures that he will no longer experience.

The history of the place is, on the one hand, its own history that shapes it and, at the same time, the history interpreted differently by the people there at different points in time, which is referred to as historicity. Angehrn establishes a link between identity and history (2018) and sees it as an interrelationship (2018: p. 7). Thus, history shapes a place, and the identity thus created affects people. "The reconstruction of history, historiography, is an instrument of reassurance of one's own and others' identity" (Angehrn and Jüttemann 2018: p. 7). Thus, in grasping the essence of place, its origins and history are of great importance – the here and now does not provide enough information for this. According to Angehrn (ibid.: p. 8), Dilthey assumes that man is shaped by history, i.e. that history is not a framework but a constitutive element of human existence. This also means that, on the one hand, man and place share history for a time, but for man the history that goes beyond this, which shapes the place and his identity, is significant. Even though a distinction must be made between the history that has objectively taken place and the interpretation of historical events by people, and it must be noted that history can hardly be thought of without narration by people, a totality of history that goes beyond human narratives is inscribed in the place and its identity. This totality of history of place means that different stories can be told at different times without changing its identity. This is because the people who live there perceive the identity of the place only in slices, especially the slice of time in which they themselves live. What is anthropologically elementary is to have connection to a story that goes beyond the individual himself, that begins before him and points beyond him. Being connected to history is one of the existential feelings of life and is an important experience, but so is being connected to historicity, to interpreting and processing history. This means that people live a part of the change of things (subjectively), which is connected with an objective and also subjectively interpreted past and future.

But what happens now when a place does not change its identity gradually and evolutionarily, but a strong rupture in history occurs? The extensive destruction of places in the Second World War, collective suicides in places before military invasions (e.g. Demmin), or devastating earthquakes represent such ruptures. The identity of the place is then destroyed or buried, and the question arises whether the place can find a new identity on this rubble or whether it must first find its way back to its old identity so that a gradual further development of its identity can then take place again.

In reality, places have had to face up to this question, and in cities such as Dresden, Frankfurt or Berlin, buildings have been rebuilt in the old style – also in order to be able to reconstruct their own history in this way. However, reconstruction according to historical patterns is controversial, as the Humboldt Forum in Berlin shows. This reflects how people position themselves in relation to history: Some want a future-oriented new building, others prefer to revive the old cityscape. It is therefore a question of how people perceive the identity of the place and whether this is suitable for their lives, whether continuity, the classification and connectivity of their own lives in and to past and future times is possible for them. Sigel (2006, p. 24f.) describes that the reconstruction and restoration of Dresden's historic city skyline is associated with a reparation and continuity that extends beyond the city and its coping with history. At the same time, the restored Old Town ensemble contrasts strongly with the fact that the areas surrounding Dresden's Old Town are characterized by "brownfields and the various sediments of post-war development" (Sigel 2006, p. 24). These types of development have little connection to each other and are therefore fractured in their expression of identity. A very different example is offered by Pompeii, which was buried by an eruption of Vesuvius in 79 AD and which to this day has failed to reconnect with its own history. Today it is exclusively a museum and a tourist site, for a time a venue that preserves and remembers, but does not live on.

5 The Power of Metaphor in the Identity of Place

The identity of places and their history often present themselves in metaphors. These metaphors can be buildings, but also squares or gardens, emblematic edifications or landmarks, fountains or statues. We often speak of an ensemble in a city that comes from a certain era and signifies a distinctiveness, but even small monuments such as the Manneken Pis in Brussels or the Gänseliesel in Göttingen have a high recognition value. Thus historical events coagulate in these metaphors and become part of the identity of the place. But also trees or squares belonging to the identity of the place invite to encounters and memorable events for individuals or groups. In the identity of the place they find their place next to other metaphors, which can be different in their meaning and charisma. It turns out that metaphors are vulnerable places in the identity of place: The destruction of the Twin Towers torn out of the famous silhouette of Manhattan, the destructive fire of Notre-Dame in Paris, the destruction of the Buddha statues of Bamiyan inscribe themselves in the identity of place.

The metaphors of the identity of places can be perceived by people in two ways. A distinction must be made between memory (Erinnerung) and recollection (Gedächtnis). Metaphors can address memory more or recollection more. Assmann assigns different characteristics to memory and recollection. Thus she describes memory as unreliable and active, i.e. connected with the energy of retrieval and evocation, it refers to time-removed values, to an impression. One suddenly remembers a flowering bush or even the scent of a dish, which one actively retrieves in order to reconstruct what happened. Recollection, on the other hand, is reliable and passive, a storehouse of data that makes facts retrievable in an objective way (cf. Assmann 1991, p. 17). For example, the temple of fame is not about the deeds and the facts associated with them, but about the fact that they are retold and sung about. The counterpart would be the library, in whose books are recorded the facts that nourish memory. If the temple commits to memory for the future, the library enables knowledge of the past (cf. Assmann 1991, p. 13 ff.).

The identity of the site will thus be of particular radiance if it has a metaphoric that at best serves both, but above all does not omit memory in its stimulating effect. A successful example is the memorial at Ground Zero in New York, the National 9/11 Memorial: The towers that stood here before the attack on September 11, 2001, have been inverted into two deep and dark pools into which water constantly flows. If you stand at the edge of the pool and look down into the depths, you get a glimpse of people falling from the windows of the towers. The names of the deceased are engraved on the edge of the pool, so you are close to them when you lean over the edge to look down into the depths. In addition to the "pools," there is a documentation center that appeals to recollection, documenting the details of the attack and how it was overcome with facts and figures. This has created a unique symbolism that incorporates history and literally turns it around to point to the future. Assmann (1991, p. 18) writes, "To identify is not to feel the same, but to recognize and relate."

6 Topography as a Trigger for Events

A certain landscape, geographical conditions or nature itself (also in the sense of trees, gardens or parks) lend an elementary imprint to the identity of a place. On the one hand, settlements are oriented towards the features of the landscape, natural harbours, opening towards the water. On the other hand, they can become historical places because they mark a crossing point or a certain location in relation to other places (e.g. trade routes, military locations, "neutral" places, etc.).

In it, Ivo Andrić, who was awarded the Nobel Prize in 1961 for his 1945 work "The Bridge over the Drina", sets out the problems of the multi-ethnic state of Yugoslavia. At the beginning of the book, he takes the dramatic landscape as the starting point for the story of Višegrad.

> For the greater part of its course the Drina flows between steep mountains, through narrow gorges, or through deep valleys with precipitous banks. Only in some parts of its course do the banks widen into open lowlands, forming on one or both sides of the river mild, partly flat, partly undulating landscapes suitable for cultivation and settlement. Such an extension also occurs here at Višegrad, at a place where the Drina bursts out of the deep and narrow gorge in a sudden bend. (Andrić 2013, p. 7)

Andrić describes the contrast in colour between the dark, almost threatening mountains and the green and churning water, the contrast between the mountains and the plain.

Geographically, the place is the connection between West and East, between Serbia and Bosnia and beyond Serbia with the other parts of the former Turkish Empire and thus also between Christianity and Islam. The city with its bridge becomes a crystallization point of history with its constant changes through its geographical location and with the scenic drama as a background foil. The bridge itself is a metaphor of memory. Ivo Andrić describes life on the bridge, which has terraces, where people have always encountered each other, celebrated, experienced dramas, etc.

The fact that the topographical imprint of identity has an impact on people can easily be seen in the significance of nature for people: One thinks of the reception of nature themes in literature, but also of the recurring discussions since industrialization about the tension between culture, nature, and technology. For example, the architecture of houses, for example in classicism, is perceived by man as an ordering and disciplining force vis-à-vis nature. Certainly, there are changing perceptions of nature in different epochs of the history of ideas, but the notion of antiquity, in which nature is understood in the sense of a cosmos to which man belongs and which also has something unifying, something familiar and fundamental, still has an effect today.

> But hardships do not last forever – and they have that in common with joys – but they pass, or at least replace each other and are forgotten. Life on the Kapija [on the terraces of the bridge, the author's note] renewed itself again and again and in spite of everything, and the bridge changed neither with the years nor with the centuries, nor with the most painful turns in interpersonal relations. All this passed over it just as the

> troubled waters flowed under its smooth and perfect arches. (The Bridge over the Drina, p. 143)

Göschel (2013) describes the emotional significance of the continuity of the topographical identity of the site in the context of Stuttgart 21 and the protest against the felling of the old trees in the city park.

> Even the fight over the trees in the adjacent park is not primarily ecologically but culturally determined. […] The old trees of the park, which had to be felled for the new building, seem to the project opponents to symbolize a 'benevolent', a protective nature turned towards man. The struggle for the park with its old trees is less reminiscent of a struggle for natural resources that are perceived as threatened than for a 'locus amoenus', a soulful place that draws its magic from memories and cultural charges. (Göschel 2013, p. 155)

7 The Identity of Places in the Context of Social Sustainability

We hold that places have their own identity that transcends the time of the current inhabitants. We further hold that people never fully realize this identity, but that their perceptions are shaped by current experiences and conditions. The identity of the place, shaped by the passage of time and the situation at hand, pushes itself ahead of the actual identity of the place that transcends time. How can one nevertheless shape the place at the same time with a view to current demands and challenges in demographic, economic and social change and with the knowledge of this own identity of the place?

Taking into account the three hypotheses mentioned at the beginning regarding the history, metaphor and topology of places that shape their identity, a cautious approach to all historical stratifications can be pointed out with regard to historical change, since the actual identity of the place will always shine through. Sigel writes with regard to the design of cities: "Successful historical reference, however, involves more than the acceptance of a certain historical imagery of our cities, it needs substance from the most diverse historical stratifications, [which guarantee them] differentiated, pluralistic and also subjective access […]" (Sigel 2006, p. 29). He speaks of a palimpsest, which ultimately refers to a changing, yet distinct identity of the city. The image of the palimpsest is emblematic of the fact that current historical events repeatedly recede into the background and fade, and that new things are inscribed on the historical foil of the place, while events from the past continue to shine through.

With regard to metaphor, it seems imperative to grasp its messages and relate them to the people who live there, while weighing their significance for the identity of the place as a whole. For architecture, Sigel points out that focusing on concrete description can lead to a lack of visibility of other images, leading to ambiguity, which is a problem especially for a collective recollection (cf. Sigel 2006, p. 13). Sigel states that the language of architecture must be one that neither follows the dictates of modernity, which means a facelessness and uniformity as a background foil for modern man, nor exhausts itself in the reproduction of historical facades, but transparently places the historicity of buildings in their proper context.

For the design of communities, the memories of the people are important for the identification with the place and thus for the quality of life of the place. In Grabow, they have not only revived the concerts in the park, but also built a wedding pavilion in the park, which gives the park new meaning based on history. Today's weddings will be tomorrow's memories, embedded in the metaphor of the park. In Riesa, people are rediscovering the concert shell, where people met in the days of the GDR and which had great significance as a place of encounter. Planning in municipalities must learn to read and interpret these metaphors, as they are part of their identity, and for each new symbol it is crucial that it reflects what is and has been, which is already inherent in them, and does not transport new content in an unconnected way, embody self-staging by artists, or is simply intended to be effective in the media.

Topographical features can be cultivated and emphasized as an elementary component of identity and represent a special challenge due to their usually long-lasting nature. This is a special task in Riesa, where the city, just as in Ingolstadt, was built away from the water and today the question arises whether an opening towards the water is possible in the context of economic and cultural changes. This raises the question of whether the core of the identity will nevertheless be preserved or whether this will result in a degree of maladjusted urbanity entering the city that endangers the identity.

It is obvious that in smaller places it is easier to design along the historically grown identity because of the greater clarity. However, the challenges remain the same regardless of the size of the place. In order to reach people, municipalities have to face the very identity of the places. Citizens need to feel connected to the past and to the future. The identity of the place must be uncovered in consideration of formative topography, nature, history, architectural heritage and their respective monuments and put in relation to the perception of the inhabitants. What is designed can only ever be a part – this is where the image of the palimpsest comes into play – because the identity of the place extends beyond the here and now of the people. The connection to the identity of the places as a signpost for the future will be measured by the willingness of the inhabitants to make it their own.

References

Andrić, Ivo. 2013. Die Brücke über die Drina, München: dtv

Angehrn, Emil und G. Jüttemann. Hrsg. 2018. *Identität und Geschichte*. Göttingen, Bristol, CT, U.S.A.: Vandenhoeck & Ruprecht (Philosophie und Psychologie im Dialog, Bd. 17)

Assmann, Aleida. 1991. Zur Metaphorik der Erinnerung. In Assmann, A. und Harth, D., Hrsg.: *Mnemosyne. Formen und Funktionen der kulturellen Erinnerung*. Frankfurt a. M.: Fischer-Taschenbuch-Verlag

Bockrath, Franz. 2008. Städtischer Habitus – Habitus der Stadt in Löw, Martina und H. Berking. Hrsg. *Die Eigenlogik der Städte. Neue Wege für die Stadtforschung*. Frankfurt a. M.: Campus Verlag

Dahme, Heinz-Jürgen und N. Wohlfahrt. 2013. *Lehrbuch Kommunale Sozialverwaltung und Soziale Dienste*. Weinheim: Beltz Verlagsgruppe

Frank, Sybille. 2012. *Eigenlogik der Städte*. In Handbuch Stadtsoziologie, (Hrsg.: Eckardt, F.) Wiesbaden: VS Verlag für Sozialwissenschaften, S. 289–309

Göschel, Albrecht. 2013. "Stuttgart 21": Ein postmoderner. In: Brettschneider, Frank und W. Schuster. Hrsg. *Stuttgart 21. Ein Großprojekt zwischen Protest und Akzeptanz*. Wiesbaden: Springer

Lindner, Rolf. 2008. Textur, imaginaire, Habitus – Schlüsselbegriffe der kulturanalytischen Stadtforschung. In Löw, Martina und H. Berking. Hrsg. *Die Eigenlogik der Städte. Neue Wege für die Stadtforschung*. Frankfurt/New York: Campus Verlag

Löw, Martina. 2018. *Vom Raum aus die Stadt denken. Grundlagen einer raumtheoretischen Stadtsoziologie*. Bielefeld: Transcript Verlag

Sigel, P. 2006. Konstruktionen urbaner Identität. In Klein, Bruno und Sigel, Paul (Hrsg.). *Zitat und Rekonstruktion in Architektur und Städtebau der Gegenwart. Konstruktionen urbaner Identität*. Erstausg., 1. Aufl. Berlin: Lukas

Mattenklodt, H.-F. 2013, Territoriale Gliederung – Gemeinden und Kreise vor und nach der Gebietsreform. In Püttner, Günter. *Handbuch der kommunalen Wissenschaft und Praxis: Band 1: Grundlagen und Kommunalverfassung*. Springer-Verlag, S. 154–182

Ulfig, Alexander (1999): Lexikon der philosophischen Begriffe. 2. Aufl. Wiesbaden: Fourier

Weissmahr, Bela. Stichwort "Identität". 2010. In Brugger, Walter und H. Schöndorf., Hrsg. *Philosophisches Wörterbuch*. Orig.-Ausg., [vollst. Neubearb.]. Freiburg im Breisgau: Alber

Internet Sources

https://www.philoclopedia.de/2017/07/07/das-schiff-des-theseus/, letzter Zugriff 30.11.2019

www.demografiewerkstatt-kommunen.de

Wegner, Martina, Prof. Dr., Faculty of Applied Social Sciences, Munich University of Applied Sciences, Germany. Martina Wegner is a professor for the organization of discourses on the future. As a philosopher, she is responsible for the area of values and norms in the Management of Social Innovations (MSI) degree program at the Faculty of Applied Social Sciences at Munich University of Applied Sciences. She teaches in the fields of business and social ethics as well as civil society and democracy. Her main topics are civil society developments with a focus on citizen participation and civic engagement. She conducts evaluation and consulting projects for municipalities as well as for federal and state ministries, including on the municipal implementation of cross-cutting issues such as sustainable development and demography.

Latest Publications:

Wegner, Martina; T. Klie. 2018 Responsibility and identity in the field. In Thomas Klie and Anna Wiebke Klie. Eds. engagement and civil society. Expertises and debates on the second engagement report. Wiesbaden: Springer Fachmedien Wiesbaden (Civil Society and Democracy), pp. 547–568.

Wegner, Martina: Ein Plädoyer für die (Bürger-)Tugend. In Federal Ministry for Family Affairs, Senior Citizens, Women and Youth (BMFSFJ). 2017. ed. Second Report on the Development of Civic Engagement in the Federal Republic of Germany. Focus topic: "Demographic change and civic engagement: the contribution of engagement to local development" (Bundesdrucksache, 18/11800), pp. 58–67.

Social Transformation Through Participation – A Communal Practice *with the* Population and Those Affected

Ingegerd Schäuble and Oranna Erb

Abstract

Everyday life in our municipalities is becoming increasingly complex, opaque and, by necessity, ambiguous. Politics and administration, which are responsible for coping with the diverse everyday tasks – such as digitalization, acceleration, diversity, environment, demography, mobility – often get into conflicts between bureaucratic regulatory logics, politically motivated guidelines, expectations of interest groups that are powerfully expressed in everyday life, as well as social, cultural, economic, transport-related and other needs of the general public. Conflicts, if not dealt with and solved, can lead to structural rigidity and hardening of conflict fronts. The consequence of this is often a self-generated renewal and investment backlog, not only in investment tasks, but above all in non-investment tasks. We at the Schäuble Institute have had very good experience with the development of precisely tailored dialogue processes, when they are used to revive communication that has come to a standstill, to jointly develop sustainable, respectful cooperation and to create resilience in the municipality with tolerance for ambiguity. Innovative communal structures, other forms of organisation and goal-oriented change processes are indispensable. Structure and outline: description of blockades in municipal developments, reflections on dialogical solution paths, favourable and unfavourable framework

I. Schäuble (✉) · O. Erb
Schäuble Institute for Social Research, Munich, Germany
e-mail: schaeuble@schaeuble-institut.de

H.-W. Franz et al. (eds.), *Sustainable Living and Business*,
https://doi.org/10.1007/978-3-658-41835-9_10

conditions, conclusion for practically active people from municipal politics and administration, those affected by innovation, moderators/mediators. On the potential for innovation: We use the positive potentials of rational as well as emotional intelligence and promote mental openness, from whose alert combination resilience and future-oriented, sustainable innovations become possible.

1 Introduction

Social transformation processes are like a promise for the sustainable solution of issues relevant to everyday life. While the usual democratic instances and decision-making processes are perceived by many as insufficiently hands-on and credible, the idea of societal transformation brings a piece of individual power back into play as a positive vision. Civic movements, initiative groups and alternative forms of society have positive connotations as a contrast to the cumbersome, often opaque political system. According to our moderation/mediation experience in working with and for communities, serious, consistently implemented participatory processes in the community hold considerable potential for shaping social transformation. They are transformation processes at the grassroots level of the population – and *with* the population. As prerequisites for successful participation we would like to cite: attentive professional guidance and the will in politics and administration to include the participatory effective everyday competencies in communal decision-making processes. In the following, we report directly from sociological-urban planning-communicative practice: from typical municipal problem situations and the participatory solution paths that municipalities have taken with us as a neutral moderation/mediation team in order to solve their tasks sustainably.

2 Typical Challenges in Urban/Community Develop ment

Everyday life in municipalities is becoming increasingly complex. Administrative structures, spheres of influence and interests often appear inscrutable and contradictory. The sustainable management of the municipal community requires not only professional skills and technical experience, but also a high level of social competence in order to find one's way in the intensely virulent group dynamics and in the ambiguity of municipal fields of action. The following are examples of the demanding social challenges that affect municipalities:

- Digitisation in the economy and everyday life with significant consequences, e.g. for forms of communication, mobility patterns, changing shopping behaviour (Harari 2018; King 2018)
- Increasing acceleration in all areas of life (Rosa 2005; Lobo 2019).
- Changed mobility behaviour due to more and more journeys/movements, also to more distant destinations, restrained trend towards ecologically compatible means of transport, introduction/establishment of alternative (apparently) ecologically favourable means of transport (Knoflacher 2014).
- Changing consumptive leisure patterns and forms of work (Schjold 2015; Crouch 2019).
- Disappearance of evolved social structures and changing demographics (Gehl 2015; Wichterich 2013)
- Living together in different cultural segments, exclusion, parallel worlds (Helfrich and Bollier 2019).
- Growth compulsion starting from the financial and economic system, branching out into all areas of life and stored by many individuals as "normality" (Felber 2012, Loske 2013)
- Ecological problems, e.g. in climate and energy, with considerable consequences due to environmental catastrophes and creeping, increasingly visible environmental destruction (Scheidler 2016; Neubauer and Repenning 2019)
- Disorientation in coping with life (Lessenich 2016; Meißner 2017)
- extreme political attitudes and exclusions (Rommelspacher 2002)
- Gap between rich and poor – both within the society of a city, a country and between individual states (Lessenich 2016; Eribon 2017)

Conflicts between the various spheres of existence and interests, if they cannot be dealt with and resolved in the long term, cause the social structures of cooperation in municipalities to stiffen, conflict fronts harden, and nothing progresses (Arras 2000). Many suffer from the resulting backlog of renewal and investment in investment and, above all, non-investment tasks. Municipal coping strategies that used to be tried and tested are losing their elasticity in dealing with new socio-political constellations, for example, as a result of heavy bureaucratisation. They succumb when the focus is on power politics instead of factual politics. Public actors then often miss their actual purposes and primary tasks; and not infrequently social unrest and discontent arise as a result. This can even lead to a loss of faith in democracy and provoke resistance on the part of those affected (Crouch 2008).

The social stress in municipalities is ignited by various topics: traffic, densification, new building projects, culture, social infrastructure supply, segregation, poverty, consequences of climate change, etc., and is not infrequently acted out aggressively. In such conflict situations, Possibilists, as L. Neubauer and A. Repenning (2019) call people with an alert, open attitude, are helpfully orienting. Possibilists consciously stand in the present and cultivate the ability to imagine a different, a good future.

The following example dealt with a settlement (cf. Fig. 1) in which the supply of goods for daily needs as well as services and social facilities was gradually declining or, in some cases, was no longer guaranteed. It is important to involve not only the citizens but *all the* actors concerned in the perception and processing of the problems and to bring them into contact with each other. Ideally, the circle of those involved should always remain open, because in the course of the dialogue process other affected parties can also be identified and included.

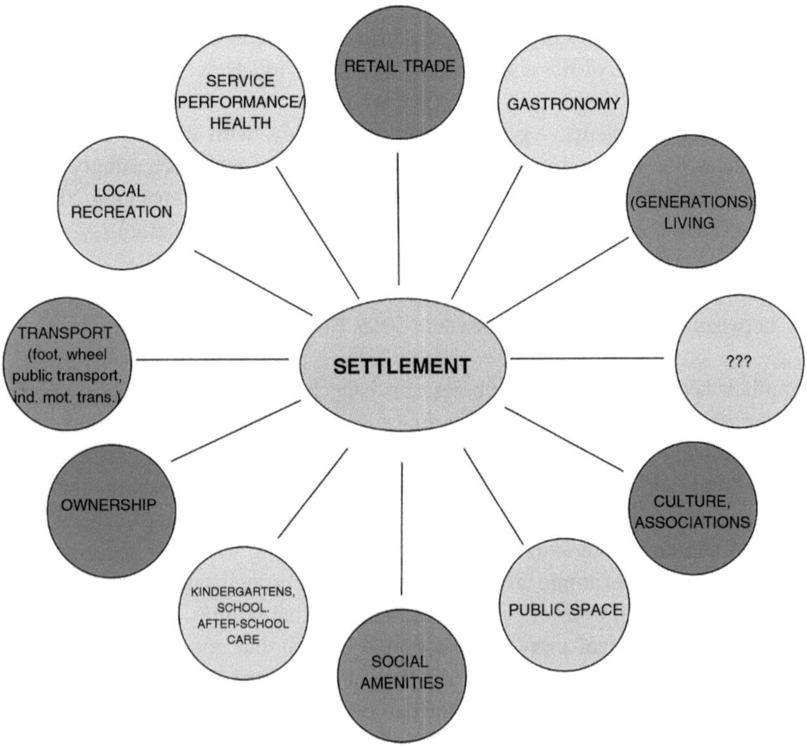

Fig. 1 Actors to be involved using the example of a settlement with infrastructure problems. (Own representation: Schäuble Institute for Social Research)

Politics and administration, which are supposed to manage changing everyday tasks quickly and sustainably, often get into conflicts between

- bureaucratic control and regulation logics
- politically motivated guidelines
- Powerfully presented expectations of local and supra-local interest groups
- social, cultural, economic, transport, … needs in the general public of citizens.

Persistent discord among the population, friction in local politics itself, but also in local government, if they increase, considerably limit the ability to act in the community. Necessary municipal developments are often slowed down, made more difficult, and sometimes even prevented by such conflict situations. The quality of life in the community decreases, as does the credibility of the actors. The supply situation (e.g. with social services, with housing, with high-quality public space) may also become patchy. Blockades not only lead to dissatisfaction among investors, the desired energizing coexistence (Knecht et al. 2015) in a constructive togetherness is thus gradually made impossible (Sennett 2018).

3 Reflections on Dialogical Solutions/Methods in Networks

Because those responsible at the municipal level are professionally determined in their function and, in addition, are generally not prepared by their professional training for social-moderating requirements, supporting, mediating and translating tasks in demanding municipal planning are, if necessary, organized externally: with the professional conception and neutral guidance of precisely fitting municipal dialogue processes (Schäuble Institute for Social Research 2005). We consciously understand these dialogues as "work in participation networks supported by many". It would be misleading to speak of "citizen" participation in this context. Participation networks that are effective in the long term span different social groups, interests, disciplines and hierarchical levels (Hüther 2013). Only for this reason can they

- revitalise the stagnation of communal communication
- develop a sustainable, respectful cooperation together and in a binding manner
- (re)building community resilience in the face of ambiguity tolerance.

Dialogue processes can vitalize communal self-understandings for lived networking and modern forms of democratic participation; they also promote the social courage to change/improve/renew (Meißner 2017). However, dialogue processes need to be designed in a well-considered and situation-specific professional manner in order to do justice to the great responsibility for the communal network. We ourselves, for example, always work in this sense in a transprofessional team on complex municipal tasks and we carefully select the dialogue methods for the respective occasion.

In the following example (cf. Fig. 2), the focus was on a town centre area in which a development plan was drawn up within a future redevelopment area ("Leben findet Innenstadt" programme). A differentiated approach was important, in which larger events for all interested parties alternated with smaller dialogue tables (DT) or with topic groups (TG) that focused on very specific aspects. Parallel to these public events, the steering group (SG) met at regular intervals to agree on the further procedure. What is important is the tailor-made offer and the flexibility in the process: The only provisionally conceived procedure remains open for changes that turn out to be necessary in the course of the participation process.

We proceed from the assumption: The human being as a community organises the provision of public services and the management of life in various social forms of society – in our latitudes, these include municipalities of varying size and quality. Ideally, municipal action should follow transparent rules and objectives that adapt appropriately to changing primary social tasks and conditions in culture, transport, education, housing, demography and the economy. The organism "municipality" lives from the interplay of numerous complementary, contradictory, promoting and restricting energy flows. Ideally, these are coordinated in such a way that the organism as a whole runs well.

4 Municipal Resilience – Municipal Intelligence

When individuals endure difficult life events, they build resilience – the more, the better they cope. Resilient people mobilise helpful social connectedness and are themselves socially committed (Eisenstein 2017), actively give meaning to their lives and feel self-efficacy (Hunecke 2013), deal flexibly with unchanging circumstances (Welzer 2019), concentrate on the essentials and focus their energies.

Municipalities, too, develop resilience by necessity in the face of major sociopolitical challenges (Fathi 2019). They, too, need (Adloff and Leggewie 2014)

- a reliable social fabric

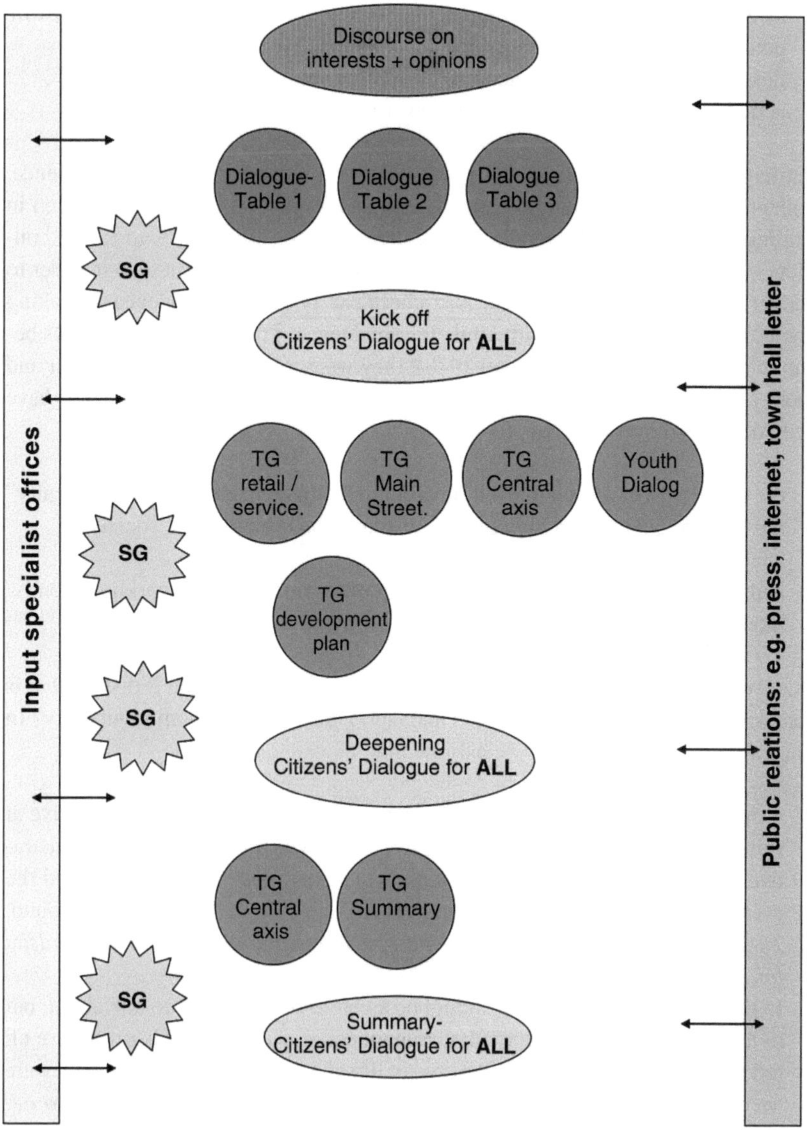

Fig. 2 Example of the course of a dialogue process for a town centre development. (Own representation: Schäuble Institute for Social Research)

- a common vision for the development of the communal society with all existing potentials
- flexibility in the activation and use of existing resources
- action competence and orientation towards communal goals.

Participation processes are a very good opportunity to make municipal resilience, understood in this way, tangible, to shape it and to make it the basis for action in dealing with conflicts. Since the 1970s, there have been impulses to tackle conflicts – triggered by social imbalances – in a participatory manner, also in order to actively involve the increasingly self-confident population in decision-making about their living situation with all their competence. The first tactile attempts began with the planning cell (Dienel 1978); they were followed by various other and more refined concepts for emancipative civic processes. Citizens' dialogues have been developed over the years for

- the one almost to an end in itself, in order to adorn themselves with "modernity"
- the other to guarantee a high quality of life in the urban/village society
- again others to solve problems in (great) need
- and for some a threat – threat e.g. for power constellations working silently/ hiddenly or by activating fears of change, or ...

But everyone was sure that participation makes a difference – and it does! What is the secret of successful planning and activation dialogues in a community/city? In the resilience thinking model we assume that

- it makes sense to use all the competencies of a community in order to arrive at suitable solutions that everyone can live with (well): Political and administrative competence are just as important as the experience of the experts and the everyday competence of those who later (have to) live with the solution found. *This corresponds to the "holding and binding social fabric" as a prerequisite for resilience.*
- In the democratic tradition, it should be a matter of course not to talk about, but to talk with *all* those concerned. Communication cultures in this regard are all too often neglected in stressful everyday life and are not available when they are needed. *This corresponds to the need to include all resources in order to develop resilience.*
- The growing complexity of municipal tasks places high demands on all those involved. Therefore, new and structured forms of teaching and learning are necessary so that flexibility can be experienced/lived in a sustainable way. These

forms can be practiced on the Planning Dialogue training field in everyday municipal life. *This is about the resilience quality "flexibility".*
- Those responsible in the municipality experience significant relief with neutral, expert guidance of the (planning) dialogue with clarification of the group dynamics among those affected (moderation and, if necessary, mediation), because they can remain focused on their actual professional roles while the balance of opinions/interests is sought and established by the neutral moderation team. *The action competence of the experts is strengthened and the goal orientation is aligned.*

In the prevailing economized thinking, the value of dialogue processes for communal peacekeeping is underestimated, as is the highly professional moderation/mediation service for the mindful bundling and alignment of the potentials themselves.

In participatory work, the following process qualities and clarifications are indispensable for a municipality to become a resilient municipality:

- The interested parties should already know at the beginning of the cooperation: Planning dialogues are work in the direct sense of the word, and for everyone.
- They are also teaching and learning pieces – for everyone as well. The competence of those affected grows, so that a later dialogue process in the same municipality can start at a higher social-communicative level than the first one.
- If professional external participation is desired, then this ideally takes place in the transprofessional team; because for the sustainable and stringent handling of the mostly complex topics, a broad professionalism is essential in the guiding moderation team.
- Dialogue processes succeed best according to the principle of "as much as necessary, as little as possible" in an effort to handle the time budget and the willingness to cooperate of the participants with care.
- Attentiveness, respect, appreciation in contact with the interested parties determine the dialogical communication culture. These qualities lived by the moderation/mediation team are an orienting example for a different quality of relationship between each other – in the ongoing dialogue process and also in other topics/tasks in the municipality. This is also an important measure of sustainability.

5 Ambiguity in Constructive Social Interaction

Tolerance of ambiguity is a growing potential and the result of well-run participations. If those concerned experience that differences tend to lead to abundance, or at any rate do not represent a threat, this is a good prerequisite for farsightedness and empathy and thus also for personal and communal resilience development. In other areas of society, instead of ambiguity, we often speak of diversity and note that many people find it difficult to allow different currents in the social environment – in society, in the community, in the neighbourhood – to simply exist side by side for the time being. If this is possible in a value-free way, a social quality is achieved that is based on peaceful forms of interaction. Here, in many social areas, there is indeed a need to catch up on experience and practice.

In the process, conventional communal self-evident facts are mixed with fast-moving modern trends whose stability and durability in the development of urban society has yet to be proven. These include, for example:

- Challenges as described at the beginning of the article, which can result in anxiety, resignation, burnout, social withdrawal, …
- The emergence of new civic initiatives that seek to deal creatively with these challenges, such as
  - innovative forms of living together/housing
  - new social forms in communities according to the principle of I-in-relation
  - Living according to the economy of exchange and sharing in social connectedness
  - Forms of mobility beyond fossil solutions (car, plane, …)
  - lived environmental awareness e.g. through sharing concepts, creation of packaging-free shops, upcycling of products, a new generation of second-hand shops and distribution channels, …
- Mobilisation of psychological and social resources in order to
  - to create and maintain the desired quality of life(s) oneself (responsibly)
  - to develop/practice social and psychological flexibility to cope with life
  - To experience connectedness and reliability with others
  - to find oneself in one's own rhythm and to empower oneself
  - Enduring unpredictability and uncertainty in the global society
  - to live with open future perspectives
  - to pause at excessive speed, and
  - stand up

- Transfer of trends from the "small" to the "large", i.e. to the municipality/to regional developments etc.
- Grassroots democracy: living here, engaging here, gathering instead of dispersing.

(Apparently objective rational) knowledge alone is not sufficient to shape such a differentiated social reality. The personal (emotional, mental, spiritual) understanding of individual and group-specific ideas and responsibilities in social structures and processes creates the prerequisite for the design competence of all participants and in all fields, which is in demand today more than ever. And there are numerous fields that need to be worked on. Here (cf. Fig. 3) is an example from the Socially Integrative City urban development programme, in which the main aim was to identify and value all the resources of the neighbourhood and to make them effective in the structurally, socially and culturally relevant redevelopment activities. During the dialogue-based development of the integrated action concept, fields of action were identified, some of which seemed feasible in the short and medium term, others only in the long term. The latter were "parked" in a memory

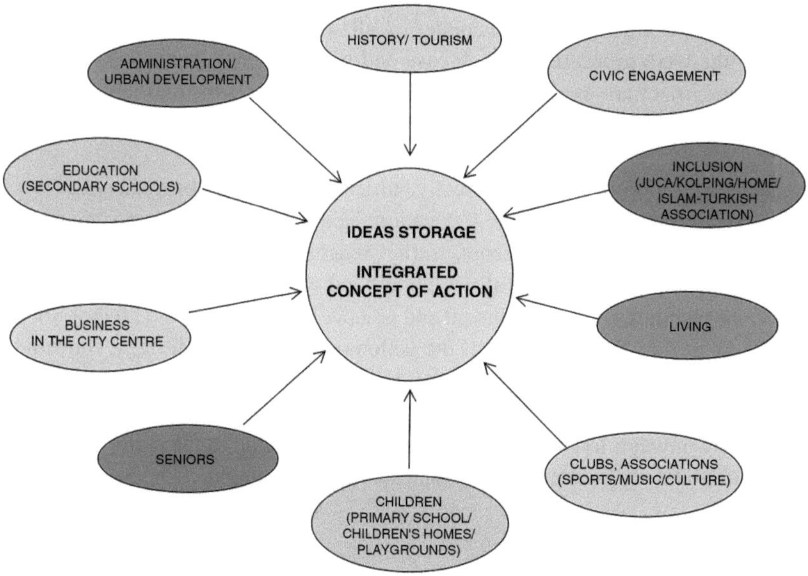

Fig. 3 Example of fields of action that may be of importance in the development of an integrated action concept. (Own representation: Schäuble Institute for Social Research)

of ideas in order to be included in the respective current action plan (application for urban development funding) at the appropriate time.

In our experience, change processes succeed best when *all* those affected are seen at eye level with their respective different competencies and interests and are actively involved.

6 Further Examples of Successful Transformative Dialogue Processes That Start at the Grassroots Level

In order to make the condensed explanations above more accessible, we will illustrate some of the key qualities of dialogues that we have implemented ourselves. The occasions for their use differ considerably in some cases; for example, a combined dialogue procedure was chosen in order to lay the basis for an integrated action concept (IAC) within the framework of an interim evaluation. Here it was necessary for the locally interested parties and those responsible to develop flexibility and competence in action, both in the dialogue procedure and in understanding the problem. Here too (cf. Fig. 4), topic-related smaller events (dialogue tables) alternated with larger citizens' dialogues for all interested parties in the small town. The results were processed in each case and reflected back in the next dialogue step. It was important for us to keep checking the interim results for their coherence and acceptance in the large group. The dialogue concept provided for the following steps:

In the redevelopment of a historically burdened settlement, the main issues were the preservation of infrastructure (education, health, provision of everyday necessities, services for senior citizens), traffic, redensification/new building district, social interaction in a respectful neighbourhood atmosphere. With a view to the resilience qualities, the establishment and practice of a "holding and binding social fabric" as well as the expansion of the action competence of all those concerned were to be ensured. The dialogue concept was even more differentiated here than in the previous examples, in order to enable the groupings, which were interwoven in a variety of ways, to learn from each other. The upswing of the entire settlement should also already be symbolically represented in the graphic (Fig. 5).

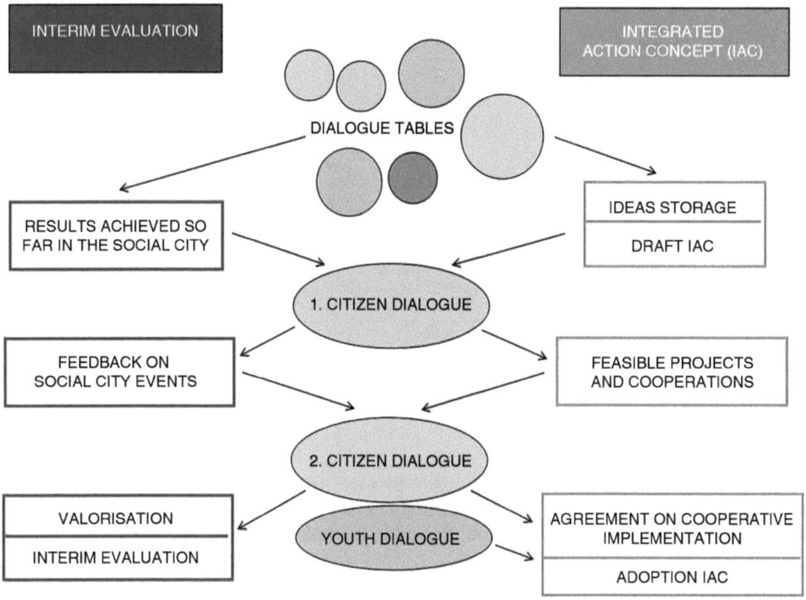

Fig. 4 Combination of development of an integrated action concept and evaluation for a project in the "Socially Integrative City" urban development programme. (Own representation: Schäuble Institute for Social Research)

7 Conclusion for Interested Parties from Local Politics and Administration, Citizens, Moderators/Mediators in Local Dialogue Processes Who Are Eager for Transformation

If the positive potentials of rational and emotional intelligence are consciously used in participation projects, this promotes the mental openness for what can be shaped, from which resilience and ambiguity in the service of future-oriented, sustainable innovations are possible in the first place. To achieve this, it is not enough to simply impart information or "knowledge" or to only control it professionally; it must also be used in a spirit of understanding, i.e. in a constructive communal atmosphere – despite the most diverse personal attitudes/interests.

For the realization of planning dialogues, it is above all advisable to approach the task with a stringent technical and dialogical concept, but open and flexible in terms of group dynamics. Moderation/mediation teams are in the middle of the ac-

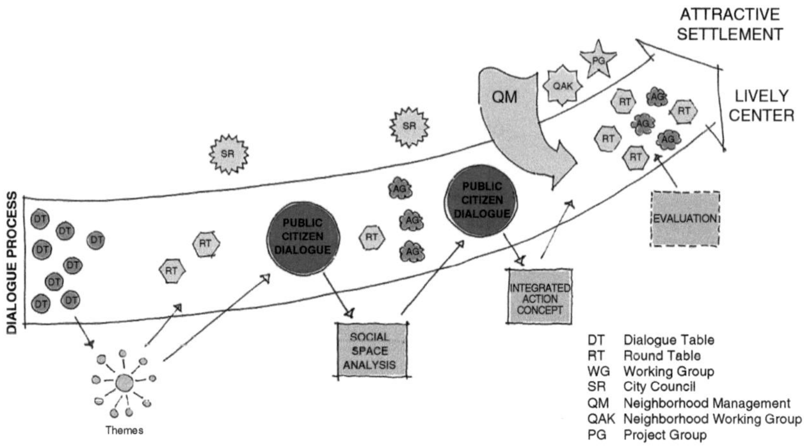

Fig. 5 Example of the course of a dialogue process for the development of a social area analysis and an integrated action concept (urban development funding programme "Socially Integrative City"). (Own representation: Schäuble Institute for Social Research)

tion and are exposed to numerous, even contradictory expectations. They need stable, alert and authentic personalities. Their credibility – one of their outstanding qualities – results from an honest and transparent strategy of action.

Anyone who is involved in planning dialogues as a municipal officer should know how important it is to find and fill their own professional role. Together with the facilitation team, municipal experts form a strong network in which municipal issues are essentially moved until they are settled. It is work to get into this network and to try it out. But it is certain that

- this effort is well worth it, because the network only needs to be set up once. Once it is in place, it is only a matter of situation-specific further development/adaptation to new challenges.
- Networks need to be nurtured so that they can develop the substance to "nourish", support, orient and socially secure the network participants themselves.

References

Adloff, Frank, C. Leggewie. 2014. *Das konvivialistische Manifest.* Bielefeld: transcript Verlag

Arras, Hartmut E. 2000. Kommunikation und Moderation – Bedeutung für nachhaltige Stadtentwicklung, in: Nachhaltige Stadt. Beiträge zur urbanen Zukunftssicherung, hg. von Kissel, Harald A. Berlin: SRL-Schriftenreihe

Crouch, Colin. 2008. *Postdemokratie*. Berlin: edition suhrkamp

Crouch, Colin. 2019. *Gig Economy. Prekäre Arbeit im Zeitalter von Uber, Minijobs & Co.* Berlin: edition suhrkamp

Dienel, Peter C. 1978. *Die Planungszelle. Der Bürger plant seine Umwelt. Eine Alternative zur Establishment-Demokratie*. Wiesbaden: Westdeutscher Verlag

Eisenstein, Charles. 2017. *Die Ökonomie der Verbundenheit*. München: Scorpio Verlag

Eribon, Didier. 2017. *Gesellschaft als Urteil*. Berlin: edition suhrkamp

Fathi, Karim. 2019. *Resilienz im Spannungsfeld zwischen Entwicklung und Nachhaltigkeit – Anforderungen an gesellschaftliche Zukunftssicherung im 21. Jahrhundert*. Berlin: Springer Verlag GmbH

Felber, Christian. 2012. *Die Gemeinwohl-Ökonomie: das Wirtschaftsmodell der Zukunft*. München: Piper Verlag

Gehl, Jan. 2015, *Städte für Menschen*, 2. Aufl. Berlin: jovis Verlag GmbH

Harari, Juval Noah. 2018. *Homo Deus. Eine Geschichte von morgen*. München: Beck Verlag

Helfrich, Silke, D. Bollier. 2019. *Frei, fair und lebendig. Die Macht der Commons*. Bielefeld: transkript Verlag

Hunecke, Marcel. 2013. *Psychologie der Nachhaltigkeit. Psychische Ressourcen für Postwachstumsgesellschaften*. München: oekom Verlag

Hüther, Gerald. 2013. *Kommunale Intelligenz. Potentialentfaltung in Städten und Gemeinden*. Hamburg: edition Körber Stiftung

King, Vera. 2018. Geteilte Aufmerksamkeit. Kultureller Wandel und psychische Entwicklung in Zeiten der Digitalisierung, 2018. in: Psyche, Heft 8

Ursula Knecht, C. Krüger, D. Markert, M. Moser, A.C. Mulder, I. Praetorius, C. Roth, A. Schrupp, A. Trenkwalder-Egger. 2015. ABC des guten Lebens, 3. Auflage. Rüsselsheim: Christel Göttert Verlag

Knoflacher, Hermann. 2014. Das Auto im Kopf. Fetisch motorisierter Individualverkehr. In: Politische Ökologie. Postfossile Mobilität. Zukunftstauglich und vernetzt unterwegs. München: oekom verlag

Lessenich, Stefan. 2016. *Neben uns die Sintflut, Die Externalisierungsgesellschaft und ihr Preis*. München Piper Verlag

Lobo, Sascha. 2019. *Realitätsschock. Zehn Lehren aus der Gegenwart*. Köln: Kiepenheuer & Witsch

Loske, Reinhard. 2013. Eine wirkmächtige Förderin der Veränderung, in: politische ökologie 133, Baustelle Zukunft. Die Große Transformation von Wirtschaft und Gesellschaft, S. 94–101. München: oekom Verlag

Meißner, Andreas. 2017. *Mensch, was nun? – Warum wir in Zeiten der Ökokrise Orientierung brauchen*. München: oekom Verlag

Neubauer, Luisa, A. Repenning. 2019. *Vom Ende der Klimakrise. Eine Geschichte unserer Zukunft*. Stuttgart: Tropen Sachbuch, Cotta'sche Buchhandlung Nachfolger GmbH

Rommelspacher, Birgit. 2002. *Anerkennung und Ausgrenzung. Deutschland als multikulturelle Gesellschaft*. Frankfurt/Main: Campus Verlag

Rosa, Hartmut. 2005. *Beschleunigung. Die Veränderung der Zeitstrukturen in der Moderne*. Berlin: suhrkamp taschenbuch wissenschaft

Schäuble Institut für Sozialforschung, Schäuble, Ingegerd, und C. Grüger, 2005. *Gemeinschaftsinitiative Soziale Stadt. Diskursive Bürgerbeteiligung.* Bericht zum Modellprojekt. München: Oberste Baubehörde im Bayerischen Staatsministerium des Innern.

Scheidler, Fabian. 2016. *Das Ende der Megamaschine. Geschichte einer scheiternden Zivilisation.* Wien: promedia Verlag

Schjold, Inger Kristine, P. Neff. 2015. Raum für Konflikte. Wenn bei der Nutzung des öffentlichen Raums verschiedenen Logiken aufeinander treffen. In: OrganisationsEntwicklung Nr. 2, S. 35–42. Zürich: Verlag Organisationsentwicklung und Management AG

Sennett, Richard. 2018. *Die offene Stadt. Eine Ethik des Bauens und Bewohnens.* Berlin: Hanser Verlag

Welzer, Harald. 2019. *Alles könnte anders sein. Eine Gesellschaftsutopie für freie Menschen.* Frankfurt/Main: Fischer Verlag

Wichterich, Christa. 2013. Im Kleinen das Große beginnen. In: politische ökologie 133, Baustelle Zukunft. Die Große Transformation von Wirtschaft und Gesellschaft, S. 86–93. München: oekom Verlag

Schäuble, Ingegerd, Dipl.-Sociologist Supervisor DGSv. Studied sociology, social psychology, economics at the LMU Ludwig-Maximilian-University Munich, research assistant at the Sociological Institute of the LMU Munich, founded AgaS GmbH Arbeitsgemeinschaft für Angewandte Sozialforschung, lectureships at the Universities of Munich, Stuttgart, Weihenstephan, FU Berlin, Lehrinstitut für Dokumentation Frankfurt, Ärztliche Akademie Munich. Certification with the DGSv (German Society for Supervision and Coaching). Founded the Schäuble Institute for Social Research with a focus on: qualitative social research, moderation/mediation/supervision of participation and dialogue processes, organisational, team and project development, training in various social and dialogue skills, supervision and coaching for individuals and groups.

Latest Publications:

see www.schaeuble-institut.de

Schäuble, Ingegerd. 2019. team development case supervision. In: Festschrift 40 Jahre Ärztliche Akademie für Psychotherapie von Kindern und Jugendlichen e. V., Seelische Gesundheit von Kindern und Jugendlichen im Fokus, ed. Manfred Endres, Munich.

Schäuble, Ingegerd, and O. Erb. 2018. voting and shaping. Motivations and attitudes of Munich women towards political participation and elections, Munich.

Schäuble, Ingegerd. 2017. new advanced training: team development and case supervision, in: Akademie aktuell 2017–2, pp. 5–9.

Erb. Oranna, and I. Schäuble. 2013. social city Augsburg and Oberhausen-Nord, Augsburg.

Distler, Andreas, and I. Schäuble: 2011. Social Urban Development Bobingen. Future of the Present, Bobingen.

Distler, Andreas, and I. Schäuble. 2011. Heuchelhof schafft Heimat. Social urban renewal, the future of the district, Würzburg.

Erb, Oranna, Dipl.-Ing.in freelance local planner, Munich, network partner in the Schäuble Institute for Social Research Munich, Germany. Studied architecture with a focus on urban planning, many years of professional experience in all areas of urban/local planning. Conception and moderation of participation processes and dialogue procedures on urban planning, gender and diversity issues. Over four years of work experience in other European countries (Poland). Significant involvement in community building processes; special interest in encounter in dance: many years of practice in conscious dance; completion of the basic level of training as a dance therapist (BTD).

Latest Publications:

Both can be found at: https://www.schaeuble-institut.de/angebot/forschung/öffentlichkeits-wirksames/

Ingegerd Schäuble and O. Erb. 2018. voting and shaping. Motivations and attitudes of Munich women towards political participation and elections, Munich.

Oranna Erb and I. Schäuble. 2013. social city Augsburg and Oberhausen-North, Augsburg.

Transformative Change in the Craft Sector

Social Science as "Infiltration" and Arrangement

Peter Biniok

Abstract

The skilled trades in general and the sanitary, heating and air-conditioning (SHA) sector in particular are confronted with an increasing shortage of skilled workers. The SHA Berlin guild has therefore initiated a model project in which a sociologist is involved in the conception of measures against training dropouts and assists in the processing of empirical-analytical questions. Model projects aim to generate social innovations as scientifically based changes in practice. In this process, social scientists themselves become creative actors in the transformation process. There are different forms of social scientific design. In the current case, empirical social research is twofold. It is firstly "infiltration" due to/by means of ethnographic access and it is secondly "arrangement" by initiating dynamics. Social science supports the self-direction of actors and instigates change that is sustained by practitioners. The research process as a whole can be understood as social enrichment (innovative sublimation), i.e. as a process of increasing reflexivity on the part of actors and the shaping of horizons of possibility. The article discusses facilitating and hindering factors as well as competence requirements for the sociologist.

P. Biniok (✉)
Guild SHK Berlin, Berlin, Germany
e-mail: p.biniok@shk-berlin.de

H.-W. Franz et al. (eds.), *Sustainable Living and Business*,
https://doi.org/10.1007/978-3-658-41835-9_11

1 Introduction: Shortage of Skilled Workers as the Object of Investigation

Social problems can rarely be solved by technical progress alone, but rather by transformation projects of science and practice (Schneidewind and Singer-Brodowski 2014). Social innovations are needed (Howaldt and Jacobsen 2010) – whether on their own or in combination with technical innovations. Linked to this insight are demands for and the emergence of transnational contexts of action. This includes forms of cooperation within the scientific community that go under the label of interdisciplinarity, as well as non-academic participation projects with civil society.

The central idea is based on the combination of heterogeneous knowledge as a basis for innovation. The actors considered relevant come together "at one table" and jointly shape a transformation process. In doing so, their specific perspectives are to be integrated and questions of, for example, individualizability, social compatibility, economic efficiency and sustainability are to be agreed upon. In this way, the actors involved learn to take on *unfamiliar roles* and to develop new problem-solving strategies. This also applies to sociologists and social scientists.[1] Depending on the field of work, they are confronted with, among other things, changed demands on themselves, new claims to validity – deviating from science – and/or limited freedom of action. The problem situation and the corresponding framework are related to the role models of social scientists and must be mutually reconciled. Accordingly, the thesis put forward here is: *Specific transformation processes each require different forms of social science.*

The starting point for this article is the discourse currently being conducted in the media, albeit barely visible, on the *shortage of skilled workers* and the attractiveness of vocational education and training in Germany (Rahner 2018; Hartmann et al. 2018; Herberg 2018; Hemkes et al. 2019). Shortages of skilled workers can be identified and/or predicted for the skilled trades and especially for specific sectors and trades (Thomä 2014; Malin et al. 2019). This includes the plumbing, heating and air conditioning (SHA) sector in Berlin, which is facing an increasing shortage of skilled workers.

[1] In this text, no differentiation is made between the two terminologies. Depending on the case, the focus is on sociologists who work in application-oriented research and development contexts. This does not preclude the transferability of the discussion to other fields of the social sciences, which is even desirable.

The SHA Berlin guild therefore initiated a *model project* to counteract this shortcoming by means of a self-responsible contribution.[2] The (self-)responsibility of the guild results not only from its existential task as a professional association of the sector, but also refers to its self-image as an innovator. The overarching goal of avoiding or eliminating shortages of skilled workers is broken down in the project to the question of how premature "contract terminations" in vocational training in the SHA trade in Berlin can be avoided.[3] In addition to questions of vocational orientation, the reputation of the skilled trades or the quality of school education in Berlin, this addresses *a concrete facet of* the shortage of skilled workers. The focus of social innovations is on both the cost-effectiveness of changing measures and their sustainability. Innovations must be integrated into the daily training routine of the players in such a way that they do not impede day-to-day business and have a long-term effect.

In the project, a *sociologist* (the author) works to identify the multiplex reasons for contract terminations and to collaborate on the design and implementation of measures against training terminations in the trade.[4] In particular, the processing of empirical-analytical questions falls within his area of responsibility, i.e. planning the research design, data collection, data interpretation and writing up.

The model project is distinguished by the achievement of scientifically based social innovations. It represents a special form of applied social science and implies its own research style/habit. In contrast to the evaluative monitoring of practical projects in the form of sub-projects or by external scientists, the social scientist himself becomes a *creative actor in* the transformation process. This specific work situation is discussed in this article as an example. The role as shaper is implicit in the model project, since the exploitation interest of the data aims at transformation. Accordingly, the sociologist is both problem founder through "infiltration" and problem solver through arrangement.[5]

---

[2] Cf. model project website at: https://www.shk-berlin.de/kompetenzzentrum/sonderprojekte/projekt-as-nb (last access 04 Oct. 2019).

[3] Contract terminations is a term from the field and means contract terminations. Early contract terminations in training are not always the same as training discontinuations, because the training can be continued in another company (Uhly 2015).

[4] This article is the result of reflection on my work in the model project. In addition to my role as a "practitioner", I also take on the role of a (theory-guided) observer. Some discussions may therefore appear shadowy, abbreviated and pointed – a more in-depth analysis is conceivable. I thank Stefan Selke and Andreas Otremba for helpful comments.

[5] The terminology *infiltration*, meant as espionage/sabotage and clandestine investigation, has a negative connotation. I use the term nevertheless because it captures the essence of purpose-based research: A scientist penetrates a field as inconspicuously as possible in order

The article first outlines the sociological understanding of the role in the context of the tension between commitment and distancing (Sect. 2). This is followed by reports from the field to illustrate the work situation, to discuss the contextual conditions and to name the competence requirements of the social scientist (Sect. 3). Building on this, the model project as a form of applied social science is contrasted with academic practice research in order to develop a type of design (Sect. 4). The final section discusses the degree of rigor of applied social research (Sect. 5).

2 Location: Applied Social Sciences as Co-designers of Society

The engagement and disengagement of sociology and the representatives of the discipline have been controversially discussed since the formation of the discipline (Elias 1983; Mevissen 2016). In ever new discourse cycles, either a stronger influence on society is demanded or a stronger restraint is urged. Questions are raised as to how much sociologists are allowed to engage with regard to their subject matter and how much distancing is necessary in order to arrive at (more) objective insights. The dual nature of sociology as a discipline that is part of its own object of inquiry requires a particular reflection on one's own position and a great deal of identity and boundary work (Gieryn 1983; Kaldewey 2016). The marking of spatial, cognitive and social distances – or precisely their abolition – necessitate an actor-centred positioning and self-description, each with specific premises of scientificity, knowledge generation and knowledge transfer. In convergence with the formation of identity, different forms of sociological work can be distinguished. Such typifications also exist for the social sciences as a whole, although specific disciplines (such as social work) per se intervene more deeply in the everyday social life of the actors and initiate and accompany changes than others (e.g. social ethics).

In a rough grid, *three forms of social science work* can be distinguished (Latniak and Wilkesmann 2005): Consultancy, application-oriented research and academic research.[6] In *consulting*, social scientists are clients and provide a service predefined

to identify problems (and solutions to them).

[6] Similarly, a distinction is made for sociology on the basis of its groups of addressees (and forms of knowledge) into the four areas of activity of professional, critical, application-oriented and public sociology (Burawoy 2005). Professional and critical sociology are aimed at academic audiences. Sociology directed at non-academic audiences is, in this view, either public sociology as a dialogical treatment of relevant problems through the use of reflexive

by the client according to the agreed specifications (Degele et al. 2001; Blättel-Mink and Katz 2004). The goal is the case-specific processing of a question in relation to a defined subject area. An action logic of quick problem solving and focused decisions dominates. Consultants have little influence on the extent to which their findings are implemented in practice. *Academic research*, on the other hand, deals with questions generated by the scientific system itself. The aim is to gain knowledge that is oriented towards scientific criteria and has general validity. The results circulate primarily within disciplinary boundaries. As a "mixture", so to speak, *application-oriented research* contains components of both forms of work. As in the case of consulting, the questions are clearly defined by a client, and the results are valorized outside the scientific system. As with academic research, the work is carried out using scientific methods and quality criteria. However, since these criteria are measured and oriented towards the practical field, they are subject to possible limitations, such as a small number of cases or selective case selection.

Application-oriented social research is considered a collective term for work contexts such as accompanying research, evaluation research or action research and is characterized by cross-border cooperation (especially transdisciplinarity), needs-oriented approaches and participatory approaches (von Unger 2014; Schemme and Novak 2017). Scientists and practitioners work together.

> Knowledge is thereby generated in direct engagement with the practice context and often in cooperation with stakeholders. This activity is characterised by the fact that close cooperation with practice partners takes place, which is reflected in the joint definition of problems as far as possible and the search for practicable solutions or 'lessons learned' that can be used further at a later stage. (Latniak and Wilkesmann 2005, p. 83)

Practitioners, non-academic actors and so-called "laypersons" take on new roles. Action research, for example, claims a particularly close relationship with practitioners, who are regarded as equal cooperation partners (Fricke 2014). And innovation partnerships that initiate cross-border dialogue are also noted for responsive types of accompanying scientific research (Sloane 2007). Society becomes a laboratory, or social change takes place in real and practical laboratories. Experimentation occupies a central place in the social sciences (Latour 2001; Böschen et al. 2017).

Model experiments (in vocational education and training) and specific varieties of *model projects* are a manifestation of such experimental and participatory forms

---

knowledge. Or this form of sociology is dedicated to the mission-related elaboration of interventions through the use of instrumental knowledge under the *yardstick of application orientation.*

of application-oriented social sciences. These projects do not have a research mandate, but aim to develop exemplary or model measures and instruments for a specific purpose – they are the starting point of social innovations (Schemme 2014).

> Model experiments aim to change practice, i.e. innovations in the reality of vocational training. Science is involved in this by scientifically justifying, developing, reflecting on and evaluating the changes and the processes involved in their practical testing. (Hemkes et al. 2017, p. 2)

Development and transformation processes are based on scientific-empirical studies. In this respect, scientists are involved in model projects if necessary.[7] If the claim of participatory and cooperative science is taken seriously, the participation of practitioners in data collection and analysis processes seems just as indispensable as the presence of scientists in the field. Model projects are then characterized by special measures to establish this participation.

At best, the scientists conduct their work on site as *field research* – that is, they stay with the actors in practice for longer periods of time. In these cases, sociology and the social sciences produce a kind of ethnology of their own society (Hitzler 1999). As professional border crossers, the scientists reconstruct the construction of social (meaning) worlds. In the original sense, ethnography is understood as participant observation without interference in the action (Geertz 1983). In science-based model projects, such a distancing from the object of investigation would be counterproductive, since the aim is precisely to change the conditions on the ground. In a modification of the distancing principle to "observing participation" (Hitzler and Eisewicht 2016), more engagement is recommended and demanded.

> Existential engagement is (for us) about getting involved or being involved in as many things as possible, slipping into different roles, participating in doing whatever is 'usual' to do, and observing not only others but also oneself – in participating as well as in observing. (Eisewicht and Hitzler 2019, p. 143)

The above explanations clarify the basic assumption of the article. Application-oriented social research engages, intervenes, meets the practitioners 'at eye level'. At the same time, social scientists distance themselves in order to reflexively classify these interventions in social structures.

[7] There seems to be no uniform definition and no binding guidelines for model projects. Model projects are also carried out in which no scientists are involved.

3 Reports from the Field: Participatory Involvement

The *SHA Berlin guild* is an independent professional representation of the regionally based companies in the fields of sanitary and heating construction, plumbing, stove and air heating construction. It is responsible for the implementation of inter-company training in its own SHA Competence Centre Berlin, for the taking of journeyman's examinations within the framework of dual training and for the job-related further training of company owners and their employees. The work in the model project integrates the sociologist into the work area of vocational training of the Guild SHA Berlin. The following field reports are a self-reflective analysis of the own position and role.

The aim of the model project is to develop measures against *premature contract terminations* and thus to reduce dropouts in the training of plant mechanics (SHA). To this end, a needs analysis was carried out using a mixed methods design, followed by the design of measures and their testing in practice. The actors relevant to training are involved in all phases of the project. The model project is located in the administrative area of the guild, while the area of investigation still includes at least the training companies, the vocational school and the inter-company workshops. The following observations portray the guild (Sect. 3.1), clarify the conducive and obstructive contextual conditions of the scientific work (Sect. 3.2) and go into the demands on the social scientist (Sect. 3.3).

3.1 SHA Berlin Guild – "A Strong Community"

The SHA Berlin guild sees itself more as a *community* at eye level than as a strictly hierarchical organisation. Low-threshold contact opportunities, daily greetings with a friendly handshake and formalities are communication and interaction rituals that pave the way for situational-pragmatic action. Informal recruitment strategies promote familiar and 'familial' team constellations and form the basis for establishing ad hoc solution strategies.

The *cohesion* between the guild and the member companies is generated more by intrinsic motives of solidarity than by external constraints and control mechanisms by management and the board. A picture emerges of (merely) restrained influence by the guild on the companies and their training quality. The guild's task could only be to "hold a mirror up to the companies" (board member). When measures to prevent the termination of contracts were discussed in the project, there were corresponding concerns about upsetting companies with demands that were too forceful.

In the last few years, the guild has been *growing:* According to the guild's head master in a figurative comparison, it is no longer a matter of the requirements for organising a 30 sqm apartment, but now it is a matter of managing a city villa,. The rapid growth requires more coordination and stronger formalization in administration and organization. The claim to be more of a network than a guild entails numerous activities that push employees to the limits. However, growth is also associated with a new zeitgeist, which has made it possible to open up to science and initiate the model project. The guild sees itself as an innovator in vocational training (in Berlin).

The *member companies* of the guild are characterized by a certain reserve in guild activities, if these do not serve to cope with the daily challenges. A solid part of the companies is committed, while a large part holds back. In the drastic formulation of one company owner, a "gap" between the guild organisation and its members is stated. However, this would not be a very fruitful basis for initiating changes in training and implementing improvements in a joint, participative and cooperative manner. Particularly when it comes to training young people and securing skilled workers, the guild would like to see a shared basis of values and collectively shared standards of action among the companies that go beyond formal training regulations.

The model project works towards achieving a higher level of *voluntary commitment on the part* of companies to high-quality training. Just as it is a joint task to train the next generation, the companies must (also) support themselves in this task.

3.2 Contextual Conditions: Openness and Closure

The success of scientific work favors the fundamental openness of the field. This includes, first and foremost, the *integration of* the scientist into the employer organization. The sociologist is part of the guild staff on a full-time basis, which guarantees participation and involvement in interactive and communicative daily events. The spatial separation of the office from the administrative apparatus has a specific relieving effect. It was set up especially for the project and promotes a certain special position that is conducive to professional work. Thus, the office offers itself as a place of retreat for analyses and paperwork, while other workspaces of the administration are exposed to an invasive culture of conversation, i.e. the temporary interruption of meetings and conversations in order to clarify one's own concerns.

The *acceptance of* the scientist as a communication partner also has a positive effect – especially with regard to the implementation of the empirical studies. The employment of the sociologist was weighed up by those responsible particularly against the background of the doctorate. How would craft businesses react to a 'doctor'? And how would a doctoral academic act in this specific environment? In retrospect, there were no negative consequences. The interviewees were by no means reserved or afraid of contact. It is even possible that the academic degree had a positive effect on the legitimacy of the project. The decisive factors in this process are the social science qualifications and habitus of the scientist (cf. Sect. 3.4).

The general openness of the guild on the ostentatious level contrasts with the relative *closedness of* the companies on the performative practical level. The guild strives for a "hermetic seal against external influences, so that we do not burn our companies [i.e. overtax them]" (management level employee). The member companies are the basis of the guild and the addressees of the guild's work. This work is characterised by a consultative orientation, which may be an obstacle for social innovations.

From a methodological-practical point of view, *field access to* the companies turned out to be difficult (see above reservation). At the practical level of training, it is argued, the companies already have to reconcile the ambivalences of training and day-to-day business, which is why there is hardly any time left for supporting the project – even though our project approach is repeatedly praised. However, the decisive factor for the reluctance of the practice is presumably much more a service programmatic: The project – and thus the guild – and the scientist work out solutions (for the companies). This applies under the premise that knowledge generation is left to the 'clever brains' and does not take place in a cooperative and participatory manner.

3.3 Contextual Conditions: Resilience and Dynamics

On the one hand, different perceptions of *time and temporality have an* aggravating effect. Model and practical projects are always expected to deliver answers quickly. The fact that an inventory is necessary for the conception of measures is given little consideration.[8] Furthermore, differences in synchronicity and work cycle between

[8] This is also proven by my experience from technology development projects.

the guild as an organisation and the scientific project work are noticeable. In the model project, work is slowed down firstly by the involvement of the other project staff in other activities and projects, and secondly by the modes of action generated in organisational life (see above, overload due to growth and little formalised division of labour).

On the other hand, the understanding of *scientific practice* diverges between sociologists and practitioners. In practice, there is a 'love of numbers', i.e. a focus on quantitative methods, measured values and statistics. This is mainly due to the justification context of the project. Graphs and statistical statements are the provable evidence for specific facts. Only the broad survey of attitudes and opinions provides reliable statements about the training relationships and helps to market the results. For the model project, this results in an understanding of empirical studies in which figures are the hard facts with which arguments can be made, while statements from interviews serve primarily as 'pre-facts' for questionnaire construction. This is a common form of mixed methods, although the professional background for this is hardly known in practice. This lack of experience led, for example, to the fact that no money was budgeted for transcriptions.

Furthermore, practitioners tend to (over)*emphasize their knowledge of* the field. This applies less to the project context than to the operational training level. Symptomatic, for example, is the empirically hardly provable assumption that trainees used to have more bite than they do today. Furthermore, the predefinition of suitable measures can already be questioned in the application text. This seems to be due to the model character of the project and the understanding of science: Testing out what can be imagined instead of in-depth exploration. Here, the discursive level overrides practical action. Measures against the shortage of skilled workers are intended "on a grand scale with a campaign character" (employees at the management level). However, individual measures are already being questioned in the planning stage, with recourse to the readiness of the companies.[9]

There is a variety of resilience: on the one hand, measures should be innovative, on the other hand, they should not disrupt everyday practice. A 'hard line' is avoided because guild members may feel patronised. This leads to latent – more or less consciously self-imposed – restrictions with regard to the development of innovations.

[9] Thus, a self-test of training quality for companies is preferred to external control bodies.

3.4 (Required) Competences of the Social Scientist

Specific forms of applied social research have facets of ethnography and this is always the case when researchers do not only go into the field for interviews and/ or are integrated into the field. Thus, Völter (2008) sees *ethnographic competence* as the basis for social work. This competence has to be acquired, at best in practical action. What is true for action research is equally true for engaged ethnography.

> The aspiring action researcher must understand that it is important to approach social situations with open questions, a willingness to engage in dialogue and collaboration with practitioners. (Fricke 2014, p. 232)

The greatest challenge probably lies in shedding the sociological or sociological-scientific habitus at least temporarily and intentionally enabling participation in the field. In doing so, it is important to overcome possible social distances and at the same time to build up sufficient professional distance. Undoubtedly, social scientists shape society in their work – but equally they are affected by the field and change their actions (Zajak 2018). It is highly necessary to be able to identify with a project (goal). For it is through engagement, and less through distancing, that social scientists appear credible and obtain the information necessary for the work.

Social scientists need to be *routine border crossers*. They cross the boundaries of their own working and living environment and participate as strangers in the everyday social life of others. Even if the concrete project work is the focus of action, a sociological view of the broader structures and contexts of action (e.g. the organisational development of the guild) arises. Through "sociological strangeness" (Villa 2006) the view becomes more objective, more perceptive, more rational with regard to the habits, traditions and norms that can be found. Learning to be inconspicuously present is important for border crossers. Every organization and field has its own 'rituals' in the broadest sense. Values and routines frame common actions and interactions. Being a border crosser therefore always means adaptation.

Social scientists are called upon to *adapt rituals*. This includes, for example, the morning handshake and a gruff, clumsy tone. At lunch, for example, they jokingly refuse to take a seat at the table by saying "This seat is taken" In the repetitive workday, this ensures communication connections. It also involves appropriating the prevailing invasive conversational culture, as deviations from it are perceived as 'irritation' by the actors. The guild is a male domain, in which it is taken for granted that people talk to each other in a formal manner. A coarse form of expression is not excluded and becomes apparent in the interviews through the regular use of vulgar language. At the same time, family and friendly relationships develop among the practitioners and in the training relationships.

It is precisely these modes of expression and manners that need to be taken into account when addressing companies and/or other actors relevant to training. In principle, social scientists should be able to *'down-phrase'*. This is especially connected to the choice of words, and it is important to use terminology such as "creating a questionnaire" instead of "designing a questionnaire". Thus, the suggestion to replace the word 'Zusammentreffen' with 'Zusammenschau' was commented on with the ironic request: "You should read a Konsalik again." And at another time it was said, "When I read texts by Mr. Biniok, I always keep a dictionary handy." In this way, negotiations about the language to be used become possible.

The three competencies mentioned above enable the professional support of the practical actors in the model project. The knowledge about the field gained through participation is made available to the actors in an adequate form in order to independently imagine and implement a possible transformation process. This is a possible form of social science design.

4 Varieties of Social Science Design

The model project of the SHA Berlin guild is a science-based transformation project in which the sociologist participates in the everyday work of the practitioners due to the specific situation.[10] Field research forms the basis of change action – but by the practice actors themselves. The analysis of the formative role of the scientist in such a constellation is carried out through the following *comparison of* two exemplary formats of application-oriented social sciences: on the one hand, the academic, practice-oriented research project (Biniok and Selke 2018) and, on the other hand, the presented model project. Both exhibit specific characteristics and condition the actions of the sociologist in a different way. Although the juxtaposition suggests distinctness, the demarcations are fluid. This is due to the claim to determine the divergent characteristics of two closely 'related' forms of application-oriented social research (cf. Table 1).

'Non-research'

A first difference is the interest in knowledge and the orientation of the respective project. In contrast to academic practice research, the non-academic model project

[10] Even if a permanent or long-term stay in the field is generally desirable in practice research, this tends to be the exception in concrete projects.

Table 1 Two forms of application-oriented social sciences. (Own table)

	Academic practice project	Non-academic model project
Focus	Research	Development
Question	(general) needs, requirements	(concrete) problems, obstacles
Freedom of action	Autonomous	Semi-autonomous
Procedure	Short-term stays in the field	Permanent in the field
Roll	Role change	Roll overlay
Function scientist	Moderation, orchestration, networking	Infiltration, consultation, arrangement
Design process	Social dynamization: process of increasing activation and participation	Social enrichment: process of increasing reflexivity and unfolding

is not declared as research. On the contrary: "We are not allowed to say research." (Management level staff) The *focus* is on the targeted development of measures and not on researching the field. A differentiation of research and science in the eyes of the practice actors is indicated, seemingly based on granting science a high degree of exactness and freedom from contradictions, while research is seen as the discovery of new phenomena. This is paradoxical insofar as innovative, i.e. novel, measures are demanded for the model project.

While the academic project is concerned with rather vague (overall societal) needs and requirements (and possible problem horizons), the model project starts from concretely identifiable challenges and *questions of* societal practice. The concreteness of the question also gives rise to the idea that instead of research work, primarily scientific development work is necessary, which manifests itself in measured values. However, the development of measures is always preceded by (qualitative) exploration, analysis of the status quo and research into the field.

Quasi-autonomy

In an academic practice project, the researchers generally have a high degree of *freedom of action*, taking into account the project plan. Of course, in the course of the project (especially in practice research) external influences change the scientific plan and procedure; how this is reacted to, however, depends on the scientists. In the model project, the social scientists fit into the decision-making routines of an organization. Especially when they are not the project leaders, their right to have a say depends on these instances. Asynchrony between organizational and project work and divergent understandings of temporality can then become challenges in scientific work.

Operational Field Research

The *procedure* of academic practice research is characterized by selective and/or short-term stays in the field. Information events and workshops are held, people are interviewed and events are observed. In the case of the model project, the social scientist works permanently in the field and is exposed to the internal dynamics of the field (such as the service culture of the guild). This includes getting closer to the 'indigenous' behaviours. Although the work in the model project has facets of ethnography, it is not field research in the true sense of the word, in which 'foreign cultures' are understood. Based on concrete objectives, it is rather 'operative field research' that creates a difference.

Duc to the permanent presence in the field, the social scientist works with a simultaneity of observation and participation, in which the *roles* overlap. The retreat into one's own office makes it possible to distance oneself from the object of research. In academic practice projects, on the other hand, a distinct role change can be observed. The social scientist is a member of university structures and communication on the one hand and a 'traveller by experience' on the other.

Infiltration and Arrangement

The settings and roles mentioned go hand in hand with different *functions* that the social scientist assumes in practice research. In the case of academic practice research, the social scientist is first of all a moderator and orchestrator in order to involve the relevant groups of actors (also from civil society) in the research and to associate and network them with each other in a needs-oriented manner. The task of participation is to create structures that will become permanent over time.

In the model project, on the other hand, actor relations already exist, and the social scientist penetrates these structures in an investigative way. In a way, he *infiltrates* the field, because his presence requires explanation and is based on the fact that something is wrong. Because of the limited autonomy and the existing structures, the social scientist has a consultative function that is linked to *arranging tasks.*[11] Arrangements arise in two ways. The scientist primarily arranges knowledge, texts, evaluations in the form of categorizations and typifications. The demand-oriented arrangement of data and knowledge is an essential part of the re-vitalization of decision-making processes in the field. In connection with the arrangement of material, artefacts and personnel that goes beyond this, the practice actors are supported in the redesign of vocational training.

[11] The term "*arrangement*"is preferred to the terminology "structuring"because structures already exist and the social scientist primarily designs new arrangements on the basis of which the practice actors (re)structure.

Social Enrichment

The *design process* and the realization of a transformation each have different connotations. The process of mutual exchange between scientists and the civilian population in the academic practice project experiences a social dynamization that, at best, results in new, sustainable structures. The actors become increasingly involved in the project, while the project team withdraws more and more. The independent self-administration of the new structures is a central element of the research, since in many cases projects generate a short-term response, but after the end of the project, further interventions rarely follow and the original state – which actually needs to be improved – is quickly restored.

In the model project, the question of social dynamization undoubtedly also arises. However, it can rather be assumed that the practice actors act in a problem-averse manner and come to terms with the resources available to them. The process can therefore be understood primarily as *social enrichment.*[12] The new arrangements are developed directly from within the project and coordinated with the relevant actors. Through scientific support, practice partners self-reflexively acquire knowledge for change processes and establish innovative measures.

5 Conclusion: A Model Project Without Practice? – Degrees of 'Hardness' in Social Science Practice Research

On a science-theoretical level, changed modes of knowledge production and new forms and formats of participation of non-scientific actors in transformation processes are discussed. Less attention is paid to the question of the extent to which addressed consumers, customer groups or technology users actually want to participate in transformation processes and/or see themselves in a position to do so. The discursive openness of the SHA sector in Berlin towards social innovations contrasts, for example, with a practical reluctance in the project context. *The present study reveals ambivalences between the (theoretical) claims of practice research and practical implementation.*

[12] Cf. systemically oriented intervention research: "The approach follows an "ecological principle"of gentle control in intervention. The practitioners from the companies, management as well as employees, are seen as 'experts' for their own problems, science and consulting support the self-control ability of the acting persons through dialogical processes of knowledge acquisition and knowledge transfer in order to sustainably develop the social processes and structures."(Klatt et al. 2014, p. 286).

The model project is legitimized in a special way by the scientific work. This is to be understood as a variable aid: It is at the same time a criterion of justification externally vis-à-vis social policy as well as a practice-related moment of change internally vis-à-vis employees and training companies. In this way, it is possible to legitimise the presence of the sociologist as an investigator in need of explanation who 'uncovers grievances' (infiltration). Moreover, the sociologist becomes the benefactor of dynamics that initiate and sustain the project team (arrangement). Nevertheless, intra-field dynamics and resilience at the operational level complicate and complicate the *collective* modification of existing structures. The regular feedback of analysis results and developed measures to the field of practice does not harmonise to the desired extent.

The case study illustrates an important aspect that tends to receive little attention in generally accepted routines of project application and project start-up. Scientific staff are hired for projects that they did not conceive. This can result in the project starting with false premises and inadequate methods, and precisely those *adjustments of engagement and distancing do* not do justice to the subject matter. What follows would be, for example, a practice project without practice. Social scientists have the opportunity to analyse the field's own characteristics in order to set the course for successful project work already when addressing the practice partners. Above all, this means becoming aware of *one's own role* in the specific project. The 'degree of rigour' of social science practice research, i.e. the degree of innovation of the transformation and the sustainability of the measures, depends on this.

The comparison of the two forms of application-oriented social science shows that specific forms of design are associated with different proximity to the object and with different degrees of 'hardness'. Structure formation and structure modification can – depending on localities, actors, etc. – proceed and be successful in very different ways. Engagement and distancing are reversible and have to be adjusted depending on the case. On the one hand, the practice researchers themselves decide on appropriate roles and procedures in the scientific work. On the other hand, the commitment of the practice partners plays an equally important role. Successful participation paves the way for sustainable innovation and a successful transformation project.

References

Biniok, P. und S. Selke. 2018. Soziale Innovation durch Bricolage: Der "Geist des Tüftelns" im ländlichen Raum. In *Soziale Innovationen lokal gestalten.*, Hrsg. H.-W. Franz und C. Kaletka, 181–196. Wiesbaden: Springer VS.

Blättel-Mink, B. und I. Katz, Hrsg. 2004. *Soziologie als Beruf? Soziologische Beratung zwischen Wissenschaft und Praxis*. Wiesbaden: VS.
Burawoy, M. 2005. For Public Sociology. *American Sociological Review* 4: 4–28.
Böschen, S., Groß, M. und W. Krohn. 2017. *Experimentelle Gesellschaft. Das Experiment als wissensgesellschaftliches Dispositiv*. Baden-Baden: Nomos.
Degele, N., Münch, T., Pongratz, H.J. und N.J. Saam. 2001. *Soziologische Beratungsforschung*. Wiesbaden: VS Verlag.
Eisewicht, P. und R. Hitzler. 2019. Diesseits der prinzipiellen Lösungen. In *Moralische Kollektive*, Hrsg. S. Joller und M. Stanisavljevic, 137–152. Wiesbaden: Springer VS.
Elias, N. 1983. *Engagement und Distanzierung: Arbeiten zur Wissenssoziologie*. Frankfurt/M.: Suhrkamp.
Fricke, W. 2014. Aktionsforschung in schwierigen Zeiten. In *Sozialen Wandel gestalten*, Hrsg. M. Jostmeier, A. Georg und H. Jacobsen, 213–236. Wiesbaden: Springer VS.
Geertz, C. 1983. *Dichte Beschreibung*. Frankfurt/M.: Suhrkamp.
Gieryn, T. 1983. Boundary-work and the demarcation of science from non-science: Strains and interests in professional ideologies of scientists. *American Sociological Review* 48(6): 781–795.
Hartmann, E. A., Brings C., Fünfhaus, A., Krichewsky-Wegener, L., Schulze, M. und I. Stamm. 2018. Eine Exzellenzinitiative für die berufliche Bildung? *iit perspektive 40*.
Hemkes, B., Srbeny, C., Vogel, C. und C. Zaviska. 2017. Zum Selbstverständnis gestaltungsorientierter Forschung in der Berufsbildung – Eine methodologische und methodische Reflexion. *bwp@ 33*: 1–23.
Hemkes, B., Wilbers, K. und M. Heister, Hrsg. 2019. *Durchlässigkeit zwischen beruflicher und hochschulischer Bildung*. Bonn: BiBB.
Herberg, J. 2018. *Illusio Fachkräftemangel*. Wiesbaden: Springer VS.
Hitzler, R. 1999. *Welten erkunden*. Soziale Welt 50(4): 473–483.
Hitzler, R. und P. Eisewicht. 2016. *Lebensweltanalytische Ethnographie – im Anschluss an Anne Honer*. Weinheim und Basel: Beltz Juventa.
Howaldt, J. und H. Jacobsen. 2010. *Soziale Innovationen*. Wiesbaden: Springer VS.
Kaldewey, D. (2016): Die Sehnsucht nach der Praxis. Beobachtungen zur Identitätsarbeit der Sozialwissenschaften. In *Sozialwissenschaften und Gesellschaft*. Neue Verortungen von Wissenstransfer, Hrsg. A. Froese, D. Simon und J. Böttcher, 129–157. Bielefeld: transcript.
Klatt, R., Ciesinger, K.G., Cohnen, H. und S. Steinberg. 2014. Systemisch orientierte Interventionsforschung als innovative Methode gestaltungsorientierter Arbeitsforschung. In *Sozialen Wandel gestalten*, Hrsg. M. Jostmeier, A. Georg und H. Jacobsen, 279–288. Wiesbaden: Springer VS.
Malin, L., Jansen, A., Seyda, S. und R. Flake. 2019. *KOFA-Studie: Fachkräftesicherung in Deutschland – diese Potenziale gibt es noch*. Köln: Institut der deutschen Wirtschaft Köln e.V.
Latour, B. 2001. Ein Experiment von und mit uns allen. *DIE ZEIT 16*.
Latniak, Erich, und U. Wilkesmann. 2005. Anwendungsorientierte Sozialforschung. *Soziologie* 34(1):65–82.
Mevissen, N. 2016. Ewig umstritten. Soziologie zwischen Engagement und Distanzierung. In *Sozialwissenschaften und Gesellschaft*. Neue Verortungen von Wissenstransfer, Hrsg. A. Froese, D. Simon und J. Böttcher, 193–231. Bielefeld: transcript.

Rahner, S. 2018. Fachkräftemangel und falscher Fatalismus. Frankfurt/M., NY: Campus.

Schemme, D. 2014. Modellversuche zur Innovation beruflicher Bildung und ihre wissenschaftliche Begleitung. In *Sozialen Wandel gestalten*, Hrsg. M. Jostmeier, A. Georg und H. Jacobsen, 251–267. Wiesbaden: Springer VS.

Schemme, D. und H. Novak, Hrsg. 2017. *Gestaltungsorientierte Forschung – Basis für soziale Innovationen*. Bonn: BiBB.

Schneidewind, U. und M. Singer-Brodowski. 2014. Transformative Wissenschaft. Marbrug: Metropolis.

Sloane, P.F.E. (2007): Berufsbildungsforschung im Kontext von Modellversuchen und ihre Orientierungsleistung für die Praxis – Versuch einer Bilanzierung und Perspektiven. In *Perspektiven der Berufsbildungsforschung. Orientierungsleistungen der Forschung für die Praxis*, Hrsg. R. Nickolus und A. Zöller, 11–60. Bielefeld: Bertelsmann.

Thomä, J. 2014. Fachkräftemangel im Handwerk? – eine Spurensuche. *WSI Mitteilungen 8*: 590–598.

Uhly, A. 2015. *Vorzeitige Vertragslösungen und Ausbildungsverlauf in der dualen Berufsausbildung: Forschungsstand, Datenlage und Analysemöglichkeiten auf Basis der Berufsbildungsstatistik*. Bonn: BiBB.

Villa, P.-I. 2006. Fremd sein – schlau sein? Soziologische Überlegungen zur Nomadin. In *Nomaden, Flaneure, Vagabunden*, Hrsg. W. Gebhardt und R. Hitzler, 37–50 Wiesbaden: Springer VS.

Völter, B. 2008. *Verstehende Soziale Arbeit*. FQS 9(1), Art. 56.

Von Unger, H. 2014. *Partizipative Forschung*. Wiesbaden: Springer VS.

Zajak, S. 2018. Engagiert, politisch, präfigurativ – Das Selbstexperiment als transformative Bewegungsforschung. *Forschungsjournal Soziale Bewegungen* 31(4), 89–105.

Biniok, Peter, Dr. phil., studied computer science and sociology at the Technical University of Berlin, worked for a long time in cross-border university projects and as a freelancer, main research interests: Digitalization and social change, sociology of science and technology, social science practice research.

Latest Publications:

Biniok, Peter, S. Selke, and J. Achatz. 2019. sociodigital neighborhoods: The transformation of neighborhoods under the influence of digitalization. In Heinze, Rolf G., S. Kurtenbach; J. Üblacker. Eds. Digitization and Neighborhoods. Erosion of coexistence or new communitarization? Baden-Baden: Nomos, 33–60.

Biniok, Peter. 2018. sociotechnical assistance ensembles. Negotiations of Needs and Acceptance of Support Technologies. In Karafillidis, Athanasios and R. Weidner. Eds. Developing Support Technologies. Heidelberg: Springer, 17–25.

Transdisciplinary Research Using the Example of the "Media Future Lab" Project

Sevda Can Arslan

Abstract

Transdisciplinary practice is *"society- or lifeworld-oriented research"* (Vilsmaier and Lang, Nachhaltigkeitswissenschaften, Vol. 104, Springer, Heidelberg, p. 89, 2014). By this, the authors mean that "questions and problems of research are not generated from a scientific tradition [...] but are oriented towards socially relevant questions or problems" (Vilsmaier and Lang, Nachhaltigkeitswissenschaften, vol. 104, Springer, Heidelberg, pp. 89f., 2014). In this article, Vilsmaier and Lang's understanding of transdisciplinary research will be explained in detail. After a brief introduction of the communication science project "Media Future Lab", the characteristics of transdisciplinarity are explained using this concrete example. The structure and content of this reflection is based on the essay "Transdisziplinäre Forschung" (Transdisciplinary Research) by Ulli Vilsmaier and Daniel J. Lang from 2014, in which the authors explain transdisciplinarity using the example of sustainability science. I summarize the points relevant to the project "Media Future Lab" and place the project in the context of transdisciplinarity on the basis of these points. Thus, the article fits well into the conference proceedings, which ask, among other things, how "we as social scientists [can] facilitate the understanding and development of sustainable social innovation and transformation processes", "[w]hat roles [...] we ourselves [play] in the respective context and [w]hat theoretical and methodological tools [...] we [make use of]."

S. C. Arslan (✉)
Ludwig Maximilian University, Mannheim, Germany

H.-W. Franz et al. (eds.), *Sustainable Living and Business*,
https://doi.org/10.1007/978-3-658-41835-9_12

1 Introduction

Transdisciplinary practice is *"society- or lifeworld-oriented research*" (Vilsmaier and Lang 2014, p. 89). By this, the authors mean that "questions and problems of research are not generated out of a scientific tradition [...] but are oriented towards socially relevant questions or problems" (Vilsmaier and Lang 2014, p. 89f.). In this article, Vilsmaier and Lang's understanding of transdisciplinary research will be explained in detail.

After a brief introduction of the communication science project Media Future Lab (MFL), the characteristics of transdisciplinarity are explained using this concrete example. The structure and content of this detailed reflection is based on the essay "Transdisciplinary Research" by Ulli Vilsmaier and Daniel J. Lang from 2014, in which the authors explain transdisciplinarity using the example of sustainability science. The points relevant to the MFL project are summarized here and the project is placed in the context of transdisciplinarity on the basis of these points. Thus, this article fits into the conference proceedings, which ask, among other things, how "we as social scientists [can] facilitate the understanding and development of sustainable social innovation and transformation processes", "[w]hat roles [...] we ourselves [play] in the respective context and [w]hat theoretical and methodological tools [...] we [use] for this purpose".

2 Presentation of the MFL Project

The MFL project is about the future of the media. As public communication channels, the media are essential for democracy. But they are currently in a crisis: The reach, acceptance and interpretative authority of traditional offerings are declining. Against this background, the project asks what we, society, expect from media offerings, what we understand by good journalism and what we want to pay for it.

In five steps, answers to these questions will be collected, which will finally be bundled in a citizens' report. In the first step, *expert interviews* will be *conducted with* media critics and media practitioners from traditional and new media providers, from interest and professional associations, from media politics, science and civil society. This is followed by the so-called "MFLs". In these labs, 20 to 25 people meet in different settings to articulate their criticism and develop ideas for alternatives. Various formats are possible in the labs, whether "fishbowl" or "future workshop". In the third step, the possibility for an *online discussion on the project topic* is *created. This is intended to enable everyone to participate* who was unable to attend the labs themselves. In this way, the material gathered in the first two project phases will be supplemented and differentiated. The heart of the project is the *"Media Future Forum". Over the course of six months,* 20 to 25 people who have either already participated in the labs or have offered to participate in the online discussion will *meet* and discuss with experts of their choice. Their task is to write a citizens' report on the future communication order. This citizens' opinion is to *be presented* at the final *Media Future Summit in* 2020.

The project has a duration of 4 years and is part of the research network "ForDemocracy – Future of Democracy", which is funded by the Bavarian State Ministry for Science and the Arts. *This brief introduction to MFL should serve as a basis for now explaining transdisciplinarity using the concrete example of this project.*

3 Starting Point and Characteristics of Transdisciplinarity

Transdisciplinary research has developed as a research practice since the "1990s" (Vilsmaier and Lang 2014, p. 89). Vilsmaier and Lang (2014) first explain the starting point of transdisciplinary research. They point out that transdisciplinarity "aim[s] to redefine the place and role of science in society" (Vilsmaier and Lang 2014, p. 88). According to the authors, the current role of science has evolved over time, so it is made:

> The very demand for cooperation between different areas of society presupposes a clear separation, a boundary between the areas. But as clearly as, for example, the terms 'science' and 'politics' are to be distinguished, the boundaries between the concepts behind them can by no means always be precisely determined – and above all they are not simply *given*, but are the result of a process. So when we speak of science and *the other* spheres of society, we must not lose sight of the fact that we are referring to a very particular image of science and society that reflects a particular order. That order which appears to us today as normal is by no means *given*. (Vilsmaier and Lang 2014, p. 88).

Vilsmaier and Lang (2014) describe the differentiation of society underlying this understanding of science. In doing so, they conclude that the development of the social division of roles ends in a paradox: Science becoming more and more specialized creates a complexity that is so high that it cannot in turn be dealt with by specialized science (Vilsmaier and Lang 2014, p. 89). In order to deal with this complexity, transdisciplinarity softens these boundaries between science and other areas of society by moving towards the production of knowledge with actors outside science. This understanding of science is compatible with the foundations of the MFL project. The project is based on a comparable understanding of science in qualitative empirical social science (Meyen et al. 2011) and participatory research (von Unger 2014).

In the following, the authors identify three characteristics of transdisciplinary research: the *contextuality of* research, the *orientation towards society* and the focus on the *learning process*. These three characteristics will now be presented and related to the MFL project.

Vilsmaier and Lang (2014) identify the *contextuality of* research as a characteristic of the transdisciplinary understanding of science. The authors draw on the understanding of "Mode 2" research by Gibbons et al. (1994). Modc 1 denotes an "understanding of science that believes in a purity of method and universally valid truth" – a "myth" for the authors (Vilsmaier and Lang 2014, p. 93f.). Instead, they follow a conception of science "that recognizes that science, too, is conducted in a specific context and by people whose thinking and actions are influenced by a wide variety of interests, passions, and thus subjective factors, and to that extent cannot produce absolute knowledge." (Vilsmaier and Lang 2014, p. 93f.). As possible contextual factors, they cite "conditions in a laboratory as well as the intellectual and cultural environment, the political and economic conditions, and historical experiences that characterize a particular era" (Vilsmaier and Lang 2014, p. 92).

For the MFL project, this implies a high demand for reflection on the different contexts in which knowledge is generated within the project. The reflection, for example, on subjective factors that influence the decisions of the core team, as well as on the specific situations of the other actors or the spaces in which knowledge is generated, must be documented and included in the synthesis of the body of knowledge in order to do justice to transdisciplinary research.

The authors also refer to transdisciplinary practice as "*society- or lifeworld-oriented research*" (Vilsmaier and Lang 2014, p. 89). By this they mean that "questions and problems of research are not generated out of a scientific tradition […] but are oriented towards socially relevant questions or problems" (Vilsmaier and Lang 2014, p. 89f.). These questions are, as described above, highly complex. Here, transdisciplinary research offers "approaches that make it possible to approach situations of high uncertainty and complexity when there is no clarity about what constitutes them *as a whole*. Transdisciplinary research is – one might casually say – about this whole." (Vilsmaier and Lang 2014, p. 90). The authors emphasize that "the whole" should not be misunderstood here as meaning that reality can be completely grasped with the help of transdisciplinarity. Instead, the point is that transdisciplinarity "acknowledges uncertainty and incompleteness and takes them into account as a framework condition of research" (Vilsmaier and Lang 2014, p. 90). Transdisciplinarity needs the

> extra-scientific perspectives in order to increase the diversity of perspectives. It recognises that a problem in the life-world can be best understood and consequently dealt with if the experience as well as the knowledge acquired in everyday life or through professional activities is also included, which constitutes 'life in this world', as well as the suffering that can arise through a problem situation. Frequently, therefore, there is talk of collaborations with 'practice actors' or extra-scientific actors. They complement the picture of a situation that scientists capture through their specific knowledge of partial aspects. (Vilsmaier and Lang 2014, p. 90)

It is precisely these extra-scientific perspectives of diverse actors that are the focus of the MFL research project. As in von Unger's (2014) understanding of participatory research, the aim is to involve social actors as "co-researchers".

The authors also point out that it is not only about understanding the world, but also about shaping it (Vilsmaier and Lang 2014, p. 97). "In this respect, transdisciplinary sustainability research sees itself as *transformative* science (WBGU 2011; Vilsmaier and Lang 2014, p. 90)." MFL is also a transformative project, with the aim of "exploring and [influencing] social reality in partnership" (von Unger 2014).

The authors also identify the *learning focus as* a further characteristic of transdisciplinary research. The goal is

> not to provide only scientifically sound answers to urgent societal challenges, but to shape *processes* that fulfil a variety of tasks. First and foremost, these are learning processes in which scientists from different disciplines as well as representatives of non-scientific sectors of society (e.g. from civil society organisations, certain professions, politics, industry or residents of a region) learn together from and with each other in order to understand and change a situation or a phenomenon in its complexity (Vilsmaier and Lang 2014, p. 91).

They emphasize the importance of the attitude of the actors involved and quote their colleagues: "Through scientists entering into dialogue and mutual learning with societal stakeholders, science becomes part of societal processes [...]. Problem-solving includes reflections, the transformation on attitudes, the development of personal competence and ownership, along with capacity building, institutional transformations and technology development (Vilsmaier and Lang 2014, p. 91)." Such learning processes are envisaged in the context of MFL. The citizens' report developed on the basis of all labs and interviews at the end of the project is understood as a handout for the transformation of the media system.

However, the authors only seem to assume a difference in the interests of the actors. A possible opposition is not addressed. Thus, it is conceivable that "a phenomenon in its complexity" is understood by all actors involved in the transdisciplinary research project, but the ideas of whether and how to change it are mutually exclusive. In the case of the MFL project, this can happen, for example, when marginalized groups demand more visibility in the media, but for media makers commercial profitability or for media politicians their re-electability are in the foreground. This raises the question of whether, in the course of the project, the perspectives of certain actors may have to be (justifiably) excluded in order to ensure further unity of purpose. Such exclusions would in turn lead to a lack of diversity of perspectives. Therefore, the decision to do so needs to be well weighed. It seems helpful here if the project is based on a normative point of view that can be used for the decision. However, the authors do not provide their own examples of possible values in this article. Later in the text, they refer to Pohl and Hirsch Hadorn (2006), who mention the "common good as a regulative principle" (Vilsmaier and Lang 2014, p. 100). For the MFL project, it would be just as conceivable to take the standpoint of a "journalism of the many" oriented towards the welfare of society as a whole from the perspective of democratic theory. In this way, the project would also be immune to instrumentalization, e.g. by the media industry, whose primary interest is to increase sales figures and thus advertising customers.

But even with such a normative standpoint, nothing is said about the outcome of the learning sought in transdisciplinarity. Beyond learning, there are power relations in current society that make the transformation sought after after learning more difficult. The authors themselves are silent on how to prepare for this. Only in the above mentioned figure on "Interdependence of the three types of knowledge (after Pohl and Hirsch Hadorn 2006, p. 35)" the power relations are mentioned (Vilsmaier and Lang 2014, p. 100, Fig. 3.1). For the MFL project, too, it seems important to develop realistic ideas about the power relations in the current media system in order to stimulate "individual and collective empowerment" (von Unger 2014) of the actors involved. All in all, both the starting point and the characteristics of transdisciplinary research seem compatible with the MFL project.

4 Zurich Understanding of Transdisciplinarity

Vilsmaier and Lang (2014) state that "the emergence of transdisciplinary research is a phenomenon resulting from different historical development processes and develop(ing) in different research fields" (p. 94). They then point to different understandings of transdisciplinarity. As a "milestone" (Vilsmaier and Lang 2014,

p. 97) of transdisciplinary research, the authors consider a conference in Zurich in 2000, which was attended by 800 representatives from science, business, politics and civil society from 50 countries. There they agreed on the "Zurich Definition of Transdisciplinarity" (Klein et al. 2001).

The first section of the five-part definition is about the benefits of transdisciplinarity:

> Why transdisciplinarity? The core idea of transdisciplinarity is that different academic disciplines working jointly with practitioners to solve a real-world problem. It can be applied in a great variety of fields. Transdisciplinary research is an additional type within the spectrum of research and coexists with traditional mono-disciplinary research. The science system is the primary knowledge system in society. Transdisciplinarity is a way of increasing its unrealized intellectual potential and, ultimately, its effectiveness. (Klein et al. 2001, p. 4)

A comparison of the first point with the characteristics of the research project MFL shows: Within the project, the discipline of communication science is in the foreground; at individual points (e.g. in the preparation of the research status and in the interviews with experts), knowledge from related disciplines such as sociology or political science is drawn upon. It is only in the "ForDemocracy – Future of Democracy" network that cooperation with other academic disciplines is realized. Here, more than 20 researchers from the humanities and social sciences work together on the theory of democracy and the organization of democratic processes – in other words, on questions that are superordinate to the individual projects. Finally, within the MFL project, "practitioners" are involved: At the level of the labs, the focus is on the perspective of media users; in the interviews, experts from journalism and politics as well as civil society actors have their say. The aim of the project is to develop a concrete utopia for a democratic future of the media system. In doing so, the project sets itself the task "to solve a real-world problem". The field of the public sphere seems well suited for transdisciplinary work.

The second point of the definition refers to the relationship between transdisciplinary and other research. Communication studies is often described as "transdisciplinary". However, what is often meant by the term here is simply that communication studies is a science in which research is conducted *across various academic disciplines* on the subject of public communication. For example, communication studies integrates theoretical approaches from sociology, political science and psychology. By contrast, the term transdisciplinarity, which is the focus here, refers to research that goes *beyond the academic disciplines.* To distinguish it from similar-sounding concepts, Vilsmaier and Lang (2014, p. 98) refer to the explanation by Jahn (2008):

> "Transdisciplinary" we can call research processes that aim at an expansion of disciplinary, multi- and interdisciplinary forms of a problem-related integration of knowledge and methods: In the *disciplinary* context, integration takes place at the level of (discipline-)internally defined research questions, in the *multidisciplinary* at the level of practical goals and problems, in the *interdisciplinary at* the level of scientific questions in the overlapping area of different disciplines, and in the *transdisciplinary* at the level of the overlapping area of these scientific questions with social problems. In transdisciplinary research processes, societal issues are taken up as lifeworld problem situations and scientifically addressed. (emphasis added by SCA)

Vilsmaier and Lang (2014), like the authors of the "Zurich Definition of Transdisciplinarity" (Klein et al. 2001, p. 4), emphasize that "transdisciplinary research is not intended to question the relevance and usefulness of disciplinary and interdisciplinary research. Rather, it is about purposefully relating insights gained through these different research approaches to one another and making them useful for one another." (S. 110). This attitude can also be discerned in the MFL project. The research approach chosen here focuses on the needs and ideas of media users. Although experts are heard during the interviews, the joint development of a citizens' report is the sole responsibility of the media users. The knowledge generated in this way can subsequently serve communication science.

In the last point, the importance of the science system for the generation of knowledge in society is emphasized. The authors argue that transdisciplinarity brings to bear the intellectual potential and effectiveness of science. This claim is also formulated in MFL. Here, science is supposed to provide the framework in which new insights are gained from the perspective of different actors, which can then be applied to improve the media system. Whether this succeeds can only be seen with the progress and the end of the project.

The second part of the "Zurich Definition of Transdisciplinarity" explains how transdisciplinarity is implemented:

> How is transdisciplinary done? Transdisciplinary projects are promising when they have clear goals and competent management to facilitate creativity and minimize friction among members of a team. Stakeholders must participate from the beginning and be kept interested and active over the entire course of a project. Mutual learning is the basic process of exchange, generation and integration of existing or newly-developing knowledge in different parts of science and society. (Klein et al. 2001, p. 4)

The "clear goal" is to produce a citizens' report with concrete proposals for the democratic design of the science system. The research questions of the project provide the rough framework for the preparation of the report. We want to know: What do we (society) expect from media offerings? What do we understand by good journalism? What do we want to pay for it? These general questions can then be further specified, e.g. by breaking them down to individual media or by distinguishing between the spheres of production, distribution and consumption of the media. This happens in the course of the research process together with the participants.

However, the various stakeholders are not involved in this project from the very beginning, nor are they involved throughout the entire duration of the project. The core team relies on the collaboration of individual actors at certain points. Thus, MFL does not fulfill the claim to transdisciplinarity formulated here. However, later in the paper the authors refer to the concept of "functionally dynamic collaboration" (cf. Krütli et al. 2010; Vilsmaier and Lang 2014, p. 109), which fits this approach:

> In principle, various degrees of intensity of stakeholder involvement can be distinguished in the cooperation between science and practice (from the perspective of the scientists). These range from purely informing the actors to working on an equal footing or the 'empowerment' of the practice actors by the scientists. It should be noted that the different intensities of involvement are also accompanied by shifts in power constellations as well as responsibilities for the process and the results (cf. van Kerkhoff and Lebel 2006a, b). In terms of functionally dynamic collaboration, however, not all actors need to be involved in the research process to the same extent at every point in time. Rather, for each step of the process, it is necessary to consider together specifically whose involvement is meaningful, goal-oriented, and insofar functional, and to what intensity (Vilsmaier and Lang 2014, p. 109).

It remains unclear here to what extent this procedure does not simply coincide with disciplinary research. But this hint can be understood as a call to regularly reflect – also together with the actors – at which points they want to be more or less involved for which goal.

The last point concerns mutual learning. The MFL project offers a lot of space for "exchange, generation and integration of existing or newly-developing knowledge" between all the different actors. This means not only the formal result of the citizens' report, but also the processes of individual and collective engagement with the research questions and answers to them. There are offers for "exchange and generation" on numerous levels: In the labs, the participants discuss with each other in person; on the accompanying research blog, the entire research activity can be followed and commented on; on Twitter, additional relevant information about the media system is shared; as soon as a suitable platform has been found for this, the project can be discussed online beyond the other online channels of blog, Twitter and YouTube; and the interviews took place in part as a public lecture series to which everyone was invited. The individual interviews and panel discussions were moderated by the core team, after which there was room for questions from the audience. As the lecture took place on a weekday morning for organisational reasons, it was also recorded in audio and video and subsequently made available on YouTube. The live events were advertised via posters, the blog and Twitter, as well as email distribution lists for the department, institute and alliance. However, we did not verify which people ultimately participated in this offering. In addition to the exchange on partial aspects of the project in the form of presentations at academic conferences, a fishbowl discussion was also organized, for example, as part of the conference "Great Transformation: The Future of Modern Societies".

The "integration" of all this knowledge generated in the different forums by such diverse actors in quite a variety of ways is a particular challenge of this project. So far, it seems that the core team alone has to synthesize the different findings. A software for the analysis of qualitative data from different sources could possibly be helpful to keep track of the collected results and to systematize them in a comprehensible way. Afterwards, the results have to be communicated to the different actors in a language they can understand.

Throughout the research process, "different parts" of society should be involved. This project has a democratic claim. Therefore, the exclusion mechanisms at work in the current society should at least be mitigated. This is to be achieved, for example, by specifically addressing marginalised groups for the labs and the interviews, as well as through further training in racism-critical organising and, where appropriate, in gender-sensitive behaviour or critical whiteness within the network. However, there are still many gaps in the project in relation to inclusion. For example, the online offer is not barrier-free. The dubbing of the blog texts, the subtitling in German and other languages, the translation of films into sign language or of texts into easy-to-understand language would be possibilities to include more groups of society in this project. Vilsmaier and Lang (2014) already point out that transdisciplinary research is usually limited by a lack of resources. By resources they mean money as well as "time, energy and patience of all participants" (Vilsmaier and Lang 2014, p. 110). Already in the conception of the project and thus in the application for funding, the financial and human resources that successful diversity efforts entail must be considered so that sufficient resources are available to make the research process accessible to all parts of society. It would be helpful to have an up-to-date guide to inclusive research that lists both the various aspects that need to be included and the likely costs and possible funding streams for doing so. Such a tool, developed by charities in collaboration with people experienced in inclusive research, would thus facilitate the entry of less experienced researchers into inclusive research.

With regard to resources, the authors also point out: "The even greater challenges, however, lie in dealing with the strange and unfamiliar, the unfamiliar and unpredictable, which comes to the fore in transdisciplinary projects." (Vilsmaier and Lang 2014, p. 110). In this project, the core team consists of Michael Meyen, an older man with a GDR background, and Sevda Can Arslan, a younger woman with an immigrant background. This combination makes it easier to deal with the aforementioned challenges because the team is diverse in terms of age, gender and origin. Thus, there are fewer perceptions of "foreignness" towards certain groups and better access to certain fields. In addition, the biographies of the core team provide for two different perspectives. This is considered an advantage in transdisciplinary research. However, in many other respects, such as degree of formal education and income, the core team – and the entire research network – are very similar. In order to increase the degree of transdisciplinarity, care should be taken to ensure more diversity among the actors in relation to these characteristics in the further research process.

5 "Knowledge" in the Integrative Understanding of Transdisciplinarity

The authors also address the concept of "knowledge", which is central to the integrative understanding of transdisciplinarity. In transdisciplinary research, the "inclusion of all knowledge and negotiation of values" is in the foreground:

> Not only scientifically generated knowledge should be taken into account in the research process, but also forms of knowledge that are acquired in professional contexts or appropriated as experiential knowledge in everyday existence [...]. In addition to knowledge and experience, values, interests and habits are also taken into account in research and negotiated in transdisciplinary processes (Vilsmaier and Lang 2014, p. 97).

Both the claim to include non-scientific knowledge and the two justifications for doing so are completely in line with the MFL project.

In addition to these forms of knowledge, the authors explain the distinction between three different types of knowledge: system knowledge, target knowledge and transformation knowledge. This distinction "often serves as a structuring element of the research process and the resulting findings" (Vilsmaier and Lang 2014, p. 100). Systems knowledge is concerned with "aspects of the genesis and possible developments of the problem and its lifeworld interpretations", target knowledge is concerned with "aspects of determining and justifying the need for change and desired goals as well as better practices", and "transformation knowledge" is concerned with "aspects of the technical, social, legal, cultural and other possibilities for action to change existing and introduce desired practices" (Vilsmaier and Lang 2014, p. 100). Figure 1 describes the different types of knowledge and their interdependence in more detail.

This distinction into different types of knowledge can also be helpful for the MFL project. Interestingly, the three forms of knowledge coincide with the procedure in the first MFL: In the future workshop method used, a three-step process is carried out from critique to utopia to practice. The results of the critique phase can be understood as system knowledge, the results of the utopia phase as target knowledge and the results of the practice phase as transformation knowledge. But the distinction cannot only be used to categorize the already collected data. They can also guide inquiry during the elicitation phase. Since, according to Bergmann et al. (2010), the future workshop method is used in the context of transdisciplinary research (p. 276), existing literature can be linked to here.

Finally, the authors present different phases of transdisciplinary research. Transdisciplinarity entails going back to earlier steps again and again during the research process because of "the specific research constellations that are fraught with many uncertainties" (Vilsmaier and Lang 2014, p. 101).

Transdisciplinary researchers thus go through the three steps described above several times, sometimes not one after the other, but rather "in each other" (Vilsmaier and Lang 2014, p. 102). The following three steps (cf. Fig. 2) correspond to the three phases presented by the authors (A), (B) and (C) in Lang et al. (2012, p. 31) or points (1), (2) and (3) in the model of the Institute for Social-Ecological Research (ISOE) (Jahn 2008, p. 31).

For the phase of *"problem identification and structuring" the* following applies: First of all, it is important to "involve the 'right' and legitimate actors in the research process" (Vilsmaier and Lang 2014, p. 102). The core team of the project consists of two communication scientists. In addition, other actors will be involved in the research process at various points. The selection of the exact groups from which the actors come, as well as the persons finally selected within these groups, still has to be justified and made transparent. It should be noted that the sampling is also shaped by the knowledge and needs of the actors involved. For example, in a lab the need for more information on a topic can be formulated, which then leads to an interview with an expert on this topic. The authors themselves already point out that "some steps are also very difficult to predict, such as the development of a transdisciplinary research team" (Vilsmaier and Lang 2014, p. 102). The knowledge of this difficulty hopefully enables a more relaxed approach to the challenges that await.

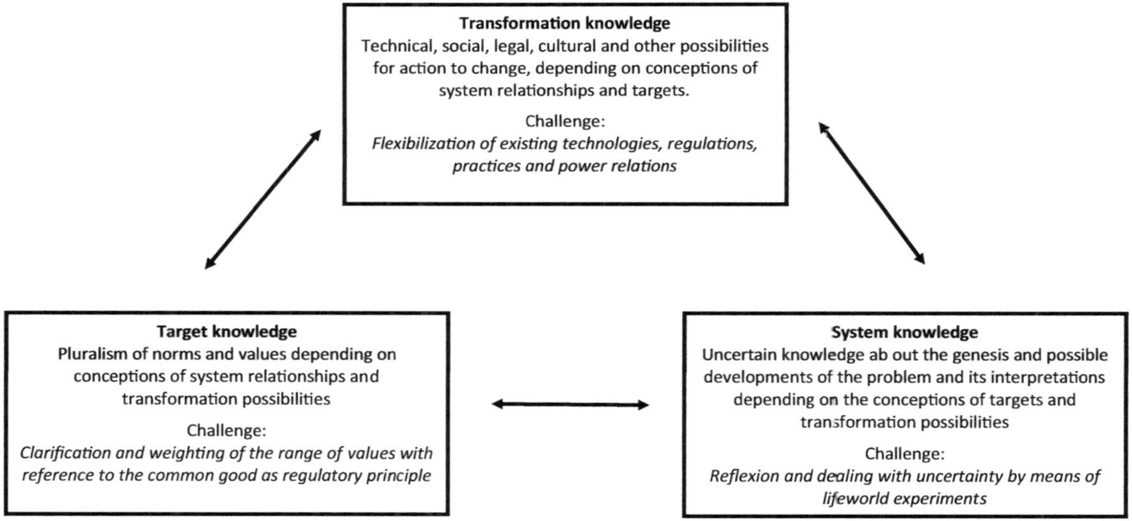

Fig. 1 Interdependence of the three types of knowledge. (Adapted from Pohl and Hirsch Hadorn 2006, p. 35; Vilsmaier and Lang 2014, p. 100, Fig. 3.1)

Principle	Guiding question
PHASE A	
Forming a collaborative research team	Does the research team represent all relevant expertise, experience and other determining 'stakes' in order to address the sustainability problem in a way that solutions and options can be proposed and a contribution to existing scientific knowledge can be made?
Creating a common understanding referring to the sustainability problem to be addressed	Has the project team created a common understanding of the sustainability problem to be addressed and does the team accept this common problem definition?
Joint defining of the research object, the research targets and the success criteria	Has the research team formulated a common research framework and guiding question (with corresponding research questions and targets) and do all partners consent to the success criteria defined?
Building a methodological framework for common knowledge production and integration	Does the project team agree with the jointly developed methodological framework defining how to achieve the research goal in Phase B and how the transdisciplinary framework is to be applied?
PHASE B	
Defining the roles of practitioners and scientists	Are the tasks and roles of all actors in the research process clearly defined?
Applying and adapting the integrative research methods and designing of a 'transdisciplinary setting' for knowledge generation and integration	Does the research team use or develop methods which i) lead to adequate solutions and ii) constitute a suitable 'setting' for inter- and transdisciplinary cooperation and knowledge integration?
PHASE C	
Achieving a bi-dimensional integration	Are the project results conceived in a way that transforms or solves the problem addressed? Are the results integrated into existing scientific knowledge in order to facilitate transfer and generalisation?
Generating of goal-oriented products for science and practice	Does the research team make the products, services and publications available to its partners in a suitable way?
Valorising the scientific and social/societal effects	Have the goals been achieved? Have additional (unforeseen) positive effects been produced?

Fig. 2 Principles and guiding questions for the design of transdisciplinary research in the sustainability sciences. (Lang et al. 2012, p. 31; Vilsmaier and Lang 2014, p. 104)

The next step is to develop a common definition of the problem. In the project, we first assume that traditional media are currently in a crisis: They have lost reach and funding as well as acceptance and legitimacy; their monopoly on information and their sovereignty of interpretation have been broken. At the same time, we ascribe important democratic functions to the media: they create a public sphere, mediate between politics and citizens, enable participation and control rulers. The need for research results in turn from the fact that communication studies currently tends to concentrate on individual media effects and treats media structures and normative questions rather on the sidelines. This problem definition has to be questioned, discussed and adapted again and again in the course of the research process. Thus, the description of the crisis of the media can certainly be led away from the perspective of the media themselves, which fear for the loss of their supremacy, and towards the needs of the media users. In the end, this project should be about improving the democratic functions of the media, the common good is in the foreground. In any case, the transdisciplinary task for the labs and the interviews is to repeatedly address the problem definition and to agree on it.

The common research framework subsequently called for initially builds on existing research in the project. The project connects to the media reform debate on financing models, journalistic professional standards, criteria for quality of journalism and legal framework conditions of the media system. The already formulated research questions on the future of the media will be further differentiated in the course of the project. Furthermore, it cannot be ruled out that both research frameworks and questions will shift or expand with the actors involved. A major challenge here seems to be to maintain the focus of the project while being open to adaptation and not to "get bogged down". So far, no "success criteria" have been formulated for the project. Here, a further look at the transdisciplinary literature is first in order to understand what exactly is meant by this. Methodologically, the core team has already determined the rough procedure (labs, interviews, planning cell/citizens' expert opinion). Adjustments are possible here – probably in consultation with the lab organizers – especially in the methods used in the lab (applied so far: future workshop and fishbowl).

In the next phase, the focus is on *"jointly generating solution-oriented and connectable knowledge":* To this end, the roles of the actors and thus the expectations of them and from them must first be jointly clarified. The first step in this direction was a workshop on "Dealing with Practice Partners" in the research network. Among other things, the text by Vilsmaier and Lang (2014) analyzed here was discussed. This was followed by another workshop on participatory research. The findings from the workshops and the related literature will result in a summary table that provides an overview of the possible roles of all actors involved in the project. This overview will then be made available on the research blog and used as a basis for consultation with the actors. In accordance with the transdisciplinary approach, this can only ever be a provisional definition of roles that can be adapted in the interaction.

The next step is the "actual investigation of the research questions" (Vilsmaier and Lang 2014, p. 102). The authors point out the following difficulty:

> A major challenge is to bring together knowledge that has been generated in different ways (e.g. through scientific research or everyday life practice). While scientific knowledge generation is safeguarded by established procedures (e.g. reference to theory, standardized methods), the situation is quite different for knowledge generated outside science. How can we determine whether such (supposed) knowledge is not mere opinion, put forward merely by a person, a company, a political party? At this point, transdisciplinary research hits the limits of verifiability (Vilsmaier and Lang 2014, p. 102).

They suggest:

> It is therefore important not simply to 'mix' the different forms of knowledge, but to relate them systematically to one another. This can be done, for example, by contrasting problem descriptions and explanations from different, non-scientific contexts of experience (often also referred to as lifeworld representations or interpretations) with those of scientific origin and relating them to one another. In doing so, it may turn out, for example, that in (inter)disciplinary research perspectives certain facets have so far been outside the horizon of observation and must therefore be included in the investigations. Conversely, (supposed) knowledge may also turn out to be mere opinion that is not resilient (Vilsmaier and Lang 2014, p. 102).

These references seem particularly important for the project. Since in this project knowledge is generated from different positions, in different settings and across different channels, a particularly reflective approach is important. It is conceivable, for example, that a point of criticism voiced by media users in the lab will be referred to scientific literature after the lab and related to it. This can show, for example, that the point of criticism can also be supported empirically or that it must be refuted. Likewise, it is conceivable that an online commentary introduces a perspective that has not yet been taken up either in the labs or in the interviews. Both scenarios raise the question of whether, to what extent, and how these two forms of knowledge can ultimately coexist or be brought into negotiation with each other. In addition, it remains to be decided whether the synthesis of all knowledge must be carried out by the core team alone, or whether, for example, in the preparation of the citizens' expert reports, the first step in a programme section is to review and systematise the knowledge that has been collected so far. Beyond the project, there is also the question of how the still larger body of knowledge from the various research projects on democracy can be synthesized within the network.

The authors admit that this point is a major difficulty of transdisciplinary research: "There is still a great need for research with regard to the integration of knowledge and experiences that differ in terms of their genesis, and the consideration of norms and values represents a major challenge, especially with regard to the generalizability of the results of transdisciplinary research." (Vilsmaier and Lang 2014, p. 110) As basic practical advice for dealing with this form of knowledge generation, the authors formulate the claim to make it as transparent and thus as comprehensible as possible. They state:

> [Transdisciplinary research] opens up space for the unpredictable and thus relinquishes some of the control that would enable an exact procedure and appropriate reconstruction. It is therefore of particular importance to plan the research process well and to document it transparently and accurately. This applies in particular to those facets of the research process that at first glance appear to be peripheral to the research, such as the emergence of contacts with potential project partners, public/political discourses that accompany the transdisciplinary process, or the course of cooperative working meetings of transdisciplinary teams (Vilsmaier and Lang 2014, p. 110).

The research blog in particular is intended to ensure the traceability and transparency of the research process. There, the core team and, if necessary, other actors document the various steps of their research throughout the entire project.

In the next phase, the focus is on *"re-integration and application of* the knowledge *generated"*: "In this phase, the aim is to transfer the knowledge developed into both social and scientific practice." For social practice, this can "mean that a concrete problem-solving approach developed in a transdisciplinary process is subsequently implemented." (Vilsmaier and Lang 2014, p. 102) However, according to the authors, "even if this does not take place in a direct form in the concrete situation, a rethinking can take place through a transdisciplinary process that influences developments." (Vilsmaier and Lang 2014, p. 102f).

The project envisages that this "concrete approach to a solution" will manifest itself in a citizens' report. This will be presented to the public in a media future summit. It remains open, however, to what extent the solutions proposed here will be implemented. It is conceivable, however, that beyond the citizens' report, self-acting groups will organize themselves out of the labs during the project. They implement certain solutions directly themselves, instead of leaving this to representatives from politics or journalism. In addition, there is also the possibility that actors come to rethink through debates in the labs. As already formulated in the project application, the benefit for society can lie in the fact that the media audience steps out of the role of spectator and becomes active, but most likely the media competence of the participants is increased. Whether these possible processes of change are also to be surveyed and then evaluated is a question that has yet to be decided for this project. For the media themselves, the project offers the space for discussions with media critics, points of reference for debates about the function of journalism and their own understanding of their role, as well as recommendations for action for those who want to develop alternative offerings.

For scientific practice

> Such cooperative research processes can lead to an increase in knowledge and understanding, which is fed into the *scientific community* and discussed there (through scientific publications) and thus unfolds its effect. An important question here is to what extent case study-based and thus strongly contextualized findings can be generalized and transferred to other cases or in other contexts (Vilsmaier and Lang 2014, p. 102f.).

For the reintegration of the knowledge into science, the usual forms of lectures and essays are planned. In these, the content-related and methodological knowledge gained in this project will be appropriately reflected and processed for communication science. The content-related knowledge concerns the knowledge and experiences of the participants; methodologically, qualitative empirical social research, especially participatory and transdisciplinary research, will be further developed in this project.

The goal-oriented products for social practice are, in addition to the citizens' report, public events, blog, Twitter and YouTube, which are intended to reflect the entire research process. Within the framework of the research network, there are various considerations in addition to the blog of the overall network. For example, there will perhaps be a democracy fair with the results of the projects and the network. The evaluation of the impact of the project will probably take place again and again in the course of the project. However, since the media future summit with the presentation of the citizens' report is at the end of the project period, an evaluation of the consequences within this project will not be possible.

The general principles shown in Fig. 3 also apply to all three phases.

Within the project, the requirement to regularly evaluate and adjust the research architecture will be ensured with meetings of the core team. Occasionally, there will be feedback from the collaborative partners. An evaluation beyond this is currently not planned. However, throughout the entire research process, feedback from different stakeholders will be taken into account, e.g. from online commentators. So far, no measures have been taken in the project to defuse conflict situations.

Principle	Guiding questions
GENERAL PRINCIPLES (apply to all phases)	
Ensuring regular formative evaluation	Was a formative evaluation carried out in which important experts in the field concerned and in the transdisciplinary project were involved?
Defusing conflict constellations	Did researchers and practitioners prevent or anticipate conflicts from the outset, and were measures taken to manage upcoming conflicts?
Increasing participation opportunities and interest	Was sufficient attention paid during the project to the tangible and intangible resources needed for effective and ongoing participation?

Fig. 3 Principles and guiding questions for the design of transdisciplinary research in the sustainability sciences. (Lang et al. 2012, p. 32; Vilsmaier and Lang 2014, p. 105)

Measures to increase participation opportunities (especially for marginalised groups) also need to be improved.

The *model of an ideal-typical transdisciplinary research process* (see Fig. 4) assigns the three phases their respective position in the research process. In addition, all possible actors are listed here, as well as possible problems and possible results. The research design of the MFL project can be well integrated here. The results for societal practice are mainly about measures, while the scientific discourse omits industrial research. Otherwise, the points mentioned in the figure correspond to different parts of the project.

All in all, the reflection of the MFL project against the background of the transdisciplinarity described by Vilsmaier and Lang (2014) shows that the structure of the project largely corresponds to transdisciplinary demands. Within the time frame of the core team and the financial framework of the project, the helpful hints of the authors will therefore be implemented here. The publication of this detailed reflection of transdisciplinarity on a concrete and currently ongoing research project in this conference volume will hopefully provide other researchers with a good insight into the practice of transdisciplinary science.

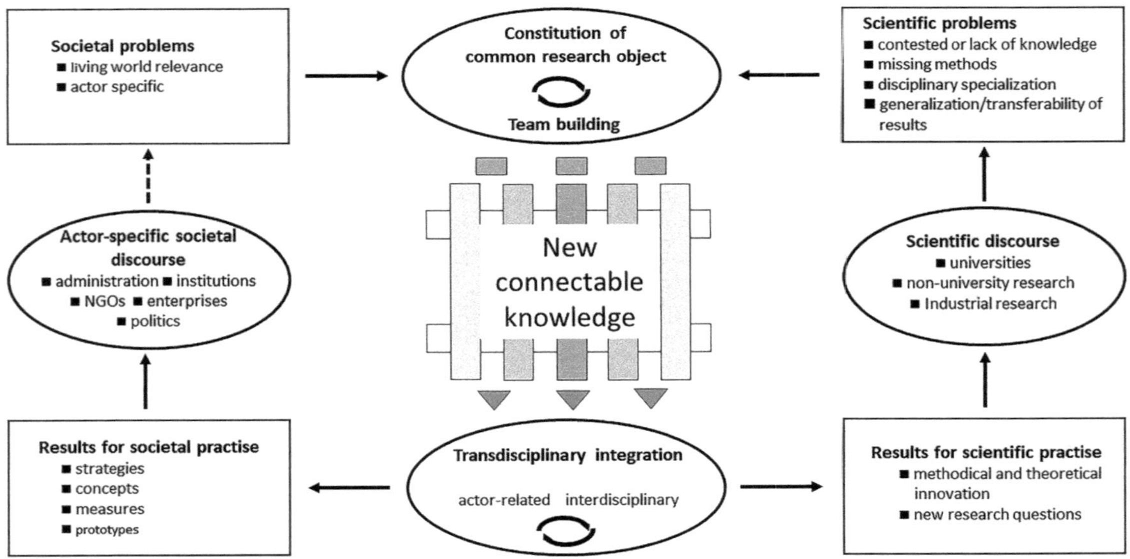

Fig. 4 Model of an ideal-typical transdisciplinary research process: the ISOE model. (Jahn 2008, p. 31; Vilsmaier and Lang 2014, p. 105)

References

Bergmann, Matthias, Thomas Jahn, Tobias Knobloch, Wolfgang Krohn, Christian Pohl, und Engelbert Schramm, Hrsg. 2010. *Methoden transdisziplinärer Forschung. Ein Überblick mit Anwendungsbeispielen*. Frankfurt a. M.: Campus.

Gibbons, Michael, Camille Limoges, Helga Nowotny, Simon Schwartzman, Peter Scott, und Martin Trow, Hrsg. 1994. *The new production of knowledge: The dynamics of science and research in contemporary societies*. London: Sage.

Jahn, Thomas. 2008. Transdisziplinarität in der Forschungspraxis. In *Transdisziplinäre Forschung. Integrative Forschungsprozesse verstehen und bewerten,* Hrsg. Matthias Bergmann und Engelbert Schramm, 21–38. Frankfurt a. M.: Campus.

Kerkhoff, Lorrae van; Lebel, Louis (2006a): Linking knowledge and action for sustainable development. In: *Annual Review of Environment and Resources* 31 (1), S. 445–477. https://doi.org/10.1146/annurev.energy.31.102405.170850.

Klein, Julie Thompson, Rudolf Häberli, Roland W. Scholz, Walter Grossenbacher-Mansuy, Alain Bill, und Myrtha Welti. 2001. *Transdisciplinarity: Joint Problem Solving among Science, Technology, and Society: An Effective Way for Managing Complexity.* Basel: Birkhäuser.

Krütli, Pius, M. Stauffacher, T. Flüeler, und R. W. Scholz. 2010. Functional-dynamic public participation in technological decision-making: site selection processes of nuclear waste repositories. In: *Journal of Risk Research* 13 (7): 861–875. https://doi.org/10.1080/13669871003703252.

Lang, D.J., A. Wiek, M. Bergmann, M. Stauffacher, P. Martens, P. Moll, M. Swilling, und C.J. Thomas. 2012. Transdisciplinary research in sustainability science: practice, principles, and challenges. *Sustainability Science*, 7 (1), S. 25–43

Meyen, Michael, M. Löblich, S. Pfaff-Rüdiger, und C. Riesmeyer. 2011. *Qualitative Forschung in der Kommunikationswissenschaft: Eine praxisorientierte Einführung.* Wiesbaden: VS.

Pohl, Christian, und Gertrude Hirsch Hadorn. 2006. *Gestaltungsprinzipien für die transdisziplinäre Forschung: Ein Beitrag des td-net.* München: Oekom-Verlag.

Unger, Hella von. 2014. *Partizipative Forschung: Einführung in die Forschungspraxis.* Wiesbaden: Springer.

van Kerkhoff, Lorrae, und L. Lebel. 2006b. Linking Knowledge and Action for Sustainable Development. *Annual Review of Environment and Resources* 31 (1): 445–477. https://doi.org/10.1146/annurev.energy.31.102405.170850.

Vilsmaier, Ulli, J. D. Lang. 2014. Transdisziplinäre Forschung. In: Harald Heinrichs und Gerd Michelsen (Hrsg.): Nachhaltigkeitswissenschaften, Bd. 104. Heidelberg: Springer, S. 87–113.

Wissenschaftlicher Beirat der Bundesregierung Globale Umweltveränderungen (WBGU). 2011. *Welt im Wandel. Gesellschaftsvertrag für eine Große Transformation. Zusammenfassung für Entscheidungsträger*. Berlin: WBGU.

Arslan, Sevda Can, Dr.in phil, studied Media and Communication Studies, Ethics and Philosophy of Culture and History (University of Mannheim). Collaborator in the project "Media Future Lab" (https://medialabs.hypotheses.org/) in the research network "ForDemocracy". Co-founder and member of the Critical Communication Studies Network (www.krikowi.net).

Interactive Formats for the Social Participation of Senior Citizens Using the Example of Socially Responsible Technology Design

Tamar Beruchashvili, Elisabeth Wiesnet, and Yves Jeanrenaud

Abstract

Our project "TP3: Technikgestaltung" (Technology Design) is part of the Bavarian-wide research association ForGenderCare (www.forgendercare.de). The challenges lie in the changed life situations and needs of older people due to demographic change and in the opportunities of participatory technology development to offer target group-oriented solutions here. "Sustainable management" can be complemented and extended by socially responsible technology development. We refer to Tronto's (Caring Democracy. Markets, Equality, and Justice, New York University Press, New York and London, 2013) notion of "personal responsibility" and to an understanding of care as mindfulness (Brückner, Care and Migration. Die Ent-Sorgung menschlicher Reproduktionsarbeit entlang von Geschlechter- und Armutsgrenzen, Verlag Barbara Budrich, Opladen, 2010). We have used this as the basis for our practice-oriented, innovative approach *New Care Spaces*. At the same time, socially responsible technology development (Rommes, Technologies of inclusion,

T. Beruchashvili (✉) · E. Wiesnet
Gender Studies in Engineering at the TU Munich, Munich, Germany
e-mail: tamar.beruchashvili@tum.de

Y. Jeanrenaud
Institute of Sociology, Ludwig-Maximilians-Universität Munich, Munich, Germany
e-mail: yves.jeanrenaud@soziologie.uni-muenchen.de

H.-W. Franz et al. (eds.), *Sustainable Living and Business*,
https://doi.org/10.1007/978-3-658-41835-9_13

Tapir Academic Press, 2011; Björgvinsson, Participatory design and democratizing innovation. Proceedings of the 11th Biennial participatory design 4 conference, ACM Library, 2010; Beruchashvili, Mensch und Computer 2018 – Workshopband, Gesellschaft für Informatik e. V., Bonn, 2018) equally as social innovation, as it has a processual and cross-cutting character that connects companies and with their environment (Stiess, Soziale Innovation und Nachhaltigkeit, Springer Fachmedien, Wiesbaden, 2013). Furthermore, we developed an experimental and interdisciplinary workshop design. We practiced direct user integration with special attention to gender- and diversity-relevant factors. As methods we used participant observation (Passaro, Anthropological Locations: Boundaries and Grounds of a Field Science, University of California Press, Berkeley, 1997) and summary content analysis (Mayring, Qualitative Inhaltsanalyse. Fundamentals and Techniques, Beltz Pedagogy, Weinheim, 2015). Thus, the transferring role of social scientists can be clarified. We propose this approach to companies, non-profit organizations and the public sector as an innovation method to dissolve skepticism between entrepreneurs and stakeholders (including the marginalized) (Rommes, Technologies of inclusion, Tapir Academic Press, 2011; Jeanrenaud et al., Study decisions, entrance and academic success of Women and Men in STEM. Gender&IT'18, Association for Computing Machinery (ACM), New York, pp. 157–160, 2018) This changes organizational cultures and opens up external collaborations. Every member of society can thus participate in "sustainable living and business".

1 Introduction

"I wish for independence and autonomy through technology, but I don't have the dream of a robot bringing me my coffee in bed." This statement comes from an interview with a senior citizen for the sub-project "The role of gender- and diversity-oriented technology development in the participation of seniors in demographic change" of the Bavarian research network ForGenderCare.[1] On the one hand, one can understand the ambivalence of this statement as an inaccessible black box. On the other hand, however, it can be seen as a challenge and an opportunity for new approaches to empowerment in old age with the help of technology. The following article would like to point out a solution for dealing with this ambivalence and define it as social innovation (Howaldt and Jacobsen 2010).

[1] www.forgendercare.de

After a brief introduction to the sub-project,[2] we explain the socio-political basis of the project. In particular, we will discuss our understanding of care, participation, demographic change and technology design and development and position it in the current scientific discussion. We will then discuss our research approach using the innovative and participatory method of innovation workshops. An important result of our research project is our approach "New Care Spaces". We will then present this approach and define it as a social innovation. The specificity of our social science work in developing this approach will be discussed separately. A discussion of the results will conclude this contribution.

2 Introduction to the Project "Technology Development" of the Research Network ForGenderCare

Senior citizens are increasingly playing an important role in public life and in the shaping of society, which they are already actively accepting and demanding to varying degrees. However, tested formats for suitable participatory processes do not yet exist. The aim of the sub-project "The role of gender- and diversity-oriented technology development in the participation of seniors in demographic change" of ForGenderCare was therefore to develop suitable communication and participation models in order to allow seniors with different requirements and life realities to participate in the development of social change. Specifically, we developed a participation model using the example of technological development that directly and indirectly affects older people.

The project is part of the Bavaria-wide research network ForGenderCare. The challenges consist in the changed life situations and needs of older people due to demographic change and in the chances of a participatory technology development to offer target group-oriented solutions here.

The project design initially included interviews with experts from science, business and politics who provided information on the necessary framework conditions for gender- and diversity-oriented communication and participation models as well

[2] Project duration 01.04.2015 to 31.12.2019. Project management from April 2015 to August 2018: Prof. Dr. Susanne Ihsen, Gender Studies in Engineering, Technical University of Munich. Project collaboration: April 2015 to September 2016: Dr. Yves Jeanrenaud, from August 2018 project management, October 2016 to October 2017: Nina Brötzmann, February 2018 to December 2019: Tamar Beruchashvili, May 2015 to December 2019: Elisabeth Wiesnet.

as on their effects on the processes of technology design. These were supplemented by self-statements of senior citizens in Bavaria regarding their private and public needs, their understanding of technology as well as existing attitude patterns. The survey was rounded off by innovation workshops for the development of gender- and diversity-oriented communication and participation models in technology design.

3 Social and Political Framework Conditions

The Leitbild Bayern 2030 (2011) already states that Bavaria's regions will change in the coming decades. Older people will be more than ever part of public life and will be needed as an important source of strength and cohesion of society in order to make their towns and villages liveable and attractive even with a decreasing population in the different sub-areas. Mainly Upper Bavaria will remain a "migration winner" due to its high-performance economy, well-connected universities and modern infrastructure, even outside the conurbations. However, this does not apply to the other regions to the same extent. The "Demographic Change Action Plan" (2011) therefore also proposes digital infrastructure measures for Bavaria in order to adequately ensure life in rural areas with a declining and ageing population. For senior citizens, demographic change already means that their familiar living environment is changing more and more: Family structures are changing due to the increasing employment of daughters and job-related migration; the proportion of senior citizens living alone is rising, leading to mobility restrictions, loneliness and ultimately to a shortage of carers from their personal environment. Accordingly, technical products and technology-supported, digital services also offer compensation opportunities in care (Brückner 2012; Aulenbacher and Dammayr 2014), in Internet communication, where participation is increasing, especially among women over 60 (D21 Digital Index 2013; D21 Digital Index 2016), and in the household and mobility sector (Ihsen et al. 2012).

With regard to their participation in society, it is evident how senior citizens actively participate in questions of demographic change in their own living and residential environment (Gebauer et al. 2011) and how their attitudes change from traditional care within family structures to public and private care and support as well as to alternative living and housing concepts (generation houses, shared flats for the elderly) (Boggatz 2011; Mahne et al. 2017). Changes can also be observed in the self-image of senior citizens with regard to public (sideline employment, voluntary work, further education, political commitment) and private activities (childcare, neighbourhood help, hobbies). Gensicke and Geiss (2010), for example, refer to the increased willingness to become more involved in civil society up to the age of about 75. Previously, Burmeister et al. (2005) had already drawn attention to the model of "senior trainers", which specifically trains older people to strengthen local networks. Federal policy is also actively engaged in the area of civil society participation, for example with the recently increased BMBF funding for citizen research (BMBF 2019).

Although for many years sufficient knowledge has been available about problems of operation, handling, functionality and complexity of technical products on the one hand and about corresponding possibilities for improvement on the other hand, only very few newly developed technologies and programs are designed to be gender- and age-appropriate or accessible (Gebauer et al. 2011). The reasons for this are a repeatedly identified "expert blindness" and little knowledge of the real needs and abilities of older people, as well as a disregard for logical and natural courses of action (Mollenkopf 2006). This is attributed, among other things, to the age difference between product developers and future customers (Shire and Leimeister 2012). At the same time, older users, but also other user groups from the fields of medicine, service, trade, etc., are hardly included in innovation processes. Many actors who influence the development of AAL systems lack applicable tools and methods with which users can be involved in the product development process (Glende et al. 2011). However, in order to design technology not only for but also with users, the needs and fears of senior citizens as well as their desire to use new technologies and participate in new developments must be addressed (ÖIAT 2015; Glende 2010).

The integration of users in technology design processes is increasing, but it unsystematically includes various diversity dimensions such as gender, age, income, geographical location, family and educational status or leisure behaviour (Gebauer et al. 2011). At the same time, we are dealing with a generation of senior citizens who are increasingly self-confident in shaping their own lives. Therefore, the question arises whether and how extended forms of participation can contribute to meaningfully address these changed needs and thus support mobility, communication and participation.

Based on the analysis of current approaches to technology development processes, four paths can be observed in practice (cf. also Fig. 1):

1. Technology design based on the (reflexive) I-methodology
2. Technology design based on stereotypes
3. Development of persona as prototype for target group
4. Participatory technology design through user inclusion

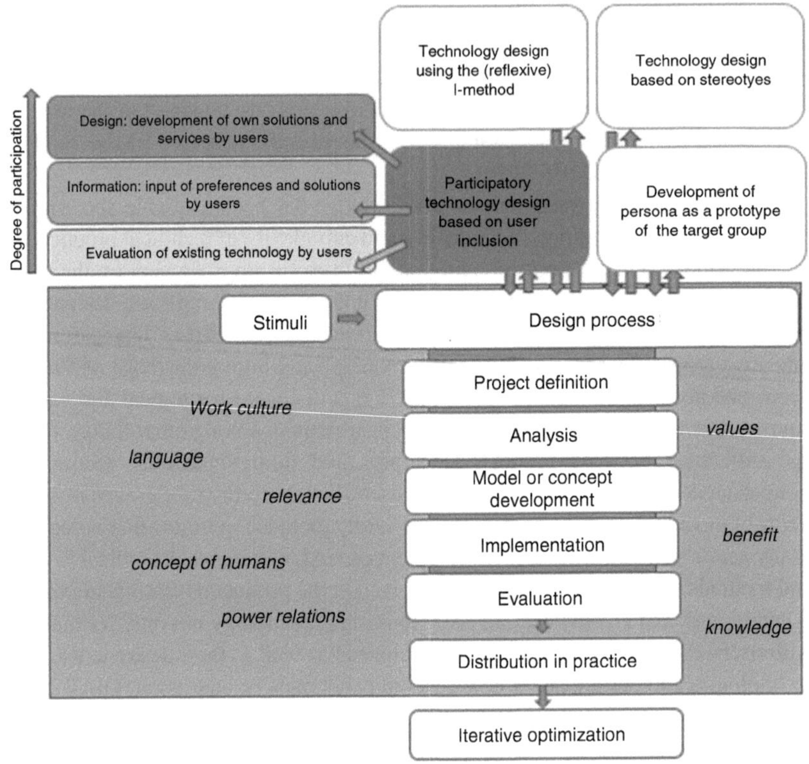

Fig. 1 Present types of technology design. (Nina Brötzmann based on Westkämper 2006: Einführung in die Organisation der Produktion, p. 121; Rommes 2011: Inclusion by design. In Sörensen et al. [eds]: Technologies of inclusion, pp. 129–146; Maaß et al. 2014: Gender/Diversityaspekte in der Informatikforschung: Das GERD-Modell. In Marsden and Kempf [Eds:] Gender-UseIT, pp. 67–78)

We understand the process of participatory technology design through user inclusion as approximating socially responsible technology development (cf. "participatory design"[3] according to Björgvinsson et al. 2010), since in this process the characteristics of the "Gender Extended Research and Development" (GERD) model can be identified through appropriate moderation. The ideal-typical concept

[3] The first transfer of "participatory design"from English to "socially responsible technology development" took place at "Mensch und Computer" 2018 in Dresden (see: https://muc2019.mensch-und-computer.de/mci-workshops/ [last access 18.10.2019]).

of New Care Spaces is based on this constellation (cf. similar models such as "Triple Helix" according to Etzkowitz and Leydsdorff 2000).

Björgvinsson et al. postulate a challenge to socially responsible technology development and define it at the same time:

> [...] exploring alternative ways to organize milieus for innovation that are more democratically-oriented than traditional milieus that focus on expert groups and individuals. It also means moving from the dominating technocratic view of innovation; a move from things to Things where differences and controversies are allowed to exist, dilemmas are raised and possibilities explored (Björgvinsson et al. 2010, p. 49 f.).

Our approach *New Care Spaces is* supposed to meet these requirements by being gender and diversity oriented, by understanding the amibivalence of the needs of seniors as an opportunity and by being moderated by social scientists. According to our research results, on the one hand, technology development mainly works with "male personas". In addition, in the development process only the usage habits of "lead users" are taken into account, who in turn are mostly technology-savvy men. On the other hand, there is a desire to participate in the design of technologies, but there is currently still a lack of a clear response on the part of the product developers. For example, a lack of response to feedback on a technical product can be demotivating. The needs, resources and fears of older people with regard to individual technologies and data protection should be taken seriously. Particular emphasis should be placed on comprehensibility, ease of use and support for an application. Empathy can be actively created if product developers themselves experience and feel the lifeworld of older people with their physical and mental conditions. This is possible to some extent, for example, by means of an old people's suit, blind people's glasses or a wheelchair. The described scepticism of senior citizens towards companies is to be dissolved by a change in the corporate culture. Companies should perceive them as a valued target group and, if possible, integrate them into technology development processes. These connections can also contribute to the development of barrier-free technology and to technologies for private and public use.

In contrast to Germany, other countries have a distinct culture of participation, which has an impact on technology development. According to Ornetzeder and Rohracher, for example, participatory innovation design through user integration is more prevalent in Denmark. This culture of participation goes beyond that from the exploitation perspective of companies. In some innovations with new forms of social organisation and socio-political objectives, civil society involvement is important. Successful examples where a sense of personal responsibility led to the collaboration of many in the development of new products and markets include the developments of wind turbines in Denmark, the self-build movement for solar thermal systems in Austria, and the emergence of organized car sharing structures in Switzerland (Ornetzeder and Rohracher 2012, pp. 176–186). These best practices of socially responsible technology design should speak for *New Care Spaces.*

4 New Care Spaces

In our new approach, *New Care Spaces,* we were concerned both to meet the needs of older people in terms of technology and to contribute to a gender and diversity-oriented culture in companies. In addition, we want to address the personal sense of responsibility of individuals to contribute to the well-being of all.

The "care" concept we use comprises two levels: On the one hand, we use Joan Tronto's (2012) mindfulness approach in relation to appropriate interaction processes (Brückner 2010). On the other hand, technology design itself has participation-oriented methods for researching, estimating and evaluating technical developments. These are closely related to questions of technology ethics and responsibility, but have so far mainly been related to engineering professions and actors (Grunwald and Saupe 1999; Hubig and Reidel 2003; Ropohl 2009). In general, it is a matter of sharpening the problem awareness for the designability of technology in order to make new technical developments responsible, socially acceptable and sustainable. In relation to participation and technology design, care is interpreted in the sense of "participation" or "being included", based on the thesis that both social and technical change is better designed *with* people than merely *for them.*

As simplified in Fig. 2, we see a reciprocal cycle between "care giver" and "care receiver" as well as between technology producers and technology users. The starting point for this consideration is that every person is dependent on care services to varying degrees in the course of his or her life (Krüger 2018). At the same time, however, everyone provides care, for example in raising children and caring for the elderly, but also in (temporarily) assuming responsibility for others. Similarly, in our postmodern society, everyone is highly dependent on technology, for example for communication. At the same time, technical devices are adapted to the buying behaviour of consumers. In addition, customers have the possibility, for example via online feedback functions, to evaluate technologies and to make suggestions for improvement. Thus, everyone is involved in the production of technology in this sense. If we understand care above as "personal responsibility", technology can also be understood as responsibility and awareness, in that in the cycle of technology development people participate just as voluntarily as in care (for example

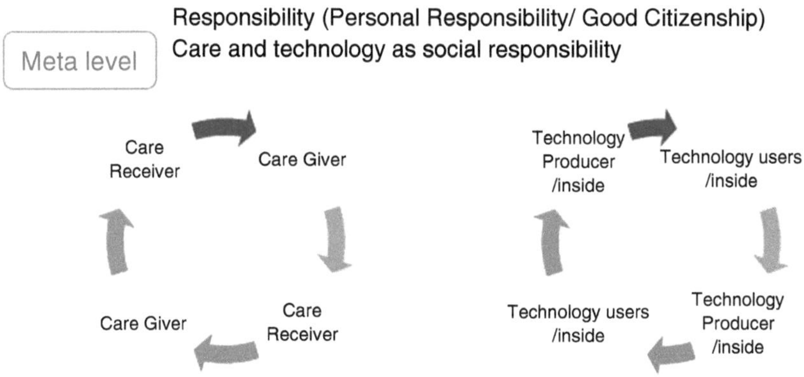

Fig. 2 Project-specific illustration "Denkwerk care". (Source: own representation)

in political or social engagement). From this analogy, technology development gains a comparable socio-political weighting as Care in society. Since we define care as (social) participation through participation in technology design and access to technology use, we also see the two cycles as interconnected.

One of the research results of our sub-project "Technology Development" is that senior citizens demand independence and autonomy through technology on the one hand. On the other hand, they wish to receive care services in old age not through service or care robots (care-giving), but through people. This ambivalence is a certain "black box" in that it reveals self-determination, social interaction and trust and at the same time hinders the acceptance of new technology (services) (cf. Figure 3). This black box also raises fears. The important requirement for technology to design individual spaces for Care can already be found in Tronto (2013). In view of the demographic change, according to our resulting thesis, *New Care Spaces* must emerge in which citizens jointly take care of the needs of all, so that social participation of diverse population groups is possible (Tronto 2013, p. 13). Based on these foundations, the sub-project offers our *New Care Spaces concept* as a space of responsibility. *New Care Spaces* are meant to fulfill frameworks of diversity-oriented communication and participation models as well as to capture fears (e.g. of the black box "technology") in an individualized way. They denote a (personal) sense of responsibility (personal responsibility) (Tronto 2013) as well as "technology-responsibility" according to the "Denkwerk Care" (see earlier in this text and Fig. 2). At the same time, they are to be understood as public spaces and thus as open innovation (Vollmann et al. 2012; Björgvinsson et al. 2010), which contribute to the participation of senior citizens in technology development and

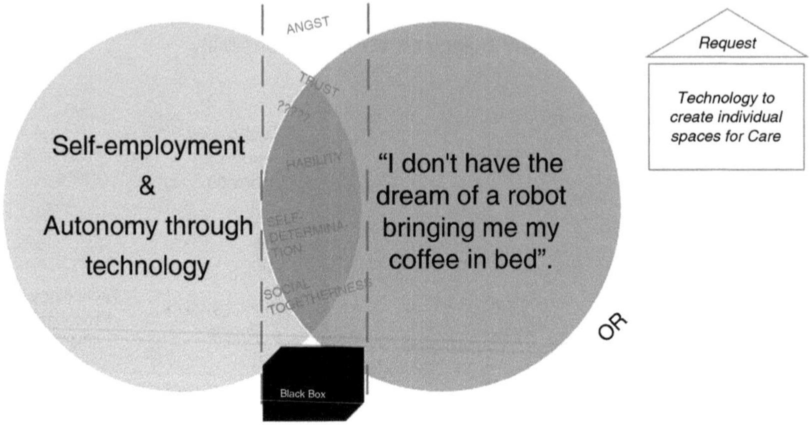

Fig. 3 Black box. (Own representation)

social change. *New Care Spaces* can be designed in a demand-oriented way with suitable cooperation partners. This requires not only premises but also moderators (including a set of methods) and multipliers who accompany the innovation processes. The principles of socially responsible technology development such as democracy orientation, the participation of non-lead users (also non-users), the abolition of a "technical view of innovation" as well as the space for ambivalences (as in the introductory statement of the article) should also be taken into account (Björgvinsson et al. 2010). Furthermore, *New Care Spaces* complement the guidelines of social space orientation (Budde et al. 2007) in the social work of welfare organisations.

The application-oriented concept of *New Care Spaces* is based on a care understanding of mindfulness and personal responsibility in the sense of awareness and serves as a gender- and diversity-oriented communication and participation model. In this way, senior citizens (and other marginalized, hitherto little-included groups) can be actively involved in technology design processes to shape their – diverse – private and public life needs and thus indirectly participate in the development of long-term and disruptive social change. *New Care Spaces* make it possible to identify the needs of senior citizens at an early stage by providing opportunities for participation. In the participatory implementation of these needs, a certain agility between users and technology developers as well as a socially responsible technology design (Björgvinsson et al. 2010) are guaranteed. Furthermore, our *New Care Spaces* approach holds the opportunity for social innovation after appropriate acceptance and practical effectiveness (Howaldt and Schwarz 2012, p. 55), because the approach simultaneously considers social needs and creates social practices. In doing so, it offers itself as an alternative path to democratic participation and intersectionality such as Living Labs (Björgvinsson et al. 2010, p. 42ff.). With the transition from an industrial to a knowledge and service society, an increase in the importance of social innovations for the contouring of a sociologically enlightened, post-industrial innovation paradigm is becoming apparent (Howaldt et al. 2008). *New Care Spaces* can thus be a component of social innovation thrusts that require numerous small and large social sub-areas that influence the lives of individual people as well as the development of a national and global society (ZSI 2008, p. 28).

5 Innovation Workshops as an Innovative and Participative Method

In addition to interviews with experts and senior citizens, an important component of our research design was the innovative and participatory method of innovation workshops. Through this, perspectives of both interview target groups were to be summarized once again. In addition, diverse teams were able to develop gender- and diversity-oriented communication and participation models in technology design. The innovation workshops took place during the technology development project at the Technical University of Munich (TUM). Senior citizens, experts and students from MINT subjects participated in the workshops. The social science oriented and experimental workshop design[4] can be rated as very successful. During the workshop scenario techniques, elements from Design Thinking (Lewrik et al. 2018) and LEGO Serious Play[5] were adapted. The aim was to generate a mixture of knowledge input, creativity techniques and a general motivational design, so that a stimulating framework is provided for the elaboration of innovative

---

[4] Structure of the workshop.

1st Challenge: Question for the workshop that targets the research project or goal of the workshop [divergent phase].
2. Define the current state of knowledge in relation to the challenge [divergent phase]
3. Brainstorming: Collecting ideas [divergent phase].
4. Reduce ideas using a technique/method so that in the end one idea is democratically chosen according to an evaluation matrix
5. Conceptualize the reduced idea and prototypes
6. Testing in the group
7. Feedback round

[5] LEGO-DUPLO elements were used for age appropriateness.

ideas. The workshop design was interactive, interdisciplinary and open. These criteria as well as the creation of an open communication culture during the workshop allowed the participants to work productively and on a linguistic level on a specific question (challenge). The workshops followed an experimental design and revealed the participants' value orientations through their approach. In doing so, the approach fulfilled the principles of socially responsible design in that the participants influenced the results, learned from each other and "went through it on an equal footing" (Klüber 2019). We used methods of participant observation (Passaro 1997) and summary content analysis (Mayring 2015) to evaluate the workshops.

Incentives were provided for the participants of the workshop. The unpaid voluntariness to participate in an event that can serve the well-being of all remains a challenge. "Personal/technical responsibility" and care (in this case as caring) are rarely found on a voluntary and unpaid basis and, especially in the case of care, have strong female connotations. However, if the awareness of Care (according to Tronto 2013) were created for all, the perceived concern (also "technical concern" according to our "Denkwerk Care", see Fig. 2) of all members of society could lead to the willingness of many to participate in the well-being of all. In the current political, economic and communal circumstances, however, the proposed mix of methods can be realised more purposefully through motivating incentives.

6 The Transferring Role of Social Scientists in the Development of Our Social Innovation Approach

In our approach *New Care Spaces* we see the chance of a potential social innovation with effectiveness and acceptance in practice. The development process of this research result can exemplify the transferring role of social scientists in the development of social innovations.

As early as 1989, Wolfgang Zapf identified important tools of the social sciences, especially sociology, for promoting social innovations, which are becoming increasingly important in society in the transition from an industrial to a knowledge and service society compared to technical innovations (Zapf 1989; Howaldt et al. 2008). Thus, in the innovation process, social sciences offer decision support in the form of survey research, personality tests, technology impact and risk assessment, human resource planning, and sources of social technologies such as quality circles, co-determination models, and group therapy, among others. In addition, approaches to general theory can better understand innovation and productivity (Zapf 1989, p. 182ff.). Although the social sciences, along with the natural and engineering sciences, are not yet equivalent innovation shapers today, they can position themselves as active innovation drivers by not seeing potential users and customers as the final stage of a linear development process, but by weaving them into highly interactive communication networks as active problem solvers and innovators (Howaldt et al. 2008, p. 68). The core competence of the social sciences in the innovation process is the design of social contexts in which knowledge exchange between problem solvers, experts, key users and users of different social subsystems can take place and learning processes are initiated (Gustavsen 2006). The integration of central social actors from the idea to the implementation can contribute to an "empowerment" of users or to an at least partial shift of socio-economic power relations in the relationship between manufacturer and user (Ornetzeder and Rohracher 2012, p. 171f.). Furthermore, loops of reflection initiated by the social sciences within an innovation process make a decisive contribution to focusing on the feasibility of a new idea and thus to breaking through an "automatism of progress" (Howaldt et al. 2008, p. 68). Since conventional structures of the division of labour between developers and users are thus dissolving and an ever greater integration of the experiential knowledge of the periphery is becoming necessary, there is a particular need for successful communication, cooperation and knowledge generation between more and more heterogeneous actors. Against this background, the importance of social science expertise for the design and analysis of such innovation processes is becoming increasingly apparent (Howaldt et al. 2008, p. 68). Nevertheless, unavoidable interdisciplinary professional characteristics should be pointed out. Björgvinsson et al. (2010) define fields of tasks for so-called "design researchers". "Design researchers" should be able to moderate and serve a group of heterogeneous participants and accept their marginality (Björgvinsson et al. 2010). Social scientists should also acquire these characteristics in order to be able to moderate Living Labs or innovation workshops as well as *New Care Spaces.*

We understand the experimental format of the innovation workshops within our research project as one of the social contexts described above, in which social innovations can be jointly figured. In this context, the ideal of a social innovation process was to be elaborated in an interdisciplinary way with the help of technical products. For this reason, the focus of our scientific interest was not the practical feasibility of a final product, but the reflexively designed, group-dynamic process. A mixed team of senior citizens, experts and students from MINT subjects collected the needs of people in old age under the methodological guidance of two sociologists. Together they used LEGO Serious Play and elements of Design Thinking to design a *New Care Space,* which should meet the various needs mentioned as far as possible. In this way we offered a protected space for the exchange of knowledge and views of different interest groups regarding a good life in old age. Working with mixed teams also means taking into account diversity in terms of age, educational background, (social) origin, professional background, personal attitudes and life situation. Despite these differences, we succeeded in social science-guided communication by including all group members equally in both the idea generation and elaboration phases and accepting each opinion as equally important. The group dynamics and our interdisciplinary approach proved to be extremely effective. We invited both lead users of technical products and non-users from the target group of senior citizens. This allowed us to tap the creative innovation potential of both groups. In addition, we deliberately included the marginal target group of senior citizens not only for the evaluation of a final product or a product concept, but also let them develop a prototype themselves in cooperation with experts and students. In their speeches it became clear that the target group of senior citizens felt that their opinions and needs were taken seriously and that their active participation was valued. This experience of self-efficacy and empowerment as a user was partly in contrast to the everyday experiences of the marginalized group of senior citizens, for example when they did not receive any answers to feedback on technical products or when many technologies were classified by the media as not suitable for their generation. The communication between the different age groups proved to be very productive and profitable for a joint exchange of experiences within the framework of the innovation workshops as *New Care Spaces*.

The innovation workshops were evaluated using qualitative social research methods such as summary content analysis (Mayring 2015) and participant observation (Passaro 1997). Through these methodological approaches, we ensured a smooth transition of the workshop results to research data. The use and application of certain methods of qualitative social research once again illustrate a repositioning of the role of social scientists in innovation processes.

New Care Spaces created through the sub-project can be designed in a demand-oriented manner with suitable cooperation partners. This requires not only premises but also moderators (including a set of methods) and multipliers who accompany the innovation processes in a suitable and goal-oriented manner. At this point, the professional field of social scientists can be considered quite suitable.

Our research project thus showed that social scientists can facilitate diversity of perspective and reflexivity in the development of social innovations as well as the inclusion of immediate target groups and marginalized users.

7 Summary of the Results

In this paper we discussed our approach to *New Care Spaces,* which was achieved through the participatory involvement of user groups via innovation workshops. We propose to consider *New Care Spaces* as a social innovation following Howaldt and Jacobsen (2010). In order to dissolve scepticism between companies and stakeholders (incl. Marginalised groups), we recommend to implement the participatory method of innovation workshops adapted for companies, non-profit organisations and public services (Rommes 2011). In order to create this willingness to participate, there must be empathy and sensitivity on the part of the product developers and a fundamental openness to the actual needs of older people. Companies should perceive them as a valued target group and, if possible, integrate them into technology development processes. This can also change organisational cultures and open up further external cooperation. Every member of society can thus participate in "sustainable living and business" (Stiess 2013). These connections can equally contribute to the development of accessible technology and technologies of private and public use. Only in this way, our research showed, the prevailing scepticism about an anticipated disinterest for older target groups on the part of product manufacturers and the often media-triggered fear of technologies will be dispelled. From this perspective, our *New Care Spaces* are a promising option to meet these challenges.

If *New Care Spaces* in public space function as Open Innovation (Vollmann et al. 2012), they serve our project for the participation of senior citizens in technological development and social change. *New Care Spaces* can be designed in a demand-oriented way with suitable cooperation partners. In addition to premises, moderators (including a set of methods) and suitable multipliers are required to accompany the innovation processes. Furthermore, *New Care Spaces* complement the guidelines of social space orientation (Budde et al. 2007) and socially responsible technology development.

Furthermore, social scientists can play a leading role in the development of this social innovation. Especially when designing spaces and working as multipliers and facilitators, the production of *New Care Spaces,* social science expertise, as we have shown, is extremely helpful and promising.

References

Aulenbacher, B. und M. Dammayr. 2014. *Für sich und andere sorgen. Krise und Zukunft von Care in der modernen Gesellschaft.* Weinheim: Beltz Juventa.

Beruchashvili, T., E. Wiesnet und S. Ihsen. 2018. Gender- & diversityorientierte Partizipationsansätze in Technikentwicklung. In *Mensch und Computer 2018 – Workshopband.* Hrsg. R. Dachselt und G. Weber. Bonn: Gesellschaft für Informatik e. V.

Björgvinsson, E., P. Ehn und P.-A. Hillgren. 2010. *Participatory design and democratizing innovation.* Proceedings of the 11th Biennial participatory design 4 conference. ACM Library.

Boggatz, Th. 2011. Einstellungen zum betreuten Wohnen bei Seniorinnen und Senioren – Eine qualitative Studie: 111–123. *Pflege* 24 (2).

Brückner, M. 2010. Entwicklungen der Care-Debatte. Wurzeln und Begrifflichkeiten. In *Care und Migration. Die Ent-Sorgung menschlicher Reproduktionsarbeit entlang von Geschlechter- und Armutsgrenzen.* Hrsg. U. Apitzsch und M. Schmidbaur Care und Migration: 43–58. Opladen: Verlag Barbara Budrich.

Brückner, M. 2012. Understanding Professional Care from Viewpoint of Care Receivers and Care givers – The Necessity of a Special Care Rationality. *Social Work and Society* 10 (2).

Bundesministerium für Bildung und Forschung (BMBF). 2019. *Karliczek: "Wir wollen Bürgerwissenschaften als selbstverständliche Forschungsmethode etablieren."* Pressemitteilung 122/2019.

Burmeister, J., A. Heller, und I. Stehr. 2005. *Weiterbildung älterer Menschen für bürgerschaftliches Engagement als seniorTrainerinnen.* Köln: ISAB-Schriftenreihe, Berichte aus Forschung und Praxis Nr. 91. Online Verfügbar unter: https://www.isab-institut.de/upload/Aktuelles/PDF/Nr.91.2_Kurskonzept.pdf. Zugegriffen 05. Juni 2020.

Budde, W., F. Früchtel, und W. Hinte. 2007. *Sozialraumorientierung: Wege zu einer veränderten Praxis.* Wiesbaden: VS Verlag für Sozialwissenschaften.

D21-Digital-Index. 2013. *Auf dem Weg in ein digitales Deutschland?!* Eine Studie der Initiative D21, durchgeführt von TNS Infratest. Online verfügbar unter dem Link: https://initiatived21.de/app/uploads/2017/02/d21-digital-index-2013.pdf. Zugegriffen 19. Oktober 2019.

D21-Digital-Index. 2016. *Jährliches Lagebild zur Digitalen Gesellschaft.* Eine Studie der Initiative D21, durchgeführt von Kantar TNS. Online verfügbar unter dem Link: https://initiatived21.de/app/uploads/2017/01/studie-d21-digital-index-2016.pdf. Zugegriffen 19. Oktober 2019.

Etzkowitz H. und L. Leydsdorff. 2000. *The Dynamics of Innovation: From National Systems and "Mode 2" to a Triple Helix of University-, Industry-, Government Relations.* Research Policy, 29 (2).

ForGenderCare – Bayerischer Forschungsverbund: Hauptseite. Verfügbar unter dem Link: http://www.forgendercare.de/home/. Zugegriffen 18. Oktober 2019.

Gebauer, S., L. Schütze und S. Ihsen. 2011. Diversity in Nachhaltigkeitsinnovationsprozessen. Diversityspezifische Auswertung von Innovationsworkshops. In *Nachhaltigkeitsinnovation durch Nutzerintegration. Wirtschaftswissenschaftliche Nachhaltigkeitsforschung.* Hrsg. F.-M. Belz, U. Schrader und M. Arnold: 233–255. Marburg: Metropolis-Verlag.

Gensicke, T. und S. Geiss. 2010. Freiwilligensurvey 2009. Methodenbericht in Hauptbericht des Freiwilligensurveys 2009. *Zivilgesellschaft, soziales Kapital und freiwilliges Engagement in Deutschland 1999-2004-2009.* Hrsg. BMFSFJ. Berlin: Bundesministerium für Familie, Senioren, Frauen und Jugend.

Glende, S. 2010. *Senior User Integration – Konzepte, Werkzeuge und Fallbeispiele: Ein Leitfaden für die Einbindung älterer Nutzer in die Produkt- und Serviceentwicklung.* Saarbrücken: Südwestdeutscher Verlag für Hochschulschriften.

Glende, S., C. Nedopil, B. V. Podtschaske, M. Stahl und W. Friesdorf. 2011. *Erfolgreiche AAL-Lösungen durch Nutzerintegration. Ergebnisse der Studie "Nutzerabhängige Innovationsbarrieren im Bereich Altersgerechter Assistenzsysteme".* Technische Universität Berlin. Berlin: BMBF/VDE Innovationspartnerschaft AAL.

Grunwald, S. und A. Saupe, Hrsg. 1999. *Ethik in der Technikgestaltung. Praktische Relevanz und Legitimation.* Berlin, Heidelberg: Springer-Verlag.

Gustavsen, B. 2006. Innovation and action research. *International Journal of Action Research* 3: 267–289.

Howaldt, J. und H. Jacobsen, Hrsg. 2010. *Soziale Innovation. Auf dem Weg zu einem postindustriellen Innovationsparadigma.* Wiesbaden: VS Verlag für Sozialwissenschaften.

Howaldt, J., R. Kopp und M. Schwarz. 2008. Innovationen (forschend) gestalten – Zur neuen Rolle der Sozialwissenschaften. *WSI Mitteilungen* 2: 63–69.

Howaldt, J. und M. Schwarz. 2012. Zur Rolle der Sozialwissenschaften in gesellschaftlichen Innovationsprozessen. In *Gesellschaft innovativ. Wer sind die Akteure?* Hrsg. G. Beck und C. Kropp: 47–64. Wiesbaden: VS Verlag für Sozialwissenschaften.

Hubig, C. und J. Reidel, Hrsg. 2003. *Ethnische Ingenieurverantwortung: Handlungsspielräume und Perspektiven der Kodifizierung.* edition sigma. o. O.

Ihsen, S., W. Schneider und K. Scheibl. 2012. *Interdisciplinary research collaborations and learning processes of engineers and social scientists during the development of a robot for seniors in Europe?* World Transactions on Engineering and Technology Education 10: 116–121.

Jeanrenaud, Yves, A. Sept, J. Schnaller, und S. Ihsen. 2018. Study decisions, entrance and academic success of women and men in STEM. In: *GenderIT '18: Proceedings of the 4th Conference on Gender & IT.* Association for Computing Machinery (ACM), New York, S. 157–160. https://doi.org/10.1145/3196839.3196864.

Klüber, S. 2019. Partizipative und sozialverantwortliche Technikentwicklung. Online verfügbar unter dem Link: https://fordemocracy.hypotheses.org/1862. Zugegriffen 19. Oktober 2019.

Krüger, M. 2018. "Geben und Nehmen". Care im Zeichen von Reziprozität. In *Fürsorge-Relationen. Theoretische und empirische Sichtweisen auf Care.* Soziologiemagazin. Sonderheft 3. Jahrgang 11.

Lewrik, M., P. Link und L. Leifer. 2018. The Design Thinking Playbook: Mindful Digital Transformation of Teams, Products, Services, Businesses and Ecosystems. Verlag: Wiley.

Maaß, S., C. Draude und K. Wajda. 2014. Gender-/Diversity-Aspekte in der Informatikforschung: Das GERD-Modell. In *Gender-UseIT – HCI, Web-Usability und User Experience unter Gendergesichtspunkten.* Hrsg. N. Marsden und U. Kempf: 67–78. Berlin: de Gruyter Oldenbourg Verlag.

Mahne, K., J. Wolff, J. Simonson und C. Tesch-Römer. 2017. Altern im Wandel. Zwei Jahrzehnte Deutscher Alterssurvey (DEAS). Wiesbaden: Springer Fachmedien.

Mayring, P. 2015. *Qualitative Inhaltsanalyse. Grundlagen und Techniken.* Weinheim: Beltz Pädagogik.

Mollenkopf, H. 2006. Chancen und Barrieren der neuen Medien – Technik auch im Alter kompetent nutzen. In *10. Enquete "Alter hat Zukunft – gerne älter werden in Tirol" "Internet verbindet – Fit fürs Informationszeitalter".* Zusammenfassung der Ergebnisse. Amt der Tiroler Landesregierung: 155–168. Seniorenreferat des Landes. Innsbruck.

ÖIAT – Österreichisches Institut für angewandte Telekommunikation. 2015. *Studie: Maßnahmen für Senior/innen in der digitalen Welt.* BMASK – Bundesministerium für Arbeit, Soziales und Konsumentenschutz. Wien.

Ornetzeder, M. und H. Rohracher. 2012. Nutzerinnovationen und Nachhaltigkeit: Soziale und technische Innovationen als zivilgesellschaftliches Engagement. In *Gesellschaft innovativ. Wer sind die Akteure?* Hrsg. G. Beck und C. Kropp: 171–190. Wiesbaden: VS Verlag für Sozialwissenschaften.

Passaro, J. 1997. You Can't Take the Subway to the Field! ‚Village' Epistemologies in the Global Village. In *Anthropological Locations: Boundaries and Grounds of a Field Science.* Hrsg. A. Gupta und J. Ferguson: 147–162. Berkeley: University of California Press.

Rommes, E. 2011. Inclusion by design. In *Technologies of inclusion.* Hrsg. K. H. Sörensen, W. Faulkner und E. Rommes: 129–146. Tapir Academic Press.

Ropohl, G. 2009. *Technologische Aufklärung. Beiträge zur Technikphilosophie.* Frankfurt a. M.: Suhrkamp Verlag.

Shire, K. A. und J. M. Leimeister. 2012. *Technologiegestützte Dienstleistungsinnovation in der Gesundheitswirtschaft.* Wiesbaden: Gabler Verlag.

Stiess I. 2013. Synergien von Umwelt- und Sozialpolitik – Soziale Innovationen an der Schnittstelle von Umweltschutz, Lebensqualität und sozialer Teilhabe. In Soziale Innovation und Nachhaltigkeit. Hrsg. J. Rückert-John: 33–49. Wiesbaden: Springer Fachmedien.

Tronto, J. 2012. Democratic Care Politics in an Age of Limits. In *Global variations in the political and social economy of care. Worlds apart.* Hrsg. S. Razavi und S. Staab: 20–40. New York: Routledge.

Tronto, J. 2013. *Caring Democracy. Markets, Equality, and Justice.* New York and London: NEW YORK UNIVERSITY PRESS.

Vollmann, S., T. Lindemann und F. Huber. 2012. *Open Innovation: eine empirische Analyse zur Identifikation innovationsbereiter Kunden.* BoD – Books on Demand.

Westkämper, E. 2006. *Einführung in die Organisation der Produktion.* Berlin, Heidelberg: Springer.

Zapf, W. 1989: Über soziale Innovation. *Soziale Welt* 1/2: 170–183.

ZSI (Zentrum für soziale Innovation), Hrsg. 2008. *Impulse für die gesellschaftliche Entwicklung.* Wien: ZSI Diskussionspapier.

Beruchashvili, Tamar, M.A., studied Management of Social Innovations at the University of Applied Sciences Munich, studied Sociology and Gender Studies at the LMU Munich, additional training Academic Program for Entrepreneurship at SCE Munich. Research associate at the Chair of Gender Studies in Engineering at the Technical University of Munich, responsible for sub-project 3 "Technology Design" of the research network ForGenderCare. Also consultant for innovation promotion and organizational development at Caritasverband München und Freising e. V. Since 2022, working as a consultant and trainer at TEAMWILLE GmbH.

Last published:

Wiesnet, E., Beruchashvili, T., Jeanrenaud, Y.: "New Care Spaces" -A Gender and Diversity Sensitive Approach to Digital Participation. In "To shape or be shaped? Perspectives of feminist economics on digitalization". 17th efas symposium. 06.12.2019. Berlin. Available online at: https://efas.htw-berlin.de/wp-content/uploads/Poster_Efas_Wiesnet.pdf (15.12.2019).

Wiesnet, Elisabeth, M.A., studied sociology, gender studies and statistics at LMU Munich, research assistant at the Chair of Gender Studies in the Engineering Sciences at TU Munich in sub-project 3 "Technology Design" of the research network ForGenderCare, doctoral student at LMU Munich under the supervision of Prof. Dr. Stefan Lessenich on the topic "*Grenzen des selbstbestimmten Informierens. Empirical perspectives and interpretations of § 219a*".

Last published:

Wiesnet, E., Beruchashvili, T., Jeanrenaud, Y.: "New Care Spaces" -A Gender and Diversity Sensitive Approach to Digital Participation. In "To shape or be shaped? Perspectives of feminist economics on digitalization". 17th efas symposium. 06.12.2019. Berlin. Available online at: https://efas.htw-berlin.de/wp-content/uploads/Poster_Efas_Wiesnet.pdf (15.12.2019).

Jeanrenaud, Yves, Dr. phil., studied Sociology, Gender Studies and Media Studies in Basel (Uni Basel) and Tübingen (Uni Tübingen). Doctorate in Munich (TU Munich/TUM). PostDoc Gender Studies in Engineering (TUM). Substitute professorship in General Sociology in Vechta (Uni Vechta). PostDoc Institute of Sociology (LMU Munich), Sociology and Gender Studies. From 2020: Visiting Professorship Gender Studies MINT and Med (Uni Ulm). EU Independent Expert H2020. Advisory board gender<ed.> thoughts (Uni Göttingen). AG Perspektiven (FG Gender e. V.). ORCID 0000–0002–8378-2831.

Latest Publications:

Jeanrenaud, Y.; A. Sept. 2019. What contributes to academic success in STEM subjects? Findings from the GenderMINT 4.0 project on study decisions, study entry and study success of women and men in STEM. DAADeuroletter (67). 2019. S. 28–31.

Jeanrenaud, Y.; A. Sept; S. Ihsen. 2018. study decisions, entrance and academic success of women and men in STEM. Gender&IT'18. new york: association for computing machinery (ACM). 2018. S. 157–160.

Jeanrenaud, Y. 2018. life concepts of female engineers. In: Onnen, C.; S. Rode-Breymann. eds. On the self-understanding of gender studies II. technology – space – education. L'AGENda vol. 2. Leverkusen: Barbara Budrich Publishers. S. 155–172.

The Art of Social Transformation

Empowerment Through Social Art for an Increase of Equal Opportunities in Europe

Christine Best and Kerstin Guhlemann

Abstract

One of the central current challenges is the (further) education and integration of people into society and the labour market who are disadvantaged due to unequal biographical opportunities. This requires new approaches and forms of cooperation between different actors. A socially innovative approach that aims to contribute to this is that of social art. In this approach, hierarchies are dissolved, and art becomes an integrative process of cooperation that in many ways creates space for the experience of success, shared understanding and personal development, and contributes to the empowerment of disadvantaged groups. On this basis, forms of combining theatre work and social work have already become established in Germany, which are far superior to traditional methods of integrating disadvantaged people into the labour market and society. The transfer of this approach to other European countries is being pursued in the EU project JobAct Europe – Social Inclusion by Social Arts with social science support. This paper presents the approach and the European forms of its adaptation. It shows how the chances of labour market integration can also be increased transnationally for biographically disadvantaged groups with the help of socially innovative artistic approaches.

C. Best (✉) · K. Guhlemann
Social Research Center Dortmund, TU Dortmund, Dortmund, Germany
e-mail: christine.best@tu-dortmund.de; kerstin.guhlemann@tu-dortmund.de

H.-W. Franz et al. (eds.), *Sustainable Living and Business*,
https://doi.org/10.1007/978-3-658-41835-9_14

1 Background and Procedure of the Investigation

Increasing equal opportunities within society is an issue that has lost none of its relevance since its integration into the Europe 2020 strategy goals. Due to the close link between the position on the labour market and social integration, two main starting points arise: (1) improving employability and (2) employment opportunities. In this paper we therefore present a social art approach that tackles both employability and employment opportunities using artistic methods. Strengthening the key competences of challenging target groups with artistic methods can have many times higher success rates than established methods of labour market integration. Based on this, this paper therefore asks how the social art approach can help to change individuals and social processes. It examines what distinguishes the method and what results can be achieved with which target groups.

After a brief look at the background of the emergence of social problems and the potentials of empowerment approaches in general, areas of application of social art for the purpose of empowering vulnerable groups are first presented. The main part is then formed by results from the Erasmus+ project JobAct Europe, in which the use and dissemination of the JobAct method in Germany and other European countries were scientifically accompanied for 2 years. Here, it is described how, with which results and for which target groups the approach is used in the different countries to achieve the common goal of reducing social inequality. In an outlook, the opportunities for social transformation through artistic approaches are reflected upon once again against the background of the findings.

2 Playfully Against Inequality – Theoretical Findings

2.1 Manifestation of Social Problems

The core dimensions of social inequality: education, occupation, income and health, are strongly interrelated and closely interdependent, reinforced by other socio-demographic factors such as marital status or migration history (Richter and Hurrelmann 2006). A strong determinism of the social situation in childhood for the biographical opportunities in the further course of life is characteristic. In a risk chain, negative influences of the domestic and social environment, disintegrative cultural habits, low material conditions and educational prerequisites and opportunities reinforce each other (Richter-Kornweitz and Utermark 2013). Particular clusters of problems, such as high unemployment, low uptake of childcare services, preventive check-ups, cultural and educational opportunities, and critical health behaviour, often occur in individual, disadvantaged neighbourhoods. The high ethnic and social segregation of residential districts and social groups contributes to the fact that inequality can be "inherited" over generations. In this context, the influence of origin manifests itself in primary and secondary effects, on the one hand in the development of competence, performance and problematic behaviour, and on the other hand in its formative power for biographical decisions in education, occupation or deviance (Blossfeld 2013). At the same time, a homogeneous social environment suppresses the motivation to change or the development of perspectives. From a social perspective, this is countered by the danger of discrimination on the basis of the aforementioned characteristics, which further reduces the chances of integration (Imdorf 2017).

The strong determinant power of low expectations or expectations of failure for the self-perception of those affected can lead to the so-called "Pygmalion effect", a spiral of self-fulfilling prophecies, which ensures permanently low room for manoeuvre in the course of employment (Koch and Dollase 2009). This relationship manifests itself, among other things, in the still low educational mobility. Thus, due to "cumulative educational poverty", the highest educational attainment of the parents is to a large extent formative for the educational paths of the following generation, which in turn determine to a large extent the employment biographical opportunities (Wolter 2016). In this sense, it comes as little surprise that studies across Germany show the link between parental unemployment and the following generation (Berth et al. 2010; Müller 2016). In addition, prolonged absence from the labour market further reduces employment opportunities. In addition to the progressive loss of self-confidence due to repeated experiences of failure, professional skills and application strategies become outdated, the risk of stigmatisation by employers and the social environment increases, and the ability to hold one's own in the face of competition from fellow applicants decreases (Heinl et al. 2008). There is thus a danger that groups of people will be permanently pushed away from the labour market and to the margins of society due to unevenly distributed biographical opportunities.

Despite efforts to address the issue, little has changed in the distribution of opportunities in recent decades (Rock 2019). The unequal distribution of social opportunities is a Europe-wide phenomenon that is reinforced rather than reduced even by better economic situations. Due to the cumulative build-up of positive and negative development potentials over the entire lifespan, the already better-off groups of people benefit to a greater extent from expanded opportunities, while part of the population improves its situation only slowly, which further widens the gap between social groups (Mielck 2005).

2.2 Transformations for Better Opportunities

Transformation refers to a particular type of social change that is characterized by processuality, long-term nature, interdependence and sequentiality. It produces new patterns of social order and development and changes social processes. Development is intentionally controlled and formative, but at the same time inherently dynamic and organic-evolutionary (Reißig 2014). It is precisely this dialectic that is found both at the level of society and at the level of the individual.

More recent approaches to improving equal opportunities in health and education respond to biographical contexts by adopting a life course perspective. One variant is the empowerment approach. It builds on the conviction that people are fundamentally "experts in their own affairs" and possess skills and resources for shaping their own biographies that can be strengthened. The underlying conception of man is that of a competent actor who can shape his own life. The aim is to increase autonomy and the scope for action in the course of life by strengthening self-efficacy and essential competences for active biographical action. People in different life situations should recognise their strengths and thus be empowered and encouraged to take their lives into their own hands. This addresses three development goals: (1) the conviction of one's own creative power, which influences the perception of one's scope for action (self-efficacy), (2) the abilities to expand this scope for action, and (3) the knowledge of one's scope for action. The approach is more open-ended than direct psychosocial counselling and support. While opportunities for individuals' development can be provided and changes initiated, life course interventions must be provided by the individuals themselves (Stark 1996). Basically, the goal is to "initiate and support processes of self-help and networking where they cannot arise on their own based on the existing resources of the individuals" (Bodenmüller 2004, p. 21). The approach does not stop with those affected, but in addition to the subject level also starts at the level of the group, institutions and politics. For example, by promoting networks in the local area through the development of self-help groups and contact points, and by striving for institutional and political changes through participation and political involvement of those affected, the aim is to achieve a comprehensive upgrading of the living situations of the target group. In this sense, empowerment means not only self-change but also social change and, in addition to the personality as a source of self-change, can also build on the collective (Herriger 2014).

Empowerment approaches for the unemployed are mainly directly related to the labour market. Projects aim to build up occupationally relevant skills (further training vouchers), integration into a meaningful activity – depending on employability in the first or second labour market (e.g. citizen work, integration vouchers, wage subsidies) or entrepreneurship training. In addition, there are projects that combine the approach with health promotion or the development of health skills, create spaces and resources for regular exchange, work on time management or integrate the job search into project management[1]. Empowerment approaches using artistic methods still play a marginal role, and their application and potential effects are the subject of the following subchapter.

2.3 Empowerment with Social Art

Artistic approaches in the field of empowerment are based on the assumption that with art there is a universal level in which an understanding and exchange between the target group and its environment is possible. Social art is based on the Beuysian approach of an expanded concept of art, but goes beyond this in its dialogical claim. The focus is no longer on a physical piece of work, but on the artistic process of its creation (Krenn 2016). It enables the processing of unpleasant or problematic situations through a "slow indirect approach to topics and experiences" (Kechaja 2017, p. 195), their (re)evaluation and processing. Essential elements here are that art is transferred from the usual top-down approach to a participatory framework in a multi-professional cooperation of actors from the fields of art/culture, education and social work (Heinrich 2016). In social work, biographical approaches are often chosen here. Artistic forms of expression can thus be used to create a space in which, protected from the dangers of failure, difficulties can be overcome, solutions to problems can be found, alternative roles can be tried out and new sides of oneself can be discovered. The participants can make new experiences, change their perspective, recognise unfavourable behavioural routines and initiate changes (Bodenmüller 2004, p. 20). Working together on an artistic product promotes self-reflection, solidarity, teamwork and creativity and the pride of creating something of high quality. Both the artistic process and the result contribute to the development of the participants. With the presentation of the result, a sense of achievement is made possible, which is important for strengthening self-esteem and is otherwise often missing in unemployment. Creativity and belief in one's own abilities are essential prerequisites for success in the job search after a long period of unemployment. It is also essential to change the perception of others and to overcome stigmatisation, which can be achieved through artistic performance. Artistic work

[1] For an overview, see exemplary https://www.gesundheitliche-chancengleichheit.de/gesundheitsfoerderung-bei-arbeitslosen/gute-praxis/empowerment/ (Oct. 27, 2019).

can thus become a kind of "lobbying for those affected" (Bodenmüller 2004, p. 22). Particularly in the case of the homogenising tendencies of socio-spatial segregation described above, this development of perspectives and the exchange across peer groups can create a counterweight that can contribute to changes in perspective. The mechanisms at work here are provocation, reflection and distancing (Larcher 2016).

Artistic approaches to empowerment draw on a wide variety of art forms. Reports include painting, literature, visual arts, music, radio, dance, radio play production and theatre. Some examples are presented below.

In one project, sculptures were made by unemployed people, accompanied by the presentation of these with text and photography via various media and participation in the organization and planning of the public exhibition. At the same time, reproductions were offered for sale. This not only promoted creativity and artistic expression, but also marketing/public relations skills as well as diligence and conscientiousness. While participants in assisted job searches operate in competitive situations, this project encouraged teamwork and support. Through contacts with companies within the project, one participant found a job (Bodenmüller 2004). In another project, unemployed people were able to paint a large picture together with pupils, people with disabilities, political and economic actors "without words", which created an opportunity to meet at eye level and to reduce prejudice (Bodenmüller 2004, p. 20).

Young people with a history of migration or flight were the target group of a project that conducted weekly workshops with rap, hip-hop dance, theatre, photography, film and graffiti, which culminated in a public performance of the results at the end of a year. The expression of their own problematic situations and experiences of exclusion was thereby made possible with texts or choreographies and accompanied by an examination of racism, prejudice and threats (Kechaja 2017). The artistic form of expression served for a fear-free analysis of one's own experiences and the impetus for an examination of one's own identity. Empowerment took place in a "dynamic interplay of self-empowerment and reinforcement" (Kechaja 2017, p. 199) by overcoming powerlessness and helplessness and triggering processes of "becoming a subject".

In theatre approaches with the aim of empowerment, the basis is the dissolution of traditional boundaries between recipients and performers in favour of a dialogical character. Developments towards a "citizens' stage" can be observed, on which "professional theatre is offered with non-professional performers" (Kunze 2014, cited in Heinrich 2016), if necessary also in combination with professional actors. This is done by involving the target group, for example refugees, people with disabilities, the long-term unemployed, the elderly, in the production of the plays, by taking up stories from the lifeworld of those affected or by writing plays together. This method serves to create a distance to one's own history among those affected and to initiate a process of reflection that seeks solutions applicable to one's own situation in the safe space of the portrayed reality (Dörflinger 2015). Another variant uses the stage to give a voice to the target group – in the case study, young people from different social and ethnic backgrounds. By enabling them to clarify their lifeworld to the adults in the audience in this way, an improved understanding of the target group and an improvement in the image of others emerged, while at the same time strengthening the young people's self-perception and ability to express themselves (Larcher 2016).

One approach that uses theatre work with the long-term unemployed specifically for labour market integration is the JobAct approach, which was developed by Projektfabrik Witten, has won several awards and has been disseminated throughout Germany. This approach is presented in the following.

3 Empirical Consideration – The JobAct Approach

In the Erasmus+ funded project "JobAct Europe – Social Inclusion by Social Art", the JobAct method was scientifically accompanied in its application for 2 years. In an exchange between science and practice, the basic elements and effects could be worked out and their applicability in other European countries could be examined. This was done through a close dialogue within the project, participatory observations of the work in the theatre projects with unemployed participants as well as the premieres and the trainings for the social artists who carry out these projects, analyses of internal documents and qualitative interviews with participants and trainers as well as experts from the Projektfabrik Witten. From these materials the following description of the method, its impact and its application in other countries was elaborated.

The JobAct method is an established artistic approach in Germany for integrating the long-term unemployed into the primary labour market and is based on the idea of empowering individuals to overcome individual problems. Conceived about 15 years ago by the social enterprise "Projektfabrik" from North Rhine-Westphalia and continuously developed and disseminated since then, the method has meanwhile been successfully applied in about 350 projects. The JobAct method is based on the social art approach.

3.1 Target Groups

The target group of the JobAct approach consists of long-term unemployed people with multiple placement barriers who are to be integrated primarily into the primary labour market and consequently into society with the help of the method. Current target groups are single parents, young people without work or training, refugees, people with language barriers and older people. The method is based on a combination of theatre pedagogical practices, classic job application training and a target group-specific approach such as language courses for people with language barriers. The approach is variable and can be applied equally to the long-term unemployed who have other potentially discriminatory characteristics such as lack of education, migration background, etc. The participants are often subject to multiple discrimination. Participants are often exposed to multiple discriminations which mutually reinforce and reproduce each other. In addition, the approach was adapted to the specific needs of people in particular social problem situations, for example single parents, taking into account their limited time resources. The Jobcentre promotes this approach particularly for people who have not been able to benefit from participation in regular activation and occupational integration measures and it has proved to be very effective (see Sect. 3.4).

3.2 Social Art in the JobAct Method

The underlying approach of the method is that of empowerment through social art, here implemented through theatre methods. The approach is based on the conviction that an artistic approach is necessary to address current social issues. Creativity, imagination and inspiration play central roles in overcoming obstacles.

In this understanding, social art enables the discovery of the self, creates space for the development of individuality and offers a new perspective on one's own problem situation as well as on ways to solve it. With the help of social art, key competences are developed, space for self-development is given and the self-confidence of the participants is strengthened. In particular, taking on new roles creates objectivity and consequently enables self-reflection. In this newly created space, facets of one's own personality that were previously hidden from the participants can be discovered and developed on the stage and in the play. In the interaction with other participants on stage, one's own role is redefined, which triggers a questioning of one's own role as an individual in social structures and enables a personal repositioning in society at a later point in time. In addition, the participants learn to appear courageously, to present themselves and to transfer and apply the creativity discovered in acting to their everyday lives. In a playful way, decision-making processes are also trained on stage, the ability to work on tasks creatively is developed, one's own awareness is sharpened and, as a result, the abilities to actively shape one's own life are improved. Of great importance and equally self-evident is the encounter of trainer and participants at eye level, in order to be able to create social art in a joint process on the one hand and on the other hand not to give the participants the feeling of unbalanced power relations. Generally, other artistic elements such as music or dance can also be integrated.

3.3 Practical Implementation of the JobAct Method

Based on the combination of social work and theatre pedagogy, the participants are empowered, equipped with the skills and competences they lack and supported in finding their way (back) into the labour market.

The practical implementation of the JobAct method consists of two phases: a six-month theater training and a subsequent two to four-month internship. In the first phase, the participants receive acting training 3 days a week, during which they rehearse a play that will later be ready for the stage. They also spend one day a week designing sets, props and costumes and one day a week receiving individual job application coaching, during which an individualised career plan for each participant is drawn up after potential analyses have been carried out to identify individual strengths and problems. In order to use the interdisciplinarity of theatre trainers and social workers, to avoid possible interface losses and to enable a holistic effect of the approach, the theatre training takes place once a week in the presence of the social workers, so that questions or problems that arise can be answered and solved at short notice. After the end of the training phase, the play is presented to a broad public. The aim here is to achieve a twofold effect: (1) to supplement the self-perception of the participants, which has already changed in the course of the training phase, through the sense of achievement of the performance, and (2) to change the perception of others in the social environment of the participants, the Job Centre staff and, if applicable, company representatives. The play is always a classic play by a well-known author; each year a different one is chosen as the focus. The fact that no biographical experiences are used for the creation of own plays pursues the goal of broadening the horizons of the participants by alternative spaces of experience. In addition, experience has shown that by participating in a well-known play, participants can gain more respect in their environment. The energy and self-confidence gained by the participants from the premiere is then used for their transition into the second phase of the project.

In the second project phase, following the premiere, the previously acquired key competencies such as the ability to work in a team, personal problem and crisis management as well as the ability to speak and express oneself are applied and expanded in a two to four-month company internship, so that the self-esteem is solidified through the experience of success in the internship. In parallel, a theatre training takes place one day a week, in which problems during the internship can also be discussed and solved. The internship position is already sought during the practical phase with the help of job coaching, in order to ideally enable a seamless transition. Often, training or employment opportunities arise during the internship, either in the same company or through previous or parallel application processes, which usually ensures continued employment.

3.4 Dissemination of the JobAct Method

The success of the JobAct method goes far beyond the usual measures of the job centres, despite the target group being more difficult to place. According to statements by the project factory management, in past years around 60–70 percent of the previously unemployed participants were placed in internships, training and further education and/or employment subject to social security contributions after taking advantage of the measure. Currently, the placement rate has dropped to 30–40 percent, because the good market situation has increased the remoteness of the long-term unemployed in the JobAct projects from the labour market. Nonetheless, this is still about twice as good as the rates achieved through other job centre measures. Around 6000 people took part in the more than 350 projects across Germany (as of October 2019) in 120 different German cities. The final theatre performances were attended by a total of around 55,000 spectators. Numerous awards and honors testify to the public recognition of the success of the method, including the award of the Federal Cross of Merit on Ribbon to founder Sandra Schürmann, the inclusion in the global support network Ashoka or the award of the Vision Award 2012 for social commitment. The approach is also used in vocational training: Profile-building courses of study such as "Theatre as Social Art" (FH Dortmund, Social Work) in the field of social work or the "School of Social Art" (Projektfabrik Witten, Social Artists) are still the exception, but testify to a growing interest in the potential of social art.

Although the method is firmly anchored as a measure in the offer in the area of responsibility of the job centres, in the context of stable employment figures and declining long-term unemployment (Statista 2019), a national diffusion saturation can nevertheless be observed. Plans for expansion, for example into the pension and health insurance sectors, are currently not being realised, although the JobAct approach has already shown promise in the past with regard to work with people suffering from mental illness. In adaptation to the current labour market situation, the JobAct method is therefore currently used in particular in the course of reintegration assistance and thus for the stabilisation of previously long-term unemployed people who have entered into a new employment relationship.

Due to its high success rate and its high applicability for a wide range of target groups, transnational diffusion processes of the approach were also initiated. Within the framework of the "JobAct Europe" project, the method was adapted in the partner countries by a total of eight partners from Italy, France, Hungary and Germany. The implementations are part of the following subchapter.

3.5 Implementation of the JobAct Approach: European Pilot Projects

In the course of the two-year project period, pilot projects were developed in all participating partner countries that adapted the JobAct approach to the target group and the respective profession-specific orientation of the organisation. The aim was always to develop sustainable and realistic new approaches for the social inclusion of disadvantaged groups.

3.5.1 France

The partner organisation La tête de l'emploi, based in Paris, applies the approach to women with a migration background, who represent a particularly vulnerable target group due to the multiple burdens of language barriers, education and ethnic and gender-related stigmatisation (Degele and Winker 2011). The target group is not subject to any age restriction, which makes participation as low-threshold as possible. Experience on the part of the project partners has shown that access can be difficult due in part to culturally conditioned barriers and domestic paternalism on the part of spouses. For recruitment purposes, therefore, close cooperation took place with the employment agencies, which were able to establish contact with the participants, sometimes with gentle pressure. The practical implementation of the pilot project closely followed the JobAct approach with the development of a play on several days per week and within 3–4 h each day. In general, as little as possible was prescribed for the participants, rather the focus was on the joint search for and formulation of goals, also in order to be able to react to and work with individually arising group dynamics.

In the course of an "Academy of Arts", the JobAct approach was implemented for a younger target group in the pilot project of the second French partner Apprentis d'Auteuil. Due to high youth unemployment in France and, in particular, high unemployment rates among young people in the northeast of Paris (Köster 2017), as well as, according to the project partner, increasing propensity to violence among students, the focus here is on young people with multiple school biographical disadvantages as well as those whose school retention is at risk and who have already attracted attention through violent behavior in the school context. The aim is to stabilise these young people and strengthen their personalities so that they can graduate from school and ideally be shown further prospects for the rest of their lives. To this end, the program is conducted parallel to regular school education and concludes with an internship. The highlight for the students is a joint trip to another country, where artistic projects are carried out together with local children. The contents taught at the Academy of Arts are identical to those of the regular curriculum, but they are taught in an artistic way, for example in the combination of mathematics and music or French and theatre, and have the planned trip as a common framework theme. Social art as an educational principle is implemented here primarily with the help of musical elements, as music is seen as a kind of catalyst of emotions and feelings. In this way, the young people should first of all be given easier access to themselves and, as a result, also to their fellow human beings.

3.5.2 Italy

In view of constantly high unemployment rates among young adults in Italy (Schraad-Tischler et al. 2017), the target group of the partner organisation Vivaio per l'Intraprendenza from Florence are young adults with and without a migration background. Vivaio relies on a combination of the JobAct approach with elements of the entrepreneurship approach. The aim is to develop an "entrepreneurial mindset" that can be used by the participants to market themselves. In the pilot projects, therefore, 4 weeks of intensive theatre work are initially carried out, followed by a public performance of the play developed. Afterwards, the participants undergo 9 days of job coaching, during which the individual potentials and weaknesses as well as career options of each participant are evaluated. Based on this, potential business ideas are then developed during a four-week project work phase using the problem-solving approach. The phase ends with a pitch of the respective business idea and leads into a two-month internship phase. Both the search and the application for the internship take place during the job coaching. In total, the pilot project consists of 9 weeks of intensive theatre, coaching and project work, followed by a two-month internship. After 13 months of Impulso, 59 percent of the participants are employed, 27 percent are studying and only 14 percent are still looking for work.

In line with its organisational orientation, the second partner organisation from Italy, Patchanka, focused on the inclusion of social work approaches when applying the JobAct approach, but otherwise adhered closely to the original method. Due to the poorer funding situation in Italy for both the projects and the unemployed persons, the time was shortened to 3 months. The target groups were former addicts and, in another project, young adults without school-leaving qualifications. In contrast to Germany, the internships in Italy are primarily arranged by the partners, who cooperate with companies in the region for this purpose, due to poorer access opportunities. Here, too, the success rates were high; for example, all 15 participants in the target group without school-leaving qualifications subsequently found a training place, employment or resumed their school education.

3.5.3 Hungary

Against the background of high poverty and unemployment rates and rising open racism, especially towards non-European migrants and non-Christians (Schraad-Tischler et al. 2017), the JobAct approach was adapted by the two Hungarian partner organizations Szubjektiv Foundation and Faktor Terminal to educationally disadvantaged young people between 18 and 24 years of age, most of whom have a migration background. The aim is to counteract the growing social inequality in Hungary and to empower those who experience the greatest disadvantages due to the above-mentioned backgrounds. In particular, the Hungarian pilot project tried to reach people who belong to the Roma society and thus face numerous discriminations, disadvantages and stereotypes anyway (Scherr 2017). However, since a reproduction of social exclusion and segregation is to be prevented, the organisations attach importance to heterogeneity of the target group. The project work here consists of theatre training, individual life and career orientation counselling, the teaching of helpful IT skills, and assistance in finding an internship or apprenticeship. The play developed during the project is presented at the end of the project in one of the Budapest theatres. Institutionalised racism in Hungary proved to be a major obstacle to the implementation of the project. Projects that are intended to work with migrants sometimes receive state funding, but these are often discontinued as soon as their purpose is publicly communicated.

3.5.4 Germany

Based on the conviction that young people can be helped out of a lack of perspective and social isolation with the help of an artistic approach, the project factory developed the pilot project "Frederick Ensemble". Young people under the age of 25, who find themselves in a situation without orientation or prospects with regard to their schooling or vocational training, can develop ideas for their future in an artistic way over a total of 10 months. The aim is to strengthen the personal will of the participants and to develop and open up their own ideas and perspectives for the future. Under the direction of a theatre pedagogue and with the support of a social worker, two productions are developed, which are later presented to the public in the context of several performances, partly also in district and citizen-oriented formats such as neighbourhood festivals. On one day per week, the participants can also voluntarily acquire a certificate of competence in culture, i.e. an educational certificate recognised throughout Europe by the Federal Association for Cultural Education. In the first weeks of the project, participants first work on the basics of acting, such as interaction in groups, improvisation on stage and working with their own bodies. In addition to the playful discovery of their own strengths and weaknesses, the weekly structure created by the project also proves helpful for the participants. The participants are acquired for the project through personal contacts as well as through the job centre.

4 Outlook

As the examples show, the unequal distribution of opportunities for labour market and social inclusion is a transnational challenge that cannot be taken lightly due to the intergenerational effects of accumulated biographical disadvantage. In order to achieve transformation at the two essential levels, the individual level and the societal level, a combination of empowerment approaches with social art seems promising. The aim of the approach is to empower the unemployed participants with the help of integrative measures from social art, in order to subsequently strengthen their chances in the search for work or training opportunities with the help of job coaching. The approach of social art, as a framework-giving instance in the center of the work, ensures that the participants free themselves from the role of social attributions in order to redefine themselves as individuals. In the project work, importance is attached to offering the participants space, time and a personal approach without restricting or influencing them in their individual creativity. In accordance with the empowerment approach, it is assumed that this will lead to a strengthening of autonomy, increase self-efficacy and expand one's own scope for action.

In addition to achieving public attention through a presentation of the results of the artistic work, a connection with elements of social work and placement in an internship stands out as essential for the success of integration. This approach works with slight adaptations under different national framework conditions and with different target groups. With the help of the pilot projects, individual job opportunities for disadvantaged groups have been demonstrably improved. The empowerment through the basic principle of social art works independently of the country or target groups, but the adjustments have to be made in order to ensure the participation of the target groups in the longer-term projects.

References

Berth, H., P. Förster, K. Petrowski, A. Hinz, F. Balck, E. Brähler, und Y. Stöbel-Richter. 2010. Vererbt sich Arbeitslosigkeit? *Zeitschrift für Psychotraumatologie, Psychotherapiewissenschaft, Psychologische Medizin* (8): 35–43.

Blossfeld, H.-P. 2013. Bildungsungleichheiten im Lebensverlauf — Herausforderungen für Politik und Forschung. In *Bildungsungleichheit und Gerechtigkeit. Wissenschaftliche und gesellschaftliche Herausforderungen*, Hrsg. Rolf Becker und Bühler, Patrick, Bühler, Thomas, 71–100. Bern: Haupt Verlag.

Bodenmüller, M. 2004. Kunst- und Kulturprojekte mit Erwerbslosen. Mit Skulpturen Öffentlichkeit schaffen. *Sozial Extra* 28 (12): 18–23.

Degele, N., und G. Winker. 2011. Intersektionalität als Beitrag zu einer gesellschaftstheoretisch informierten Ungleichheitsforschung. *Berliner Journal für Soziologie* 21 (1): 69–90. https://doi.org/10.1007/s11609-011-0147-y.

Dörflinger, T. 2015. *Der Beitrag des Theaters der Unterdrückten zu einer Praxis der Freiheit bei Jugendlichen in Österreich – eine Analyse am Beispiel der vom SOG. Theater Wiener Neustadt behandelten Themen*. Masterarbeit.

Heinl, R., W. Semmelmann, und M. Gottwald. 2008. Selbstorganisation als Strategie? "AktivFirma" als Instrument eines beteiligungsorientierten Integrationsansatzes. In *Integration älterer Arbeitsloser. Strategien – Konzepte – Erfahrungen*, Hrsg. Herbert Loebe und Eckart Severing, 121–130. Bielefeld: Bertelsmann.

Heinrich, B. 2016. Kunst oder Sozialarbeit? Eckpunkte eines neuen Beziehungsgefüges zwischen Sozialer Arbeit und Kulturarbeit. https://www.kubi-online.de/artikel/kunst-oder-sozialarbeit-eckpunkte-eines-neuen-beziehungsgefueges-zwischen-sozialer-arbeit. Zugegriffen: 27. Oktober 2019.

Herriger, N. 2014. *Empowerment in der Sozialen Arbeit. Eine Einführung*. Stuttgart: Verlag W. Kohlhammer.

Imdorf, C. 2017. Das Integrationspotenzial nutzen. Es braucht eine sozial innovative Berufsbildung. *skilled* (2): 2–5.

Kechaja, M. 2017. Jetzt rede ich! – Das TALK Projekt: Kunst und Empowerment gegen Rassismus und Diskriminierung. In *Flucht. Herausforderungen für Soziale Arbeit*, Hrsg. Johanna Bröse, Stefan Faas und Barbara Stauber, 191–202. Wiesbaden: Springer VS.

Koch, K.C., und R. Dollase. 2009. Diskriminierung im Kontext von Bildung und Bildungskarrieren. In *Diskriminierung und Toleranz. Psychologische Grundlagen und Anwendungsperspektiven*, Hrsg. Andreas Beelmann und Kai J. Jonas, 337–355. Wiesbaden: VS Verlag für Sozialwissenschaften.

Köster, T. 2017. *Jugendarbeitslosigkeit in Europa. Eine europäische Verantwortung*. Berlin: Konrad-Adenauer-Stiftung.

Krenn, M. 2016. Das Politische in sozialer Kunst. Intervenieren in soziale Verhältnisse. https://www.p-art-icipate.net/das-politische-in-sozialer-kunst/. Zugegriffen: 27. Oktober 2019.

Larcher, A. 2016. Jugendliche erfahren Empowerment. Eine Begleitforschung des Theaterstücks "Ausblick nach oben". *Soziales_kapital* (16): 130–142.

Mielck, A. 2005. *Soziale Ungleichheit und Gesundheit. Einführung in die aktuelle Diskussion*. Bern: Huber.

Müller, S. 2016. Vererbung von Arbeitslosigkeit: Wie der Vater, so der Sohn? *Wirtschaft im Wandel* 22 (2): 30–32.

Reißig, R. 2014. Transformation – ein spezifischer Typ sozialen Wandels. In *Futuring. Perspektiven der Transformaton im Kapitalismus über ihn hinaus*, Hrsg. Michael Brie, 50–100. Münster: Westfälisches Dampfboot.

Richter, M., und K. Hurrelmann. 2006. *Gesundheitliche Ungleichheit. Grundlagen, Probleme, Konzepte*. Wiesbaden: VS Verlag für Sozialwissenschaften | GWV Fachverlage GmbH Wiesbaden.

Richter-Kornweitz, A., und K. Utermark. 2013. *Werkbuch Präventionskette. "gesund aufwachsen" für alle Kinder! Herausforderungen und Chancen beim Aufbau von Präventionsketten in Kommunen*. Hannover: Landesvereinigung für Gesundheit & Akademie für Sozialmedizin Niedersachsen.

Rock, J. 2019. Not sehen und handeln. *Sozialwirtschaft* 29 (4): 24–25.

Scherr, A. 2017. Diskriminierung von Roma und Sinti. In *Handbuch Diskriminierung*, Hrsg. Albert Scherr, Aladin el Mafaalani und Emine Gökçen Yüksel, 529–543. Wiesbaden: VS Verlag für Sozialwissenschaften.

Schraad-Tischler, D., C. Schiller, S.M. Heller, und N. Siemer. 2017. *Social Justice in the EU – Index Report 2017. Social Inclusion Monitor Europe*. Gütersloh: Bertelsmann Stiftung.

Stark, W. 1996. *Empowerment: neue Handlungskompetenzen in der psychosozialen Praxis*. Freiburg i. Br.: Lambertus.

Statista. 2019. Anzahl der Langzeitarbeitslosen in Deutschland im Jahresdurchschnitt von 2007 bis 2019. https://de.statista.com/statistik/daten/studie/666199/umfrage/anzahl-der-langzeitarbeitslosen-in-deutschland/. Zugegriffen: 17. Oktober 2019.

Wolter, A. 2016. Soziale Barrieren – Wege ins Studium und Wege im Studium. Beitrag zur Tagung: Soziale Durchlässigkeit – Wege ins Studium und Wege im Studium. https://www.boeckler.de/pdf/v_2016_05_20_wolter.pdf. Zugegriffen: 25. Oktober 2019.

Christine Best, M.A., studied Gerontology at the University of Vechta, Aging Societies at the Technical University of Dortmund. Researcher in the research area of labour policy and health at the Social Research Centre Dortmund, ZWE of the TU Dortmund, tutor at the Apollon University of Applied Sciences in Bremen, member of the Dortmunder Forum Frau und Wirtschaft e. V. (Dortmund Forum for Women and Business).

Latest Publications:

Best, C. (forthcoming). Workplace co-determination under the sign of generational change: knowledge transfer in the event of a change of chairmanship in the works council. Sozialforschungsstelle Dortmund, Beiträge aus der Forschung, Vol. 204. Accessible online after publication at: http://www.sfs.tu-dortmund.de/sfs-Reihe/Band_204.pdf

Kerstin Guhlemann, M.A., studied Sociology and Media Studies at the Ruhr University Bochum. Coordinator of the research area Labour Policy and Health of the Social Research Center Dortmund, ZWE of the TU Dortmund, module supervisor at the Apollon University of Applied Sciences in Bremen, member of the DGS and working groups of the HBS and IGM.

Latest Publications:

Janda, V.; K. Guhlemann. 2019. visibility and implementation – digitalization amplifies known and generates new challenges for occupational safety and health (baua: Focus); Dortmund: Federal Institute for Occupational Safety and Health (BAuA). Accessed online: https://www.baua.de/DE/Angebote/Publikationen/Fokus/Digitalisierung.html.

Guhlemann, K. 2019. advocacy and co-determination in the digital transformation. In GfA. Hrsg. Arbeit interdisziplinär analysieren – bewerten – gestalten, Dortmund: GfA-Press, A.1.3.

Guhlemann, K.; A. Georg. 2019. effectiveness of occupational safety and health structures in the flexibilized world of work. In Kock, K. Eds. researching and shaping work. A cross-section of work research at the Social Research Center Dortmund. Beiträge aus der Forschung, vol. 201, pp. 24–35. Accessed online: http://www.sfs.tu-dortmund.de/sfs-Reihe/Band_201.pdf.

Get Online Week 2019 – An Intervention to Improve Digital Participation

Bastian Pelka and Study Group Get Online Week

Abstract

In the course of digitalisation, many lifeworlds are shifting to digital media. However, certain groups of people benefit less than others. This is where the Europe-wide campaign "Get Online Week" comes in since 2010. Students of Rehabilitation Education at TU Dortmund University participated in this campaign for the fifth time in a row in March 2019, offering around 40 free courses on digital topics for disadvantaged people. The aim was to sensitize society to digital exclusion and to impart media competence to target groups as well as to social and health care institutions. The subsequent evaluation examined the effectiveness and sustainability of the interventions (survey of participants and guideline-based interviews in institutions). The article presents the evaluation results and outlines approaches for transferring the campaign to other institutions.

Study Group Get Online Week: Julia Heidegger, Hannah Klamroth, Friederike Kober, Hannah Leibig, Henrike Naß, Larissa Oliverio, Adina Pauksch, Nathalie Schmitte, Cynthia Seemann, Floriane Thies, Pia Wolf, Ina Zawadka

B. Pelka (✉) · Study Group Get Online Week
Social Research Center Dortmund, TU Dortmund, Dortmund, Germany
e-mail: bastian.pelka@tu-dortmund.de

H.-W. Franz et al. (eds.), *Sustainable Living and Business*,
https://doi.org/10.1007/978-3-658-41835-9_15

1 Introduction

As part of the project studies of the degree programme Rehabilitation Education at the TU Dortmund University, students work on a professional field-oriented project for two semesters, in which they scientifically investigate a rehabilitation education issue (Technische Universität Dortmund, Faculty of Rehabilitation Sciences 2018, p. 4). This report presents the results of the project *Get Online Week Dortmund – 2019 (GOW Dortmund)*, which 12 students conducted in the winter semester 2018/2019 and summer semester 2019 under the supervision of Dr. Bastian Pelka.

The "Get Online Week" is an international campaign with the aim to draw attention to the social challenge of digital exclusion and to show ways to combat it. As part of the project study, the students acted as a local initiative of the campaign. They developed workshops for disadvantaged people and carried them out in Dortmund. In addition, the topic of digital participation was launched through accompanying public relations work.[1] This report describes the workshops and the didactic concepts on which they are based, but is also devoted to their scientific evaluation. The aim is to prepare the intervention itself, but also its conditions for success for possible transfer to other local campaigns and for subsequent student cohorts in Dortmund for imitation. The Get Online Week has already been carried out four times in Dortmund and documented three times (Becker et al. 2019; Pelka et al. 2016, 2017). This indicated first approaches of recommendations for the design of pedagogical interventions with the aim of strengthening digital competences of different marginalized target groups. For example, a strong individualisation of the workshop formats to the needs of the target group is recommended. Interviews with potential participants and employees in the institutions as well as job shadowing are suitable for this purpose. In addition, technical equipment should be checked and tested on site. A third block of measures concerns the adjustment of the number of participants to their socio-demographic characteristics and the contents of the workshops. The aim of this paper is to go beyond these recommendations and to point out steps that support the transfer.

In order to explain the necessity of the campaign, the theoretical background is first outlined with the starting point and problem situation as well as the current state of research. The following chapter presents the development of the campaign and the workshops.

The research design is then presented, which includes the development of the research question and the methodological approach. The following chapter presents the research results and carries out an evaluation so that the results can be used to answer the main and sub-questions. This is followed by a reflection on the de-

[1] The public relations activities of the project group will not be taken up further here, as they are not part of the study of rehabilitation sciences.

sign of the questionnaires. Finally, a conclusion of the *GOW Dortmund 2019* campaign is drawn with regard to rehabilitation education.

2 Theoretical Foundations

In this chapter, the social problem of the digital divide and its effects are first described and then substantiated by an explanation of the current state of research.

2.1 Initial Situation and Problems

Progressive digitalization is influencing more and more areas of society. Everyday activities are shifting to the Internet, and communication is also taking place to a large extent via digital media. Political participation and opinion-forming are also shifting online (Initiative D21 e. V. 2019, p. 21 ff.). The merging of different media technologies, known as media convergence, means that they are becoming increasingly compact, are permanently available everywhere and are used in many social contexts (Krotz and Hepp 2012, p. 7 f.). One example of this is the smartphone, which combines many different functions.

In addition to new opportunities, the development described above also leads to new risks and barriers that make it difficult or impossible for some people to access digital media and thus also information and communication technologies. A division in society is emerging, the so-called digital divide (Dudenhöfer and Meyen 2012, p. 7 f.). On the one hand, there are digitally included people who possess, use and benefit from digital skills. On the other hand, there are digitally excluded people who lack the necessary competencies, access or interest in digital environments or who cannot fully exploit their competencies. This can lead to digital exclusion. "The more digitisation becomes a natural part of most people's everyday lives, the more those on the sidelines lose out" (Initiative D21 e. V. 2019, p. 7 f.).

This is followed by a presentation of current research on the topic of the digital divide and a reference to its social consequences.

2.2 State of Research

The problem of the digital divide discussed above and the associated consequences can be demonstrated using various indices and studies. In the following, concise results are briefly presented.

The Digital Economy and Society Index (DESI) measurement tool describes the development of the digital society and economy in the EU countries (European

Commission 2019a). The level of digitalisation in the individual EU countries is recorded on the basis of five different categories. In an international comparison, Germany ranks 12th out of 29 in terms of the average score (European Commission 2019g, p. 1). Looking at the individual categories in more detail, we find the following results: The *human capital* category shows that 20 percent of Germans have only insufficient competencies in Internet use. For 5 percent, digital skills were even categorized as non-existent (European Commission 2019d, p. 6). The category of *digital public services,* on the other hand, shows that appointments with public offices are increasingly being arranged via websites (European Commission 2019b, p. 3 f.). It can be assumed that more and more digital procedures will potentially replace analogue alternatives to the greatest extent possible in the future (European Commission 2019b, p. 3) and that the exclusionary consequences for people with digital disadvantages will be more far-reaching. Therefore, as digitalisation continues, digital competences will become increasingly important in order to be able to situate oneself in today's society and to participate critically as well as safely in the diverse, digital opportunities (Vourkari and Punie 2016, p. 1).

Not only within the individual states, but also within the different population groups, strong differences become visible with regard to use and competences (European Commission 2019d, p. 6 ff.; 2019e, p. 4ff.; 2019f, p. 5 ff.). For these inequalities, the DESI identified correlations primarily in the categories of education, income and occupation (European Commission 2019c, p. 1).

These findings are also supported by the Digital Index (D21). The measuring instrument combines the categories of *access, usage behavior, competencies and openness* in Germany into one index value. The *access* category illustrates that technical equipment has improved significantly over the last five years. In the *competencies* category, it is clear that citizens' knowledge of digital topics has increased further on average compared to last year. In addition, the D21 records seven different user types, which are summarized in the three main groups of *digital pioneers, digital keepers* and *digital outsiders* (Initiative D21 e. V. 2019, p. 36 f.).

In Germany, 13 million people still belong to the last group of *digital offliners,* which in turn is divided into *offliners* and *minimal online users*. This group of people sees little or no advantage in using the Internet and is largely overwhelmed by Internet applications (Initiative D21 e. V. 2019, p. 35 f.). In the D21, aspects are mentioned that would make internet use easier for the so-called *offliners* according to their own statements. These include recognizing personal benefits (19 percent), learning how it works with the help of others (12 percent), easier use (11 percent), and better understanding of technical terms and functions (9 percent). 5 percent of respondents indicated that more knowledge about the protection of personal data online would be helpful for use (Initiative D21 e. V. 2019, p. 19). The D21 identifies gender, age and education as reasons for the existing differences between the various groups of people (Initiative D21 e. V. 2019, p. 38 f.). Due to the large differences within the German population, one continues to speak of the digital divide.

With regard to the participation of people with disabilities in the Internet, existing barriers have been examined in various studies. The Web 2.0 study was the first to survey people with disabilities who already use the Internet about their Internet applications and identified disability-related barriers (Aktion Mensch e. V. 2010, p. 10 ff.). For example, for deaf people who want to communicate via video telephony, download and upload speeds that are too low represent a barrier (Aktion Mensch e. V. 2010, p. 46f.). People with a visual impairment have major problems finding their way around the Internet in general and benefit from responsive web designs (Aktion Mensch e. V. 2010, p. 48f.). The study Mediennutzung von Menschen mit Behinderung (MMB 16) shows, among other things, that people with learning difficulties use the Internet less than people with physical disabilities. The research presented indicates that the population of people with impairments is restricted in their use by various barriers on the Internet, so that they are more likely to forego the applications. As a result, people with impairments are restricted in their participation in Internet-based applications (Bosse and Hasebrink 2016, p. 45 ff.).

In order for everyone to participate fully in the digital society and benefit from digitisation, it must be designed accordingly. Moreover, the teaching of media literacy must become an important social and political goal. Thus, the development of appropriate ways and means to counteract the digital divide and promote digital participation is needed. The *Get Online Week Dortmund* as part of the Europe-wide campaign *ALL DIGITAL Week* is one way to pursue the global goal of digital participation of all people and is explained in more detail below.

3 The Intervention: *Get Online Week Dortmund 2019*

3.1 The Campaign

The European *ALL DIGITAL Week* campaign started in 2010 under the name *Get Online Week*[2]. Every year since then, during the last week of March, workshops

[2] The original goal of introducing people to the online world has since been expanded by the umbrella organisation of digital learning centres coordinating the Europe-wide campaign (until 2018 "Telecentre Europe", then "All Digital") to the global goal of supporting people in the competent use of media. This change of goal was also reflected in the name in 2018

have been held in over 20 European countries to help participants achieve digital empowerment, i.e. the ability to use digital technologies profitably, independently and on their own. The activities take place in a wide variety of settings such as libraries, schools, community centres and non-profit organisations, and cover a wide range of content. Since its launch, the campaign has reached over one million people.

In 2015, the Dortmund location was added as part of the Europe-wide campaign. Here, students of rehabilitation education at TU Dortmund University develop workshops on digital topics together with Dr. Bastian Pelka as part of the project studies, which are evaluated after implementation. In 2018, the fourth *GOW Dortmund* reached 560 participants with 40 workshops on four topics in 30 institutions – conducted by 12 students within 7 days.

3.2 Workshops

The following is a brief description of the four workshops offered by *GOW Dortmund.*

- *#augenauf* (open your eyes) *– counter cyberbullying*

In this workshop, parents and students were sensitized to the topic of cyberbullying. To this end, the participants were taught practical skills that help them to recognise cyberbullying at an early stage and to deal with it appropriately. The workshop was conducted in two parts: as a parents' evening and as a workshop for students.

- *Facebook- and then?*

This workshop was aimed at people with disabilities and introduced the participants interactively to a safe handling of Facebook. Through practical assistance, the necessary skills were acquired and expanded.

- *Online to the job*

when "Get Online Week" was renamed "All Digital Week". However, the students decided to continue with the established name "Get Online Week" in Dortmund.

In this workshop, the tools around the topic of "online applications" were taught interactively. Contents of the course included practical exercises and the creation of checklists for later use. The workshop was aimed at all those who are looking for a job, whether to start a career or after a period of unemployment.

- *GoTalkNow*

This workshop provided skills for using the Talker app "GoTalkNow". Furthermore, helpful tips on the use of digitally supported communication were given. The workshop was aimed at teachers and, if necessary, also at integration assistants and parents.

4 Research Design

The aim of this essay is to describe the local campaign in a way that lends itself to replication. To this end, the paper goes beyond a mere description of the interventions and evaluates them. The assumption is that an evaluation of the effects and conditions of success of the campaign is important for potential imitators. It was also known from previous GOW campaigns and their evaluations that cooperating institutions are interested in questions of sustainability of the interventions: How can the effects of the workshops be perpetuated for the participants, but also for the cooperating institutions? These contexts of use guided the research design described below for the evaluation of the workshops designed and offered in the project.

4.1 Research Questions

The following research question was formulated quasi as an operationalization of the imitation interests: To *what extent can the workshops offered within the framework of the GOW Dortmund contribute sustainably to an increase in digital participation?*

Three sub-questions were then developed to provide methodological support for this main question:

1. *How can the workshops be designed to increase the digital literacy of the participants?*
2. *What aspects in the different workshops can bring about sustainability?*

3. *How does the usage behaviour of the participants change with regard to digital media?*

The aforementioned research questions served as guiding principles throughout the research process and were to be answered in the course of the evaluation. From the point of view of the project group, the increase of digital competences, the sustainability of the contents conveyed as well as the change in user behaviour represent central components of digital participation. Accordingly, the answers to the three sub-questions should allow contextual conclusions to be drawn about the main question. In addition, a total of nine hypotheses were derived from theory, assigned to the sub-questions. These are addressed in detail in Sect. 5.

4.2 Methodological Approach

In accordance with the formulated research interest, a quantitative research approach was chosen. The data was collected through a written survey of all workshop participants. Since the increase in media competencies, their sustainable effect and the change in usage behaviour were relevant for answering the research questions, the project group decided to conduct a longitudinal study (panel research). As a result, the implementation of a pre- and posttest as well as a follow-up were determined. Thus, the survey was conducted at a total of three measurement points: before the workshops, immediately afterwards and a third time another 5–6 weeks later.

4.2.1 Research Instrument

The project group used written questionnaires to collect the data. Since the contents of the workshops and the associated competencies varied greatly, these questionnaires were developed in two parts. One main questionnaire covered workshop-wide statements in order to ensure comparability of the entire sample. A respective supplementary sheet specifically identified competencies related to each workshop. A separate main questionnaire with different statements was designed for each of the three survey dates. The supplementary sheets, on the other hand, were identical at all survey points.

In principle, the questionnaires were written in *plain language.* The project group decided to use a rating scale for frequencies and evaluations as an answer option for all formulated statements (with the exception of socio-demographic data). This was chosen as a four-point scale to avoid neutral responses. For the ratings, the gradations were supported by coloured smileys to increase the comprehensibility and thus the reliability of the answers. In order to counteract the feeling of being forced to answer, the answer option *no information/ I don't know* was additionally offered. For all questionnaires, a closed answer format was chosen in order to offer a simple comparability of the sample and to facilitate the evaluation.

4.2.2 Sample

The basic population of the research consists of all 560 participants of the workshops, of which 532 could be considered for the evaluation. It includes on the one hand pupils of the third, fourth and seventh grade and partly their parents as well as a large number of professionals. The sample also includes people with cognitive impairments and people with mental impairments, as well as digitally disadvantaged adults and young people. Overall, this represents a heterogeneous sample. As a rule, homogeneous samples can be identified in the individual workshops.

4.2.3 Evaluation Methods

Data collection based on questionnaires T0 (before the workshop), T1 (immediately after the workshop) and T2 (5–6 weeks after) was followed by data analysis using *IBM SPSS Statistics (SPSS)* statistical software.

In the following chapter, the results as well as their analysis and interpretation are presented in detail.

4.2.4 Gaining Competence

The competence gain of the participants was determined by the values of the supplementary sheets (cf. Sect. 4.2.1). These were added up at time T0 and compared with the values of the subsequent survey points. A competence point describes the change by one scale unit. In order to obtain an unbiased result, persons who had *not* ticked *any box* could not be taken into account. The differences between the competence scores at time T1 and T0 or T2 and T1 result in a value that represents the average competence gain per workshop. The competence gain at time T1 is abbreviated as *KompGewT1 in* the following, the competence gain at time T2 as *KompGewT2*. A *KompGewT1* of 2 points means that the participants had on average 2 competence points more at time T1 than at time T0.

The competence development of the individual workshops can be compared by showing the *averaged* competence gains per question in Fig. 1. They are shown at the survey times T0, T1 and T2. For example, at time T1 the participants of the workshop *GoTalkNow* stand at an average of 3.58 points (between *agree rather* and *agree completely*) per question.

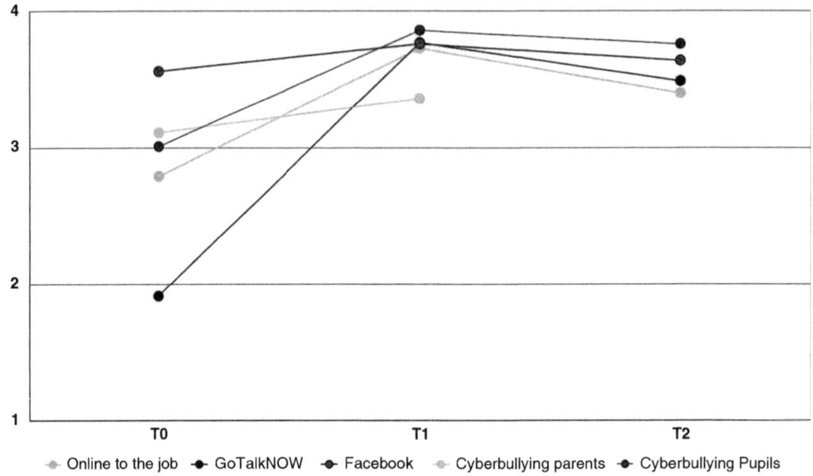

Fig. 1 Averaged skill gains at time points T0, T1, T2. (Own representation)

At time T2, the competence gain of the participants of the parent workshop #augenauf – *Cybermobbing begegnen* could not be determined, as none of the 12 questionnaires of the parents answered this question.

5 Research Results

This chapter presents the results of the evaluation. Based on these results, the research question: *To what extent can the workshops offered as part of the GOW contribute sustainably to an increase in digital participation?* will then be answered. The chapter is thus also intended to provide potential imitators of the campaign with indications of conditions for success and possibilities for improvement.

The basis for the analysis and interpretation of the results was the evaluation of the questionnaires using the statistical software *IBM SPSS Statistics* (SPSS). The results are presented, analysed and interpreted according to the respective hypotheses. The hypotheses represent well-founded assumptions derived from theory, the testing of which should facilitate the answering of the research questions.

5.1 Answer to the First Sub-Question

This chapter addresses the first two hypotheses, which will *be* addressed by the first sub-question: *How can workshops be designed* to *increase participants' digital literacy?*

Hypothesis 1: The framework conditions of the workshops (number of participants, duration, premises) must be suitable for the target group in order to increase competences.

The statement: "I liked the room, the group size and the duration of the course" was fully or rather agreed with by 91 percent of all participants. Based on the positive feedback received by the teams after the workshops and the participants' high level of satisfaction with the framework conditions, it can be assumed that the framework conditions had a positive effect on the gain in competence.

Hypothesis 2: For competences to be increased, both knowledge and the practical applicability of this knowledge must be imparted (theory-practice transfer).

Overall, 78.2 percent of the participants agreed that they were able to actively participate in the workshops and learned something new. This shows that the goal of making the workshops practice-oriented was achieved. A transfer of knowledge by linking theory and practice has taken place.

Result of sub-question 1:

The interpretation of the results from the cross tables, the frequency distributions as well as the feedback from the institutions show that a precise agreement with the cooperation partners and the resulting target group-oriented design of the workshops have a positive effect on the transfer of knowledge. Furthermore, these results confirm that a practice-oriented workshop, which takes up the theoretically imparted knowledge, has a positive effect on the learning success.

5.2 Answer to the Second Sub-Question

In the course of this chapter, the second sub-question: *Which aspects in the different workshops can bring about sustainability?* will be analysed and answered by verifying hypotheses 3 to 7.

Hypothesis 3: Through an interactive workshop design, learning content can be conveyed more sustainably.

At survey time T2, 72.6 percent of the participants agreed both that they were able to actively participate in shaping the workshop they attended and that they could still remember the content taught after six weeks. Furthermore, 64.1 percent still remembered after six weeks that they had the opportunity to actively participate in shaping the workshop, as well as that they were still applying the content taught. It can be seen that interactive participation in the workshop by the participants both "stayed in their heads" and led to the contents being conveyed more sustainably.

Hypothesis 4: In order to achieve sustainability, the workshops must be practice-oriented.

The correlations between the variables of sustainability and practical orientation were clearly recorded as positive. Here, the findings on the question of whether the participants were able to actively participate in the workshop are used once again to operationalise the practical orientation: 64.1 percent of the respondents stated that they were able to actively participate in the workshop as well as that they were still using the workshop contents after six weeks. It can be seen that a practice-oriented workshop can positively influence the sustainable applicability of the workshop content.

Hypothesis 5: The materials used support the deepening of the learning content.

91.3 percent of the respondents found the materials used in the workshop helpful and useful. 79.6 percent of the respondents at time T2 who felt the materials were good were still able to remember the contents of the workshops after six weeks. 71.1 percent of the participants who rated the materials positively further agreed with the statement that they were still using the workshop contents after six weeks. In conclusion, it can be said that the design of the materials has a positive effect on the learning success of the participants.

Hypothesis 6: Materials for further use that can be referred to in the long term increase the lasting learning effect.

A total of 78 percent of respondents indicated that they were still using the developed materials as a resource after six weeks. 66.1 percent of the participants stated that they found the handouts helpful, they were able to remember the learning content and were still using the workshop content after six weeks. An appealing handout thus contributes to a sustainable learning effect, because the workshop content is consolidated through constant repetition with the help of the handouts.

Hypothesis 7: The workshops should arouse the interest and motivation of the participants to continue to apply the learning content taught there.

At survey time T1, 89.3 percent of all participants fully or somewhat agreed that they would continue to apply the learning content taught in the workshops. At survey time T2, 78.3 percent of the 401 respondents stated that they would still apply the learning content. The cross tabulation of the two items shows that 73.1 percent of the participants agreed with both statements. It can thus be concluded that the content taught in the workshops was both interesting and useful for the target groups.

Result sub-question 2:

Five aspects that bring about sustainability could be identified: the interactive design of the workshops, the practical orientation of the workshops, the workshop delivery materials, the materials for further use, and the arousal of interest and motivation among participants during the workshop. Each of these aspects was included in the research with an associated hypothesis. The hypotheses were investigated and could be verified, thus sub-question 2 can be finally answered. It can be stated that all mentioned aspects positively influence the sustainable learning effect.

5.3 Answer to the Third Sub-Question

The following chapter answers the question *How does the usage behaviour of the participants change with regard to digital media?*

Hypothesis 8: The variation of digital media used has increased.

To test this hypothesis, six items on usage behavior were asked at the time points T0 and T2. The participants indicated how often they use search engines, online shopping, entertainment services or social networks and how often they chat or play online games. It is worth mentioning that the participants' usage behaviour changed in the areas that were addressed in the workshops. However, the hypothesis could not be clearly verified. Due to imprecise items in the questionnaires, no variation in usage behaviour could be measured. Only a shift in the frequencies in the areas could be determined.

Hypothesis 9: Participants will continue to engage with the content taught even after a longer period of time.

84.8 percent of the participants at time T2 agreed that they can remember the contents taught in the workshop. 78.3 percent stated that they would continue to use what they had learned in the workshop. This suggests that the content taught was adapted to the needs of the participants.

Outcome Sub-question 3:

It can be seen that the results obtained do not allow a clear interpretation of a change in usage behaviour. The questions asked in the questionnaire do not provide any meaningful results to answer hypothesis 8. However, tendencies in the variation of usage behaviour suggest that the learning content taught has an influence on a reduction or increase in the use of digital media. Hypothesis 9 can be verified more clearly as the items are exactly aligned with the hypothesis. The results show that the participants continue to use the learned content even a longer time after attending the workshops.

5.4 Answer to the Main Question

The following is a concluding answer to the main question.

The main question: To *what extent can the workshops offered as part of the GOW Dortmund contribute sustainably to an increase in digital participation?* can now be answered with the help of our empirical survey results. The results show that the practice-oriented teaching of learning content has just as positive an influence on the learning of theoretical knowledge as does a target group-oriented design of the framework conditions. It was found that a practice-oriented workshop in which the participants have opportunities to shape the content positively influences the sustainable applicability of the workshop content. Materials linked to the content and designed with the target group in mind have a positive influence on the learning effect both during and after the workshop. Interest in the workshop content persists and motivates further independent application. The results show that target group-oriented and interest-driven workshops have contributed to a sustainable increase in digital participation.

With regard to the questionnaires, it was noticed positively that they were designed in a target group-oriented way and were easy to understand due to the *simple language and* smileys. The questionnaires had a high recognition value due to their uniform design and wording, which was particularly advantageous at time T2 after the workshops.

During the transfer of the questionnaires into *plain language*, compromises had to be made in the complexity of the items, which had a negative effect on their validity. As a result, not all hypotheses could be answered adequately or using different items. One item had to be used twice, which meant that the specificity of the interpretations was lost.

Due to the panel design of the study, questionnaires of the same participants from different waves had to be assigned to each other. In order to guarantee the anonymity of the respondents, a code system was used that was based on characteristics of the respondents unknown to the researchers (first letter of the first name of the mother and father, own year of birth, see Sect. 4.2.2). Critically, the assignment of individual codes on each questionnaire resulted in a large dropout rate. Contrary to expectations and the results from the pretests, there was a high error rate in the creation of the codes, meaning that a large proportion of the panel mortality can be explained by this. In order to minimize the errors, the sample codes require a more detailed description. Alternatively, the anonymised list of participants, which is also used, can be used (Sect. 4.2.2). The questionnaires that were coded using simple numbering could be assigned more clearly.

6 Conclusion

In addition to psychosocial support, nursing and care for its clientele, rehabilitation education is primarily dedicated to promoting their participation in all areas of social life. In the course of digitalisation, many areas of life are shifting into the digital world. Technological innovations offer new forms and opportunities for participation. In order to promote these, rehabilitation educators must combine their knowledge of the clientele and the application of the technologies.

This year's campaign reached a total of over 500 people with 40 workshops in Dortmund and the surrounding area. The heterogeneity of the target groups, which includes both the previous digital knowledge and the socio-demographic backgrounds of the participants, required a high degree of flexibility during the planning and implementation of the workshops. Overall, it can be stated that the project group was able to gather both action and research-relevant knowledge against the background of scientific working methods with the implementation and evaluation of the *GOW Dortmund.* Furthermore, the design of the interventions made it possible to work in an individual-centred way. This gave the students the opportunity to gain practical experience in the field of rehabilitation education.

Various success factors and challenges were outlined for potential replicators of the campaign – including subsequent cohorts of students. The reports of the 2018 (Becker et al. 2019), 2017 (Pelka et al., 2017), and 2016 (Pelka et al. 2016) campaigns are recommended for further reading.

References

Aktion Mensch e. V., Hrsg. 2010. *Web 2.0/ barrierefrei. Eine Studie zur Nutzung von Web 2.0 Anwendungen durch Menschen mit Behinderung*. Bonn: Aktion Mensch.

Becker, Manuela, A. Benner, K. Borg, J. Hüls, M. Koch, A. Kost, A. Korn, M.C. Lueg, D. Osthoff, B. Pelka, C. Rosenberger, H. Sattler. 2019. How to Design an Intervention to Raise Digital Competences: ALL DIGITAL Week – Dortmund 2018. In: Antona, M. und Stephanidis C. (eds) Universal Access in Human-Computer Interaction. Theory, Methods and Tools. HCII 2019. Lecture Notes in Computer Science, vol. 11572. Springer, Cham.

Bosse, I., und U. Hasebrink. 2016. *Mediennutzung von Menschen mit Behinderung. Forschungsbericht.* http://www.kme.tu-dortmund.de/cms/de/Aktuelles/aeltere-Meldungen/Studie-Mediennutzung-von-Menschen-mit-Behinderung-MMB16_/Studie-Mediennutzung_Langfassung_final.pdf. Zugegriffen: 16. Januar 2019.

Dudenhöfer, K., und M. Meyen. 2012. Digitale Spaltung im Zeitalter der Sättigung. Eine Sekundäranalyse der ACTA 2008 zum Zusammenhang von Internetnutzung und sozialer Ungleichheit. *Publizistik – Vierteljahreshefte für Kommunikationsforschung* 1: 7–26.

European Commission. 2019a. *DESI 2019 – Key Findings.* https://ec.europa.eu/digital-single-market/en/desi. Zugegriffen: 23. Juni 2019.

European Commission. 2019b. *Digital Economy and Society Index Report 2019. Digital Public Services.* https://ec.europa.eu/digital-single-market/en/desi. Zugegriffen: 12. Juni 2019.

European Commission. 2019c. *Digital Economy and Society Index Report 2019. Digital Scoreboard Visualization.* http://bit.ly/2F46bhQ. Zugegriffen: 12. Juni 2019.

European Commission. 2019d. *Digital Economy and Society Index Report 2019. Human Capital. Digital Inclusion and Skills.* https://ec.europa.eu/digital-single-market/en/desi. Zugegriffen: 12. Juni 2019.

European Commission. 2019e. *Digital Economy and Society Index Report 2019. Integration of Digital Technology.* https://ec.europa.eu/digital-single-market/en/desi. Zugegriffen: 12. Juni 2019.

European Commission. 2019f. *Digital Economy and Society Index Report 2019. Use of Internet Services.* https://ec.europa.eu/digital-single-market/en/desi. Zugegriffen: 12. Juni 2019.

European Commission. 2019g. *The Digital Economy and Society Index. Desi 2019.* https://ec.europa.eu/digital-single-market/en/desi. Zugegriffen: 23. Juni 2019.

Initiative D21 e. V., Hrsg. 2019. *D21 Digital Index 2018/2019. Jährliches Lagebild zur Digitalen Gesellschaft.* https://initiatived21.de/publikationen/d21-digital-index-2018-2019/. Zugegriffen: 27. Mai 2019.

Krotz, F. und A. Hepp. 2012. *Mediatisierte Welten: Beschreibungsansätze und Forschungsfelder.* Wiesbaden: VS Verlag für Sozialwissenschaften.

Pelka, Bastian und Projektgruppe Get Online Week 2017. Hrsg. Get Online Week 2017. Eine Woche zur Verbesserung der digitalen Teilhabe in Dortmund. Beiträge aus der Forschung. Dortmund. Online: http://www.sfs.tu-dortmund.de/sfs-Reihe/Band_198.pdf.

Pelka, Bastian und Projektgruppe Get Online Week Dortmund 2016 (2016): Get Online Week Dortmund 2016. Eine Woche zur Verbesserung der digitalen Teilhabe in Dortmund. Sfs Eigenverlag, Beiträge aus der Forschung. Online: http://www.sfs.tu-dortmund.de/sfs-Reihe/Band_195.pdf.

Technische Universität Dortmund, Fakultät Rehabilitationswissenschaften. 2018. *Handbuch. Kompetenzorientiertes und selbständiges Lernen im BA Rehabilitationspädagogik,* Aufl. 4. https://www.fk-reha.tu-dortmund.de/fk13/de/Studium_und_Lehre/Projektstudium/20180619-Handbuch_Broschuere_Projektstudium.pdf. Zugegriffen: 13. Juni 2019.

Vourkari, R. und Y. Punie, Hrsg. 2016. *JRC Science for Policy Report. Der Referenzrahmen für digitale Kompetenzen für Verbraucher.* Luxemburg: Amt für Veröffentlichungen.

Bastian Pelka, Dr. phil. Studied communication science, sociology, political science in Münster. Lectureships in Münster, Hanover, Bielefeld, Dortmund. Dr. Pelka conducts research at the Sozialforschungsstelle Dortmund, central scientific institution of the TU Dortmund University, on the topics of (digital) social innovation, digital inclusion, professional orientation and acts there as coordinator of the research area “Work and Education in Europe”. Dr. Pelka teaches at the Faculty of Rehabilitation Sciences at TU Dortmund University on the topic of digital participation and digital media for empowerment of marginalized groups of people.

Latest Publications:

Tamami Komatsu Cipriani, C. Kaletka; B. Pelka. 2019. transition through design: enabling innovation via empowered ecosystems, In: European Planning Studies, https://doi.org/10.1080/09654313.2019.1680612.

Bosse, Ingo; D. Krüger; H. Linke; B. Pelka. 2019. the maker movement’s potential for an inclusive society. In Jürgen Howaldt; C. Kaletka; A. Schröder; M. Zirngiebl. Eds. Atlas of Social Innovation. second Volume: A World of New Practices. 2019. munich: oekom.

Eckhardt, Jennifer; C. Kaletka; B. Pelka. 2018. observations on the role of digital social innovation for inclusion. In Technology and Disability, vol. 29, no. 4, pp. 183–198, 2018. https://doi.org/10.3233/tad-170183. Online: https://content.iospress.com/articles/technology-and-disability/tad170183

A Story About Storytellers – Innovation Potentials in Community Foundations and Volunteer Agencies

Janine Kuhnt

Abstract

How do community foundations and voluntary agencies, taking into account their organizational constitution, fulfill the innovation function attributed to them by promoting engagement? With a look at the social science discourse around the "newer" organizations that promote engagement (Roß/Roth, Engagement und Zivilgesellschaft, Springer Fachmedien Wiesbaden, Wiesbaden, p. 225, 2018; Klein et al., Engagementpolitik. Die Entwicklung der Zivilgesellschaft als politische Aufgabe, VS Verlag für Sozialwissenschaften, Wiesbaden, p. 55, 2010; Jakob, Engagementpolitik. Die Entwicklung der Zivilgesellschaft als politische Aufgabe, VS Verlag für Sozialwissenschaften, Wiesbaden, p. 233, 2010), this question is explored in a secondary analytical way. In doing so, empirical data will be used to assess the organizational forms of community foundations and volunteer agencies with regard to their constitution, which favors the fulfillment of the innovation function attributed to them. The relevant aspects of the secondary analysis include both quantitative data such as the number of organisations, their financial resources and personnel structure, as well as qualitative data generated from scientific findings on the self-assessment of the professionals working in the organisations and their organisational environment (e.g. Wolf and Zimmer, Lokale Engagementförderung, VS Verlag für Sozialwissenschaften, Wiesbaden, 2012; Speck et al. 2012). As a result, it is clear that organisational forms are gaining in importance quantita-

J. Kuhnt (✉)
Institute of Educational Science, Friedrich Schiller University Jena, Jena, Germany
e-mail: janine.kuhnt@uni-jena.de

H.-W. Franz et al. (eds.), *Sustainable Living and Business*,
https://doi.org/10.1007/978-3-658-41835-9_16

tively and releasing innovation potential qualitatively. Legitimacy for innovations is especially created in organizations through the "telling" of a credible or a "success story" (Luhmann, Organisation und Entscheidung. 3rd edition, VS Verlag, Wiesbaden, p. 440, 2011). In the competitive social economy, the organization that gains advantages is the one that is *perceived* as innovative(er) by the funders. Resource-rich donors act as the *fuel of* innovation in organizations, and at the same time the resource endowment of committed individuals is a *prerequisite for* their commitment and thus also for the possibility of co-deciding on *legitimate* innovations.

1 Introduction

> It becomes clear that traditional forms of engagement (such as within churches and other religious institutions) continue to exist, can assert themselves and are essential, but that diverse new and innovative forms of engagement are also developing or are needed under changed conditions. It is these changed spheres of life and social conditions that must be increasingly shaped on the part of politics and those active in the promotion of engagement in order to enable engagement and participation in traditional and/or innovative forms for all people. (BMFSFJ 2017, P. 39)

The quote from the "Second Report on the Development of Civic Involvement in the Federal Republic of Germany" indicates a mandate for action for political actors and those active in promoting involvement, which is aimed at developing innovative forms of involvement and enabling participation through innovative forms of involvement promotion. The engagement-promoting organisations (EPOs) that can be identified locally differ in terms of their organisational structures, their "missions" and guiding principles, their staffing and financial resources, their histories and their local visibility. As traditional EPOs, for example, the welfare associations and their member organisations have a local presence, which is expressed in the fact that, supported by the principle of subsidiarity and their legal recognition in §§ 3, 4 SGB VIII – for the provision of services within the framework of youth welfare – they are accorded a "privileged" position in terms of regulatory and funding policy. The associations benefit from this position when it comes to the provision of services for compulsory tasks within the framework of youth welfare. At the same time, the welfare associations with their facilities and services can point to a diverse and decades-long tradition of engagement (cf. Backhaus-Maul et al. 2015, p. 15). According to the most recent overall statistics of the Bundesarbeitsgemeinschaft der Freien Wohlfahrtspflege e. V. (BAGFW)

(2018, p. 6), the largest area of engagement is youth welfare with 35 percent of all facilities, followed by elderly welfare and disability welfare with 16 percent each of all facilities in which both full-time employees and volunteers are deployed. Fields of activity in welfare organisations in which people volunteer include organising and running events, practical work, committee and management work, as well as public relations and administrative activities (cf. Backhaus-Maul et al. 2015, p. 485).

In addition to the "traditional" contexts in which engagement is promoted, two organizational forms can be observed empirically that can be described as comparatively new. In social science discourse, citizens' foundations and volunteer agencies are considered "newer" and "more modern" organizational forms for promoting local engagement (Roß and Roth 2018, p. 225; Klein et al. 2010, p. 55; Jakob 2010, p. 233). The genuine organisational purpose of both forms of organisation is directed towards promoting local engagement. Engagement, on the one hand, functions as a social and organisational resource, especially when it is integrated by EPOs for social, person-centred service delivery (Kuhnt 2018). Furthermore, engagement is ascribed an *innovation function* (Liebig and Rauschenbach 2010, p. 267). The innovative power of engagement is based on its function as a "seismograph of social conditions" (ibid.). This function is based on the potential for criticism by those involved, who organise themselves in many different ways (from citizens' movements and self-help associations to club and association structures), in relation to state grievances and on the assumption of personal responsibility (ibid.). In this context, the state assumes a "guarantee responsibility" (Schönig 2006, p. 27) for social services, to which special importance is attached in the promotion of engagement within the framework of a state activation policy (ibid.). Citizens' foundations and voluntary agencies, which emerge parallel to other EPOs, could be understood in this context as organisational forms of an "activated citizens' society", which contribute locally to the development of "innovative" solutions for social service needs by activating the personal responsibility of the users of public services (on this Kessl 2006, p. 71). *How they fulfil the innovation function, taking into account their organisational constitution, by promoting commitment,* is largely unanswered.[1]

[1] Two exceptions are the study by Annette Barth (2012) and the dissertation by André Christian Wolf (2009). The former examines, on the basis of a qualitative case study, the tensions between (politically desired) demands placed on the organizational form of "community foundations" and their realization in a selected region of Baden-Württemberg. The statement that innovation in itself is not a value and cannot sufficiently legitimize the existence of an organization (ibid., p. 33) is relativized in the process – and this should be anticipated at this point – in that a credible narrative about the redemption of the innovation function, assuming

In the following, an understanding of innovations is first presented. In the following, based on a secondary analysis of empirical data, the organisational forms of community foundations and voluntary agencies are examined with regard to their constitution, which favours the fulfilment of the innovation function attributed to them. The relevant aspects of the secondary analysis include quantitative data such as the number of organisations, their financial resources and personnel structure, as well as qualitative data generated from scientific findings on the self-assessment of the professionals working in the organisations and their organisational environment. Finally, a field of tension is outlined, which can be understood as a critical answer to the leading question and the expectation of innovative forms of engagement cited at the beginning as enabling participation of as *many* people as possible.

2 Innovations or a History of Irritable Organizations

In social science discourse, the term innovation is discussed in particular for researching and analysing organisational or entrepreneurial action and with reference to social challenges to be solved. It is discussed in the context of the design of "new welfare arrangements" (Brinkmann 2010, p. 118), of networks (cf. Straßheim 2013), of the potential of narratives to initiate organisational change and learning processes (cf. Fahrenwald 2013, p. 87f.), and as discourse and social practice in organisations, i.e. with a view to changing social practices in and around organisations, taking into account actor relations and arrangements (Weber 2018). Innovations are viewed in terms of organisational structures and processes, and innovation management – from an organisational pedagogical perspective – in terms of "the presuppositional nature of the new in structural, procedural, methodological, (organisational) cultural and discursive settings" (Weber 2018, p. 521).

In nonprofit organizations (NPOs), the concept of innovation raises both the question of the quality and the impact of (social) person-related services. Although the impact is primarily developed outside the own organization (cf. Schuhen 2009, p. 108f.), within the organizations the impact as quality question of their services

the reciprocity of organization and environment, does have an existential character for infrastructural institutions that promote engagement; namely, when social impact is also narrated via innovativeness and held out in prospect, and thus the self-purpose of the organization can be assumed to be fulfilled or not. Through an analysis of case studies, Wolf (2009) points out that the term "originality" is more appropriate than the concept of innovation, since the civic foundations studied do not primarily initiate innovations, but rather change processes and test concepts (ibid., p. 217).

arises. The impact discussion is a quality discussion in a different guise (Rock 2017, p. 109). Investments are made in those areas and services that promise impact and "pay off", taking into account quality claims. The fulfilment of the innovation function represents a competitive advantage for the organisations of the social economy:

> The ability of charities to meet the needs of their target groups economically and with high quality, and thus to be competitive, stands and falls with innovative capacity, also in the social economy. (Nowoczyn 2017, p. 8)

Then (2017, p. 41) cites the criteria of *need, urgency and legitimacy* for determining social innovations in order to clarify how welfare organisations relate to social innovations and to innovation impulses from different origins. According to this, innovations must be oriented towards a need that must be articulated and negotiated (ibid., p. 51); "this need must be accompanied by a social perception of urgency, and the approach must be considered legitimate" (ibid., p. 40). Legitimacy and an associated possibility of mobilising resources to implement innovations should furthermore be generated on the basis of performance competition, i.e. an orientation towards the effectiveness of problem solutions (ibid., p. 51).

An indication of the prominence of the issue of impact and the relevance of public presentation on the one hand, and the self-authentication of the (social) impact of community foundations and voluntary agencies on the other, is provided by quality seals (e.g. from PHINEO, bagfa or the Association of German Foundations). According to these, NPOs are considered to be effective if changes can be observed in the abilities, opportunities for action or living conditions of the target groups of their services (outcome) or in society (impact) (cf. PHINEO gAG 2014, p. 6f.).

The[2] intermediary function of NPOs and the existing relationship to other actors in this context mean that innovations do not only trigger goodwill and/or resistance within an organisation, but also outside it. The management level in NPOs is of particular importance for dealing constructively with resistance to innovation. On the one hand, the importance of the leadership level is rooted in the "core dilemma of management and governance of nonprofit organizations" (Schröer 2009, p. 148), according to which NPOs "serve" multiple stakeholder groups, which in turn often have contradictory interests and needs and thus also place different expectations of success on the organizations (ibid., p. 149). On the other hand, "... it is not only about the financial return, but also about the fulfilment of the organisation's mis-

[2] For typical concerns and objections to innovation ideas, such as 'ingrained cultures' in organisations or the need to justify them to their controlling bodies, see Kerka et al. (2012, p. 253 f.).

sion, its social impact or its sustainability." (ibid., p. 148). In this regard, the unfolding of social impact is not only a measure of the fulfilment of the innovation function of organisations, but challenges the level of management of organisations. Management's actions generate legitimacy gains when stakeholders, supported by reciprocity, see their expectations fulfilled. The core dilemma of management is met in organizations by filing away at the organizational façade "to meet, at least on the surface, the different expectations." (Kühl 2011, p. 142).

Innovations in NPOs thus appear as discursive constructions, which are superficially expressed in the self-description (and self-exaggeration, if innovative capacity is linked to competitiveness) of the organisations and are primarily based on imitation processes within the organisation. Krücken (2006, p. 269f.) formulates this "play" aptly from a perspective of neo-institutionalist organizational research: "While, metaphorically speaking, novelty, innovation and uniqueness are played out on the social front stage, primarily copying, imitation and structural alignment processes take place on the back stage."

Empirically, both a complete copy and a complete rejection of an innovation proposal are rare; rather, it is to be expected that, taking into account the specific organisational and application contexts, recombinations, hybridisations and miscopies will arise (ibid., p. 270). Innovations would then be a "'paradoxical effect' of mimetic behaviour" (ibid., p. 271), in that structures *perceived* as successful are copied and conditionally labelled as new by the context in which they are produced. Through processes of copying, imitation, and structural alignment, organizations prove irritable on the backstage. Irritation pays off in the form of innovation and "above all in that it forces a decision in the first place and that innovations that are tested or rejected ('for which the time is not yet ripe') are then also retained in the system memory." (Luhmann 2011, p. 220).

For the organizational forms of community foundations and volunteer agencies, the question arises as to how they generate innovations from *needs that are* perceived as *urgent by* society, which (due to their assumed effect) generate *legitimacy.* Or, to put it differently, the question arises as to how they fulfil the *innovation function* attributed to them, i.e. how they allow themselves to be *irritated in a* self- and external-referential way.

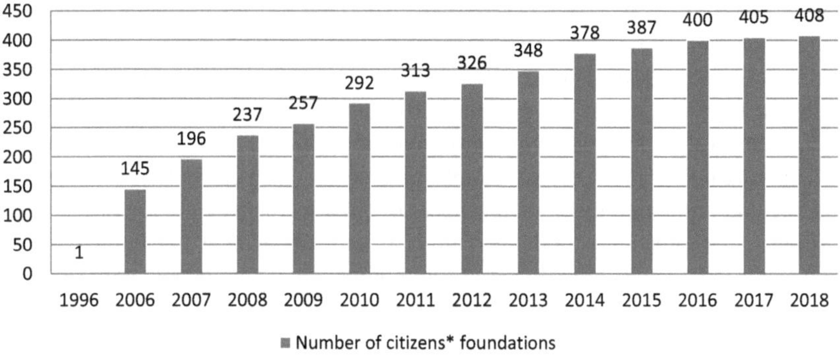

Fig. 1 Development of community foundations in Germany

3 Citizens' Foundations

Citizens' foundations are part of organised civil society[3], which, based on the US model of the community foundation, have now also been established in Germany since 1996 with the establishment of the first citizens' foundation in Gütersloh (cf. Figure 1).

(Source: Own representation based on the data of the continuously published reports of the Stiftung Aktive Bürgerschaft: "Länderspiegel Bürgerstiftungen Fakten und Trends" [published 2006 to 2014] or "Report Bürgerstiftungen Fakten und Trends" [published since 2015]).

According to their conception, community foundations are non-profit, economically and denominationally as well as party-politically independent organisations (cf. Bundesverband Deutscher Stiftungen 2000). The people organised in community foundations work at local or regional level for social issues in the areas of education and upbringing, art and culture, social affairs, health and sport and, since 2015 in particular, also for the integration of people with refugee experience (cf. Stiftung Aktive Bürgerschaft 2017, p. 12; Wolf 2010, p. 106). The form of project work is particularly relevant for actively shaping these areas of society (cf. Wolf

[3] In the discourse on structures that promote engagement, organised civil society includes clubs, associations and initiatives in which engaged individuals act as co-producers and co-designers of services within the framework of the municipal division of tasks and responsibilities (cf. Jakob 2010, p. 252). Since there is a lack of a uniform definition, foundations, non-profit limited liability companies and cooperatives are also counted as organised civil society, taking into account the legal form of EfO (cf. Priemer et al. 2019, p. 9).

and Zimmer 2012, p. 65). Local project work focuses on the fields of action "education and upbringing" (47 percent of the projects are located in this field of action) (Stiftung Aktive Bürgerschaft 2017, p. 7) and "refugee work" (ibid.); the latter has been part of the surveys since 2016 and is worked on as a focus topic in 20 percent of the surveyed community foundations (ibid.). The area of education and upbringing can include, for example, projects in which citizens are involved as reading and arithmetic mentors in schools in order to "convey the joy of reading, writing and arithmetic to children" (Bürgerstiftung Wiesloch 2019), in the context of which school books are purchased for children and young people with refugee experience in order to be able to use them in lessons (cf. Bürgerstiftung Bad Bentheim 2015) or scholarships are awarded to pupils "who, due to their family or social situation, need additional support to develop their potential" (Bielefelder Bürgerstiftung 2019). For the area of sport and health, the project "Sport in the Park" can be mentioned as an example, with the aim of pursuing health-promoting activities in nature (cf. Bürgerstiftung Gütersloh 2019). It is characteristic of the projects mentioned as examples that the community foundations – as project initiators and project sponsors – enter into cooperation with other local actors (including associations from the cultural and sports sector, schools, the municipality and universities). On the organisational level, the potential willingness of community foundations to cooperate with other local actors can be used to derive the hypothesis that there is a potential for innovation here. The cooperation of organizations and actors that are actually in competition with each other for resources (e.g. for financial resources, infrastructure, spokesperson positions in the political discourse, committed people) is innovative insofar as the participating organizations open up to each other and become more "permeable" in order to be able to react efficiently to local needs that are perceived as urgent, for example by bundling the resources of the participants. However, this potential for innovation through collaborations is fragile and prerequisite-rich; Priemer et al. (2019, p. 44), for example, summarise that in 2016 only just under a third of all foundations (including community foundations) entered into collaborations (31.8 per cent, n = 255), that foundations with a high foundation capital in particular entered into collaborations, that cooperation partners were primarily other foundations, and that "financial support" was usually given as the priority reason for collaborations. The relevance of cooperations that are entered into for financial reasons is also evident with regard to the founding phase and development of community foundations. In this context, reference can be made to the close cooperation of community foundations with cooperative banks. Cooperative banks are active in 252 community foundations in a founding capacity and in 147 community foundations in a funding capacity (BVR 2017). However, the close connection of community foundations to financial institutions is controversially discussed. For the community foundations, this connection may be advantageous in terms of securing financial resources. From the perspective of potential volunteers, however, this connection "could also discourage them from making their money and time available in this context" (Jakob 2010, p. 247).

Furthermore, the discourse on social innovations states that the major societal challenges will not be overcome without the organisation of cross-sectoral cooperation and networks (cf. Howaldt 2019, p. 18). This addresses not only the sectors in general – in the "ecosystem of social innovations" (ibid. 2019, p. 21), the sectors of civil society, politics, business and science are mentioned – but also the executive level of citizens' foundations. Finally, the implementation and long-term maintenance of collaborations requires people who organise, coordinate and mediate between the sectors. The staffing in community foundations makes it clear that full-time employees, i.e. those persons who could take on an organizing, coordinating and mediating function between sectors (also in the long term), tend to be in the minority. According to the Stiftung Aktive Bürgerschaft (2018b, p. 20), 180 full-time employees work in 70 community foundations, but mostly on a part-time basis. Although project work is usually the responsibility of full-time employees (cf. ibid.), the main human resources are volunteers. The involvement of volunteers takes place regularly in 68 percent of the organizations and occasionally in 32 percent (cf. ibid., p. 15). A constitutive element here is the participatory and democratic organizational structure of community foundations. Decisions, e.g. on the allocation of funding for projects, are not only made by individual donors, but by several committed citizens, the board of directors and the foundation council (cf. Jakob 2010, p. 245). In 69 percent of the citizens' foundations surveyed by Stiftung Aktive Bürgerschaft, committed citizens are systematically involved in decision-making processes, and in 23 percent of the citizens' foundations, committed citizens also receive voting rights as members of the founders' assembly, on an equal footing with founders (cf. Stiftung Aktive Bürgerschaft 2018b, p. 18).

In addition to the connection to financially strong founding donors and cooperation partners, endowments and donations are essential for the implementation of the projects. The endowment capital of community foundations in Germany has grown significantly over the last ten years: at the time of the survey on 31 December 2006, it amounted to € 84.1 million (cf. Hellmann 2007, p. 8) and at the time of the last survey on 31 December 2016, it was already € 360 million (cf. Stiftung Aktive Bürgerschaft 2017, p. 4). Furthermore, the sum of funds used for project funding is considerable and characterized by continuous growth. The highest amount used for project funding in a comparison of citizens' foundations rose from 499 thousand euros in 2006 to 1.7 million euros in 2016 (cf. ibid., p. 8).

According to their self-description, community foundations have a social impact as "participatory foundations" (Stiftung Aktive Bürgerschaft 2018a) through the commitment of citizens for citizens; thus, in addition to society in general (1.2 percent), the state (5.6 percent), and companies (12.8 percent), the vast majority of donors are private individuals (80.4 percent) (cf. ibid.). Maintaining legitimacy for innovations thus poses a number of challenges for the leadership of community foundations. On the one hand, it is necessary to acquire and cultivate stubborn citizens as (resource) givers and to understand and integrate them as irritating innovators. At the same time, it is necessary to create positions for full-time employees in order to be able to fulfill one's own mission as well as to assume a relevant, i.e. visible position in the ecosystem of social innovations and to be "maneuverable" as an organization in order to be able to serve cooperation requests by third parties or to initiate them oneself and to enter into them in the long term. Furthermore, one's own competitiveness goes hand in hand with being able to hold out the prospect of success and "impact" to potential funders. If innovations are determined by the criteria of need, urgency, and legitimacy, the potential for innovation can be attributed to community foundations at least in the sense that they react to local needs in the form of projects, the urgency of which is decided primarily by the donors, who can be activated to contribute their resources (time, knowledge, money) to the organization, to co-decide on the eligibility of projects on site with self-authorization, or to follow up on needs that are assessed as urgent locally through commitment. If innovativeness is linked to the impact of projects in community foundations, three aspects should be considered: Since projects are limited in time, they would have to 1) be transferred into structures in which full-time employees continue the work, 2) in this context, cooperations with other sectors would have to be cultivated, and 3) the addressees of the projects would have to be questioned as to what (out)effects participation in the projects has from their perspective, in order to do justice to the claim with which impact is told through quality and cachet on the face of the organizations. As a reminder, NPOs are considered to be effective if changes in the abilities, opportunities for action or living conditions of the target groups of their services (outcome) or in society (impact) can be determined (cf. PHINEO gAG 2014, p. 6f.). For the community foundations, the criteria selected here for innovations do reveal a potential, but this is based primarily on the attribution of relevance or eligibility of the projects and ideas in community foundations by the funders. To what extent the claim can be served to develop innovative forms of engagement as a way of enabling participation of as *many* people as possible in community foundations is an empirical question that needs to be further researched and discussed. However, in view of their endowment capital and the activation of private individuals as the largest group of donors, community foundations seem to succeed in telling credible stories about innovations and impact on the front side of the organizations – from the perspective of the donors – and to show themselves as irritable on the back stage through the implementation of concrete project ideas of the donors.

4 Voluntary Agencies

The first voluntary agency was founded in Munich in 1980 (cf. Wolf and Zimmer 2012, p. 46). The scientific data available for assessing the quantitative development of this form of organisation is limited. Essentially, there are three studies in which the organisational form "voluntary agency" was examined. The studies differ in terms of their guiding research interest and their methodological approaches.

1. The Generali Engagement Atlas (2015) is the most recent study in which, on the basis of quantitative and qualitative data, a broad range of local infrastructural institutions that promote engagement (citizens' foundations, volunteer agencies, municipal staff units, multi-generation houses, mothers' centres, self-help contact points, senior citizens' offices and socio-cultural centres) are recorded and, in particular, their number, tasks, goals and equipment are mapped.
2. The study Speck et al. (2012) is based on a nationwide questionnaire survey and qualitative case studies on the organisational form of voluntary agencies. With the help of this comprehensive study, statements on the context, input, process and result quality of voluntary agencies are made on the basis of the quantitative questionnaire survey. Through guideline-supported partially standardised expert interviews with leading employees in voluntary agencies and their local organisational environment, self-assessments and external assessments of this organisational form were collected and analysed. The analysis of the interview material leads to case studies that provide information about the organisational structure, the task profile and the local environment of volunteer agencies.
3. As in the Generali Engagement Atlas, the study by Wolf and Zimmer (2012) examines the breadth of local infrastructures that promote engagement. Based on a selection of six model municipalities, guideline-based interviews were conducted with senior staff in infrastructure institutions that promote engagement, as well as in staff or contact points of the municipal administration, and a questionnaire was used to collect "key data" (ibid., p. 14) from the organisations. In addition, the results of the surveys will be discussed with representatives of the organisations in the model municipalities.

The varying objects of research (infrastructural institutions in their local breadth on the one hand and voluntary agencies as the exclusive object of research on the other) and the time frames in which the surveys were carried out make it difficult to compare the findings and make it clear that there is little *current* and empirically generated data for assessing the existence and "constitution" of this form of organisation.

The available quantitative findings show that the organisational form of voluntary agency is gaining in importance locally. The Speck et al. (2012) study refers to data from 2011, according to which the number of volunteer agencies in Germany rose from 190 in 2001 to 360 in 2011 (cf. ibid., p. 126). At the time of publication of the study, the authors of the Generali Engagement Atlas (2015) assumed a number of 667 volunteer agencies, including organisations that combine more than one organisational form under one roof and are referred to as "combination institutions" (ibid., p. 12) (e.g. organisations that are both a senior citizens' office and a volunteer agency). The available data therEPOre do not allow for a longitudinal view of the quantitative extent of voluntary agencies.

Most volunteer agencies are located in North Rhine-Westphalia (with 83 percent the leader), followed by Bavaria, Lower Saxony and Baden-Württemberg (cf. Speck et al. 2012, p. 31). They are usually run as an independent association (28 per cent), by a welfare association (26 per cent) or by a local authority (21 per cent), while foundations or churches are the exception as sponsoring organisations (cf. ibid., pp. 37 and 44). With regard to the financial resources of voluntary agencies, the findings of the Generali Engagement Atlas (2015) correspond to those of the study by Speck et al. (2012). In both studies, it is clear that municipal funding is by far the most dominant source of funding; in 62 percent (cf. Generali 2015, p. 31) and 41% (cf. Speck et al. 2012, p. 49) of volunteer agencies, municipal funding is used. The financial support of voluntary agencies through donations comprises 10 per cent private donations and 13 per cent corporate donations (cf. Generali 2015, p. 31). In terms of their inflow of funds, voluntary agencies thus differ from citizens' foundations, which, as already described, are supported in particular by private individuals, followed by companies, and to a much lesser extent by public funds. The financial resources of many voluntary agencies – in relation to the community foundations – are to be assessed as "meagre" or "precarious": More than half of the volunteer agencies included in the Generali study have a total annual budget of up to €50,000 (cf. Generali 2015, p. 30). This finding is consistent with that of the Speck et al. study (2012, p. 45), which retrospectively asked about the annual budget of voluntary agencies in 2008, albeit at a much later point in time. According to this study, 42 percent of the agencies have an annual budget of up to €10,000 and 32 percent of the agencies have an annual budget of up to €50,000.

If the qualitative relevance of this form of organisation is examined on the basis of an analysis of its self-image, it can be seen that voluntary agencies see themselves as "social development agencies in matters of engagement and as protagonists of innovations within associations" (Speck et al. 2012, p. 20). In this context, they assume a bridging function "between people willing to get involved and institutions oriented towards the common good" (Wolf and Zimmer 2012, p. 46). The range of tasks performed by voluntary agencies is diverse and, according to their self-assessment, includes first and foremost the task area of "information and advice for volunteers" (98 per cent of metropolitan, 92 per cent of medium-sized and 82 per cent of small-town rural voluntary agencies say they cover this area "strongly"), the "placement of volunteers" and "cooperation with organisations" (Speck et al. 2012, p. 70). In concrete terms, this means that volunteer agencies inform and advise people who are interested in volunteering about possible fields of activity (e.g. in kindergartens, schools, senior citizens' facilities, in nature conservation and monument protection, in the sports or cultural sector) and refer them to organisations that offer volunteering opportunities in these areas and are looking for volunteers. In this context, voluntary agencies take on an intermediary function between those interested in getting involved and the local organisations looking for volunteers. A key premise on which the intermediary service rests is the establishment of fit between the demands placed on the engagement (e.g. by the organisations seeking engaged people) and the self-interests of the engaged people (cf. Kuhnt 2018, p. 564). The suitability of volunteers for their fields of work is optimised through the expansion of qualification opportunities on site (cf. ibid.). In addition to the local volunteer agencies that those interested in volunteering can visit, some volunteer agencies also offer online portals so that those involved can find a "suitable" volunteering activity on their own. For example, the volunteer agency Erfurt (2019) advertises with a reference to the online volunteering exchange: "We are convinced that you will find the task that suits you." The Freiwilligen-Agentur Halle-Saalekreis e. V. (2019) offers an online database where interested people can search for fields of volunteering according to various criteria and directly contact the desired volunteer agency. The services offered by local voluntary agencies depend above all on the size of the organisation (budget and number of full-time staff) and its environment (small-town rural, medium-town, metropolitan) (cf. Speck et al. 2012, p. 71). Compared to the other main tasks, the main task "cooperation with companies" is considered to be less "strongly covered"; 31 percent of the metropolitan voluntary agencies cover this area strongly, while this applies to only 8 percent of the medium-sized and small rural voluntary agencies (cf. ibid., p. 72). To implement activities in the above-mentioned areas of responsibility, almost a third of the voluntary agencies rely exclusively on volunteers; in 27 percent of the agencies there is no full-time staff and in 43 percent there is one staff position (cf. ibid., p. 56).

In view of their organisational constitution, the question arises as to how voluntary agencies can fulfil the innovation function. In the following, innovation potentials are attributed to voluntary agencies: (1) with regard to their mediation function and (2) in the context of professional volunteer management. The financial dependence of voluntary agencies on municipalities is discussed as a condition that inhibits innovation.

1. Innovation potential can be attributed to voluntary agencies with regard to their mediation function. The mediation function is geared both (i) to the interests of people who are willing to get involved and to taking into account their expectations and demands for meaningful involvement (Jakob 2010, p. 237), and (ii) to the needs of organisations that are looking for volunteers and to which volunteers are referred. Furthermore, the intermediary function (iii) is geared towards mediation between companies and NPOs, e.g. to support companies in the context of their self-image as corporate citizens and, more specifically, the corporate volunteering of their employees (on forms of corporate citizenship, see Bartsch and Biedermann 2018). For voluntary agencies, stimulating innovation through the intermediary function means serving different stakeholders and identifying local *needs*, having them communicated by other organisations and companies, and responding to them. Innovation is thus defined – directed towards the organisational environment – primarily *reactive*. With the assumption of the mediation function, a potential for innovation emerges from which the organisations to which the committed are referred profit. Through the intermediary function of an "agency", the engagement-seeking organisation can outsource its own recruitment function[4]. The outsourcing of recruitment of human resources can be interpreted as a copying and imitation process of an organisational action perceived as successful, for which the copying foil in the organisational environment is e.g. recruitment agencies. Outsourcing recruitment is particularly attractive for "functionalist organisations" (Backhaus-Maul et al. 2015, p. 435) of the Freie Wohlfahrtspflege, in which both intensive public relations work is carried out and recourse is made to infrastructural facilities such as volunteer agencies in order to recruit volunteers (cf. ibid.). One advantage of outsourcing the recruitment function is primarily the saving of resources. By

[4] On the recruitment function of NPOs, see Liebig and Rauschenbach (2010, p. 268).

transferring or delegating responsibility to an external agency, the organisations are relieved of having to use their own resources. At the same time, the agency provides the prospect of professional task performance; instead of developing their own organisational structures, recruiting and deploying and training staff to pursue this purpose, it can be efficient to draw on professional structures and responsibilities outside. Viewing the intermediary function as an innovation in the context of engagement promotion, because it relieves other organisations of their recruitment function and in this respect represents an innovation of tradition-based, inwardly closed organisational processes, does however entail that there are sufficient professional and full-time staff and structures in place to fulfil the function.

2. The assumption of an innovation function in the internal orientation of voluntary agencies entails the need for professional management. The professional management must – in order to maintain the appearance of the organisation – carry out public relations work and at the same time (further) develop the advisory, information and mediation services (i.e. volunteer management). Since in 27 percent of volunteer agencies services are provided exclusively by volunteers, resistance to innovation is ostensibly due to the lack of resources in volunteer agencies; without a permanent, full-time staff structure, it is sometimes a challenge to secure the core business. In voluntary agencies where the structural conditions are comparatively more favourable, i.e. where two or more staff are employed (this is the case in 15% of the voluntary agencies surveyed; cf. Speck et al. 2012, p. 56), professional management could also be used to raise the profile of the voluntary agency and its range of services in order to be able to hold one's own in competition locally and to gain legitimacy on the "front stage" (discursively). With regard to the assessment of the impact of the mediation function and the volunteer management – as innovative action – appropriate evaluation instruments would have to be developed and studies continuously conducted, in which on the one hand the perspective of the committed as "activated users" of the offers are recorded, but also the expectations and impact assumptions of possible cooperation partners and funders.
3. Municipalities act as an essential source of funding for voluntary agencies to offer services to third parties, which creates a pressure for voluntary agencies to legitimise themselves vis-à-vis municipalities. Voluntary agencies face the challenge of *holding out* the *prospect of* successfully fulfilling their "latent promise of innovation" (Speck et al. 2012, p. 11) in their self-image to local authorities as funders. The possibility of acquiring alternative sources of funding and thus competing with other EPOs, which in turn potentially address funders, does not minimise the challenge of addressing the social impact question. It is question-

able to what extent the innovative and thus effective identity of the individual organization, certified or authenticated by seals of quality, is still useful (or generates legitimacy) if the number of socially effective organizations in the local area increases and effectiveness no longer applies as a differentiating criterion. With Luhmann, one could answer this question by saying that organizations use their self-descriptions "to highlight their individual specificity in a terminology that, one hopes, will gain general recognition. The most important form of resolving the paradox of uniqueness [while forming the organization from the same values as those of its environment; d. V.] seems to consist in *strategies of outdoing*." (Luhmann 2011, p. 438; emphasis in the original). Innovation as an identity strategy is only convincing in the mode of outbidding if the one organization is assessed as more innovative, in the case of the volunteer agency under consideration here as more (socially) effective, than other organizations in the description of itself and others. Outbidding strategies of this kind can be seen in the fact that organisations, given the right facts, write a "success story" (ibid., p. 440) and distinguish themselves.

With regard to the voluntary agencies, it can be noted that success stories are written by the annual awarding of an innovation prize by the umbrella organisation, but the factual situation lacks scientifically sound, continuous surveys. In addition to the writing of success stories, there must be those – well aware of the reciprocity of organisation and environment – who believe these stories and feed their money, time and knowledge into the organisations. In the case of voluntary agencies, according to the quantitative distribution of funders, it is the local authorities who (must) believe the success stories. In addition to the municipalities – taking into account the hesitant willingness of some municipalities to provide basic support for this form of organization in return for a promise of effectiveness and success – the management level in volunteer agencies is challenged to acquire cooperation partners and funding providers through broader public relations work[5] and to visibly communicate success to the outside world as measurable in terms of funding or the fulfilled "mission" (placement and management of volunteers).

[5] Following the ecosystem of social innovations, the sectors of business and science should be addressed and convinced as potential cooperation partners and providers of funds, in addition to the municipalities as the dominant financiers and those interested in engagement as users of the services offered. According to the quantitative data, cooperation with companies is less pronounced and science has not been systematically (scientifically) recorded as a sector to be considered.

5 Innovation as an Investment by and for Funders

In the debate on the promotion of engagement and engagement policy, there is agreement that "the active and participatory forms of engagement can have an important political, more precise, democracy-promoting effect" (Roth 2010, p. 625). In organised contexts, engagement becomes the possibility of redeeming or claiming an active right of co-decision and co-determination, for which the actors of organised civil society form organisational structures. At the same time, this is connected with challenges for the organisations and institutions that want to mobilise and promote engagement, which lack a corresponding "role offer" (ibid.) for engaged people and which have to be irritated by the engaged people against routine procedures and inertia. At the same time, this irritability is accompanied by the fact that engagement, although it receives positive public and political recognition, is not quasi "naturally" democratic or democracy-promoting. Rather, the organizations and actors promoting engagement are challenged to produce the "democratic substance of engagement" (ibid., p. 616) themselves. The democratic potential of the organizations is also measured by the extent to which they succeed in mobilizing not only those engaged who are already privileged due to individual resources (money, knowledge, time), access (networks, social relationships) and participation experiences (cf. ibid.).

This flanks a practical area of tension: The acquisition of resources is accompanied by an invitation to the participation of resource-rich donors[6], whereby resource-poor persons are (at best) considered as addressees of services, but not as persons who decide on the use of resources. On the other hand, the acquisition of resources is a decisive "fuel" for the implementation of the innovation function.

Organized promotion of engagement does not come for free (Hartnuß 2018, p. 123); thus, municipal structures or infrastructural facilities, such as citizens' foundations and volunteer agencies, are needed to facilitate organized opportunities for engagement. The involvement of organised civil society in the provision of social services in the context of municipal services of general interest, i.e. the local division of tasks and responsibilities, within the framework of which citizens are activated as users and co-producers of services, requires basic funding so that EPOs can develop lasting organisational structures that are largely independent of the influence of particularly resource-rich funders and, in this sense, sustainable. With regard to basic funding and the associated recognition of the potential of the infrastructural institutions that promote engagement, Jakob (2010, p. 235) notes

[6]You also have to be able to afford time for commitment.

that this has so far been perceived by only some of the municipalities. In this respect, the promotion of engagement is not a matter of course for municipal policy.

The ability to innovate includes creativity in dealing with the institution of social services of general interest as a political-administrative framework. Creativity is not exhausted by falling back on tried and tested structures and cooperation partners (such as the classic promotion of associations by municipalities or the consideration of welfare associations in the neo-corporatist system), but emerges from an understanding of the local division of tasks and responsibilities and a related financing mix, in which new partners on the socio-political terrain are recognised and new modes of promoting engagement are tested locally. The modes of local engagement promotion, taking into account the range of organised civil society and its political-administrative framework conditions, need to be further empirically investigated.

Within the organisations, full-time and professional structures are needed that develop engagement promotion as a task in the sense of organisational development and establish "a modern volunteer management" (Hartnuß 2018, p. 123). At the same time, it becomes clear that engagement promotion is based on a competitive principle between local organisations. In the competition for resources (volunteers, financial resources, knowledge, time, spokesperson positions in the political discourse), those organisations are perceived as "innovative" that manage to be irritated by civil society, to react to civil society *needs that are* assessed as *urgent,* and to offer solutions that generate *legitimacy* through assumptions of impact. In doing so, those organizations gain a competitive advantage that succeed – on the front stage – in telling high-profile, compelling stories about quality, impact, and their own organization as the innovative one(s).

Finally, it must be critically noted that if innovativeness is the criterion by which organizations' eligible activities are measured, it is the funders who decide what is considered an urgent need, which impact assumptions they believe, and which solutions to local needs seem legitimate. Local needs that the funders do not perceive as urgent and communicate to the organizations, or that they do not want to help solve, remain under the radar. The "activated citizen society" or its engagement is therEPOre discussed on the one hand as a "middle class project" (Kessl 2006, p. 75). On the other hand, the results of the most recent Volunteer Survey regarding a gender-specific distribution of engagement "speak for a still existing orientation towards the traditional gender-specific division of labour" (Vogel et al. 2017, p. 643). The perception of an opportunity to get involved locally is thus less an activation problem than a compatibility problem; and engagement promotion, as has become clear in this paper, particularly favours those who can afford to get involved because they have the necessary and required resources to be able to participate in decision-making and shaping locally.

References

Stiftung Aktive Bürgerschaft e. V. 2007. *Länderspiegel Bürgerstiftungen. Fakten und Trends 2007*. 2. Auflage. Berlin.

Stiftung Aktive Bürgerschaft e. V. 2008. *Länderspiegel Bürgerstiftungen. Fakten und Trends 2008*. Berlin.

Stiftung Aktive Bürgerschaft e. V. 2009. *Länderspiegel Bürgerstiftungen. Fakten und Trends 2009*. Berlin.

Stiftung Aktive Bürgerschaft e. V. 2010. *Länderspiegel Bürgerstiftungen. Fakten und Trends 2010*. Berlin.

Stiftung Aktive Bürgerschaft e. V. 2011. *Länderspiegel Bürgerstiftungen. Fakten und Trends 2011*. Berlin.

Stiftung Aktive Bürgerschaft e. V. 2012. *Länderspiegel Bürgerstiftungen. Fakten und Trends 2012*. Berlin.

Stiftung Aktive Bürgerschaft e. V. 2013. *Länderspiegel Bürgerstiftungen. Fakten und Trends 2013*. Berlin.

Stiftung Aktive Bürgerschaft e. V. 2014. *Länderspiegel Bürgerstiftungen. Fakten und Trends 2014*. Berlin.

Backhaus-Maul, Holger, K. Speck, M. Hörnlein, und M. Krohn. 2015. *Engagement in der Freien Wohlfahrtspflege: Empirische Befunde aus der Terra incognita eines Spitzenverbandes*. Wiesbaden: Springer VS.

Barth, Annette. 2012. Bürgerstiftungsschelte. Anspruch und Wirklichkeit von Bürgerstiftungen. Eine Fallstudie am Beispiel der Region Vorderes Fließtal/Baden-Württemberg. Hrsg. MAECENATA Institut an der Humboldt-Universität zu Berlin, *Opusculum*, 53.

Bartsch, Gabriele, und C. Biedermann. 2018. Varianten und Formen des gesellschaftlichen Engagements von Unternehmen. In *Gesellschaftliche Verantwortung von Unternehmen in Deutschland*, Hrsg. Holger Backhaus-Maul, M. Kunze, und S. Nährlich, 333–49. Wiesbaden: Springer Fachmedien Wiesbaden.

Bielefelder Bürgerstiftung. 2019: "aufwind" – Das Bielefelder Schülerstipendium. https://www.bielefelder-buergerstiftung.de/projekte/aufwind/. Zugegriffen: 11.07.2019.

Brinkmann, Volker. 2010. *Sozialwirtschaft: Grundlagen – Modelle – Finanzierung*. 1. Aufl. Gabler Lehrbuch. Wiesbaden: Gabler.

Bundesarbeitsgemeinschaft der Freien Wohlfahrtspflege e. V., Hrsg. 2018. *Gesamtstatistik 2016. Einrichtungen und Dienste der Freien Wohlfahrtspflege*. Berlin.

Bundesministerium für Familie, Senioren, Frauen und Jugend. 2017. Zweiter Bericht über die Entwicklung des bürgerschaftlichen Engagements in der Bundesrepublik Deutschland. Demografischer Wandel und bürgerschaftliches Engagement: Der Beitrag des Engagements zur lokalen Entwicklung. Drucksache 18/11800. Berlin: BMFSFJ.

Bundesverband der Deutschen Volksbanken und Raiffeisenbanken e. V. (BVR). 2017. Stiftungskapital von Bürgerstiftungen. https://www.vr.de/privatkunden/news/stiftungskapital-von-buergerstiftungen.html. Zugegriffen: 06.11.2018.

Bundesverband Deutscher Stiftungen e. V. 2000. 10 Merkmale einer Bürgerstiftung. https://www.stiftungen.org/fileadmin/stiftungen_org/Verband/Was_wir_tun/Veranstaltungen/AK-Buergerstiftungen/10-Merkmale-einer-Buergerstiftung.pdf. Zugegriffen: 25.04.2019.

Bundesverband Deutscher Stiftungen e. V. 2018. Das Gütesiegel für Bürgerstiftungen. https://www.buergerstiftungen.org/de/guetesiegel/guetesiegel/. Zugegriffen: 21.12.2018.

Bürgerstiftung Bad Bentheim. 2015. Schulbücher für Flüchtlinge. https://buergerstiftung--badbentheim.de/bildung-erziehung/schulbuecher-fuer-fluechtlinge/. Zugegriffen: 11.07.2019.

Bürgerstiftung Gütersloh. 2019. Sport im Park. https://www.buergerstiftung-guetersloh.de/fileadmin/files/Informieren/Projekte/Sport_im_Park/Flyer_Sport_im_Park_2019_Web.pdf. Zugegriffen: 11.07.2019.

Bürgerstiftung Wiesloch. 2019. Eine Patenschaft … damit Grundschulkinder einen besseren Start beim Lesen, Schreiben und Rechnen haben. https://buergerstiftung-wiesloch.de/wp-content/images/BueStiPatenschaft18-3-1.pdf. Zugegriffen: 11.07.2019.

Fahrenwald, Claudia. 2013. Narration und Partizipation im organisationalen Kontext. In *Organisation und Partizipation*, Hrsg. Susanne Maria Weber, M. Göhlich, A. Schröer, C. Fahrenwald, und H. Macha, 83–91. Wiesbaden: Springer Fachmedien Wiesbaden.

Freiwilligenagentur Erfurt. 2019. Willkommen bei der Freiwilligenagentur Erfurt. http://freiwilligenagentur-erfurt.de. Zugegriffen: 11.07.2019.

Freiwilligen-Agentur Halle-Saalkreis e. V. 2019. Engagementsuche direkt. https://www.freiwilligen-agentur.de/fuer-freiwillige/engagementsuche-direkt/. Zugegriffen: 11.07.2019.

Generali. 2015. Generali Engagementatlas 2015. Rolle und Perspektiven Engagement unterstützender Einrichtungen in Deutschland. https://www.generali.de/ueber-generali/verantwortung/gesellschaftliches-engagement/alter-demografie-buergerengagement/. Zugegriffen: 18.07.2018.

Hartnuß, Birger. 2018. *Bürgerschaftliches Engagement und Soziale Arbeit: ein Studienbuch für die Praxis*. 1. Auflage. Studienbuch. Bremen: Apollon University Press.

Hellmann, Bernadette. 2007. Bürgerstiftungen in Deutschland: Fakten und Trends 2007. In *Länderspiegel Bürgerstiftungen. Fakten und Trends 2007.*, Hrsg. Aktive Bürgerschaft e. V., 2. Auflage, 7–9. Berlin.

Howaldt, Jürgen. 2019. Soziale Innovation im Fokus nachhaltiger Entwicklung – Die Bedeutung von Kooperationen und Netzwerken für den Erfolg sozialer Innovationen. In *Netzwerke und soziale Innovationen*, Hrsg. Christian Neugebauer, S. Pawel, und H.Biritz, 13–30. Wiesbaden: Springer Fachmedien Wiesbaden.

Jakob, Gisela. 2010. "Infrastrukturen und Anlaufstellen zur Engagementförderung in den Kommunen". In *Engagementpolitik. Die Entwicklung der Zivilgesellschaft als politische Aufgabe.*, Hrsg. Thomas Olk, A. Klein, und B. Hartnuß, 233–59. Wiesbaden: VS Verlag für Sozialwissenschaften.

Kerka, Friedrich, B. Kriegesmann und T. Kley. 2012. (K)eine einfache Frage: Wie überwinden innovative Kräfte Innovationswiderstände? In *Gesellschaft innovativ.*, Hrsg. Gerald Beck und C. Kropp, 251–270. Wiesbaden: VS Verlag für Sozialwissenschaften.

Kessl, Fabian. 2006. Bürgerschaftliches/zivilgesellschaftliches Engagement. In *Aktivierende Sozialpädagogik*, Hrsg. Bernd Dollinger und J. Raithel, 65–77. Wiesbaden: VS Verlag für Sozialwissenschaften.

Klein, Ansgar, T. Olk, und B. Hartnuß. 2010. Engagementpolitik als Politikfeld: Entwicklungserfordernisse und Perspektiven. In *Engagementpolitik. Die Entwicklung der Zivilgesellschaft als politische Aufgabe.*, Hrsg. Thomas Olk, A. Klein, und B. Hartnuß, 24–59. Wiesbaden: VS Verlag für Sozialwissenschaften.

Krücken, Georg. 2006. Innovationsmythen in Politik und Gesellschaft. In *Kluges Entscheiden.*, Hrsg. Arno Scherzberg, T. Betsch, H.-J. Blanke, P. Walgenbach, A. Waschkuhn, und G. Wegner, 259–73. Tübingen: Mohr Siebeck.

Kühl, Stefan. 2011. *Organisationen*. Wiesbaden: VS Verlag für Sozialwissenschaften.

Kuhnt, Janine. 2018. Engagementförderung zwischen Professionalisierung, Deprofessionalisierung und Selbstpotimierung. *neue praxis: Zeitschrift für Sozialarbeit, Sozialpädagogik und Sozialpolitik* (6/2018): 547–70.

Liebig, Reinhard, und T. Rauschenbach. 2010. Die engagementpolitische Rolle von Akteuren des Dritten Sektors. In *Engagementpolitik. Die Entwicklung der Zivilgesellschaft als politische Aufgabe.*, Hrsg. Thomas Olk, A. Klein, und B. Hartnuß, 260–81. Wiesbaden: VS Verlag für Sozialwissenschaften.

Luhmann, Niklas. 2011. *Organisation und Entscheidung*. 3. Auflage. Wiesbaden: VS Verlag.

Nowoczyn, Tobias. 2017. Föderalismus in der Sozialwirtschaft: Hindernisse überwinden und Chancen nutzen. Innovative Antworten auf die Herausforderungen der föderalen Wohlfahrtsverbände. In *Die Wohlfahrtsverbände als föderale Organisationen*, Hrsg. ders., 3–19. Wiesbaden: Springer Fachmedien Wiesbaden.

PHINEO gAG. 2014. Engagement mit Wirkung. Die PHINEO-Analysemethode im Detail. https://www.phineo.org/phineo/analysemethode. Zugegriffen: 15.01.2019.

Priemer, Jana, A. Bischoff, C. Hohendanner, R. Krebstakies, B. Rump, und W. Schmitt. 2019. Organisierte Zivilgesellschaft. In *Datenreport Zivilgesellschaft*, Hrsg. Holger Krimmer, 7–54. Wiesbaden: Springer Fachmedien Wiesbaden.

Rock, Joachim. 2017. Die Antwort ist 42: Vom Hokuspokus der Wirkungsmessung in der sozialen Praxis. In *Privates Kapital für soziale Dienste? Wirkungsorientiertes Investment und seine Folgen für die Soziale Arbeit.*, Hrsg. Monika Burmester, E. Dowling, und N.Wohlfahrt, 41:108–20. Baltmannsweiler: Schneider Verlag Hohengehren.

Roß, Paul-Stefan, und Roland Roth. 2018. Bürgerkommune. In *Engagement und Zivilgesellschaft*, Hrsg. Thomas Klie und A. W. Klie, 163–268. Wiesbaden: Springer Fachmedien Wiesbaden.

Roth, Roland. 2010. Engagementförderung als Demokratiepolitik: Besichtigung einer REPOrmbaustelle. In *Engagementpolitik. Die Entwicklung der Zivilgesellschaft als politische Aufgabe.*, Hrsg. Thomas Olk, A. Klein, und B. Hartnuß, 611–36. Wiesbaden: VS Verlag für Sozialwissenschaften.

Schönig, Werner. 2006. Aktivierungspolitik. Eine sozialpolitische Strategie und ihre Ambivalenz für soziale Dienste und praxisorientierte Forschung. In *Aktivierende Sozialpädagogik. Ein kritisches Glossar.*, Hrsg. Bernd Dollinger und J. Raithel, 23–39. Wiesbaden: VS Verlag für Sozialwissenschaften.

Schröer, Andreas. 2009. Professionalisierung und Nonprofit Leadership. In *Leadership in sozialen Organisationen.*, Hrsg. Johannes Eurich und A. Brink, 141–58. Wiesbaden: VS Verlag für Sozialwissenschaften.

Schuhen, Axel. 2009. Leadership und Nonprofit Governance. In *Leadership in sozialen Organisationen.*, Hrsg. Johannes Eurich und A. Brink, 101–10. Wiesbaden: VS Verlag für Sozialwissenschaften.

Speck, Karsten, H. Backhaus-Maul, P. Friedrich und M. Krohn. 2012. *Freiwilligenagenturen in Deutschland.* Wiesbaden: VS Verlag für Sozialwissenschaften.

Stiftung Aktive Bürgerschaft. 2018a. Über uns. https://www.aktive-buergerschaft.de/ueber-uns/. Zugegriffen: 30.1.2019.

Stiftung Aktive Bürgerschaft. Hrsg. 2015. *Report Bürgerstiftungen. Fakten und Trends 2015.* Berlin.

Stiftung Aktive Bürgerschaft. Hrsg. 2016. *Report Bürgerstiftungen. Fakten und Trends 2016.* Berlin.

Stiftung Aktive Bürgerschaft. Hrsg. 2017. *Report Bürgerstiftungen. Fakten und Trends 2017.* Berlin.

Stiftung Aktive Bürgerschaft. Hrsg. 2018b. *Report Bürgerstiftungen 2018. Zusammenarbeit mit Ehrenamtlichen.* Berlin.

Straßheim, Holger. 2013. Vernetzung als lokale Krisenstrategie? In *Lokale Politik und Verwaltung im Zeichen der Krise?* Hrsg. Michael Haus und S. Kuhlmann, 121–38. Wiesbaden: Springer Fachmedien Wiesbaden.

Then, Volker. 2017. Innovative Weiterentwicklung in den Netzwerkstrukturen der Wohlfahrtsverbände. Chancen für soziale Innovationen und deren Verbreitung. In *Die Wohlfahrtsverbände als föderale Organisationen*, Hrsg. Tobias Nowoczyn, 39–55. Wiesbaden: Springer Fachmedien Wiesbaden.

Vogel, Claudia, J. Simonson, J. P. Ziegelmann, und C. Tesch-Römer. 2017. Freiwilliges Engagement von Frauen und Männern in Deutschland. In *Freiwilliges Engagement in Deutschland*, Hrsg. Julia Simonson, C. Vogel, und C. Tesch-Römer, 637–46. Wiesbaden: Springer Fachmedien Wiesbaden.

Weber, Susanne Maria. 2018. Innovationsmanagement als Gegenstand der Organisationspädagogik. In *Handbuch Organisationspädagogik*, Hrsg. Michael Göhlich, A. Schröer, und S. M. Weber, 17:517–27. Wiesbaden: Springer Fachmedien Wiesbaden.

Wolf, André Christian. 2009. *Bürgerstiftungen als Akteure der Stadtentwicklung. Erkundung der Beiträge von Bürgerstiftungen zur Entwicklung von Stadt und Region.* (Dissertation) Rheinisch-Westfälische Technische Hochschule Aachen. http://publications.rwth--aachen.de/record/50790/files/Wolf_Andre.pdf. Zugegriffen: 31.01.2019.

Wolf, André Christian. 2010. Zivilgesellschaft konkret: Bürgerstiftungen als Akteure der Stadt-entwicklung. In *Stadtentwicklung, Zivilgesellschaft und bürgerschaftliches Engagement*, Hrsg. Elke Becker, E. Gualini, C. Runkel, R. Graf Strachwitz, 99–118. Stuttgart: Lucius & Lucius.

Wolf, André Christian, und A. Zimmer. 2012. *Lokale Engagementförderung*. Wiesbaden: VS Verlag für Sozialwissenschaften.

Kuhnt, Janine, M. A., studied Educational Science at the Free University of Berlin and the Martin Luther University Halle-Wittenberg. Since April 2016, she has been a research assistant at the Chair of Social Pedagogy and Out-of-School Education at the Institute of Educational Science at Friedrich Schiller University Jena.

Latest Publications:

Kuhnt, J. (to be published in mid-2020). Generating quality of life through engagement – Equal living conditions between utopia and self-activation. In: Staats, M. (ed.). Quality of life. A Metathema, Weinheim: Beltz Juventa.

Kuhnt, J. and J. Finzi, (forthcoming mid-2020). Less house, more life(quality)?! The Tiny House movement between revolt and return. In: Staats, M. (ed.). Quality of life. Ein Metathema, Weinheim: Beltz Juventa.

Kuhnt, J. (forthcoming). The dynamics of local responsibility sharing: Engagement-promoting organizations and structures in Germany, in: Voluntaris: Zeitschrift für Freiwilligendienste.

Kuhnt, J. (forthcoming). Addressing housing need in a minimalist, self-reliant and/or social work way? In: Blätter der Wohlfahrtspflege Heft 2/2020.

Kuhnt, J. 2018. Engagement promotion between professionalization, deprofessionalization and self-optimization. In: np: Journal for Social Work, Social Pedagogy and Social Policy 6/2018, pp. 547–570.

RePair Democracy – Social Innovations as Workshops for Democratic Design

Gerald Beck and Robert Jende

Abstract

This paper discusses social innovations as workshops for democratic design. Against the background of the "crisis of representation" (Diehl, Aus Politik und Zeitgeschichte, 40–42: 12–17, 2016) and the "ecological-economic pincer crisis" (Dörre, Große Transformation? Zur Zukunft moderner Gesellschaften. Sonderband des Berliner Journals für Soziologie, Springer VS, Wiesbaden, pp. 3–33, 2019), shaping social change appears increasingly urgent and complex. Social innovations can provide examples of alternative social practices and thereby be models for shaping change. Looking at initiatives in the repair scene, we explore the question of the possibility of democratic design of sustainable living. Can "democratic micro-practices" practiced in social innovation initiatives such as repair cafés, open workshops or solidarity-based agriculture help to carry political self-efficacy into other areas of life? The "democracy café" presented in the article aims to offer a space for people to meet with their local concerns, where these concerns can be worked on collaboratively and problems solved together.

G. Beck (✉) · R. Jende
University of Applied Sciences Munich, Munich, Germany
e-mail: gerald.beck@hm.edu

H.-W. Franz et al. (eds.), *Sustainable Living and Business*,
https://doi.org/10.1007/978-3-658-41835-9_17

1 Sustainable and Democratic Living – An Aporia?

Modern society is often described as functionally differentiated (Luhmann) and based on the division of labour (Durkheim). Thus, individual functional areas have emerged, and social problems are dealt with in small packages by specialists within a delimitable sphere. In this country, representative democracy is regarded as a comprehensive principle of organization in order to make directional statements of political control attempts electable. This principle of control is increasingly coming under pressure; there is much talk of a "crisis of representation" (Diehl 2016). This is directly related to the way in which social coexistence is economically organised. In relation to the crisis of democracy, there is also talk of an "ecological-economic pincer crisis" (Dörre 2019). This means, shortened to its essentials, that the global economic system is growth-driven and that this dynamic is destroying the natural foundations of life. Conversely, a resource-efficient economy would cause the current global economic system to collapse and lead to immense social dislocations.

Against the backdrop of these acute multiple crises, the shaping of social change with the growing "desire for alternatives" (Wright 2017, p. 9) appears increasingly urgent in order to "act in the here and now in a way that increases the likelihood of implementing the alternative in the future" (ibid., p. 11). In recent years, "social innovations" have increasingly been thematized for dealing with these crises (cf. Howaldt and Jacobsen 2010, Beck and Kropp 2012, Moulaert et al. 2014, among others). Following Frank Moulaert and colleagues, we understand social innovations as innovations that address human needs, create new social constellations and thus promote social cohesion (Moulaert et al. 2014, p. 16f). We are particularly interested in locally embedded, civic innovations "from the middle of society" (Beck and Kropp 2012, p. 15), as these are less suspected of serving socio-technological fantasies, but rather function as a breeding ground for the establishment of sustainable and grassroots democratic ways of life. We thus explore the question of the extent to which sustainable living can be realized democratically. In doing so, we do not equate democracy with representative parliamentary democracy, but represent a dynamic concept of *democratization.*

As a means of *democratization,* we understand open workshops, repair cafés, solidarity farms and other social innovations as a contribution to the establishment of *local democracies.* These are characterized above all by low-threshold participation access, direct effectiveness and informal exchange. Our guiding thesis is based on Albert Bandura's (1997) concept of *self-efficacy* and states that citizens need to experience themselves as politically effective in order to build an inclusive and satisfying political community. Conversely, this means that a corresponding decoupling of citizen will and political decision-makers leads to an erosion of democracy. Because citizens feel that they are 'not being heard', they turn away from the idea of democracy and towards radical fringes. Sustainable living and economic activity are thus systematically lost from view because political conflicts are fought out in other arenas. Large-scale societal weather patterns are rapidly shifting according to the media wind that can capture the attention of the many. The rituals of democracy, such as elections or parliamentary debates, can be inserted into these simulations of design intentions (cf. Blühdorn 2013). However, no necessary changes are made in the simulations. These are practiced on a small, experimental scale in the *laboratories of sustainable life*.

The principle of repair seems to be a proven starting point for the transformation of an institutionalized "politics of unsustainability" (cf. Blühdorn 2013, p. 258ff.) to forms of life in fluid equilibrium with the natural foundations of life. "Repair, far more than other knowledge cultures, is built on practical experience and collaboration" (Bertling and Leggewie 2016, p. 275). Here, an "art of living together" (Les Convivialistes 2014, p. 47) is at the heart of action, based on both care for things and people, and non-growth-oriented giving. Repairing in small communities resists the capitalist logic of growing, consuming, and profiting, and is per se oriented toward use value. Simply put, repairing is sustainable, promotes technology literacy and sociable togetherness (Bertling and Leggewie 2016, p. 277). Thus, we focus on social groups that already manage without growth (or are excluded from it) in order to "participate in the formation of counterpublics that illuminate possibilities for social transformation" (Dörre 2017, p. 56). But not only illuminate, it is about the real experiment on a small scale that can give us insights into how sustainable forms of life organize themselves as democratic ones. The city as space and urban society as *social power* (Wright 2017, p. 184ff.) move to the centre of shaping local democracies. "Moreover, the city, like the workshop, allows the concentration of the means of production – tools, raw materials, labour – in a limited space" (Lefebvre 2016, p. 35).

This is linked to a second implication of Re-Pair: the connection (pair) of citizens' needs to political design. In this we see the potential of a communal understanding of democracy for the participatory design of local living spaces. Social innovations such as Repair Cafés, Open Workshops, Commons or Maker Labs are reminiscent of a way of living that benefits the development of local self-efficacy. Collaborative practices of appropriation, reshaping, recycling, and appropriation become alternatives to current consumption and growth orientations as *real utopias*. Through the experience of self-efficacy, actors of social innovation seem apt to replicate the grassroots and sustainability-oriented practices learned in the initiative in other contexts (cf. Dumitru et al. 2016). Specifically, we are therefore concerned with the question of the extent to which social innovations can develop politicising and democratising potential and the organisational practices practised in social innovations can also lead to the activation of democratic values and sustainable lifestyles in other contexts.

In addition to the overarching question of the potential of social innovations for the practice, legitimization and dissemination of democratic practices, we are interested in these very practices in detail. What characterizes the *real utopias* that are lived out in open workshops? To what extent are sustainable forms of life lived in the initiatives, which are predominantly based on grassroots democratic self-organisation? And what can be learned from this for the democratization of highly complex societies?

In order to get closer to these questions, we start with the main sites of environmentally and resource-friendly forms of practice by presenting the repair principle (2). The workshop turns out to be a *practice space for productive sociability*, in which *democratic micro-practices* are lived and practiced. Although open workshops or repair cafés carry politicising potential, this is not explicitly addressed. In order to connect sustainable ways of living with political possibilities of realization *(re-pair)*, we explore in a next step a *repair café for democracy* (3). We understand such a local space, the democracy café, as a laboratory for a participatory development of local living spaces by the inhabitants in collaboration with structure-building institutions. Finally, we summarize the conclusions in the conception of a *collaborative democracy in order* to draw attention to a *democratization of democracy* that has structurally anchored sustainable life and economy in a grassroots democratic way (4).

2 Sustainable Life and Economy: The Principle of Re pair

"If you can't fix it, you don't own it!" – This motto of the repair movement shows that there is much more behind the simple idea of Repair Cafés than helping people to help themselves. The social innovation of the Repair Café is embedded in a larger movement that builds on the principle of repair and can be considered a rallying point of post-capitalist practices (Baier et al. 2016). The motto clearly aims at an appropriation of products that is no longer foreseen in capitalist logic. If a product can only belong to us when we can repair it, then the purchase itself is no longer the decisive factor. The appropriation process in DIY or repair is also on another level. If you have made a table yourself in an open workshop, you are unlikely to replace it with a cheap item from a furniture store the next time you move house. Resources are thus conserved and products are given a new appreciation. It is the same with products that are repaired together with others in a repair café. Here, too, a bond is created with the product, which leads to a longer useful life (Simons et al. 2016).

Jürgen Bertling and Klaus Leggewie (2016) highlight three achievements of the repair movement in particular for the politically aspired "Great Transformation" (WBGU 2011). Firstly, repair practices are an important element of sustainability strategies; secondly, repair promotes the technological literacy of citizens; and thirdly, repairing together creates new social connections and opportunities for interaction (Bertling and Leggewie 2016, p. 277). These three elements of the repair society can be observed very well in repair cafés. The third point in particular is interesting from a democratic theory perspective, because in Repair Cafés actors not only acquire technical knowledge, but also experiment democratic practices. They learn to organize themselves and to make decisions in groups. Both often function in social innovations in the form of democratic micro-practices (see below). The function of repair cafés as a meeting place in the neighbourhood or district should also not be underestimated. Guests spend the waiting time with others at the coffee table, and this opportunity is used for conversations about various topics.

The acquired democratic and technical competencies are subsequently used by actors in other contexts as well. This step of social learning is a building block of transformative social innovation (Dumitru et al. 2016), which will be examined in more detail in the project. Specifically, the question is to what extent social innovations can develop democratizing potential and whether the democratic practices practiced in social innovations also lead to the activation of democratic values in other contexts.

2.1 The Workshop: A Training Space for Productive Sociability

In the chapter on the *workshop in* his book *Zusammenarbeit*, Richard Sennett posits that "physical work can promote dialogic social behavior" (Sennett 2012, p. 267). We also follow this observation, as it has been shown that successful social innovations can generate discard effects (Kropp 2014) and stimulate social learning processes (Dumitru et al. 2016). Both manifestations of transformative potential are pursued in the RePair Democracy project. Our considerations are based on the assumption that actors of social innovations experience positive self-efficacy in the successful initiatives. Learned skills and certainties can in turn be brought into community shaping processes "by transferring experiences gained in the workshop to society" (Sennett 2012, p. 268). Thus, the workshop serves as a symbol of shaping common living space in collaboration. Here, the connection between craftsmanship – for example, repairing things together – and social coexistence is of central importance. "Those who acquire skill in making things as craftspeople develop physical skills that can also be applied to social life" (ibid., p. 267).

The workshop can thus be reconstructed as the basic form of cooperation and is thus also a serious burning glass for a grassroots democratic way of life that solves problems cooperatively on the spot. To this end, some rules of interrelated behavior in social innovations are empirically observable and conducive to society as a whole to develop an economy that is both sustainable and democratic. Democratic micro-practices indicate in the immediate interaction with each other – as the smallest unit of equal interaction – the basic skills and attitudes as a condition for the possibility of democratic design processes.

2.2 What Are Democratic Micro-practices?

> For humans, action exists solely because it is action on the part of the other. (Ziemer 2013: 86)

A first essential characteristic of successful understanding is the principle of *dialogue.* This goes from the recognition of the other as a you (cf. Buber 1996) to the ability to listen and speak "at eye level" – the first is a prerequisite for the second. The recognition of the interlocutor as an Other requires a *distancing,* that he/she has an independent being. Listening and speaking allows us to *enter into a relationship* with the other person. "The foundation of being human-with-human is this twofold and one: the desire of every human being to be affirmed by human beings as what he is, indeed what he can become, and the innate ability of human beings to affirm their fellow human beings in just the same way" (Buber 1951, p. 33f.). Buber sees this principle as already being permanently disturbed in his time. Directly related to the dialogical principle are *openness,* allowing for surprise and loss of control, and *unreservedness,* that is, being free from judgment about the unknown. These two qualities are part of the distancing that is necessary in order to be able to negotiate rules together as equals and different at the same time.

This is already very presuppositional for a world that tends to produce narcissistic subjects. In order to acknowledge the Other unconditionally and openly and to enter into a relationship with him/her under this precondition, we need a *tolerance of ambiguity,* i.e. a relaxed way of dealing with contradictions and differences, and *trust in* the sense of a positivization of uncertainty and strangeness. "Precisely because in modernity we increasingly encounter the Other as a stranger, as someone with whom we share neither characteristics nor symbolic frames of reference, we are both compelled and free to encounter him [...] with 'inner unreservedness'" (Hetzel 2010, p. 248). Trust, however, cannot be *manufactured,* but is "given and accepted" (Luhmann 1989, p. 46); it belongs to the realm of *unavailability* that accompanies and enriches all of life (cf. Rosa 2018). Because one moves out of a realm of one's own controllability, trust can easily come into conflict with other values such as security, certainty, or expectability, because it is convenient to call for the "big other" to resolve conflicts qua positing (e.g., by the state). For democratic micro-practices, however, trust is constitutive, since in the context of an immediate dialogical understanding there is no determiner who decides on a dissent.

For democratic coexistence, it is therefore essential to "endure" ambiguities and uncertainties. Another characteristic of democratic micro-practices helps here: *Diversity sensitivity.* This somewhat cumbersome term – for lack of a better one – describes a *milieu-, context-, age- and culture-sensitivity* without which a broad inclusion of different positions as equals can only fail. Moreover, diversity sensitivity promotes tolerance of ambiguity, because *being sensitive to* the *other as equal* also leads to a relaxed approach to uncertainties, contradictions and the extraordinary.

And being sensitive to divergence does not take place in a cultureless space, but presupposes *reflexivity.* Reflexivity is the awareness of the partiality *(perspectivity) of* one's own perception of the world, which a person has developed through his or her specific experiences. In order to develop an awareness of one's own perspectivity, methodical *self-observation* is required. This in turn enables *self-criticism* as a prerequisite for seeing and acknowledging other perspectives in their otherness (cf. Moldaschl 2010, p. 10). This partly overlaps with the distancing mentioned above in order to "look away from one's own egocentric perspective" (ibid., p. 4). *Decentering* one's perspective allows one to become aware of the *time- and location-bound nature of thinking* (cf. Mannheim 1978). This insight makes it possible to know about the genesis of other perspectives and to always understand one's own standpoint as relational to others. "The mental situation at stake theoretically offers the possibility of switching back and forth between mutually logically exclusive systems of meaning." (Berger 1984, p. 62).

These very presuppositional and idealistic characteristics of democratic encounters base their presence and effectiveness on the *binding nature of* the effects of joint efforts. If political commitment does not lead to consequences, confidence in one's own effectiveness dwindles. If the same logic always prevails in the shaping of the common living space, reflexivity is corroded in favour of strategic benefit orientation. This in turn results in an aloofness, instrumentalizing other people and objects and making them objects of one's own point of view – and so on. Only through commitment can political self-efficacy manifest itself and thus promote democratic micro-practices. The conditions for this are very fragile.

In order to make political self-efficacy at the local level more likely, certain forms of practice are particularly suitable for realizing collaboration. *Complicity* (Ziemer 2013) and *collaboration* (Terkessidis 2015), often used in criminal or war contexts, both refer to purposeful cooperation that is entered into unbureaucratically and flexibly between people for a limited time. Complicity, derived from criminal law, means a purposeful, temporary complicity based on trust (cf. Ziemer 2013, p. 167 f.). It is based on voluntariness and the desire to form alliances and leads to close entanglements "between different elements" (ibid., p. 70). The diversity of social origins or perspectives involved recedes into the background in comparison to the jointly entered practice. Thus, surprising changes can be made in complicity. The principle of collaboration as solution-oriented, cross-border and mediating cooperation aims in a similar direction. Self-efficacy is experienced in the direct impact on the (social) environment. Moreover, collaboration is decoupled from education, background or skills – it does not require "more education!" as a prerequisite for social participation. Collaboration is *communal self-care with radicalized inclusion.*

The characteristics and elements of democratic micro-practices described above are more or less lived out in the social innovations or real utopias described above. In-depth empirical studies must provide further clarity as to whether these are merely theoretical idealizations or whether democratic micropractices can actually be realized in practice. The principle of collaboration will be discussed again below. It embodies such a presuppositional possibility of rethinking and practicing a *democratization of democracy* from local fields. First, however, we would like to present a possible form of institutionalisation of how local political self-efficacy can be developed.

3 A Repair Café for Democracy

In the project "RePair Democracy"[1], a format for a place where urban commoning can take place is being developed from the experiences of repair cafés and other social innovations. Commoning refers to practices that are based on "sharing or

[1] The project "RePair Democracy. Social Innovations as an Experimental Field of Demo-

using together *and at the same time* producing lasting social structures in which we can cooperate and create something useful" (Helfrich and Bollier 2019, p. 19). Urban commoning thus refers to the "commons-making" (Stavrides 2018, p. 22) of urban living conditions such as the sharing of public spaces or the cooperative shaping of urban policy. Commoning refers to a logic of cooperation and self-organization that begins where neither state nor market solutions are effective (Helfrich and Bollier 2012).

Under the name *Demokratiecafé (Democracy Café),* these events, designed and carried out together with practice partners, function as laboratories for experiments with forms of collaborative democracy (Rohr 2013).

3.1 Workshops for the Development of Local Democracies

The multiple crises of democracy discussed in the introduction suggest that democracy as we know it no longer works. There is thus a need to test alternatives for democratic design, at least in the local.

The format of the Democracy Cafés is closely based on the process of Repair Cafés. Visitors are greeted at the entrance and given a handout on which they should note, among other things, what concerns they have come to the event with. On the one hand, this serves the purpose of self-reflection, on the other hand, the collection of concerns offers the possibility to bring people with similar concerns together. In contrast to Repair Cafés, there are no experts for democracy in Democracy Cafés who can help the visitors to deal with their concerns. Rather, self-help groups with similar concerns form spontaneously – not necessarily with similar ideas for solutions to these concerns. Thus, with the help of moderation techniques, the Democracy Café primarily brings together people who see a need for action on similar issues. Depending on the occasion and the group, the methods range from future workshops to design thinking workshops (cf. Nauditt and Wermerskirch 2018). The aim should always be to make concrete action the goal. The next step should be a reconnection of concerns to processes of democratic design (re-pair). For example, in the first democracy cafés in Munich, a group of civil society actors solidified their desire to participate in the process of introducing an online participation platform for the state capital of Munich. By developing criteria for such a platform from the perspective of civil society, the group was able

cratic Micropractices" is one of eleven subprojects in the Bavarian research network "ForDemocracy. Future of Democracy" (https://www.fordemocracy.de/)

to approach city politics and the administration with concrete concerns and was subsequently involved in the still ongoing design of the platform.

It does not have to be about direct demands, but participation can also mean that citizens formulate concerns for which they demand a process of democratic design. This would be a further development of previous formats of direct democracy, such as referendums, which are based on yes/no decisions.

In the sense of urban commoning, the visitors of democracy cafés deal with the joint shaping of local living conditions. This reference to the local is a reaction to the realization that national and international agreements are increasingly difficult to negotiate. This is currently most evident, among other things, in the example of climate policy, which, in the face of the "ecological-economic pincer crisis" cited above (Dörre 2019), seems increasingly helpless the larger the scale it works on becomes. National climate protection plans seem incapable of really dealing with the crisis, and transnational agreements are torpedoed out of nation-state interests and seem doomed to failure. A feasible democratic lever for dealing with climate change seems to be the cooperation of actors from different sectors at the local level (cf. WBGU 2016).

3.2 Just Do It!

With the development of the Democracy Café, we are connecting to the ideas of the repair movement in many ways. Firstly, it is about the democratic principle of appropriating design options. In Repair Cafés, this is the re-appropriation of products that are repaired and thus withdrawn from the logical course of the throwaway society. Democracy Cafés are about the re-appropriation of political shaping of the local environment.

Secondly, both cases are about direct *action*. What social innovations from the field of repair and open workshops have in common is that the actors are concerned with finding and tackling pragmatic solutions. No grand visions are needed at the beginning, the entire system is not changed, but it is about working on current concerns: "concrete, precise and solution-oriented" (Baier et al. 2016, p. 35). In doing so, one's own contribution to systemic transformation is not ignored, but in the "mode of repairing the world" (ibid.), the processing of concrete matters dominates over discourse.

The Democracy Café also starts with this principle. In this context, "RePair Democracy" means reconnecting concerns to processes of democratic design rather than repairing political institutions that have fallen into crisis. Even if the connection to existing institutions becomes more and more important in the course of the processes in order to ensure the implementation of the results of the Democracy Cafés, it is nevertheless crucial at the beginning to set a dynamic in motion and to get into action.

4 Collaborative Democracy and the Question of Representation

What happens when politics no longer reflects the needs and wishes of the citizens, when the concerns for a sustainable society are not heard? The alienation between elected decision-makers and voters, *not being heard* and *remaining ineffective* in their own concerns, is a major cause of the crisis of democracy. For: "Modern democracy is […] fundamentally based on the idea that its form of politics gives each individual a voice and makes them audible, so that the politically shaped world becomes an expression of their productive polyphony" (Rosa 2016, p. 366). An intensive exchange between representatives and the represented is a basic prerequisite for the success of a representative democracy (Diehl 2016, p. 12). However, if one understands democracy as a *way of life* (cf. Dewey 1996, 2011), then the practical practice of coordinated behaviour moves to the centre. Democracy then takes place everywhere in everyday life, in the realm of the interpersonal. Repair cafés, open workshops or solidarity farms are an experimental field for this.

In such social innovations, counter-strategies to ecological collapse are already being practiced. And they are able to counteract both the "ecological-economic pincer crisis" and a "crisis of democracy". For on the one hand, they are exercised *beyond the market and* the *state* (cf. Helfrich and Heinrich-Böll-Stiftung 2012) and thus escape the logic of permanent economic growth, which entails a dwindling of ecology. On the other hand, these initiatives mostly function in a grassroots democratic way. They thus represent precisely those concerns that are virulent on the ground and institutionalize their practical management on flexible and manageable scales through *collaborative production* and *joint consumption.* Depending on the size of the initiative, decisions are made from the grassroots or by an elected board or in interaction. For the partly formalized, partly informal organizing principles, we have proposed the term *democratic micropractices* and made some substantive determinations. By the term we mean the smallest dialogical unit of interaction for negotiating common goals and their ways to achieve them on a local scale.

4.1 For a Policy of Collaboration

In a graduated model of political participation, the following systematization can be made, which successively increases the intensity of participation of the individual in the shaping of the community: informative, deliberative and collaborative participation (Rohr 2013, p. 33). *Informative participation* in the shaping of living spaces means the passing on of information about building projects or other planning by politicians to citizens. *Deliberation is* based on mutual exchange on questions of future coexistence and includes the hope that the best ideas will prevail in the end. However, this does not yet imply that political participation in deliberative processes also implies decision-making power and that corresponding consequences will become visible. Collaboration, on the other hand, is directly related to political self-efficacy in that "participants actively collaborate and cooperate on concepts, results and ideas" (ibid., p. 34).

Collaboration, from the Latin *co-laborare,* in its most general sense means working together. The principle of repair and the place of the workshop already pointed to such practices. Moreover, collaboration is determined by starting "from the contradictoriness of relations and the activity of individuals" (Terkessidis 2015, p. 11f.). Thus, it does not only mean collaboration of those with the same interests, but, as this was elaborated in the determination of democratic micropractices, a *collaboration of those who are different as equals.* Collaborations, then, take place across the board where different interests, desires, and abilities meet in order to "foreground [the] actual, multitudinous, complicated concerns of the heterogeneous population" (ibid., p. 54). To this end, there are many possible additions to existing democracy to reconnect *(re-pair)* the concerns of citizenship and policy implementation – for example, the (partial) composition of parliament by drawing lots (cf. Van Reybrouck 2016). A *politics of collaboration* enshrines the principle of cross-cutting cooperation of the diverse – without boiling down to the principle of majority voting.

4.2 Re-pair Democracy

In this paper we have tried to show how a sustainable way of life can be practiced. A considerable resistance to the possibility of a comprehensive realization can be found in the conception of democracy and the practice of democracy. We proposed to locate democratic processes of habitat design in local *connectives* (cf. Ziemer 2013, p. 64ff.). This promises a higher likelihood that concerns of both the inhabitants of a neighbourhood and demands that the climate will make on us in the future will be implemented. The practices that have a model character for this can be found in repair cafés and other workshops, which on the one hand have a local connection and on the other hand cultivate an environmentally friendly and sustainable way of dealing with their co-world. Sustainable lifestyles are structurally anchored in the thematised social innovations in a grassroots democratic way. Against this, it can be argued that the "liberal democratic society [...] has elevated the 'politics of non-sustainability' to its principle" (Lessenich 2019, p. 103). In terms of the "ecological-economic pincer crisis", the current political system is fundamentally caught in a dynamic of producing disasters. There are no links between environmental concerns and institutional design power. Therefore, it is beneficial to focus on *democratic micro-practices* that subvert the institutional structure of unsustainability and already practice alternatives "in the here and now".

These practices follow a politics of collaboration based on the inclusion and interaction of the diverse. Collaboration is grassroots democracy, without realizing the will of a majority. Rather, it is a matter of concretely coming into joint action, as suggested by the principle of the workshop. The Democracy Café presented in this article – and to be further developed in the course of the research project – is conceived as a workshop for the development of local democracies. In it, the concerns and needs of a city, a neighbourhood or a neighbourhood come together and, as it were, the skills and abilities come together to address the concerns in a practical way. The goal is to anchor democracy cafés in urban society in order to connect the wishes and needs of citizens with new possibilities for shaping them.

The development of the Democracy Café is subject to a dynamic of practical co-production. In the sense of *responsive science*, this co-production of the practice of the Democracy Café is an "interaction between science and society" (Matthies et al. 2015, p. 21). The dynamics of the field have captured and propelled the project from the first moment. This means that we had to rearrange the originally envisioned project steps and could not develop the Democracy Café following an extensive empirical study of Repair Cafés, but that the development has become part of a collaborative and transdisciplinary process that is still ongoing. Thus, as a project of transdisciplinary research, we open the protected space of scientific preparation, but benefit from the influences of our practice partners and ongoing experiences from the workshop "Democracy Café".

References

Baier, Andrea, T. Hansing, C. Müller und K. Werner. 2016. Die Welt reparieren: Eine Kunst des Zusammenmachens. In *Die Welt reparieren: Open Source und Selbermachen als postkapitalistische Praxis*, Hrsg. Andrea Baier, Tom Hansing, Christa Müller und Karin Werner, 34–62. Bielefeld: transcript.

Bandura, Albert. 1997. *Self Efficacy: The Exercise of Control*. New-York: Freeman.

Beck, Gerald und C. Kropp, Hrsg. 2012. *Gesellschaft Innovativ – Wer sind die Akteure?* Wiesbaden: Springer VS.

Berger, Peter L. 1984. *Einladung zur Soziologie. Eine humanistische Perspektive*. Reinbek bei Hamburg: Rowohlt.

Bertling, Jürgen, und C. Leggewie. 2016. Die Reparaturgesellschaft. Ein Beitrag zur Großen Transformation? In *Die Welt reparieren: Open Source und Selbermachen als postkapitalistische Praxis*, Hrsg. Andrea Baier, Tom Hansing, Christa Müller und Karin Werner, 275–286. Bielefeld: transcript.

Blühdorn, Ingolfur. 2013. *Simulative Demokratie. Neue Politik nach der postdemokratischen Wende*. Frankfurt a. M.: Suhrkamp Verlag.

Buber, Martin. 1951. *Urdistanz und Beziehung*. Heidelberg: Verlag Lambert Schneider.

Buber, Martin. 1996 [1923]. *Ich und Du*. Stuttgart: Reclam.

Dewey, John. 1996. *Die Öffentlichkeit und ihre Probleme*. Darmstadt: Wissenschaftliche Buchgesellschaft.

Dewey, John. 2011. *Demokratie und Erziehung. Eine Einleitung in die philosophische Pädagogik*. Weinheim: Beltz.

Diehl, Paula. 2016. Demokratische Repräsentation und ihre Krise. *Aus Politik und Zeitgeschichte 40–42*: 12–17.

Dörre, Klaus. 2017. Nach dem schnellen Wachstum: große Transformation und öffentliche Soziologie. In *Öffentliche Soziologie. Wissenschaft im Dialog mit der Gesellschaft*, Hrsg. Brigitte Aulenbacher, Michael Burawoy, Klaus Dörre und Johanna Sittel, 33–67. Frankfurt a. M./New York: Campus.

Dörre, Klaus. 2019. Risiko Kapitalismus. Landnahme, Zangenkrise, Nachhaltigkeitsrevolution. In *Große Transformation? Zur Zukunft moderner Gesellschaften. Sonderband des Berliner Journals für Soziologie*, Hrsg. Klaus Dörre, Hartmut Rosa, Karina Becker, Sophie Bose und Benjamin Seyd, 3–33. Wiesbaden: Springer VS.

Dumitru, Adina, I. Lema-Blanco, M. Ricardo-Garcìa, I. Kunze, T. Strasser und R. Kemp. 2016. Social Learning for Transformative Social Innovation. *TRANSIT Deliverable 2.3. TRANSIT:EU SSH.2013.3.2-1 Grant Agreement n.613169*. http://www.transitsocialinnovation.eu/resource-hub/transit-deliverable-23-social-learning-for-transformative-social-innovation. Zugegriffen: 04. April 2019.

Helfrich, Silke und D. Bollier. 2012. Commons als transformative Kraft. In *Commons: Für eine neue Politik jenseits von Markt und Staat*, Hrsg. Silke Helfrich und Heinrich-Böll-Stiftung, 15–23. Bielefeld: Transcript.

Helfrich, Silke und D. Bollier. 2019. *Frei, fair und lebendig – Die Macht der Commons*. Bielefeld: Transcript.

Helfrich, Silke und Heinrich-Böll-Stiftung. 2012. *Commons: Für eine neue Politik jenseits von Markt und Staat*. Bielefeld: Transcript.

Hetzel, Andreas. 2010. Vertrauen als Affekt der radikalen Demokratie. In Das Politische und die Politik, Hrsg. Thomas Bedorf und Kurt Röttgers, 235–251. Berlin: Suhrkamp.

Howaldt, Jürgen und H. Jacobsen, Hrsg. 2010. *Soziale Innovation: Auf dem Weg zu einem postindustriellen Innovationsparadigma*. Wiesbaden: VS Verlag für Sozialwissenschaften.

Kropp, Cordula. 2014. Homo socialis – auf der Suche nach dem anderen Glück. In *Jahrbuch Ökologie 2014*, 71–81. Stuttgart: Hirzel Verlag.

Lefebvre, Henri. 2016. *Das Recht auf Stadt*. Hamburg: Nautilus.

Les Convivialistes. 2014. *Das konvivialistische Manifest: Für eine neue Kunst des Zusammenlebens*. Bielefeld: Transcript.

Lessenich, Stephan. 2019. *Grenzen der Demokratie. Teilhabe als Verteilungsproblem*. Stuttgart: Reclam Verlag.

Luhmann, Niklas. 1989. *Vertrauen. Ein Mechanismus der Reduktion sozialer Komplexität* Stuttgart: Enke.

Mannheim, Karl (1978 [1929]). *Ideologie und Utopie*. Frankfurt a. M.: Schulte-Bulmke.

Matthies, Hildegard, D. Simon und M. Torka. 2015. *Die Responsivität der Wissenschaft. Wissenschaftliches Handeln in Zeiten neuer Wissenschaftspolitik*. Bielefeld: transcript Verlag.

Moldaschl, Manfred. 2010. *Was ist Reflexivität?* Papers and Preprints of the Department of Innovation Research and Sustainable Resource Management (BWL IX). Chemnitz University of Technology, No. 11/2010.

Moulaert, Frank, D. MacCullum und J. Hillier. 2014. Social innovation: intuition, precept, concept, theory and practice. In *The International Handbook on Social Innovation: Collective Action, Social Learning and Transdisciplinary Research*, Hrsg. Frank Moulaert, Diana Maccallum, Abid Mehmood und Abdelillah Hamdouch, 13–24. Northampton: Edward Elgar Pub.

Nauditt, Kristina und G. Wermerskirch. 2018. *Radikal beteiligen: 30 Erfolgskriterien und Gedanken zur Vertiefung demokratischen Handelns*. Köln: EHP Edition Humanistische Psychologie.

Rohr, Jascha. 2013. *In unserer Macht. Aufbruch in die Kollaborative Demokratie*. Klein Jasedow: Oya.

Rosa, Hartmut. 2016. *Resonanz: Eine Soziologie der Weltbeziehung*. Berlin: Suhrkamp Verlag.

Rosa, Hartmut. 2018. *Unverfügbarkeit*. Wien/Salzburg: Residenz Verlag.

Sennett, Richard. 2012. *Zusammenarbeit. Was unsere Gesellschaft zusammenhält*. München: Hanser Berlin.

Simons, Arno, U. Petschow und J. Peuckert. 2016. Offene Werkstätten – nachhaltig innovativ? Potenziale gemeinsamen Arbeitens und Produzierens in der gesellschaftlichen Transformation. *Schriftenreihe des IÖW* 212/16 1–73.

Stavrides, Stavros. 2018. Common Space: Die Stadt als Gemeingut. Eine Einführung. In *Gemeingut Stadt. Berliner Hefte zu Geschichte und Gegenwart der Stadt #4*, Hrsg. Mathias Heyden, 18–92. Berlin: EECLECTIC.

Terkessidis, Mark. 2015. *Kollaboration*. Berlin: Suhrkamp.

Van Reybrouck, David. 2016. *Gegen Wahlen. Warum Abstimmen nicht demokratisch ist*. Göttingen: Wallstein Verlag.

WBGU. 2011. Welt im Wandel. Gesellschaftsvertrag für eine Große Transformation. (Hauptgutachten). https://www.wbgu.de/de/publikationen/publikation/welt-im-wandel-gesellschaftsvertrag-fuer-eine-grosse-transformation. Zugegriffen: März 2017.

WBGU. 2016. Der Umzug der Menschheit: Die transformative Kraft der Städte. http://www.wbgu.de/hg2016/. Zugegriffen: März 2017.

Wright, Erik Olin. 2017. *Reale Utopien: Wege aus dem Kapitalismus*. Berlin: Suhrkamp Verlag.

Ziemer, Gesa. 2013. *Komplizenschaft. Neue Perspektiven auf Kollektivität*. Bielefeld: transcript.

Beck, Gerald, Prof. Dr. (sociologist). Since 2014 Professor for Social Innovation and Organizational Development at the University of Applied Sciences Munich. Head of the BA Management of Social Innovations and MA Social Change and Participation. Current research project: RePair Democracy. Social innovations as an experimental field of democratic micro-practices. Funded by the Bavarian State Ministry for Science and Art in the research network ForDemocracy. Gerald Beck researches and teaches in the fields of sustainability, social transformation, social innovation, design and democracy.

Latest Publications:

https://www.sw.hm.edu/die_fakultaet/personen/professoren/beck_gerald/Gerald_Beck.de.html

Jende, Robert, sociologist (Magister Artium), research assistant at the University of Applied Sciences Munich in the research project "RePair Democracy. Soziale Innovationen als Experimentierfeld demokratischer Mikropraktiken" funded by the Bavarian State Ministry of Science and the Arts in the research network ForDemocracy. Research interests: Performative sociology, public sociology, social transformation, social theory, aesthetics.

Latest Publications:

https://www.sw.hm.edu/die_fakultaet/personen/wissenschaftliche_mitarbeiterinnen/jende/jende.de.html

When Many Do Something Differently – Social Innovations and Sustainability in the Phenomenon of Bottle Collecting

Florian Engel

Abstract

The consensus of the conference on innovation was: "When many do something differently". I would like to demonstrate such defined innovative action using the example of bottle collecting. Instead of seeing this solely as the last resort of an exhausted underclass, I propose to understand those who give and take deposits as communicatively acting subjects in interaction with objectified matter. Innovative action then already begins in the smallest communicative contexts, in which deposit bottles, for example, do not merely stand around to be collected as garbage. It is precisely the free-standing bottle that connects the reciprocal subjective attention of the person giving and receiving the deposit. The object of the deposit bottle culminates objectified and obstinate (action) knowledge about the phenomenon of 'collecting deposits'. The bottle in the publicly visible space is not *free,* but establishes a different kind of communicative relationship. In the form of the deposit rings, it then becomes apparent, for example, that urban space is specifically rethought and reshaped on a material and symbolic level by 'many who do something different', following the references offered by the free-standing bottle. By means of a combined textual and pictorial analysis, I would like to trace these communicative entanglements, which often

F. Engel (✉)
University of Applied Sciences, Fulda, Germany
e-mail: florian.engel@pg.hs-fulda.de

H.-W. Franz et al. (eds.), *Sustainable Living and Business*,
https://doi.org/10.1007/978-3-658-41835-9_18

take place invisibly, in the form of the deposit bottle. For in its spatiotemporal references I understand it as a relevant aspect of social innovations in urban living spaces.

1 Introduction

"When many do something differently": This was the consensus at the conference "Sustainable Living and Management – Managing Social Innovation as a Shaping of Social Transformation" on the concept of social innovation. It depends on the object of the innovation exactly whom this "many" should represent. For social science sustainability research, it seems that primarily actors of the middle and upper classes are meant and implicitly addressed here. Especially economically less capable members of society are supposedly hardly interested in environmental issues (Schad 2018), precisely because they 'lack' capital, (problem) awareness and the will to engage themselves (Bögenhold 1991; Heinrichs and Grunenberg 2012). This fundamental problem of a blind spot on the part of social science sustainability and innovation research on social inequality appears all the more glaring, as such a narrowed view unquestioningly grasps the subject of interest to it in the sustainability discourse as an actor acting consciously, operating with a relatively clear consideration of goals and means. The 'doers' who are instead considered relevant and drive innovation exist, of course, e.g. in Gabriele Christmann's avant-garde spatial pioneers (2018) or in the diverse research on entrepreneurs (Aulinger 2003). However, both research perspectives, similar to recent approaches to the sharing economy, narrow their view to certain aspects of innovation, in the form of class-specific attitudes and particularly empowered actors.

In contrast, I would like to trace social innovation using the example of bottle collecting, whose sustainability dimension is rooted in the deposit legislation of the early 2000s (Federal Ministry for the Environment, Nature Conservation and Nuclear Safety 2001; Moser 2014). In such a marginalized social context as bottle collecting, innovation does not only depend on the creative class. Rather, it can be traced in connection with everyday communicative acts in which many do things differently. Instead of seeing deposit collection as the last resort of an exhausted underclass, I propose to understand deposit givers and takers as communicatively acting subjects in the public space of our cities in interaction with objectified matter. These contexts of communicative action can then be traced, for example, under the aspect of innovatory action, in which many do something differently.

By means of a combined text and image analysis[1] I would like to trace these communicative entanglements in which deposit bottles represent objectified matter and are an element of social innovation. For in their micro-sociologically comprehensible spatio-temporal references I understand them as a relevant aspect of macro-sociologically effective, social innovation processes in urban living spaces, which often happen unobserved, but certainly uncoordinated. Therefore, a pointed theoretical embedding in communicative constructivism (Knoblauch 2017) is followed by a main empirical section divided into three parts. In the first part, I will trace the communicative actions between pledgers and pledgees by means of interview excerpts.[2] This is followed by the second analysis of objectivation as an objectification detached from the situation, which is to be reconstructed primarily on the basis of visual materials. In the third analytical section I would like to trace the connection of those smallest communicative acts with the 'observable' socio-spatial change 'on a large scale'. The conclusion deals with the connection between innovation processes understood in terms of society as a whole and the micro-sociologically investigable connections between the acting subject and objectivation. Furthermore, I would like to make a short reflection on the process of analysis.

2 Ego – Alter Ego – Objectification – The Deposit Bottle in Communicative Constructivism

> Some children are romping through the lunch break of a businessman. He, too, is sipping a bottle of Radler. When he leaves, he just leaves the bottle. It'll soon be gone, he'll think to himself. It will. (Rüttenauer 2019)

I open with this quote from the taz of 17.05.2019, because in it the topic of collecting bottles connects in a concise way with a key concept of communicative constructivism: "All cases of communicative action necessarily include a bodily act-

[1] The data is taken from classic print media, the short news service Twitter and my master's thesis on "Combined forms of employment of bottle collectors in the Ruhr area – on the income structure of an urban social figure" from 2013. Names and data that could enable traceability have been anonymised.

[2] Written data is not the most appropriate material for an analysis according to communicative constructivism. To fall back on such pieces of data serves above all to successively introduce the central concept of objectivation, which in turn is to be analysed in more detail in its effects on the basis of image data.

ing." (Knoblauch 2017, p. 150) Where is bodily action and agency taking place here, or where does it come from? To get to the bottom of this introductory question, in this sect. I will first give a brief introduction to objectification of objects as a core concept of communicative constructivism. The aim will be to elaborate this epistemological basis for the more advanced concept of objectification by means of the deposit bottle in the empirical first part.

Communicative constructivism represents a further development of phenomenologically based constructivism. I am first interested in what Hubert Knoblauch calls the smallest unit of the social, the triadic relation of communicative action (cf. Fig. 1).

Following Grenz et al. (2018), I would like to exemplify this connection in Fig. 1: from a certain age, subject(2), which represents the alter ego in this constellation, learns that subject(1)/ego, the initially physically acting subject who brings a weapon to bear, is not concerned with this weapon itself, but with what (1)/ego is aiming at; so possibly subject(2)/alter ego. The gun together with the finger on the trigger is then perceived by both subjects (1) and (2) as part of a common environment and is an elementary component of mutual coordination (of, among other things, aiming, dodging, re-aiming and moving into cover). The rifle is therefore not simply an *object*, but an *object-in-action,* or more precisely: a part of the execution of social action, because it is a perceptible and thus effective expression of joint action executions. Objectifications thus contribute to meaningful processes of negotiation. They achieve this by transporting, through their specific form and application, a sense and knowledge that can be experienced and comprehended intersubjectively, which would not function in this way without their specific presence. The very idea that subject(1)/ego would use a toy weapon instead of the weapon

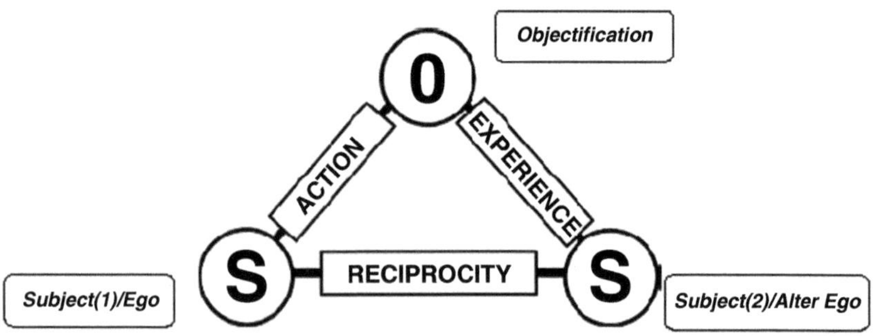

Fig. 1 The triadic relation of communicative action. (Source: Knoblauch 2017; p. 112, italics in the boxes added by the author)

changes the reciprocal meaning, the possibilities of experience, the action and thus also the negotiation process as a whole.

Although both objects are similar or even appear identical, their inherent meaning and the knowledge necessary for their use (as part of objectification) are not. And even if ego and alter ego behaved similarly – aiming, dodging, taking cover – their movements would presumably lack urgency and acute fear for their own survival. As already indicated, objectifications can also be gestures, facial expressions, verbal expressions and much more. For Hubert Knoblauch, however, it is central that objectifications, as in the above quotation, are always part of observable and experienceable action processes between subjects and objectified objects. Following on from this, how can we imagine the deposit bottle as an objectified object in such acts of action? Here is a piece of data from my master's thesis, in the course of which I conducted open-narrative interviews with bottle collectors in the Ruhr region in 2012.

> And then it even happens that other football fans say: 'Hey, leave him alone'. Or, if you're walking through the train and they see you, *they'll reach out to you with* the *bottle* or take it from the shelf or from the bag. Or they call out: *'Master, come back here'. And they give you the bottle.* You're not really a second-rate person, it's perfectly okay. [...] So that's actually quite positive. (Michael, author's emphasis)

It becomes apparent that the deposit bottle is perceived by both interacting people as an object of interest and assumes a constitutive role in the reciprocal bodily-sensual action of the involved subjects. This is referred to in the last emphasized sentence: "And they give you the bottle". The triadic schema in which the bottle effects something as an experiential and effective aspect of the environment shared with the two subjects is again apparent here. The 'bottle' of the last sentence thus refers on the gestural level to its inherent sense of being accepted. The objectified bottle thus coordinates the possibility of experience and action in the triadic communicative action. This becomes more understandable again if we form new readings in a hermeneutic sense. Without the contextual information that the bottle is being held out towards, and only with the sentence "Master, come back here!", this could be – because it is located in the Ruhr area – the teasing of a Dortmund fan towards a Schalker. Or someone is actually calling for a master mechanic. There are an infinite number of possibilities.

Only through the perception of the bottle as a relevant object in the specific action situation or action process (object-in-action) does it, as a third moment, place both subjects, acting and perceiving in its inherent way, in a meaningful and knowledge-charged specific relation[3] to each other. The bottle thus accomplishes something in communication, representing the "embodiment of subjective processes in occurrences and objects" (Schütz and Luckmann 1979, p. 317, cited in Grenz et al. 2018, p. 99) of the everyday lifeworld. Such scenes of gift exchange (on the paradigmatic meaning of the gift following Marcel Mauss in particular detail: Caillé 2008) in which meaning and knowledge are intersubjectively negotiated can be observed daily and also performed by oneself. But the vast majority of bottles are not handed over in this way, but find *more anonymous* paths.

2.1 Analysis I: The Bottle Detached from the Action – From Objectification to Objectivation

In the following short interview sequence a past situation for bottle collectors is described, which can be described as typical.

> Let's say at the station you *look* in the trash cans, *all the* people *look, they stare*. I mean, that's a phenomenon anyway. […] *There's a bottle there now* and sometimes I *don't* go *there because people are looking*. […] But that I have to be aware of it at that moment and say: 'Go there, take it, that's all'. And a lot of people have that shame, too, and other collectors have told me that, that you have that shame when other people are looking. (Michael, author's emphasis)

What takes place here? First of all, the established triadic communication situation between subjects and objectification becomes recognizable. However, the subjects do not come into direct contact with each other or with the bottle. Despite the absence of face-to-face interaction, the bottle nevertheless accomplishes something in this context. This is because its material properties are recognized as socially relevant, "[as they] contribute to the performance" (Knoblauch 2014, p. 134).

Their participation in the communicative negotiation causes Michael to perceive how people (supposedly) perceive someone, what he perceives. In doing so, however, he turns to several perceptible subjects in addition to the object of the bottle. Once again, an objectification similar to the earlier examples is present in the materiality of the bottle, which also contains the additional level of shame. The difference, however, lies in the fact that the inherent meaning of the bottle and the knowledge stored in it is not (any longer) communicated explicitly and in direct, bodily exchange between the subjects.

[3] Relationality is another concept or property that underlies Knoblauch's basic triadic scheme.

Let's remember the handover on the train. There, the pawner still clearly indicated his request to hand over the bottle via the interplay of language, gesture and material object. Nothing like that happens here. This detachment from direct, bodily interaction does not, however, change the meaning associated with the bottle, but rather transforms it from the original observable action into longer-term temporal and spatial processes. And it is precisely this spatiotemporal transformation of knowledge that Michael connects to here. The very perception of these attendants as possibly perceiving the bottle triggers highly specific interpretations and a tension expressing expectation[4], which includes, among other things, the feeling of shame. In the first interview excerpt, we have been able to see the meaning of the rifle as well as the deposit bottle as an object perceived as embedded in clearly delimitable spatial, temporal and bodily contexts of action. The bottle in this third piece of data is something different even in its beginnings. Michael describes the bottle as an objectivation in the Grenzian sense, detached from direct communicative action, with which a similar sense and a similar (action) knowledge are nevertheless associated. The bottle as objectivation is thus seen "not merely as a means to an end" (Grenz et al. 2018; p. 101), as it might appear in the first examples. It also possesses "a sensually perceptible dimension [...] which, although bound to the concrete situation of grasping, always contains from its shape a trans-situational (meaning) part that is not determined by its material boundness, but also not arbitrary (i.e. symbolically contingent)" (ibid.).

In the anticipatory communicative action of ego (Michael) with other subjects (alter egos) and objects – as objectivations – presented here, it becomes apparent that the materialization of the latter is anchored in the process of acting, but is not necessarily bound to its explicit spatiotemporal performance (Grenz et al. 2018). We are thus dealing here with a temporally as well as spatially delimited situation with a process character. In this situation, the object, which is detached from direct bodily interaction, nevertheless proves to have an effect on something and therefore to participate in a situation. In interaction with the subjects, the bottle causes perceptions, observations, interpretations and ultimately actions of the bottle collector reporting here, even without him or another subject entering into bodily interaction with it. Her perceived material presence alone constitutes a relevant moment to be analyzed. Expressed in Hubert Knoblauch's triadic schema, the bottle in

[4] With James Gibson (1982) and, building on this, Donald Norman (2004), this situation could also be understood as 'perceived affordances', which are closely associated with questions of the materiality of design and perception. I am particularly grateful to Tilo Grenz for this reference, which illuminates the proximity of sociological and psychological concepts to the connection between expectation and action.

this example would also be part of ego (action), alter ego (reciprocity) and objectification/objectivation (which is experienced), but without all three having to interact directly with each other.

2.2 Analysis II: Pledge as (Affecting) Objectivation

The Twitter feed of a bottle collector (see also Fig. 2) offers a further shift in perspective that sharpens this logic. She is a lady who walks regular routes and documents them online. I deliberately refer to a combined image-text tweet in which she describes one stop on this route to give a sense of the composition of image and text that is sometimes inherent in this medium. The route takes her across playgrounds, sports fields, schoolyards, through housing estates and natural spaces in her immediate living environment. We also learn that she actively scans these spaces for pawns. Similar to Sebastian Moser's (2014) findings, it becomes clear that many collectors do not only have the value of their bottles in mind. They roam

Fig. 2 Screenshot from Twitter of bottle collector who wishes to remain anonymous

through urban living space and comment, for example, that open bookshelves would be an offer worth preserving or even expanding. I chose this tweet, however, primarily because of the bottles concentrated in the bin here. Because on the basis of the comments, the action and expectation knowledge associated with them or stored in them becomes more comprehensible for collectors. The collector describes this very succinctly on a very intuitive, sensual level, which is difficult to access for most of us who have never had to collect bottles (Schmitt 2015). She writes: "No deposit there today? ... YES, there is!:-)". Written in capital letters, with an exclamation mark and a smiley beaming with joy.

People who do not collect probably do not feel such joy. They lack such joy, excitement and sensual/bodily affection/being attracted to this conglomerate. For them, this is first and foremost an accumulation of various identifiable objects that ultimately trigger no action or even major sensory response. For subjects who do not regularly collect bottles, these are precisely not a 'tappable store of knowledge'; objectification passes them by. Indeed, the bottles are presumably not even seen as a significant component of the ensemble 'garbage' that exists on its own, but are 'only' part of a conglomerate of what is thrown away. The bottle collector, however, has consciously and purposefully searched for the object of interest to her, found it and linked it as with an obstinacy and knowledge of action that is understandable to her. We can understand it theoretically, but that theoretical knowledge still wouldn't persuade us to follow her example, I would argue. Why this tweet is so intriguing is that, according to Grenz et al, "the interpretation of products as objectivations of specific knowledge is extremely rare in everyday life" (2018, p. 101). It is the knowing gaze of the collector that is expressed in this, transforming our everyday into their extra-ordinary or special.

Here we can also briefly return to the beginning of the article. Remember the – fictional – businessman and how he could obviously know that someone will come who will take the bottle. The bottle, as the third moment in the spatially and temporally separated action, communicates meaning and knowledge between two subjects through its specific shapes, smells and colours, and connects them without the ego and alter ego having to meet in the flesh. The bottle, understood as objectivation, is detached from the immediate consummation of action, reciprocity and perception, but without losing its effecting character.

2.3 Analysis III: Institutionalized Objectivations

In a third step, I take up the original question again. What does the phenomenon of bottle collecting have to do with innovation and sustainable action? For although the actions of many people are visible in what I have described so far, this seems to point rather to life contexts of poverty and urban pollution. But the bottle, with its associated meaning and knowledge, does not merely transform the actions of individual subjects towards and towards each other, as described in Sections I and II. For these diverse communicative actions that have spread uncoordinatedly since 2004 as an unintended consequence of the deposit legislation are the starting point of an intentional, innovating social action associated with the idea of sustainability. Deposit rings are not the only example of this, but they are one of the better-known ones (Fig. 3).

These installations, created consciously (by the then design student Paul Ketz) and with a specific intention (to facilitate collecting), are easily recognizable as an element of small-scale social change in the city. Precisely because of the unity of intention, action and person, this object is also recognizable as an innovation (e.g. through prizes: Bundespreis Ecodesign 2012) and usable (by municipalities, residents and the press).

The appearance of the deposit rings results directly from the phenomenon of bottle collecting. Accordingly, Paul Ketz names the humanization of collecting as well as the protection of the collectors from dirt and injury as an explicit goal and motivation. How deposit rings work, on the other hand, remains implicit. This is understandable, because the idea of deposit rings adapts nothing other than the (action) knowledge stored in the bottle. However, they provide a new, materially tangible connection for the spatio-temporally asynchronous, triadic scheme of action (see Section II) and, in this respect, a social innovation that becomes more compre-

Fig. 3 Deposit ring. Hildesheimer Allgemeine (2019)

hensible in concert with the smallest communicative action contexts of subjects and objects.

3 Conclusion

In the course of this article, the following should have become clear:

- Bottle collecting can be analysed as a phenomenon that takes place in the smallest communicative acts.
- From the point of view of communicative constructivism, deposit bottles can be understood as matter that conveys meaning and knowledge, in the form of objectification even beyond direct bodily action. Deposit rings dock both to sense and knowledge objectified in the deposit bottle, but from a communicative constructivist point of view they also represent an institutionalization of the triadic scheme's action processes.[5]
- From this perspective, social innovations such as deposit rings can be seen as dualistic processes whose creative, intentional side cannot be understood without the often unnoticed, uncoordinated communicative action of many (over long periods of time), as can be found in bottle collecting.
- The sustainable change of urban living space does not only depend on the intentional creativity of its inhabitants. An analytical approach that attempts to understand the visible and invisible contexts of action in their interconnectedness appears to be fruitful.

It is precisely with the extension of the definition to the effecting material level that it becomes clear that social innovation can involve profoundly everyday processes. Objects play a specific role in these processes, as should have become clear in the analyses of the deposit bottle. They can be the consciously perceivable third moment in communicative actions (analysis section I). But they can also bring about communicative perception and action without actually being moved (analysis section II). In interaction with individuals acting in a purposefully innovative way, impulses and feedbacks for a more sustainable urban society emerge.

Innovative action thus already begins in the smallest communicative contexts in which deposit bottles are collected. It is precisely the free-standing bottle that con-

[5] Institutionalization has been a central aspect of the concept of knowledge for constructivist approaches at least since Berger and Luckmann (Knoblauch 2017: 58) as well as for the question of the connection between subjectification and objectification (ibid.: 69).

nects the reciprocal perception of subjects who give and take deposits. The object of the deposit bottle is the culmination of objectified and materialized (action) knowledge about the phenomenon of collecting. The bottle in the publicly visible space is not *'free as the wind'*, but offers material points of contact for a variety of new communicative references. Deposit rings innovatively continue these materially perpetuated stocks of knowledge and meaning. They show, for example, that urban space is being rethought and reshaped socially by the 'many and the many who do things differently', following on from the material and symbolic level. We see social innovation at work.

Section III in particular brought an unexpected insight in the course of the analysis. Objectifications and also objectivations initially exclude possibilities of interpretation and options for action. The knowledge of action inherent in them is a fundamental component of communicative action and helps to shape these situations. This is initially also true in the context of the materially institutionalized action-completion represented by the pledge rings. If we look at the picture again, however, we see no bottles there at all. The deposit ring is full of one-way plastic cups – the exact opposite of the deposit bottle. When objectivations as part of innovative processes such as the construction of deposit rings re-enter the sphere of visible action, subjects have the chance to reject the offer of knowledge conveyed by the bottle, to break it ironically, but also, of course, to simply misuse it. The circle of communicative action closes.

References

Aulinger, Andreas. 2003. Entrepeneurship – Selbstverständnis und Perspektiven einer Forschungsdisziplin. Schriftenreihe am Lehrstuhl für Allgemeine Betriebswirtschaftslehre, Unternehmensführung und Betriebliche Umweltpolitik. https://uol.de/fileadmin/user_upload/wire/fachgebiete/laub/download/Arbeitspapier_Entrepreneurship_Aulinger.pdf. Zugegriffen: 01.10.2019.

Bögenhold, Dieter. 1991. "Alternative" Wirtschaft oder Atoll des Kleinunternehmertums? Rückblick auf ein soziologisches Konstrukt. *Zeitschrift für Soziologie 20/3*: 223–236.

Bundesministerium für Umwelt, Naturschutz und nukleare Sicherheit (Hrsg.). 2001. Bundesumweltminister Jürgen Trittin: Pfand auf Einweg ab 2002 wird Vormarsch der Dose bremsen. Pressemitteilung des Bundesministeriums für Umwelt, Naturschutz und nukleare Sicherheit. https://www.bmu.de/pressemitteilung/bundesumweltminister-juergen-trittin-pfand-auf-einweg-ab-2002-wird-vormarsch-der-dose-bremsen/. Zugegriffen: 31.10.2019.

Bundespreis Ecodesign Hrsg. 2012. Preisträger 2012. https://bundespreis-ecodesign.de/de/wettbewerb/vorjahre/2012/preistraeger.html. Zugegriffen: 01.10.2019.

Christmann, Gabriele B. 2018. Städtische Raumpioniere, kommunikative Figurationen und Raum(re)konstruktionen in Quartieren. In Die mediatisierte Stadt. Kommunikative Figurationen des urbanen Zusammenlebens, Hrsg. Andreas Hepp, S. Kubitschko, I. Marszolek, 121–138. Wiesbaden: Springer VS.

Caillé, Alain. 2008. *Anthropologie der Gabe*. Frankfurt a. M.: Campus.

Gibson, James J. 1982. *Wahrnehmung und Umwelt. Der ökologische Ansatz in der visuellen Wahrnehmung*. München: Urban & Schwarzenberg.

Grenz, Tilo, M. Pfadenhauer und H. Kirschner. 2018. Die Unabgeschlossenheit von Objektivation. In Kommunikation – Medien – Konstruktion. Wissen, Kommunikation und Gesellschaft (Schriften zur Wissenssoziologie), Hrsg. Jo Reichertz und R. Bettmann, 93–116. Wiesbaden: Springer VS.

Norman, Donald. 2004. Affordances and Design. Persönliche Website des Autors. https://jnd.org/affordances_and_design/. Zugegriffen: 01.10.2019.

Heinrichs, Harald und H. Grunenberg. 2012. Sharing Economy – Auf dem Weg in eine neue Konsumkultur? Lüneburg Centre for Sustainability Management. https://www.ssoar.info/ssoar/bitstream/handle/document/42748/ssoar-2012-heinrichs_et_al-Sharing_Economy__Auf_dem.pdf. Zugegriffen: 01.10.2019.

Hildesheimer Allgemeine Zeitung (Hrsg.). 2019. Versuch gescheitert: Stadt baut Pfandringe ab. Hildesheimer Allgemeine Zeitung vom 01.02.2019. https://www.hildesheimer-allgemeine.de/news/article/versuch-gescheitert-stadt-baut-pfandringe-ab.html. Zugegriffen: 14.10.2019.

Knoblauch, Hubert. 2014. Das Subjekt des kommunikativen Handelns. In: Wer oder was handelt? Wissen, Kommunikation und Gesellschaft, Hrsg. Angelika Poferl und N. Schröer, 37–94. Wiesbaden: Springer VS.

Knoblauch, Hubert. 2017. *Die kommunikative Konstruktion der Wirklichkeit*. Buchreihe *Neue Bibliothek der Sozialwissenschaften, Bd. 15, Hrsg. Reiner Keller*. Wiesbaden: Springer VS.

Moser, Sebastian. 2014. *Pfandsammler. Erkundungen einer urbanen Sozialfigur*. Hamburg: Hamburger Edition.

Rüttenauer, Andreas. 2019. Wanderarbeiter in Europa. Ein Münchner aus Pasardschik. Tageszeitung 17.05.2019. https://taz.de/Wanderarbeiter-in-Europa/!5592917/. Zugegriffen: 01.10.2019.

Schad, Miriam. 2018. Typisch prekär? In Typologische Konstruktionen. Erlebniswelten. Hrsg. Nicole Burzan und R. Hitzler, 235–251. Wiesbaden: Springer VS.

Schmitt, Christian J. 2015. Ethnographische Gameness. In Ethnographische Erkundungen. Erlebniswelten. Ronald Hitzler und M. Gothe, 273–294.Wiesbaden: Springer VS.

Engel, Florian, Master of Arts, Studies in General Social Science (Uni Bochum), Studies in Sociology with focus on Restructuring Gender Relations at the University of Bochum. Research assistant at the House of Competence of the Karlsruhe Institute of Technology (KIT) with a focus on scientific presentation. Since 2015 research assistant at the Department of Nursing and Health at the University of Applied Sciences Fulda in the field of poverty and inequality research.

Latest Publications:

Engel, F. 2018. basic security experiences in families. Crises, worries and (out-)action practices. In: Betzelt, S., I. Bode. Eds. Anxiety in the new welfare state – critical views on a diffuse phenomenon. Baden-Baden: Nomos.

Singh, A., F. Engel, S. Kreher. 2018. adolescents in the triangle of SGB II benefit receipt. In Social meaning: journal of hermeneutic social research. Jg. 19, H. 1, pp. 11–43.

Hirseland, A., F. Engel. 2016. "Ich meine, das reicht hinten und vorn nicht": Ansätze nachhaltigen Wirtschaftens bei Hartz IV-Beziehenden. In: Quarterly Journal of Economic Research. Jg. 85, H. 3, pp. 69–79.

FSC
www.fsc.org

MIX
Papier aus verantwortungsvollen Quellen
Paper from responsible sources
FSC® C105338

If you have any concerns about our products, you can contact us on
ProductSafety@springernature.com

In case Publisher is established outside the EU, the EU authorized representative is:
Springer Nature Customer Service Center GmbH
Europaplatz 3, 69115 Heidelberg, Germany

Printed by Libri Plureos GmbH
in Hamburg, Germany